advance, but had
warned Dublin
Castle, & not even
Birrell in London — one
of them saying that it
was better to let things
come to a head! (But
this may not be true)
She expressed a very
poor opinion of Sir
John Simon, as
unwilling to take
off his coat to a
political fight, and
disliking his associates
in such a fight.
Lady Barlow called,
& gushed as usual.

# The Letters of Sidney and Beatrice Webb
## Volume II
### Partnership 1892–1912

Sidney and Beatrice Webb
*circa* 1909. Drawings by
Jessie Holiday; the originals
are at Beatrice Webb House
near Dorking. Reproduced by
permission of John Parker,
M.P.

# The Letters of
# Sidney and Beatrice Webb

EDITED BY
NORMAN MACKENZIE

## Volume II
## Partnership
## 1892–1912

Cambridge University Press

CAMBRIDGE   LONDON   NEW YORK   MELBOURNE

PUBLISHED IN CO-OPERATION WITH

The London School of Economics
and Political Science

Published by the Syndics of the Cambridge University Press
The Pitt Building, Trumpington Street, Cambridge CB2 IRP
Bentley House, 200 Euston Road, London NWI 2DB
32 East 57th Street, New York, NY 10022, USA
296 Beaconsfield Parade, Middle Park, Melbourne 3206, Australia

First published 1978

Printed in Great Britain
at the University Press, Cambridge

*Library of Congress Cataloguing in Publication Data* (*Revised*)
Passfield, Sidney James Webb, Baron, 1859–1947
The Letters of Sidney and Beatrice Webb.
'Published in co-operation with the London School
of Economics and Political Science.'
Includes index.
CONTENTS: v. 1. Apprenticeships, 1873–1892. –
v. 2. Partnership, 1892–1912. – v. 3. Pilgrimage,
1912–1947. I. Socialists – Great Britain – Correspondence.
I. Webb, Beatrice Potter, 1858–1943, joint author.
II. Mackenzie, Norman Ian. III. London School of
Economics and Political Science. IV. Title.
HX243.P295   1978   335'.14'0922   77–1665
ISBN O 521 21681 8 Volume I
ISBN O 521 21682 6 Volume II
ISBN O 521 21837 3 Volume III
ISBN O 521 22015 7 Set

# Contents

# Introduction

Sidney Webb and Beatrice Potter were married on 23 July 1892, when he was thirty-three and she was thirty-four. By the time of this late marriage each had an established career – he as a civil servant, part-time journalist and Fabian politician, she as a social investigator – but each realised that marriage was the beginning of a partnership in work as well as in their private lives. The prospect of such an alliance of their complementary skills, indeed, had been a strong motive in Beatrice's decision to accept Sidney as a husband, and a significant though lesser motive for him. From the first they intended to collaborate on research and writing. Sidney was anxious to leave the Colonial Office and, if necessary, support himself by political journalism. With marriage, since Beatrice had a private income of more than a thousand pounds a year, they were sufficiently well-off for him to resign: additional earnings from articles and books would be a bonus on top of their assured income, helping to pay for travel and research assistance for their work.

Before their marriage they had already begun on their first joint book, *The History of Trade Unionism*, which was published in 1894, and followed three years later by *Industrial Democracy*. From 1906 they began to issue their volumes in English local government, and that series remained a continuing commitment for almost thirty years. In all their work the pattern of collaboration remained much the same. Beatrice, more intuitive and speculative, normally conceived the shape of a project and did much of the field-work herself or directed their research assistants. Soon after their honeymoon, spent in part on research in Ireland and Scotland, she was off visiting trade unions in the provinces. Sidney, who disliked interviewing, ground through the paper-work of official reports and other sources, and did much of the actual writing. Much less imaginative than Beatrice, as the style of her diaries shows, he nevertheless wrote quickly, but ponderously and with a thorough attention to detail.

The Webbs lived a busy life and, apart from long summer breaks, they had to find time for writing in the intervals of other commitments. They also took on almost unmanageable tasks which only Sidney's capacity for grinding toil enabled them to complete. And Beatrice was an erratic worker. She drove herself hard, and overwork then led to minor nervous collapses in which her morale was sustained only by Sidney's unflagging support, both personally and in their work: it was the rock on which the achievement of the partnership was always firmly based.

Gradually, as Beatrice came to realise how much Sidney uncomplainingly gave to their marriage in all its aspects, the respect and cautious affection with which she regarded him turned to love. It was never the passion she had felt once and for all for Joseph Chamberlain; it never satisfied her deeper emotional needs, for Sidney – though feeling profoundly for her – was a matter-of-fact man who preferred blue books to philosophy. Yet it was a marriage that made her life bearable amidst the torments of self-doubt and unappeased guilt, partly because it satisfied her intellectual needs and her craving to do useful work in the world, partly because Sidney consistently encouraged her to come out in the world and was a steady comfort in the periods of illness and depression. He was necessary to her; and in a different way she was essential to him. He never ceased to wonder at the good fortune of what he had called the story of 'Beauty and the Beast' – of marrying one of the most striking and able women of the century who was the exact foil to his own temperament and abilities. Without the stimulation of her flair he might have been a worthy man, of solid achievement in journalism, scholarship and politics, but he would not have flown so high.

All through the years of partnership it was Beatrice who made the decisions which shaped their life and work. During their courtship Sidney had repeatedly asserted that she was to be his 'mentor', guiding him on matters of manners, criticising his work, advising him about his career. Cast in that role from the outset she maintained it to the end: even when he had doubts he complied with her leadership. In one sense, therefore, he was her subordinate in their joint undertakings, as he was in social status, though he never saw their relationship in that light. It seemed to him a simple consequence of the division of labour between them, in private as well as public life. As Beatrice came to use the editorial 'we' to express their opinions he accepted it as the natural pronoun to exemplify their collective outlook on life.

Immediately after their marriage, for instance, Beatrice made it clear that Sidney's parliamentary aspirations would be an impediment to their intended partnership. It would take too much of his time, and she felt him ill-suited to the House of Commons. His membership of the London County Council seemed sensible however, especially as he had given up full-time work in the civil service, for she thought that 'more is to be done by administration, experiment on the one hand and educating the constituencies on the other than by the political game carried on in Parliament'. That belief, which matched Sidney's already-formed predilection for backroom work, was the basis upon which the Webbs became the proponents of 'permeation' as a political tactic. They saw themselves, in effect, as a pair of brains-trusters, supplying ideas and tactics to such practising politicians as might choose or be persuaded to adopt them. They were to be enlightened specialists, on the model of Comte's 'priests of humanity' which had influenced both of them in their formative years.

They called themselves socialists, but in the first phase of their partnership they were closer to the Radical wing of the Liberal Party and particularly to the municipal reformers who followed Chamberlain than to the contemporary socialist sects. They were, moreover, Londoners: despite their travels and their contacts with the trade union movement, they saw politics in terms of the capital – and the social life which revolved round Parliament and Fleet Street. They were aloof from and suspicious of the evangelistic enthusiasms which led to the formation of the Independent Labour Party in 1893. Even when their disillusionment with the Liberal Government later that year led to a breach with Gladstonian Liberalism, with long-lasting implications for their own political future, they did not turn to the emerging alliance between socialists and trade unionists for the formation of a Labour party: they chose, instead, to persist with a policy of permeation which by the end of the century had led them in a working relationship with Conservatives and imperialist collectivists. They were not associated with the Labour Party in any serious way until after 1914.

The Webbs, nevertheless, were closely involved in politics throughout the period covered by this second volume of letters. They were, with Shaw, the dominant figures in the Fabian Society, asserting its independence of party politics, concentrating largely on measures of social and municipal reform, and endeavouring to influence practising politicians to accept them. They were, through Sidney's membership of the L.C.C., much concerned with London government, especially in matters of educational policy. Through their association with such Liberal Imperialists as Haldane and Asquith, and then through their personal friendship with Arthur Balfour, they were drawn into the whirl of lunches and dinner parties through which political Society did much of its business – and through which the Webbs lobbied for their own schemes. And from 1905 they were heavily engaged in the controversy about the future of the Poor Law. Beatrice's singular role in the Royal Commission on the Poor Law was a prime though unsuccessful example of permeation by salon politics combined with persevering research – the essence of Fabianism.

The Webbs were collectivists, interested in cleaning up the morass of poverty and promoting national efficiency. To that end they believed in using whatever political instruments came to hand – a posture which earned them the reputation of being unreliable allies and even unscrupulous wirepullers. If they had succeeded in permeating the Liberal Party effectively (a task they abandoned after 1893), or if, as they hoped, a new 'national efficiency' party should come from a merger of Chamberlain's Liberal Unionists and Rosebery's Liberal Imperialists, they might have been drawn into party activity in middle life rather than in old age.

They were led astray because their policy of permeation, though logically consistent, did not fit the realities of the British party system.

This commitment to permeation led them to make three critical mis-judgements. The first, and most understandable, was their failure to see the potential of the I.L.P. It was left to Ramsay MacDonald, with whom they quarrelled, to be the means of permeating the I.L.P. with Fabian policies of gradualism. The second was their separation from and their antagonism to the Radicals, which was intensified by their association with the imperialist Liberals during the Boer War and their subsequent flirta-tion with the Conservatives during the controversies over education policy. This meant that when the Liberal Government of 1906 was elected with a huge majority the Webbs were outsiders, having lost the contacts through which they might have influenced its policy. The third error followed from Beatrice's strong emotional commitment to the Royal Commission, and from the obsession of the Webbs with the Minority Report, their own comprehensive formula for dealing with poverty. Though they made a fruitless effort to persuade the Liberal leaders of its merits, they were actually in competition with Lloyd George and Winston Churchill. They were convinced that their own scheme was intrinsically better than the Lloyd George proposals for social insurance, but intrinsic merit was no substitute for political power. With the Tories out of office and absorbed in Tariff Reform, and with the Liberal reformers caring little about the complex collectivism of the Webb Poor Law scheme, the Webbs then turned from permeation by manipulation to public agitation. But they lacked a political base and their campaign left the two main parties unaffected. They were, in any case, forming up for their set-piece battle over the powers of the House of Lords in which the single-minded Webbs showed little interest. Soon afterwards the passage of Lloyd George's insurance scheme led to the collapse of the Webbs' campaign. As John Burns cruelly observed, they had been 'dished' by Lloyd George. They consoled themselves by leaving on a long tour of Asia to recoup their energies and to plan their course for what then seemed the few remaining years of active middle-age.

The Webbs had run themselves into a political impasse by 1910, but the most energetic part of their careers had nonetheless been marked by some real achievements. There were their books, apart from the flow of Fabian tracts and articles which had come from Sidney's untiring pen. Most important, perhaps, was their foundation of the London School of Economics in 1895. Making skilful use of a small bequest from a Fabian solicitor, Henry Hutchinson, they launched the School to promote efficient administration – underpinned by disinterested research – as a means of solving social problems. Conceived, in Beatrice's phrase, as their 'child', it was Sidney's direct and continuing concern. He watched over every detail and every penny, from the academic programme and the appointment of staff, to the establishment of a first-class library, the level of fees and the quality of the linoleum on the floors. In educational matters he was at his best – not merely in the complex business of creating a new college of London University, and of reforming that university as a whole, but also in the in-fighting over the Tory Education Bills of 1902 and 1903. He was not the prime designer of those Bills, but their passage owed much to him. During the eighteen years he served on the London County Council he made himself the outstanding authority on the city's schools and colleges.

Throughout the period covered by this volume the Webbs were, with Shaw, the dominant figures in the Fabian Society. With Hubert Bland, Graham Wallas, Sydney Olivier and Edward Pease they formed the 'Old Gang' which gave the Society a coherent leadership and provided a stabilising influence on its policy. Despite the disagreements between them, especially on political tactics, imperialism and educational policy, the Old Gang stood firmly together on the principles which enabled the Society to weather the kind of storms that wrecked other socialist sects. They insisted upon its independence from direct involvement in party politics; they ensured that its activities gave a high priority to research and propaganda; and they created a tolerant style of controversy which treated differences upon their merits and avoided personal bitterness. It is true that Shaw and the Webbs set the direction of the Society; at times they treated it as if it were a family business in which they were co-directors. Yet they saved it from splits and silliness, time and again; and they jealously protected it against waves of enthusiasm which threatened to enlarge it beyond manageable proportions and thereby change its character.

The most dramatic of these surges of expansion came in 1906, when the leftward swing of middle-class opinion swept hundreds of new members into the Society. The Webbs and Shaw had seen a similar boom in 1893, and had been glad when the over-enthusiastic recruits drifted away into the I.L.P. Between 1906 and 1909 it was not the attraction of independent labour representation that threatened the stability of the Society but the demagogy of H. G. Wells, who proposed in effect to convert the Fabians from a family business into a public company, committed to large-scale activity and possibly to the formation of a new middle-class socialist party which he fancied he might lead. Although the Webbs were heavily committed at the time to their Poor Law campaign, and although Shaw was devoting less time to Fabian affairs as his dramatic career soared to its zenith, the triumvirate had to turn back to fight a long battle to preserve the curious Fabian identity they had shaped in the previous fifteen years, That battle was not only the heyday of the Fabian Society; the winning of it was the guarantee that Fabianism survived as a distinct element in British public life and became an important component of the modern Labour Party.

# A brief chronology

A fuller but far from complete bibliography is available in *Publications of Sidney and Beatrice Webb: An Interim Checklist* (British Library of Political and Economic Science, 1973).

1893    Webbs lease 41 Grosvenor Road, Millbank as permanent home. Shaw and Webb publish 'To Your Tents O Israel' on 1 November in *Fortnightly Review*.

1894    Webbs begin *Industrial Democracy*. In July they learn of legacy from H. H. Hutchinson and decide to use greater part of it to found a London School of Economics. Sidney and Beatrice Webb: *The History of Trade Unionism*. Sidney Webb: Fabian Tracts 51, *Socialism: True and False* and 60, *The London Vestries*.

1895    Foundation of L.S.E. Webbs are neutral in General Election.

1896    On 29 January Webbs introduce the Irish heiress Charlotte Payne-Townsend to Bernard Shaw. Webbs begin to support Conservative Government's proposals for educational reform. Sidney Webb: Fabian Tract 69, *The Difficulties of Individualism*. Beatrice Webb: Fabian Tract 67, *Women and the Factory Acts*.

1897    Sidney and Beatrice Webb: *Industrial Democracy*. Sidney Webb: Fabian Tracts 75, *Labour in the Longest Reign* and 84, *The Economics of Direct Employment*.

1898    Sidney re-elected in Deptford. Webbs decide to take 'sabbatical' journey to United States, New Zealand and Australia. Bernard Shaw and Charlotte Payne-Townsend marry during their absence. Sidney and Beatrice Webb: *Problems of Modern Industry*.

1899    In January Webbs return to England. Permanent site found for L.S.E. off Aldwych, and negotiations begin to give the School university status.

1900    Webbs break with anti-war Fabians who, led by Ramsay MacDonald, resign from the Society.

1901    In national politics Webbs openly support Lord Rosebery and Liberal Imperialists. On Shaw's initiative Webb writes 'Lord Rosebery's Escape from Houndsditch' in *Nineteenth Century* for September. Sidney Webb: Fabian Tracts 106, *The Education Muddle and the Way Out* and 108, *Twentieth Century Politics*.

1902    Sidney closely involved in drafting of Conservative Education Act 1902, though it is opposed by his own party, the Progressives, on the L.C.C.; he helps to launch the Imperial College of Science. Advent of A. J. Balfour, a personal friend, as Conservative Prime Minister increases Webb links with Conservative administration. In September Webbs found the 'Co-efficients' as dining club or 'shadow cabinet' for supporters of 'National Efficiency'.

1903    Sidney Webb supports Conservative Education Act for London; Webbs neutral on Tariff Reform controversy. Sidney and Beatrice Webb: *The History of Liquor Licensing in England*. Sidney Webb: Fabian Tract 114, *The Education Act, 1903*.

1905   Beatrice appointed as member of the Royal Commission on Poor Law, set up as last act of Balfour government.

1906   Landslide electoral victory for Liberals. Unable directly to influence the programme of the new Liberal government, Webb publishes his proposals in June *National Review*, 'The Liberal Cabinet. An Intercepted Letter'. H. G. Wells bids for control of Fabian Society: Webbs and Shaw forced to defend leadership of Society. Sidney and Beatrice Webb: *English Local Government I – The Parish and the County*.

1907   Webb narrowly saves Deptford seat when Progressives are routed in L.C.C. election. Beatrice, unable to dominate Poor Law Commission, decides to produce a comprehensive policy on Pauperism in the form of a minority report. Sidney Webb: Fabian Tracts 131, *The Decline in the Birth-Rate* and 135, *Paupers and Old Age Pensions*.

1908   Webbs endeavour by backstairs manipulation to secure government support for their proposed reform of Poor Law. They antagonise crucial Ministers (Lloyd George and Winston Churchill), and become emotionally committed to their minority report. Sidney and Beatrice Webb: *English Local Government II–III – The Manor and the Borough*.

1909   Minority Report published in January as personal manifesto of the Webb partnership, who then launch national campaign for the 'Break Up' of the Poor Law.

1910   Liberal struggle for Lloyd George budget, and against House of Lords (which involves two general elections) largely ignored by Webbs who press their own campaign. In November Beatrice sets up research department for Poor Law campaign. Sidney and Beatrice Webb: *English Local Government X – English Poor Law Policy; The State and the Doctor*.

1911   Sidney leaves London County Council. In June the Webbs leave for a long-planned journey around the world, visiting Canada, Japan, Korea, Manchuria, China, Malaya, Burma and India. Sidney and Beatrice Webb: *The Prevention of Destitution*. Sidney Webb: Fabian Tract 159, *The Necessary Basis of Society*.

1912   The Webbs return from world tour in May.

# Location codes

The following abbreviations are used in this volume to identify the location of letters.

| | |
|---|---|
| AP/BLPES | Acworth Papers (BLPES) |
| BEV | Beveridge Papers (BLPES) |
| BL | The British Library |
| BLPES | The British Library of Political and Economic Science |
| BOD | The Bodleian Library, Oxford |
| BUL | Birmingham University Library |
| BWD | Beatrice Webb's Diary (BLPES) |
| CCO | Corpus Christi College, Oxford |
| FP | Fabian Papers, Nuffield College Library, Oxford |
| GLC | Greater London Council |
| HL | House of Lords Record Office |
| HP | Hutchinson Trust Papers (BLPES) |
| HRCUT | Humanities Research Center, The University of Texas at Austin |
| HSP | Historical Society of Pennsylvania |
| LP | The Lansbury Papers |
| LSE | The London School of Economics and Political Science Papers (BLPES) |
| MMLMU | Mills Memorial Library, McMaster University |
| MUL | Manchester University Library |
| NH | Dr Henriette Noufflard (Halévy Papers) |
| NLNZ | National Library of New Zealand |
| NLS | National Library of Scotland |
| NUL | Newcastle University Library |
| PF | Sir Horace Plunkett Co-op Library, Oxford |
| PP | Passfield Papers (BLPES) |
| PRO | Public Record Office |
| SCA | Salop County Archives, London |
| SCL | Shaw *Collected Letters* |
| SHSW | State Historical Society of Wisconsin |
| SUL | Sheffield University Library |
| UI | University of Illinois |
| WP/BLPES | Wallas Papers (BLPES) |
| WSC | In W. S. Caine, *The Founding of the London School of Economics* |

# 1. Marriage
## August 1892 – July 1894

The letters in the first section in this volume cover the first years of the Webb marriage when they were primarily concerned with their joint research on trade unionism and with Sidney's membership of the London County Council. During this period, moreover, Sidney was beginning to swing away from his close association with the radical wing of the Liberal Party. In 1892 he still had high hopes that the Radicals might eventually be able to dictate Liberal policy, gain greater control over the constituency associations and prove amenable to Fabian permeation. By the end of 1893, partly under pressure from Shaw and partly disillusioned with the performance of the Liberal Government, he had become disaffected with Gladstonian Liberalism. Both within the Fabian Society and in his public posture he was becoming more concerned with the role of social research as an instrument of change – a line of thought which led fairly directly to the notion of founding a School of Economics which would embody disinterested research and teaching of what he conceived to be a science of society – an approach which seemed to him and to Beatrice to be far more promising for the future than the knock-about of Radical politics.

### 269 FP   SIDNEY WEBB TO EDWARD PEASE

Beatrice reacted unfavourably to the Dubliners, deciding that they were a 'pathetic people – with high pretensions and low purposes!' and 'unfit to be yoked with other races'. Going on to Belfast for the Trades Union Congress the Webbs noted the better discipline of the low-paid Protestant Ulstermen, exploited by employers who 'were in the primitive stage of money-getting'. (BWD 16 August 92)

> Shaftesbury Hotel, 6 College Square,
> Belfast
> 12th August, 1892

Fabian Society here composed of a good sort of fellows – taking a new start – and well worth encouraging – I see that only the *News* has come to them – not the Circular re Education, nor yet copies of Shaw's lecture. I don't know what has happened to the former – it ought to go out soon. As to Shaw's lecture I thought it was agreed that all local members should have a copy free (as with the *News*). I think this is important. Ask Shaw about it. I stay here until Wednesday morning.

> Sidney Webb

I

At the T.U.C. Beatrice noticed the efforts of Sir Charles and Lady Dilke to ingratiate themselves with the trade unionists as a means of political rehabilitation. They were, she remarked, entertaining the delegates wholesale to lunch, tea and dinner, but she found them 'unpleasant figures – now creeping back well-thrashed to public life'. (BWD 17 September 92). She also noticed the difference in the temper of the Congress from that which she had attended at Dundee three years earlier, when the socialists 'were at daggers drawn' with the old moderate leaders: now Sidney 'hobnobs with all the older men and we are as friendly with Mawdsley as with Tillett'.

Wallas was now working hard on research for his biography of Francis Place.

The Webbs went on to Glasgow. During their month-long stay they spent one day with Auberon Herbert on Loch Awe; another weekend was given to a visit to R. B. Haldane's family home at Cloan in Perthshire where they met some of 'The Souls', the nickname given by Lord Charles Beresford (1846–1919) to a group of Society intellectuals, much interested in literature and art, which included Arthur Balfour and his personal secretary, the cultivated Conservative M.P., George Wyndham (1863–1913), Alfred Lyttelton (1857–1913), a lawyer and Liberal Unionist M.P., Margot Tennant (1864–1945), who became the second wife of Herbert Asquith in 1894, and the well-known hostesses Lady Elcho and Lady Desborough. Through their later friendship with Arthur Balfour the Webbs became marginally involved in the social life of this group. On this occasion they met at the home of Sir Charles Tennant (1823–1906), a wealthy chemical industrialist and patron of art in Scotland. Beatrice was impressed by 'the exquisite deference and ease which constitutes good breeding' but felt that 'The Souls' had 'a vain restlessness of tickled vanity'. (BWD August 92)

The Webbs returned to their first home – a flat between Swiss Cottage and Hampstead. Shaw wrote to them on 12 August saying that there was a need for 'a salon for the cultivation of the socialist party in Parliament' and asking: 'Will Madame Potter-Webb take it on?' (PP)

6 Blythwood Square, Glasgow<br>[? September 1892]

My dear Graham

We are delighted to hear of your safe return from the wiles of Norwegian beauties and the dangers of Norwegian Stolbuchers (however do you spell that word) and trust you are grappling with the monster Chartism with the strength of a refreshed giant.

I have sent Sidney off to inspect Calico Printing and as it is a pouring wet day I am staying at home to write letters and generally 'tidy up'.

Imagine us *wie alle Leute* settling down each day to the day's work: usually flying off first thing after breakfast to inspect Works on opposite sides of the Clyde – then perhaps re-uniting for lunch or tea; evening spent I, in interviewing T.U. secretaries here; he in wandering through all the working-class suburbs in search of informants. (He grumbles dreadfully about his evening work!)

We are getting on very well – tho' I fancy we are generally informing ourselves more than we are collecting material of any great value. But we are very happy – if that be the end of human life.

We spent one Sunday with Auberon Herbert on Loch Awe, another with Haldane. The latter was profitable as we left Haldane with excellent instructions to be handed on to all the ministers.

But the most serious part of our visit was our formal introduction to a company of fair 'Souls', who came over in a bevy to tea from a neighbouring home.

Under Haldane's beneficial gaze Souls looked at us with eager curiosity and we on the Souls with wondering admiration for they were good to look at. But tho' they offered to mount up to our Flat at Hampstead we sorrowfully refused to enter into their Paradise – and so parted each on our own way.

Congress week will be interesting – I hear that Sir C. Dilke is to be here – amusing to watch how he is received.

Ever yours affectionately

Beatrice Webb

We come home end of September.

## 271 PP   BEATRICE TO SIDNEY

Beatrice had gone to Manchester to continue research. The Webbs had settled into a working routine in London. They normally worked at their book until lunchtime. In the afternoons Beatrice often took a walk while Sidney went to his committees, returning about 7.30 'full of the doings of the L.C.C. or carrying back news of an interview with a Cabinet minister or some proposed reform'. They entertained little, spending most of their evenings quietly. 'Perhaps also', Beatrice reflected, 'the calm of married happiness deadens, in the first instance, one's intellectual energies.' Sidney was fully occupied. In addition to serving as chairman of the Technical Education Board he also sat on the Parliamentary, Local Government, Taxation, Education, Housing and Water Committees of the L.C.C. He had, Beatrice noted happily, become the 'trusted confidant and helpmate of the great officials of the Council', was 'steadily acquiring influence with the official Liberals' and was becoming 'the chief instigator of policies, the source of Liberal doctrine'. (BWD 1 December 92)

[Manchester]

[late September 1892]

My own dearest

It is certainly boiling hot and the hotel is very noisy. I made a mistake not to go to the Grand Hotel which I had discovered was the one I before stayed at. What with the heat and the noise I have not been able to get much sleep.

[?Owen] comes tomorrow 11.30 so I cannot come up till 2 o'clock train. I am glad I came down if only to see something of Gaiton. I went through the minutes of the Trade Council yesterday. Today I am seeing some employers from which I do not expect much but who may be useful. Collins has certainly done his level best; entertained both me and Orford Smith to a sumptuous lunch here yesterday. I was glad I saw Orford Smith, for I think I took his measure. I think we can leave it to his self-importance and amour propre to do his best to make the Commission's work successful. He was rather put out because the Commissioners were not sitting next week owing to the L.C.C. not being ready with their case. Is that committee doing the work well and expeditiously? I have an intuitive impression that it is rather a muddle! and wants a little 'one man power' to drive it through. Maggie's [?Margaret Hobhouse] letter is amusing – it is your diplomatic ways that have misled her.

Now dear one, goodbye for today – you will work all the more tomorrow and perhaps about 4 o'clock you will saunter down the Finchley Road. You shall not carry up the bag, so don't be afraid of that. It will be delightful to get back to our 'dovecot', and to be again with my darling old boy – who twists his strong-minded wife round his little finger – by soft sounds and kisses.

BW

## 272 FP SIDNEY WEBB TO EDWARD PEASE

No surviving letter from either of the Webbs refers to the foundation of the Independent Labour Party at a conference in Bradford in January 1893. The Society's delegates were Shaw and William S. De Mattos: within a few months most of the provincial Fabian groups had been reconstituted as I.L.P. branches, or were closely associated with the I.L.P., but the parent Society in London showed little sympathy for the new venture, whose roots and strength lay in the textile districts of Yorkshire and Lancashire. The Webbs did not care for the heady rhetoric of the provincial enthusiasts or for Keir Hardie, Robert Blatchford and other leaders of the new party; for the next twenty years they remained aloof from and critical of the I.L.P., opposing recurrent attempts within the Society to achieve a closer relationship.

This letter is typical of many chivvying notes from Webb to Pease during the next two decades, most of which are omitted from this collection because they deal simply with routine matters. Webb treated Pease as his man of business and though they had a close working relationship – Webb could always count on Pease's loyalty – they were not personal friends or even social associates. Beatrice did not greatly like either Pease or his wife.

10 Netherhall Gardens, South Hampstead
8th April, 1893

Dear Pease

(1) It occurs to me that I saw but one review of the Guardians leaflet: I suppose it went automatically to the press as a matter of course?

I notice that neither the *Labor Prophet*, nor the *Financial Reformer* nor

4

the *Church Reformer* mentioned it. Did *Justice*? I do not know about the *Labor Elector*, the *Workman's Times*, or the *Labor Leader* (Keir Hardie's paper) or the *Labor Tribune*.

It was not in the *Cotton Factory Times* nor the *Co-operative News*. I suppose these are all on your press list? The provincial papers, too, would have noticed it.

(2) It occurs to me that it would be well to compile a statement, at any rate for Executive use, as to how much literature has been bought during the year by each local society. Some take very little, and ought to be admonished. I do not know whether it might not be well to publish the statement to excite emulation. I suppose we could hardly give a banner or a bonus to the society taking most? Mention this to publishing committee.

Yours

Sidney Webb

### 273 FP   BEATRICE WEBB TO EDWARD PEASE

There was an edge to Beatrice's sarcasm. On 10 March she had noted in her diary that 'I tell Sidney laughingly that I miss the exciting relationships with marriageable or marrying men – that I feel "hemmed in" by matrimony. Fortunately I have a bit of solid work in hand: I doubt more than ever whether I could have been long satisfied with a life in which intellectual effort were not the main or rather the most prominent part'. At the same time she imposed constraints upon Sidney's public ambitions. 'Parliament seems farther off than ever; we are content for the present with the prospect of intellectual study and the more humble role of C. Councillor . . . Personally I think more is to be done by administration, experiment on the one hand and educating the constituencies on the other than by entering into the political game carried on in Parliament.' Beatrice's approach to politics, conditioned both by temperament and by her earlier life in London political society, undoubtedly reinforced Sidney's predilection for the tactics of permeation and his reluctance to support independent labour activity.

Albemarle Club, 13 Albemarle Street, w.

[18 April 1893]

Dear Mr Pease

I have duly considered your flattering invitation to speak from the Fabian Platform on May Sunday. But not only does my vow of courage fail me, but the hidden masculinity of Sidney's views of women are discernable in his decided objection to my figuring among the speakers. See how skin-deep are these professions of advanced opinion, with regard to women, among your leaders of the forward party!

The upshot is that I fear you must omit me from your list.

Yours truly

Beatrice Webb

10 Netherhall Gardens, South Hampstead
22/4/1893

Dear Pease

I started this morning to do another paper of economic questions but found I had totally forgotten what point we had reached!

I asked once before that you should treat me like a Cabinet Minister – put the whole matter before me each time in applepie order. It seems a good deal to ask, but I fear I am too much occupied in other ways at present to be able to work on any other terms.

Send me the last paper; any suggestions; and name a date.

Yours

Sidney Webb

275 PP SIDNEY TO BEATRICE [*incomplete*]

Beatrice was on a round of family visits. She went to stay with the Hobhouses at Hadspen, at Castle Cary in Somerset, and then went on to The Argoed, where Sidney joined her for Easter. This letter is similar to many written throughout their married life when separated. In May, while they were attending the Co-operative Congress at Bristol Beatrice's sister Theresa Cripps died. Meeting her sisters at the funeral Beatrice reflected on the manner in which she had drifted away from her relations and old friends since her marriage: she particularly felt the breakdown of her close ties with the Booths, 'the stay of my life during the real struggle of it'. (BWD 22 May 93) Going to The Argoed again in summer, on the sixth anniversary of Chamberlain's decisive visit, she sorrowfully noted: 'he is always there'. (BWD 29 July 93)

*Justice* was Part IV of Herbert Spencer's *The Principles of Ethics* and it was available in a separate volume.

10 Netherhall Gardens, South Hampstead
28.4.93

My own dear Bee

It wasn't from want of love that I wrote such a scrubby letter, nor from not missing you, but because I made the characteristic mistake of trying to write in a committee room! I did the same yesterday and ultimately had to hurry off my letter unfinished. Now this morning (as I made up my mind to do yesterday) I am writing in 'your' time – instead of going off to the Museum at once I am enjoying myself talking to you.

Do come back; it is so lonely without you. I do not get to sleep, and I wake up so early, and then am no longer content, as I once was, to lie and dream, but I toss about and want you. And then the breakfast is so lonely, and the evening so dreary without my loving partner.

I have nothing sweet to tell you: the Museum seemed waste and hideously dull, and I could not find what I wanted – and the Council Work was bothersome – and then Stuart, Costelloe, Grant and I settled the terms of a long resolution of implied censure on the Govt, to be passed Monday week – and then I came home and found Herbert Spencer's new volume *Justice*, which I looked through – a *very* bad piece of work indeed – e.g. women have no right to the vote because they can't serve in the army: he says they should have a vote for all local. . . .

During a six-week summer holiday at The Argoed the Webbs entertained both Shaw and Wallas. Shaw, Beatrice observed, was 'an artist to the tips of his fingers – and an admirable *craftsman*. I have never known a man use his pen in such a workmanlike fashion or acquire such a thoroughly technical knowledge upon any subject upon which he gives an opinion'. But she could not understand his personality. He was 'a delightful companion' but also 'a born Philanderer . . . disliking to be hampered either by passion or by conventions and therefore always tying himself up into knots which have to be cut before he is free for another adventure'. Wallas was very different: he was 'a loveable man' but 'in spite of his moral fervour he seems incapable of directing his own life'. (BWD 17 September 93) Shaw, Wallas and Sidney formed the Fabian 'Junta'. Shaw provided 'sparkle and flavour', Wallas 'morality and scrupulousness, Webb 'practical initiative'. What was missing, Beatrice felt, was 'a personality of *weight*' – a role in which she sometimes wanted to cast John Burns, though she recognised that his egotism and inability to collaborate with others made this a vain hope. Beatrice's fear that the Fabian leaders were not temperamentally suited to practical politics – neither members of the ruling class nor men who had served their time in labour organisations – probably played a significant part in turning the Fabians to a policy of permeation: it was certainly her taste and experience which led the Webbs to put so much reliance on salon politics.

By the summer the Webbs had decided to move to a more convenient house and they took a long lease on 41 Grosvenor Road, on the Thames embankment near the Tate Gallery and not far from the Houses of Parliament. This remained their home for the next thirty-five years. It was a severe ten-roomed terrace house, renting at £110 p.a., and served by a maid and a cook. Neither of the Webbs had sybaritic tastes, though they appreciated the splendid outlook on to the river; Beatrice recognised their lack of 'a wider culture – knowledge of other and higher forms of intellectual effort'. She sadly confessed that 'all the world of art and literature is closed to me'. (BWD 30 July 93) Yet she made an effort to soften the harsh interior of their new home, going shopping for Morris furniture and wallpapers. 'I do not wish it to be thought that simplicity of daily life means ugliness and lack of order and charm', she wrote. Feeling uneasy at such self-indulgence she comforted herself with the thought that 'efficiency only demands plenty of nourishing food, well-ordered drains and a certain freedom of petty cares. It is somewhat softening to contend that you *need* beautiful things'.

F. H. Millington's *The Housing of the Poor*, the Warburton Prize Essay at Owen's College, Manchester, was published in 1891.

7

Dear Pease

I have written direct to Firth of Rochdale as to Common Lodging Houses – practically I know nothing more than is stated in the 'London Programme' – see also Millington's *Housing of the Poor* (Cassell: 1/-). Huddersfield, Glasgow and London are the only cases.

With regard to [?Maund] of Leicester, I think you should tell them that the London County Council has hitherto totally failed to secure the payment of T.U. wages in the tailoring trade, as no T.U. of any standing or extent exists in the branch of trade in question, i.e. factory tailoring. The Amalgamated Union of Tailors, for instance, work under a 'log' or price list which does very well for your clothes, but which would figure out for policemen's uniforms to about £4 or £5 a piece, instead of a quarter of that sum. It is therefore nothing to the point that they object, but as this is seldom understood by people, it would be desirable to explain it fully.

The fact is that factory tailoring is a new process of industry – worked under division of labor, and cutting wholesale – with ample machinery. Under this system the price for *each garment* is infinitesimal: nevertheless, such is the speed, that a worker can earn good wages per week. The old tailors, (who make a garment right through) object to the factory industry just as the handloom weavers did to the powerloom. But as a matter of fact it is much better for the community to have its work *done in factories*, instead of in the workers' homes (against which the Tailors Unions have always been protesting).

Now, I don't know anything about Pearce. But if it is true, as alleged, that his work is all *done in his own* factory – then I do not hesitate to say it is better for London than if it were put out to be done at home, even under the Union 'log'. The Amalgamated Tailors Union will not admit workers who do not work by the 'log' i.e. those on the new factory system. This may be good policy, but in such case the Union ought not to raise the objection that the 'log' rates are not paid. Burns and others have done all they can to make a Union among these factory workers, but hitherto without that amount of success as warrants anyone in saying there is a Standard Rate at all in this branch of trade. Of course the 'log' is no more the standard rate of the new trade than the handloom weavers list was the rate for the powerloom.

All we have been able to do in the L.C.C. is to go to a good firm, known to have its own factory, *out of London*, and to bind it not to sublet, and so execute the work in the factory. What Worcester ought to do is to insist that in the new contract, which will apparently be made at once, as the present one expires December, a clause such as that put in the Commissioners of Police contract – you might buy and send a copy of the Parliamentary Report on *the steps taken by Govt. Depts to carry out H. of C. resolutions against* Sweating, 1890 or 1891, moved for by Mr [Sydney] Buxton.

Yours

Sidney Webb

### 277 WP/BLPES  SIDNEY WEBB TO GRAHAM WALLAS

While Wallas was visiting the Webbs at The Argoed there was much discussion about Fabian tactics. The Webbs had pinned their hopes on the influence that Haldane, Asquith, Grey and Acland might exert upon the Liberal government, both to secure policy changes that could be achieved by ministerial action and to implement some of the legislation envisaged in the Newcastle Programme. By the early autumn of 1893 it was clear that such hopes were fruitless. Gladstone had thrown all his failing energies into the cause of Home Rule and had run into difficulties with the House of Lords. There was considerable industrial unrest; the Trades Union Congress had established a fund to support labour and socialist candidates; and the I.L.P. had managed to set up a considerable number of local branches in the first months after its foundation in January. Shaw felt that the initiative was slipping away from the Fabians, after the boom the Society had enjoyed since the publication of *Fabian Essays* in 1889; he also saw that there was a danger that he, Wallas and Webb might lose their commanding position in the Society if they could be dismissed as mere hangers-on to the Liberal Party. Both he and Webb wrote to Wallas arguing the case for a change of front. Wallas was reluctant to agree: he felt that they were acting hastily for fear of being thought too complacent by the I.L.P. and its sympathisers in the Fabian Society.

The Argoed, Monmouth
12.9.93

Dear Wallas

It was angelic of you to arrange that matter of McCrae's reports so promptly, and to relieve our minds by a telegram. I felt wicked in asking you to do the job, but there seemed no other method.

Shaw will probably stay on with us until the 18th, and return with us that day. He has written to you as to the Fabian meeting. I agree that if anyone wants a private meeting, we ought to meet it halfway.

The time has come I think, for a strong tract showing up the Liberal Party, and advocating as many decent Labor candidates as possible. But it ought not to be so difficult to make clear to the members that, with the I.L.P., the various Trade Union attempts at political action, and the innumerable other Labor Parties in the field, any attempt at S.D.F. sectarian exclusiveness must be fatal.

However, it does not matter all that much what is decided about the Joint Committee. Neither Shaw nor you nor I will go on it. And I can't imagine it ever becoming of any real force. But I am dead against hampering ourselves with it.

Yours

Sidney Webb

Herbert Samuel graduated from Balliol in 1893; he was the Liberal candidate for South Oxfordshire in 1895 and 1900. In 1902 he was elected for Cleveland.

41 Grosvenor Road, Westminster Embankment
14 Oct/93

Dear Mr Samuel

I am much obliged for your prospectus of the English Land Colonisation Society – an interesting experiment, which may prove much.

Frankly, I am afraid that I have but little sympathy – probably, too little – with any attempts to 'settle the people on the land' or to stay the rural exodus.

Do you really want *more* people to 'obtain a living from the land'? Would you not rather increase the proportion of cotton spinners and engineers, at the expense of even the most intelligent agriculturalist? I confess that, whether we look to France, New England, Ireland or England, agricultural pursuits *seem* – whatever may be the reason – to produce less of what we regard as civilisation or citizenship, than other forms of manual labor. However, I am perhaps prejudiced as a townsman.

Moreover, does not industrial and economic development fight against you? We do not need much more food – practically no more bread – in the world than is now produced. Surely every step in the progress of 'command over nature' implies a diminution in the proportion of those required to till the soil for the rest.

But you have studied this question so much more closely than I that I can only wish you every success in whatever experiments commend themselves to you.

Yours very truly
Sidney Webb

## 279 FP   SIDNEY WEBB TO EDWARD PEASE

On 1 November 1893 the *Fortnightly Review* published 'To Your Tents, O Israel!', written jointly by Webb and Shaw as a diatribe against the Liberals for their failure to implement a reformist policy. It was a sharp, tendentious article, ridiculing the Liberal leaders severally and collectively, which suggested that the time might soon come when a Labour Party should be formed. 'Pending the formation of a Labour Party the working classes need not greatly care which party divides the loaves and fishes', the article concluded with a temporary deviation from Webb's commitment to the tactics of permeation; it proposed that the T.U.C. should find the money to run fifty independent labour candidates at the next general election.

The article was revamped by Shaw for publication as Fabian Tract 49, *A Plan of Campaign for Labour*. It did not mollify the I.L.P., whose members were distrustful of the apparent Fabian conversion to independent action; and it greatly upset Radical members of the Society who had hitherto considered Webb one of themselves. Henry Massingham and the Scots philosopher David George Ritchie (1853–1903) both angrily resigned from the Society in protest against what Massingham denounced as 'mischievous' behaviour. R. B. Haldane also complained that most people would assume that Shaw and Webb had declared war on their former Liberal associates. By the following March, however, Webb's irritation with the Liberals had abated and he had reverted to his old tactic of seeking to influence Liberal policy. As Rosebery succeeded Gladstone as prime minister, and as Haldane and such colleagues as Asquith and Grey appeared to be increasingly influential, Webb had new hopes for permeation. At a Fabian meeting during the winter the I.L.P. leader Keir Hardie attacked Webb and Shaw as 'superior persons' who tried to be generals without an army.

Tract 48, *Eight Hours by Law*, was written by Henry W. Macrosty, a civil servant and statistician who served on the Fabian executive from 1895 to 1907. Tract 32 was Webb's 'The Municipalization of the Gas Supply', first issued in 1891.

Beatrice's lecture was on 'The Sphere of Trade Unionism' and it was reported in *Fabian News* for December 1893.

41 Grosvenor Road, Westminster Embankment<br>19/11/1893

Dear Pease

(1) Wallas tells me he can and will go to the School Board Election Conference on Tuesday. Send him a card to remind him. I am not sure that Headlam is otherwise delegated: I think you might usefully send him for us on chance. There would be no harm in sending 4 – I should say Lowerison before De Mattos.

(2) I am sorry I know nothing about a paper for (a) class economics. If I have been asked for it, I have forgotten it. But I have *several times* said that the matter must be put formally before me each time, *with copy of the last paper*. My mind is a blank about it until that comes.

(3) Shaw is very much pressed for time just now, and should be spared as much as possible – especially as he has the manifesto to revise. For instance, who is doing the Eight Hours tract? Rather than put it on Shaw, please send all the corrections *to me*.

(4) Tract 32 must be brought up to date by new figures which I will *try* to get tomorrow.

Yours

Sidney Webb

(5) Kindly make your own report on Mrs Webb's lecture for [*Fabian*] *News*, and let her see ms or proof.

280 FP   SIDNEY WEBB TO EDWARD PEASE

William Evans was returned unopposed to the Brighton town council in November 1893, serving for three years. There were no party designations at that time: the main local issue was temperance option.

41 Grosvenor Road, Westminster Embankment

3rd Dec. 1893

Dear Pease

Here at last is the Circular on Economics Classes – please see if it is what is required. I take it we only want 2/6 for each set of papers. I suggest that you should see B. T. Hall of Club and Institute Union about its issue. He will certainly put it in their journal and might be willing to print 500 copies for all their clubs, and circulate them. If not, I am inclined to think it might pay us to print rather than to manifold. In that case, it ought to bear our List of Tracts on the back as a valuable advertisement.

I shall not be able to come to Exec. on Tuesday. I have been over the manifesto and have by excising all Shaw's most objectionable efforts, *reduced* it to 32 pages! We can't print more, so please resist additions or restorations.

Yours

Sidney Webb

By the way is not Evans of Brighton a member? He got in for Town Council. Get particulars and members.

SW

281 FP  SIDNEY WEBB TO EDWARD PEASE

Webb was a conscientious collector and maker of mailing lists. This method of publicity suited the relatively small scale and selective propaganda of the Fabians; it was also employed by the Webbs to promote their own books, for fund-raising for the London School of Economics and for political lobbying. Webb had more faith in the effectiveness of the printed than the spoken word, both to inform and persuade.

London County Council, Spring Gardens, s.w.

[January 1894]

Tract No. 49 might be sent to

(a) the 100 Trades Councils

(b) the Secretaries of I.L.P. Branches (3 already sent)

(c) the Secretaries of S.D.F. Branches (11 already sent) – with a printed slip stating terms for sale in quantity.

(d) The 17 Cabinet ministers

(e) Liberal and Labor M.P.'s (about 350)

(f) The General Purposes Committee of the National Liberal Federation (about 20)

This gives a total of something under 600 = £5 postage about 25/-, which is a small part of the £20 subsidy from the *Fortnightly Review*.

Webb and Pease had met Richard T. Ely (1854–1943) in Baltimore, when he taught at Johns Hopkins University, during their American visit in 1889; they had not then been much impressed, considering that he was nervous of being called a socialist for social and academic reasons. Ely's book *The Labour Movement in America* (1886) led to his creation at the University of Wisconsin, where he spent most of his academic career, of the school of labour economists which included Frederick Jackson Turner and John R. Commons.

The T.U.C. declaration was the policy of encouraging labour candidates.

The joint *Socialist Manifesto* came from an attempt to bring together the Fabian Society, the Social Democratic Federation and William Morris's Hammersmith Socialist Society after – and in reaction to – the formation of the I.L.P. It was drafted by Shaw, Henry Myers Hyndman and Morris for publication on May Day 1893. It made no impact. It was, Shaw wrote to Walter Crane (SCL 15 December 95) 'a string of the old phrases and a few ambiguities by which Hyndman meant one thing and I another'.

41 Grosvenor Road, Westminster Embankment

1 February, 94

Dear Dr Ely

I am glad to hear your book on Socialism is at hand. As regards progress in England, the best I can say 'in a few words' is the introductory chapter to the Second Edition of my *Socialism in England* which I send you herewith. There are no statistics of Socialism; indeed, I doubt whether the nominal membership of the few avowedly Socialist propagandist bodies varies very much. They are all actually what the Fabian Society is explicitly, rather nuclei of educational influence, than numerically strong voting armies. Their relations *inter se* remain much as I described them in 1889.

I think your selection of programmes is good. But you might add the Trade Union Congress declaration at Belfast last September. (It is in Fabian Tract 49); and whatever may be done at the ensuing Conference of the Independent Labor Party at Manchester in the next few weeks. I would not revive the *Communist Manifesto*. On the other hand the *Joint Socialist Manifesto of England*, 1893, deserves a place.

I am sending you a few stray pamphlets which may interest you.

With kind regards,

Yours very truly

Sidney Webb

41 Grosvenor Road, Westminster Embankment

Feb. 21st 1894

Dear Professor Ely

I am glad to receive your slips on Socialism.

(1) If you are incorporating them in book form may I say that your

reference to the London County Council salaries is misleading. It is true that Burns did let slip in the heat of debate the unhappy phrase you quote. But his *action* has been much more sensible. And no one would gather from your statement that the London County Council pays no fewer than 47 of its officials over £500 a year, 20 of them getting £1000 or over – no bad sums according to English scale.

(2) Not the 'trust', but the National Post Office, the Municipal Water-works or the Parish School is the model of Socialists.

Throughout your articles I think you ignore too much the steady growth of actual Socialism, i.e. Municipal or National administration – see my *Socialism in England*, and my essay in *Fabian Essays*. I think you write too much as if Socialism could be established, or even conceived as established *uno ictu*. The day will never come when Socialism will be 'established' in any sense that it was not established the day before.

(3) Agriculture and the export trade will probably be the last industries to be brought under collective ownership. But we already see our way to collective *ownership* of the land, even if the 'parish council' lets it out to individual farmers or groups of farmers.

(4) We only suggest that extensions of collective administration become possible *pari passu* with the growth of the motive of social esteem.

(5) Do you really believe that the opposition would come from the exceptionally gifted? It seems to be on the contrary that these are the first to place their services at the disposal of the Community 'for love', as we say. It is the ordinary man who 'stands on his rights', and it is the *stupid* men and women now living on rent and interest – not the able ones – who are our bitterest opponents. Socialism implies '*la carrière ouverte aux talens*' in the fullest sense – the career of social esteem.

(6) I am sorry you disbelieve somewhat in Democracy. However that is not particularly our affair as Socialists anymore than Democratic Indi-vidualism. We suggest that culture and learning come off better in Ger-many where they exist on public funds – (and thus under Collectivism) than in the United States where, in spite of your many universities, Individual-ism draws your able men off to make money. Surely a multiplication of endowed professors, and teachers, a shutting off of the avenues of mere money-making, a growth in social feeling offers a better chance for a natural aristocracy than Individualist Commerce.

I send these free criticisms and suggestions because I know you always welcome such, and because it is the way in which we can all best help one another's thought.

Yours very truly

Sidney Webb

Burns, Beatrice noted, was a man of 'splendid physique, fine strong intelligence, human sympathy, practical capacity' who seemed the most promising labour leader of his day. (BWD 12 October 93) Realising that he was marred by vanity and by jealousy of Keir Hardie the Webbs knew that he could never emerge at the head of a labour party; yet they continued to hope much from him. Burns was equally ambivalent towards them. At the time of this letter Beatrice thought he showed 'an excessive admiration for the brain-working class'; in later years Burns turned against the Webbs as manipulators who, he believed, intrigued against him.

41 Grosvenor Road, Westminster Embankment
[21.2.1894]

Dear Mr Burns

Here at last is a copy of our *History of Trade Unionism* to be published *on the 1st of May*. I hope you will find it some little use as a book of reference, and that it will supply some modicum of powder to your constant cannonade against existing evils.

I am rather afraid it will be a little too heavy and costly for the ordinary trade unionist, but I cannot help thinking that the young officials of the big societies would find a good deal of useful information in it, if they could be persuaded to ask for it at public libraries. So indeed would the ordinary M.P. – do boom it in the Lobby!

Ever yours
Sincerely

Beatrice Webb

285 PP  SIDNEY WEBB TO PROFESSOR BRENTANO

In the two years that Beatrice and Sidney worked through the mass of historical data on trade unionism they developed the style of collaboration which persisted throughout their partnership. Beatrice enjoyed research and took pleasure in interviewing; Sidney was never comfortable in face-to-face situations. Beatrice, said Frank Galton looking back on their collaboration, was 'largely responsible for the plans . . . while all the actual construction was done by Sidney . . . in the large flowing handwriting which he wrote with great speed'. Beatrice's ingenuity and imaginative range were the admirable complement to Sidney's 'executive power and driving force'. (MS autobiography: BLPES)

On completing the *History*, which was more a report of the facts which they had assembled than an analysis of the development of trade unionism, the Webbs realised that they had written the book without any definite theory of trade unions. They therefore decided to begin at once on another book, which became *Industrial Democracy*, in an attempt to weave their data into a comprehensive theory.

Lujo Brentano's *Hours and Wages in Relation to Production* was published in English in 1894.

41 Grosvenor Road
Westminster Embankment
13.4.94

Dear Professor Brentano

Mrs Webb and I were glad to receive your *Hours and Wages in Relation to Production* which comes opportunely just when our big capitalists are dismayed at the Government adopting the Eight Hours Day in the War Office and Admiralty. Scarcely a week passes without an announcement of some small firm or another following their example, but the great establishments in the shipbuilding trade, and the textile mills, are still obdurate. The movement for a legal limitation of hours gathers way rapidly – the doctrinaire objection has been largely abandoned – and John Morley's own Cabinet now blesses the Miner's Eight Hours Bill, though the House of Commons situation makes the actual passing of any Bills whatsoever very doubtful.

Our own book – *The History of Trade Unionism* – will be published by Longman's about 1st May. We shall of course send you one of the first copies, and we would fain hope to be encouraged by the approval of one who will always be regarded as the discoverer of trade union history! Working in your footsteps we have produced what will, I fear, be considered a very ponderous volume of 558 pages, entirely devoted to the history of the general movement. The analysis we reserve for another volume.

Do you think we could possibly get any sale in Germany? The book has been expensive to produce and will be published at 18/-. But it ought to delight the German student, for we have tried to make it *thorough*. Perhaps some of the university or other public libraries might take copies. Would you advise us to send any copies to German periodicals for review, and if so, to which? The publishers rather doubt whether there will be any Continental sale for so English a book.

We have had a proposal from P. H. W. Dietz of Stuttgart to translate the book – that is, he has asked on what terms he might do so. We have replied suggesting that he had better wait until he has seen the volume, as we think it would prove an expensive work to translate, as needing so much annotation to make it intelligible.

Would it be troubling you too much to ask you what you think of Dietz in such a matter? Of course we should be glad to be honoured by a German translation, but the volume will be read only by students, and we do not feel sure that Dietz could command more than a popular circulation, and perhaps our book would not really suit him.

Is there any chance of you being in England this year? When you come, you must, of course, come to see us. We shall be very pleased indeed if we can have the pleasure of discussing some of these problems with you.

Yours very truly

Sidney Webb

Mrs J. R. Green's *Town Life in the Fifteenth Century* (Macmillan. 2 vols. 32/-) will interest you, as dealing graphically with much new material about English towns.

## 286 BL BEATRICE WEBB TO JOHN BURNS

Burns was an energetic collector of books, pamphlets and newspapers on labour history and in the course of his life built up a notable personal library in this field. The *Beehive* was edited by George Potter (1839–93) a building worker who played a significant part in the mid-century revival of trade unionism.

41 Grosvenor Road, Westminster Embankment
April 18th [1894]

Dear Mr Burns

I am sorry to say that we never had the old *Beehive* Vol. Nov. 1861; if you will look in page 501 of *The History of Trade Unionism* (Bibliography), you will see the entry

'*Beehive* London 4° *Weekly*'
'1861–2 [no copy known]'
'1863–9 Burns Coll.'

That, I think, will convince you that so far as we know, you never had this volume.

I am sorry that we have drifted so far apart since those far off days, when we were all working for the same camp. But such is life!

Ever yours sincerely
Beatrice Webb

## 287 FP SIDNEY WEBB TO EDWARD PEASE

In May the Webbs went on a holiday to Venice and the Italian Lakes. Their first real vacation since their marriage was, Beatrice noted, 'a true honeymoon of common love and enjoyment'. (BWD 21 May 94) In July they rented Borough Farm, near Godalming, for their summer recess. They found the new book 'a horrid grind'. (BWD 10 July 94) Wallas, who already knew the house from visits when it was occupied by Mrs Humphry Ward, stayed with them to work on his Place biography. During the summer Beatrice regretted the fact that she would have no children. The deliberate foregoing of motherhood, she felt, thwarted the nature of a woman: 'we chose this course on our marriage – but then I had passed the age when it is easy and natural for a woman to become a child-bearer – my physical nature was to some extent dried up at 35 after ten years stress and strain of a purely brain-working and sexless life . . . as it is I sometimes wonder whether I had better not have risked it and taken my chance'. (BWD 28 July 94) Beatrice found the 'analytical deductive' work on *Industrial Democracy* difficult, noting that she and Sidney were attempting to do three things at the same time – to combine a study of trade union development with a homily to trade unionists and an apology for the unions to the middle classes. (BWD 10 August 94)

The continuing reorganisation of local government opened new opportunities for Fabian publicity and the training of the new entrants into public life. Tract 53, *The Parish Councils Act: What it is and How to Work it*, was written by Herbert Samuel, not a member of the Society. In the course of 1894 he wrote three other tracts on rural problems.

The suggested helpers have not been further identified. Joseph Arch (1826–1919) organised the rural workers: he was Liberal M.P. for N.W. Norfolk 1885–6, and 1892–1902.

Borough Farm, Milford, Surrey.
21.7.94

Dear Pease

1. Will send some pars for *News*.

2. As regards District Council Question re Cottages, I don't know what I was thinking of. I suppose it should be

'Will you vote for pressing the County Council to provide new cottages out of the rates in the villages in which they are needed.' The District Council, as responsible for sanitation, ought to stir in the matter.

3. I concur in sending only the Tract to the country papers this time. By the way, don't forget the various papers published in London for country circulation (*Lloyds, Reynolds, The People, The Dispatch, Weekly Budget, Weekly Times* etc.). You will, I suppose, send a Circular letter with the Tract, calling the Editor's attention to it? This seems well worth printing.

4. It is of the utmost importance not to drop the scheme of sending the Questions into every parish. Wallas and I strongly urge that you should push this actively forward. To get the names, we recommend the following:

(a) Exhaust Verinder, offering to send someone to copy out any names he will place at your disposal.

(b) Write to Theodore Dodd consulting him, and asking every help he can give.

(c) Write specially to Hamilton (for Wilts) Hines (for Oxford) and so on, requiring them to send full lists for these counties.

(d) Ask Samuel to give you someone in each parish in his constituency for future use and reference.

(e) Go and consult privately Donald Murray, the Secretary of the N.L.C. and get from him on the quiet whatever names he has for his village libraries scheme.

(f) Remember that *most* villages are not agricultural but mining, or textile etc. Galton can give much help in the way of T.U. branch addresses in Lancs, Durham, Northumberland etc.

(g) Get Galton to exhaust the National Agricultural Labourers Union (Arch's) and its newspaper – also the various branches of Verinder's Unions.

(h) You might try Hudson and the Nat. Lib. Federation, asking them to allow you to use the names they have collected. At any rate, get the list of delegates to the Laborers Conference in 1891(?)

(i) Above all, try Corrie Grant. He probably has a pile of letters asking questions. You might offer to sort and index these letters, if he would let you copy the addresses.

One way and another it ought to be possible to compile a list of several thousand country addresses, which will be very useful in future. I suggest that you should start 40 or 50 little penny books, one for each county.

5. It will be quite worth while sending the 'Questions' and leaflets to your 1000 country newspapers in a couple of months time and so repeat the advertisement.

The Parish Councils Election is of the utmost importance to us, as opening a new field of influence.

6. Will think about T. Union class and write you in a day or two.

Yours

Sidney Webb

# 2. A School of Economics
## August 1894 – December 1897

On 26 July the Derby solicitor Henry Hunt Hutchinson shot himself. By a will signed in the previous October he left about half his estate to be used over ten years for 'the propaganda and other purposes' of the Fabian Society 'and its Socialism' and to advancing Fabian objects 'in any way' that Webb and other Fabians nominated as trustees should 'deem advisable'. Hutchinson knew De Mattos, William Clarke and Pease through his previous gift of money to support Fabian provincial lectures. But he was scarcely known to the London Fabians he chose to implement the ambiguous provisions of his bequest: the legacy came as a complete surprise to Webb and his colleagues. As soon as Sidney and Beatrice learned of it at Borough Farm they decided that they would not permit the Society to make 'a big political splash' with the money; they were determined that it should not be frittered away on futile parliamentary campaigns, used as a general subsidy 'to save the pockets' of ordinary subscribers, or dissipated on 'mere propaganda of the Shibboleths of Collectivism'. What was needed was '*hard thinking*'. The fact that Hutchinson had left the money in the hands of trustees rather than to the Society as such enabled Sidney to divert the money to the Webb plan of founding a School of Economics in London 'which would train experts in the task of reforming society'. (BWD 21 September 94) Such a diversion, however, was arguably legal in the letter and Webb's critics among the Fabians thought it was undeniably a violation of the spirit of the bequest. From the moment he heard of the Hutchinson gift Webb realised that he must move warily and conceal his manipulations from the mass of the membership. A year later, on 1 July 1895, Shaw still found it necessary to write to Beatrice complaining that Sidney was giving an impression of shady behaviour and antagonising the Fabian executive. In the longer run Webb's use of the money was a recurring source of difficulty, especially with Ramsay MacDonald who, quarrelling with the Webbs on other grounds, often sought to discover how Webb had actually spent the money in order to expose him as a man of bad faith. For the whole decade in which Webb was responsible for the Hutchinson Trust he was at pains to keep its accounts protected against Fabian scrutiny.

Miss C. was Hutchinson's daughter Constance.

Borough Farm, Milford,
Surrey
3/8/94

Private

Dear Pease

Hutchinson is dead leaving, I am told, some £13,000 or so, about half in family legacies, and the other half in trust for Socialist propaganda – Miss Constance and I sole executors – the trustees of the half to be Miss C. and I, together with you, De Mattos and Clarke!!

Don't tell anyone all this – we ought to keep it as quiet as we can, lest there be huge claims from everyone. It does not seem to me clear that the Will might not be disputed. Anyhow it is a great trouble.

Yours

Sidney Webb

Hutchinson's solicitor was doubtful whether the will was valid: it might be shown that Hutchinson was not of sound mind and that its terms were too vague. Hutchinson, moreover, had left his wife only a hundred-pound annuity and lesser bequests to his two sons and two daughters.

Borough Farm, Milford, Godalming
22/8/94

Dear Pease

Touching the will I wrote about, I have seen the Co-Executor who reports that opposition is probable on the part of widow and son – so don't say anything about the matter at present. It may clear itself up later.

I append a few notes on other side.

Galton has been stirring around to get rural addresses and there should by this time be many hundreds at least. Now that harvest is over I think the sooner we send to them the better.

He will also be able to supply you presently with a list of a couple of hundred Continental Economists to whom I think we might send specimen tracts.

Yours

Sidney Webb

Add to *Press* List

*The Single Tax*, 7 Argyle St., Glasgow.
*The Scottish Co-operator*, Glasgow.

21

I have just arranged for 25 copies of the *History of Trade Unionism* to go to the Co-operative Union for cash, on best trade terms. These are

$$
\begin{array}{ll}
\text{25 as 24 – at 12/10} & \text{15. 8. 0} \\
\text{5\% discount} & \underline{\hphantom{15. }15. 5} \\
& \text{14. 12. 7}
\end{array}
$$

equal to 11/8½ each. If the Fabian Society did the same, they could thus retail at 11/9 or 12/- a copy.

---

290 FP   SIDNEY WEBB TO EDWARD PEASE

Only Wallas and Shaw had so far been told of the scheme to promote a School of Economics.

Borough Farm, Milford, Godalming
25/8/94

Dear Pease

I can't possibly go to Glasgow. But it is an interesting move, and if you can get someone, send him. MacDonald would be very useful there, I should think.

As regards leaflets, I do not think you should count on any subsidy from the source I wrote about. It seems very possible that the whole matter will be contested, and it would be quite unsafe to rely on our getting anything. Moreover, the view that I take very strongly is that (even if it comes off) the Trustees ought to make it a strict rule not to help the ordinary, current purposes of the Society (or else we shall merely dry up all other contributions, and thus gain nothing at all) but that any funds should be kept exclusively for special work of a larger kind. I look for important additions to our supply of books from it: we need this more than anything. Another, I should like to attract the clever young economists to the working out of Collectivism, and thus get some 'research' done.

After all, the lecturing and tract distributing comes to naught unless there is some solid work of costly but not showy character going on behind it. Unless we can 'keep up the sacred fire' there will be no sparks to carry about presently, and the whole thing will peter out.

However, we will talk this over when the time comes. But meanwhile don't commit us to any, even the least, liability.

Yours
Sidney Webb

---

291 FP   SIDNEY WEBB TO EDWARD PEASE

A number of letters to Pease on minor aspects of the Hutchinson legacy during the remainder of 1894 have been omitted.

Dear Pease

I shall not be able to attend Exec. on Friday.

With regard to the legacy, things have progressed merely to point that I have now formally authorised the Derby solicitor to prove the will, and he is going to do so. I think it is necessary that a communication should be made to the Executive. Will you kindly inform them (you had better read this letter) that under Hutchinson's will, his daughter and I are left Executors: that after specific legacies to the family, the residue is left in trust to be administered by 5 trustees in any way they may think fit for the 'purposes of the Fabian Society and its Socialism' within 10 years: the trustees being myself as first Chairman, yourself, Miss Constance Hutchinson, Clarke and De Mattos – that there is every prospect that the sum coming to the trustees may be several thousand pounds, but that there is quite a possibility of the will being upset by the family, as there are several awkward points – and that accordingly it is of the utmost importance that it should be kept a dead secret. Nothing dries up the subscriptions so much as a rumour of a legacy, and if any word of it gets out – especially in the papers – we shall get no more money. Any sums receivable will not come in for a long time, if at all, and will not come to the Society as such. They ought moreover in any case to be applied for special objects, quite outside the Society's usual expenditure.

Yours

Sidney Webb

292 FP   SIDNEY WEBB TO EDWARD PEASE

Tract 60 was written by Webb: *The London Vestries: What They are and What they Do.*

Dear Pease

The Vestry tract is as you say, urgent. Do what you can to hurry it up.

Country lectures. These are important, and I would keep them up if we can possibly afford it – I cannot judge as to this. But please make it quite clear that nothing is to be expected from the Hutchinson fund for such expenses. Even if all goes well, I do not think the trustees would be wise to do anything which the Society itself is doing. If the trustees begin to meet deficits, subscriptions will fall off, and there will be no end to it.

This would not in my view exclude the possibility of the trustees occasionally making a grant for some specific purpose. However, a more immediate reason is that I do not see how the trustees (even if all goes well) could be in a position to begin operations for some months to come – perhaps more – as their trust, being a residue, does not come into existence until all the other business is done.

But at the present juncture I believe very much in country lecturing, and doing all we can to keep the local societies alive. Hence my vote is distinctly for going on, if the cash will at all run to it.

Yours

Sidney Webb

### 293 FP  SIDNEY WEBB TO EDWARD PEASE

One clause in Hutchinson's will gave five hundred pounds to cover the cost of examining his unpublished writings with a view to publication and donated his books to the Fabian Society.

Borough Farm, Milford, Surrey<br>24/9/94

Dear Pease

I saw the Hutchinson brothers today. What they want is £200 a year for their mother, instead of £100; and some ready money for her, as she is left practically penniless, and cannot draw the annuity for six months. I answered sympathetically on both points, and said I would consult the trustees. They much want a definite answer this week if possible, so I have written to Clarke and De Mattos, summoning them to a meeting of the trustees on Wednesday *next*, 26th inst. at *noon*, at Fabian office. Please attend yourself as a trustee.

Of course I think we should grant both demands. I have asked that the deceased's books be sent direct to you, carriage unpaid – debit the trust. I have told Clarke and De Mattos, if they can't attend, to call and see you. Please explain, and get their consent if they come.

The brothers Hutchinson propose to call on you – merely friendly, tomorrow. Be sympathetic and say you cannot pledge the others, etc.

Yours

Sidney Webb

### 294 FP  SIDNEY WEBB TO EDWARD PEASE

Only Webb, Pease and De Mattos were at the meeting of the Hutchinson trustees on the previous day. They decided that they needed the approval of the Fabian executive before they could proceed with the proposed composition with Mrs Hutchinson, which was an arrangement quite outside the terms of the will. Webb also wanted the executive to endorse his decision that the trustees rather than the Society should control the spending of the money. It was a tricky position to take and it fell to Shaw, in Webb's absence, to defend it at the executive meeting on 28 September. That evening Shaw sent a full account of the difficulties caused by Webb's contradictory desires to secure the executive's

24

approval without conceding that it had any say in the disposition of the bequest. (PP) Both Hubert Bland and Sidney Olivier were openly critical and Shaw foresaw further friction. Webb, he felt, was treating his executive colleagues as children and risking his standing in the Society by apparent evasion and concealment. Always meticulous and honourable in financial matters he insisted that 'a monetary transaction cannot be too clear'. The idea of consulting Haldane had been mooted at the executive and on 6 October Sidney formally requested Haldane to give counsel's opinion on the powers of the trustees and the rights of the Fabian Society: in his reply Haldane broadly endorsed the position that Webb had taken. By now Webb had privately let it be known that the trustees planned to make *ex gratia* grants to the Fabian Society to support its educational work of lectures and publications: Haldane had firmly declared that none of the money could legally be used for the support of candidates at elections.

Borough Farm, Milford, Godalming
27th Sept. 1894

Dear Pease

Will you please bring before the Fabian Executive tomorrow the following position of the Trustees under Hutchinson's will.

It appears that the estate is larger than was supposed – about £20,000 – and that the residue coming to the trustees, if no opposition is made, and all goes smoothly, may amount to some £9,000.

But it has been very forcibly pressed on the Executors and Trustees by Mrs Hutchinson, by her two sons and her daughter, and by the solicitor, that it is practically impossible to leave Mrs Hutchinson with the miserable sum of £100 a year, (her bequest under the will) which is her *sole* resource. After considerable enquiry and discussion, it was yesterday agreed at a meeting of the trustees, to purchase for her an annuity of £200 a year, instead of the £100 and to pay her, in addition, one year's annuity in advance (£200), as she would otherwise be without means of support. The trustees also agreed to forego any claim to the furniture and personal effects which the testator – clearly by inadvertence – left to them. The value of these is said to be trivial (not more than £20 or so).

I think it will be easily understood that these concessions, (which seem to me to be called for by common humanity) can be justified by considerations of prudent administration, as any opposition to the will on the part of the widow, even if entirely unsuccessful, would involve considerable costs.

The decision is a matter for the trustees alone, as the bequest is to them, and not to the Fabian Society. But, by strict law, the trustees have no power to make any such compromise with the family, without a friendly action at law, and an order of the Committee. As there is no person who would have any right to object, it seems unnecessary to go to this expense. But in view of the fact that the trustees' decision might hereafter be criticised by any stray member of this or any other Socialist organisation, as diverting to private purposes funds intended to advance Socialism, the trustees would like to be fortified in their decision by an expression of approval from the Fabian Executive.

Yours truly

Sidney Webb

## 295 PP  BEATRICE WEBB TO MARY PLAYNE

After Alice Green's visit Beatrice noted that her friend had become 'disillusioned' with the Webbs' 'sordid simplicity, lack of culture and general lower middle-class-ness'. Mrs Green, she felt, had succumbed to the aristocratic embrace as eagerly as she had formerly embraced 'Demos in all his most objectionable forms'. Unless the Webbs speedily became distinguished, Beatrice added, 'that is, thought well of by London Society (a fate which is not likely to befall us) I fear we shall see little more of Alice Green'. (BWD 9 October 94)

London local government was an archaic patchwork of vestries, based upon parish boundaries, with lay elected members: there were over five thousand elective places in all. They dealt with sanitation, street cleaning and lighting, and similar minor services. The Webbs tried to activate the London Reform Union, which served as the electioneering arm of the Progressive Party, to play a larger role in the coming elections in December. They formed a branch of the L.R.U. in Westminster and made their house the campaign headquarters for a list of ninety candidates. Elections for the London School Board took place at the same time, the Webbs being particularly concerned with the successful attempt by Graham Wallas to secure re-election. In the event only five of the Progressive candidates were returned in the Westminster vestry contest.

Mademoiselle Gaudier was a French investigator of women's work and education who was attending a conference in London. Noel Williams was the son of Beatrice' sister Rosalind.

Borough Farm, Milford, Surrey<br>[?early October 1894]

My dear Mary

I was delighted to see your handwriting and to get your nice letter of news. With regard to Mlle Gaudier, if she can stay three weeks from the 22nd that will suit me as well as the 14th. But I have worn out every article of clothing I possess down here and want a completely new outfit so I cannot give up any part of the time. Perhaps you would ask her whether she could stay as long as she arranged to from the 22nd October. You did not send me her letter so I cannot tell what she proposes.

We are still down here and do not return until the 12th to London. Rosie and Noel are with us. She seems to me very happy just now and fairly strong, and Noel is a charming little fellow and very pleasant in the house. Graham Wallas has left us to look up his School Board companions, and Bernard Shaw is coming back this afternoon after three weeks in Italy, Mrs Green and Mr Taylor paid us a flying visit, otherwise we have been very quiet working away at our second volume, Sidney running up to town once or twice a week on L.C.C. business. When we get back to London we shall be very busy in the Technical Education Board with its daily increasing work in all directions [it] gives Sidney a good deal to think about especially in finding out who are the best men in each department of science and art. It is difficult to spend £100,000 a year easily! But Dr Garnett is turning out a good Director and the Board is wonderfully docile so that I hope the work will not be so heavy after this year. Miss Pycroft continues to be, so far as one can judge, very successful. She certainly manages to get on with 'all sorts and conditions of men' in a quite surprising manner. Her absence of conventionality seems to stand her in good stead with the rum and scratch lot of persons whom you have to work with in any London organisation. But I imagine you taught her a good deal of wisdom in Gloucestershire.

We are beginning to prepare for the Westminster Vestry Election at which both Sidney and I will probably stand. It is a horrid reactionary neighbourhood but we may possibly 'surprise' the seat as the old gang seem to have gone fast asleep. That takes place the middle of December. We should much like to come down and see you in November, perhaps the last Sunday in November. Sidney could get away for the Sunday and I would stay on for a day or two. But he will see about that later on and you will let me know whether that would suit you. I shall be interested to know something of your School of Cookery – I am glad those Meinertzhagen girls are having a spell of hard work! It will do them a world of good.

Ever yours affectionately<br>Beatrice Webb

## 296 HP   SIDNEY WEBB TO HUTCHINSON TRUSTEES AND FABIANS

To protect himself against the charge that he had not consulted Fabian opinion about the Hutchinson money Sidney sent a letter to each of the trustees and to a number of prominent Fabians to invite suggestions. Eight replies were received: one suggested a Fabian newspaper; another a project on international affairs; a third proposed a correspondence school to teach Fabianism, with examinations before admission to the Society.

The Hutchinson Trustees would be very glad if you would help them with any suggestions as to the best way of using their funds.

They feel that so large a bequest places on them the responsibility of setting on foot important and substantial work, not necessarily all of one kind, which may be calculated to exercise a solid and lasting influence in aid of Collectivist progress. It seems clear that this work should be educational in character, and there might be some advantage in the Trustees paying special attention to any department which is not being adequately attended to by existing agencies. The most pressing needs of the Collectivist movement in England at the present moment appear to be (1) a wider diffusion among the people and especially among Socialists and I.L.P. members of accurate knowledge as to the economic bearings of public administration; (2) further research into the unsolved problems of municipal and national government, so as to renew and freshen the propaganda; (3) the attraction to these studies of clever and educated recruits.

Whether these, or any other ends should be specially aimed at by the Trustees, and if so, in what way they can best be attained, demands careful consideration.

The Trustees would be very grateful for any suggestions, however slight, that you could give them. They should be sent to me within the next fortnight.

[Sidney Webb]

### 297 SUL  SIDNEY WEBB TO W. A. S. HEWINS

William Albert Samuel Hewins (1865–1931) was an economist and tutor at Pembroke College, Oxford. The Webbs, who had met him casually in the Bodleian Library while doing research in Oxford during the previous autumn, were impressed by his unorthodox economics and his interest in university extension work. They had already had some general discussion with him about their idea of creating a specialist college for teaching economics.

Sidney had begun his campaign for re-election to the L.C.C. It was clear that the political tide was setting towards the Tories and Lord Salisbury encouraged his party to intervene vigorously in the London elections. On 23 January the Webbs gave a dinner party to explore the possibility of electoral collaboration between the Fabians and the I.L.P. Pease and Shaw came for the Fabians; Ramsay MacDonald, Keir Hardie and Tom Mann for the I.L.P. Nothing came of the discussion because the I.L.P. refused to support Liberal or Progressive candidates. Beatrice concluded that the Fabians should stick to their 'policy of innoculation – of giving to each class, to each person, coming under our influence, the exact dose of collectivism that they were prepared to assimilate. And we should continue to improve and enlarge such machinery of government that came into our hands'. (BWD 23 January 95)

The L.C.C. elections on 2 March resulted in a dead-heat between the Moderates and the Progressives, the latter retaining technical control of the Council. Sidney held his seat in Deptford but his running-mate was defeated. He was disappointed by the results, blaming in part the economic depression, in part the failure of the Liberals in national affairs: he noted unhappily that the newer Progressives who stood for an advanced social policy had done less well than better-known but conventional Liberals.

My dear Hewins

The estate business has taken longer than I expected, and even now the funds are not yet handed over to the trustees. However this is, I hope, only a matter of a week or two now.

More serious is the fact that I have only two hemispheres to my brain, and ten fingers! This County Council Election is a very big fight.

But I will try to get some preliminaries settled in a week or two. Thanks for all your help. Will write you again as soon as I can.

Sidney Webb

### 298 HP  SIDNEY WEBB TO HUTCHINSON TRUSTEES

The Hutchinson trustees met on 8 February and approved this memorandum from Webb. They also agreed to offer the post of Director of the proposed School to Graham Wallas, personally acceptable to Fabians yet sufficiently moderate to avoid antagonising academic and commercial opinion on whose goodwill the success of the venture might depend. It has been suggested that this was merely a manoeuvre on Webb's part to conciliate the Fabians, that he knew Wallas would decline and that he had already decided upon Hewins. This view is not supported by the tone of a letter to Pease on 25 March in which Webb said that the refusal of Wallas 'rather upsets our plans' or by the tenor of his letter to Hewins on 24 March.

8 February 1895

After a great deal of discussion with all sorts of authorities, it seems to me clear that we should make it our main object to promote *education* – not mere propaganda in the parties or controversies of the hour, but solid work in economic and political principles.

The greatest needs of the Collectivist movement in England appear to me

(a) An increase in the number of *educated* and able lecturers and writers, as apart from propagandist speakers;

(b) The further investigation of problems of municipal and national administration from a Collectivist standpoint. This implies original research, and the training of additional persons competent to do such work;

(c) The diffusion of economic and political knowledge of a real kind – as apart from Collectivist shibboleths, and the cant and claptrap of political campaigning.

All this means attracting and training clever recruits, setting them to do work on social problems, and then using them to educate the people. Ten years of this work might change the whole political thinking of England.

We might, of course, throw ourselves unreservedly into organising a kind of 'University Extension' lecturing on social and economic subjects all over England. But the difficulty would be to find the staff of lecturers, able and trained in our questions, sympathetic to our views, and really competent to do what we want. I do not know more than one or two such persons who would be at all likely to be available for the work. A mere increase in the number of Socialist orations, however good, is not what we want.

Moreover, even from the propaganda side the material needs 'freshening'. We have all rather worked ourselves out. New investigations and original research – historical, statistical, economic and political, is indispensable. We want, too, new blood.

Putting together all these views and requirements it seems to me that we should do well to establish two distinct sides to our work, and develop each of them as circumstances demand. We need a *School of Investigation and Research*; and we need *educational lecturing* to spread the results of such a school. At first, the investigation and research should take the greatest place. Gradually the educational lecturing might expand as we obtained lecturers.

The following outlines may serve as a basis for discussion.

### The London School of Economics and Political Science

To arrange for original lectures on all topics within its scope: to pay well for such lectures, and to order them in advance, so as to secure new work; to be scientific, not partisan; to be under a Director, who should receive a salary, part of his time, perhaps taking always one course of lectures. The object of the School to be primarily research, and the training of researchers – the public lecturing being only a part of the purpose (a means rather than the end). The subjects I thought about as such as we could take up at once and get good work done are the following. (Chosen rather because I know of suitable men available.)

The History of the Regulation of Wages by Law, and its results.
Growth and development of English Working Class movement (Chartism, etc.).
The Working of Democratic Machinery (home and foreign).
Arbitration and Conciliation, Sliding Scales, etc.
Railway Economics.
Factory Act experiments.

Of course many other topics could be suggested, when the men can be found.

I can see my way to starting such a *School* in London next October, if it can be agreed upon at once. The experiment would not cost more than £500 for the first year. It would make a great public sensation, and would, I am convinced, 'catch on'. If not, it need not be continued.

I should propose that £500 be appropriated to the purpose, and the experiment be tried. I can give details at the meeting.

I believe such a School could get support from the Technical Education Board, to enable it to have other lectures – e.g. on Currency, Commercial Geography, etc. – which would supplement ours.

In connection with the *School*, we should I think, start a series of publications (say half-a-crown books). *Not more propaganda* but serious and original studies, or else translations and reprints. These would pay their way, if well done, but we should have to find the capital. It would be all-important to start with volumes of solid and real merit. I have thought of the following:

Translation of Condorcet's *Vie de Turgot*, with introduction and notes (The Economist as Administrator).

Documents illustrative of the Legal Regulation of Wages.

Documents illustrative of the Industrial Revolution.

These two proposals, viz.

£500 to start, experimentally, a London School of Economics and Political Science;

£150 for the Fabian Society to organise, during 1895–6, country lecturing on the 'University Extension' plan

are all that I make at present. These two plans (with their developments) would, if successful, soon take all our funds, and I suggest trying the experiments first.


299 SUL   SIDNEY WEBB TO W. A. S. HEWINS

On 28 March the Hutchinson trustees formally decided to invite Hewins to become Director of the L.S.E.

41 Grosvenor Road, Westminster Embankment

24.3.59

Dear Hewins

The project of the 'London School of Economics' – necessarily dormant during elections as far as I was concerned – was, I hoped, progressing. But Graham Wallas now decides after all that he cannot undertake the Directorship!

This is an unexpected blow. I write in haste to ask whether it would be possible for you to come and see me any day during the coming week. We should be very pleased to put you up. It is now a matter of serious import whether the scheme can be carried through. I am still keen on it, and if it should be possible for you to help to a greater extent than we contemplated it might still be done.

Yours very truly

Sidney Webb

41 Grosvenor Road, s.w.
29 March/95

Dear Pease

Will you please inform the Fabian Executive that at a meeting of the Hutchinson Trustees yesterday, it was decided to place at the disposal of the Executive during the ensuing year, under certain conditions, a sum not exceeding two hundred pounds for the purpose of providing educational lectures in the provinces on a definite plan.

It is proposed that the arrangements for these lectures should be carried out by the Fabian Society, and on this ground £50 out of the £200 is specifically allocated as a contribution towards the general office expenses. The balance will cover the following proposals.

(a) Printing syllabus of courses which Miss Enid Stacey has already arranged in and about Manchester on her own account – Autumn 1895.

(b) Series of Courses by Miss Stacey in Spring of 1896.

(c) Expenses of study and preparation by her in summer of 1895.

(d) Expenses of series of courses by J. R. MacDonald in Autumn of 1895.

These proposals are elaborated in the annexed report. The idea, in brief, is to have courses of 6 or 8 weekly lectures, going on simultaneously at 6 or 8 towns, worked from a centre. The arrangement made, and any proposed changes, to be reported to the Trustees from time to time for their approval.

Yours

Sidney Webb

### Country Lecturing

This must wait, for the most part, until we have men and matter. But I think we can do a little at once. I think we could, for £150, arrange each year two sets of courses (six lectures, simultaneously in five or six towns worked by one man from a centre), one in the Autumn and one in the Spring. These could each be done for £50, which would leave £50 as a contribution to cover Fabian office and organising expenses.

I should propose to offer to the Fabian Society to bear the expense up to £150 of such courses of lectures. It might be well to *pay* the lecturers £25 down in advance, to enable them to *work* up their subjects in the summer. In this connection the annexed letter from J. M. MacDonald is interesting.

[A note from Graham Wallas setting out arrangements for the lectures which followed upon the suggestions attached to Webb's letter and upon discussion with MacDonald is attached to the Webb letter]

The money available to the Hutchinson trustees was a pathetically small base on which to rest ambitious plans. Their first allocation was just sufficient to provide a salary for Hewins, wages for a secretary and a porter, and the services of part-time lecturers. On 6 May Webb persuaded the Technical Education Board to provide £500 to support courses on commercial subjects. For the rest he was taking a great gamble on the ability of the new institution to attract enough funds to survive.

41 Grosvenor Road, Westminster Embankment

29 March/95

Dear Hewins

The Hutchinson Trustees decided yesterday to go ahead with the proposal of a London School of Economics and Political Science on the lines which you and I worked out together. They attach great importance to securing your cordial assistance and, indeed, unless you can undertake the Directorship and carry out the scheme, it will probably have to be abandoned. They recognise that there must be sufficient time for a fair trial, and they are prepared to set aside £2,000, so as to enable the scheme to go on for three years, unless it should become patently impossible, and be abandoned by common consent.

If you can move to London, and take up the work, they offer you an inclusive sum of £300 a year, to include Directorship, your own lectures (one course, or more as you may decide) and the editing of *the series* of books (as distinguished from the separate volumes).

This is not so much as they or I would wish, but it is as much as can be afforded. I hope it will prevent your actually losing by the move, and of course, if the School grows, the position would grow with it. The salary would begin from the 1st April 1895, so as to secure your thought and organising ability at once, and to afford some slight compensation towards your moving expenses – the School itself starting in October.

If, as I sincerely hope, you can help us on these terms, the sooner you set to work the better. The Trustees desire you to work out the project – in consultation with me – in the way you think best; and to enter into any necessary provisional negotiations – which can be reported to them in due course for their covering approval. If you can take up the work, the course is now absolutely clear for making every preparation, and I shall be glad to move in any matter that can best be done by myself, or by us together.

Yours very truly

Sidney Webb

302 SUL SIDNEY WEBB TO W. A. S. HEWINS

William Cunningham was professor of economics at King's College, London, Herbert Somerton Foxwell (1849–1936) was professor of political economy at

University College, London, from 1891 to 1927. He was one of the first lecturers at the L.S.E. He had built up a remarkable collection of books on economics which Webb sought to acquire for the L.S.E.

During the Easter holiday the Webbs went to what became a favourite place for their short vacations – the Beachy Head Hotel near Eastbourne. A party of Fabian friends including Shaw went with them and the group spent their time learning the newly-fashionable hobby of safety-cycling. Both the Webbs became enthusiasts and made long cross-country journeys in the next few years: Beatrice often shipped a cycle to towns where she was staying for research.

41 Grosvenor Road, Westminster Embankment
9 April 95

Dear Hewins

I have just seen Murray, the Secretary of the London Chamber of Commerce, who thinks there would probably be no difficulty in lending us their room (holding 100 or more) at St Botolph House, Eastcheap for the 'Higher Commercial' side of the School – for one or two evenings a week, free. Cunningham has just been giving a private course there to the clerks of their subscribers, and has had audiences averaging 50 or so. He thought there might be some difficulty in having Foxwell there, objection being made to his Bimetalism.

This seems to be [?me] to solve the difficulty. If we could begin by having some lectures at the Society of Arts, and some at the Chamber of Commerce – thus tapping two distinct audience fields – probably a single large room in John St would do us. Formal application to the Chamber of Commerce should go in by the end of the month. The importance of getting the name of the Chamber of Commerce is great – *inter alia* it may be worth £500 a year at the Technical Education Board.

It might be worth while getting a short course from Cunningham to carry on the tradition. Think about this.

Sidney Webb

303 SUL   SIDNEY WEBB TO W. A. S. HEWINS [*incomplete or unsigned*]

On 31 May the Hutchinson trustees agreed to rent premises at 9 John Street, Adelphi, for two years; they arranged with Longman's, Green to publish a list of books for the new School; and they set the fees at three pounds a session.

41 Grosvenor Road, Westminster Embankment
31.5.95

Dear Hewins

(1) Trustees approve generally (a) prospectus and lectures; (b) its communication to press next week; (c) publishing with Longmans; (d) our arrangements up to date.

(2) I am authorised to take the 3 rooms at 9 John St at £100 if you see

nothing to be done – the one room from Midsummer, the others from Michaelmas.

Nothing to be got at Statistical Society's house, and I know of nothing else. What do you think?

We ought to get the one room *very cheap* for the one quarter as the solicitor could get nothing for it for so short a time, in full vacation season – I should say, a few pounds only.

For the rest (I return the overlord's letter). I see no need of a *lease* for so short a term as 18 months – surely an agreement should serve? What would the housekeeper charge? How much do you reckon for furniture?

(3) Meanwhile, for press purposes, the Society of Arts might be the best address. Why not Chamber of Commerce also? – for similar reasons. Address, the Director at either place.

(You can decide and arrange to take 9 John St at once).

## 304 PP  SIDNEY WEBB TO EDWARD PEASE

*Ramsay MacDonald had drafted a leaflet for the expected general election: revised and expanded it was published as Tract No. 64, How to Lose and How to Win an Election.*

*The Webbs had a busy summer. Apart from Sidney's concern with the L.S.E. and the L.C.C. they were busy with their book and Beatrice went to Huddersfield in June for the Co-operative Congress. They showed little interest in the elections in July. On 8 June Beatrice noted that the Fabians were 'sitting with their hands in their laps'. She added: 'We wish the Liberals to be beaten but we do not wish the Tories to win'. The Liberals, obsessed with the problem of Home Rule, showed no interest in the social policies that the Webbs favoured; at the same time Beatrice dismissed the I.L.P. as 'babies in politics'. She felt that the best hope for the Webbs and their friends lay in 'permeating the young middle-class men – catching them for collectivism before they have enlisted on the other side'. The plan for L.S.E. was part of that design. After the polls, which gave Salisbury and Chamberlain's Liberal Unionists a substantial majority, Beatrice decided that 'the result is not altogether unsatisfactory': the 'official' Liberals, she felt, had been discredited and 'the I.L.P. has completed its suicide'. This rout 'leaves us free, indeed, to begin afresh on the old lines – of building up a new party on the basis of collectivism'. For the next ten years, by various means, the Webbs sought to find a way of establishing such a collectivist party as distinct from the Radical wing of the Liberals or the nascent labour party promoted by the I.L.P. and their sympathisers in the trade unions.*

*J. F. Oakeshott was an official employed at Somerset House who was a leading member of the Fellowship of the New Life and for some years on the Fabian executive. He was also a member of the Administrative Committee of the L.S.E.*

41 Grosvenor Road, Westminster Embankment

2 June, 1895

Dear Pease

*Election leaflet*

My view is that we should do better to expand this into a penny tract. The leaflet as it stands, seems to me too vague and general to be of much use. Perhaps I am wrong – in that case, I suggest that we should do better to have a really instructive tract on Electioneering first – for the use of the officers and non-commanding officers, so to speak – and then boil it down to a leaflet for the rank and file.

I have written some pages of such a tract, starting from MacDonald's opening, and intended to be sandwiched in his leaflet.

Will you submit this idea to him and Oakeshott? *I don't disapprove* the short leaflet, but think a fuller and more exact statement would be *more* useful.

Yours

Sidney Webb

305 FP  SIDNEY WEBB TO EDWARD PEASE

Miss Priestley was the 'typewriter' at the Fabian office.

Castle Top Farm, Cromford, Derbyshire

9.6.95

Dear Pease

You will have seen that the 'London School' is launched into publicity. Hewins is taking 9 John St but meanwhile enquirers should be referred to him at 26 Leckford Road, Oxford. I think that the Fabian Society had better be kept *quite* out of it for the moment; hence please be absolutely discreet. The right answer is to say that it is done by trustees, of whom Webb is Chairman. It is better not even to give the names of the trustees, and certainly not to mention Hutchinson. Above all, *show no one* the copy of the will. It is vital to get started without any compromising suspicions.

I shall leave here Friday, and be back in London next Monday, 17th June.

Yours

Sidney Webb

I have suggested to Hewins to consult you as to clerical assistance (could not Miss Priestley give him some hours a day for a small sum?) and furniture.

306 PP  SIDNEY WEBB TO LUJO BRENTANO

The German translation of the Webb's trade union *History* was published in Stuttgart in 1895.

36

41 Grosvenor Road, Westminster Embankment

9 June 95

Dear Professor Brentano

We were very pleased to receive your long and appreciative criticism of our book. You are perhaps the only person who understands how difficult it was to gather up the material from so many different sources, and to piece together into a consecutive history so many separate threads of distinct corporate existence. We quite feel that you are justified in deprecating a dogmatic refusal to believe in the existence of English journeymen fraternities in the Middle Ages. We fully admit that, when English town and gild records get published, it is possible, and even probable, that many journeymen organisations will be brought to light. The attitude we desired to take is best expressed by the peculiar Scotch verdict of 'Not proven'. But it is difficult to express this without giving the impression of a negative attitude. We *do* think that Ashley (whose work we like and largely agree with) has been premature in his judgements on this point.

By the way, we do not consider the printers' 'chapel' as a trade union; anymore than we should the 'workshop committee' of an industrial partnership or benevolent employer. We can find no evidence of any durable combination of compositors *as a trade* before the middle of the 18th century. If Franklin had, in 1725, been importuned to join a union (as he was his 'chapel') he would certainly have mentioned it.

However, as you will recognise, we have printed or cited every scrap of evidence that we know of, in order that others might draw their own conclusions.

You will be interested in an attempt we are making to start a 'London School of Economics and Political Science', of which I send a preliminary prospectus by book post. We propose to make it especially (a) an *evening* lecture school; (b) a post-graduate school, with 'seminar' etc; (c) a centre of research. Hewins, who is to be Director, you may know as the most promising of our younger economists especially devoted to historical research. We hope to make the School specially useful to foreign students as, between us, we can put them in the way of almost any subject of investigation, and serve them with introductions etc. We trust that we may at last be able to do in London some of the good work, in the way of specialist studies and research, which German universities excel in, and in which America has perhaps shot ahead of us. I am sure we may count on your friendly co-operation. We shall hope to secure a few lectures from you next time you visit us; meanwhile you can perhaps send us students to whom, I can promise you, we should be very useful.

Mrs Webb sends her kindest regards, and warmest invitation to visit us when you come over.

Yours very truly

Sidney Webb

37

On 1 July Shaw wrote to Beatrice about Sidney's failure to convince the Fabian executive that he had kept faith with Hutchinson's intentions. To win support from commercial interests and the L.C.C. Sidney had emphasised the practical value of the proposed L.S.E. courses; to protect the new School from accusations of socialist propaganda he had also stressed that it would engage in disinterested research. These attempts to demonstrate the respectability of his plans had left a general impression, Shaw said, 'that the Hutchinson trustees are prepared to bribe the Fabians by subsidies for country lectures and the like' to allow them to commit an atrocious malversation of the greater part of the bequest. He feared 'the temporary (let us hope) suspension of Webb's wits' and urged him to avoid shocking his Fabian critics by talking about academic impartiality. 'Even if such a thing were possible, its foundation out of Hutchinson's money would be as flagrant a breach of faith as handing it over to the Liberty and Property Defence League, since it was expressly left to endow Socialism.' (PP) These strictures did not deter Webb, who went ahead with his plans and depended upon his high standing among the Fabians to retain their confidence. The first list of lecturers showed, as Shaw anticipated, that 'the Collectivist flag' was not to be waved at the L.S.E. They were all men of moderate views and academic repute. In the first session 291 students, among them 87 women, were enrolled.

Castle Top Farm, Cromford, Derby.

12.6.95

Dear Pease

I am sorry I was not at the Fabian Exec. last Friday, as I should have been glad to have explained the Hutchinson Trust projects. And I had already made arrangements which will keep me away until Monday next, so that I should be obliged if the consideration of the matter could be deferred for a week.

Certainly, the preliminary notices in the press do not look very much in our line; and I do not wonder that some questions were asked. But we are, as you know, playing for a much larger advantage than could be gained by a few propagandist lectures; and when this is the case it is not always easy to see the object of each move. But I am sure that the Exec. will agree with us when the matter is explained to them.

Yours very truly

Sidney Webb

## 308 MMLMU SIDNEY WEBB TO BERTRAND RUSSELL

The Webbs had met Bertrand Russell (1872–1970) through the Pearsall Smiths. Russell had made his mark at Cambridge as a mathematician and then turned to philosophy, becoming a fellow of Trinity College. He married Alys Pearsall Smith in 1894. During their travels in Europe they had become interested in the German Social Democratic Party – then under such pressure that Webb could joke about possible exiles – and Russell had begun to prepare his first book on this subject. He extracted six lectures from his notes and delivered them at the L.S.E. When he was elected to his Trinity fellowship he donated the income as a contribution to the School's slender resources.

41 Grosvenor Road, Westminster Embankment

11 Dec./95

Dear Russell

Hewins thinks – as I most decidedly do – that your syllabus is *first rate*. We have no suggestions to make. We both feel that there must be six lectures, if you don't mind. It would be wasting a great opportunity to crush it into fewer. And we both agree that now is the time. Next term will begin about January 18th, and the six lectures had better begin the last week in January. All the powers that be seem determined to co-operate towards making the subject of thrilling interest. I suggested that there might by that time be no party to describe. Pease, on the other hand, said the whole party might be in London, prepared to crowd our largest hall!

The School is progressing most splendidly – the great economic luminaries are most cordial. We have just decided to have a 'Summer Meeting' in August, especially for provincials – the Centre to be Toynbee Hall. But this is merely for Elementary Economics, *etc. etc.*

We shall hope to see much of you and Mrs Russell next year.

Yours very truly

Sidney Webb

### 309 FP  SIDNEY WEBB TO EDWARD PEASE

The Webbs spent Christmas at Welcombe, Lady Trevelyan's home, with her sons Charles (1870–1958) and G. M. Trevelyan. Charles, Beatrice thought, was 'a dear loveable boy' who needed 'only a dash of talent to make him a considerable politician': he became a lifelong friend, holding office first as a Liberal and then as a Labour politician. G. M. Trevelyan (1876–1962), Beatrice said, was 'bringing himself up to be a great man': he became an outstanding historian and Master of Trinity College, Cambridge. By this time Beatrice had noticed a change in Sidney. She felt that the 'perfect happiness of our life has cured his old defects of manner – he has lost the aggressive self-assertive tone, the slight touch of insolence which was only another form of shyness and has gained immeasurably in persuasiveness': his work on the L.C.C. had 'taught him how to manage men and get them to adopt his views'. (BWD Xmas 1895) During the holidays the Webbs also visited the Hobhouses at Hadspen and Alfred Cripps at Parmoor. Reflecting on their work during the past year Beatrice noted that they were caught in a dilemma: 'it is intensely difficult to be at once investigators and agitators'. (BWD 5 January 96)

E. A. Hutchinson was the elder son of H. H. Hutchinson. His sister Constance had gone to America and died there on 24 November 1895. She had strongly supported Webb's use of her father's bequest and left a legacy of her own of a little over one thousand pounds to L.S.E. It was effectively treated as part of the main Hutchinson fund, though it was wound up much later; the accounts were closed in 1924.

Welcombe, Stratford on Avon
until 27 Dec./95

Dear Pease

E. A. Hutchinson writes from Maylaw Corner, Althorne, Essex – the Colony where F. Green and other Socialists are – to say that his sister Constance is dead, in California, leaving me executor of her will. I have written for copy of this (it is no doubt with the solicitor to whom I introduced her). Will you please write a friendly letter to E. A. Hutchinson?

(2) MacDonald's syllabus is excellent – put it in some such form as Miss Stacey's. Tell him I suggest freely recommending books: it helps the lonely student.

(3) I agree with what you have told Miss Stacey. She ought to go into lodgings.

Yours

Sidney Webb

### 310 BL   BEATRICE WEBB TO CHARLOTTE PAYNE-TOWNSHEND

The Webbs met Charlotte Payne-Townshend (1857–1943) in the autumn of 1895. She was a wealthy unmarried woman of Irish origin who had 'drifted about', Beatrice noted (BWD 16 September 96), 'seeking occupation and kindred spirits'. By nature a rebel she was 'genuinely anxious to increase the world's enjoyment and diminish the world's pain'. After a few meetings Beatrice had broached the idea that some of her ample resources might be used to assist the L.S.E. The separation of the Library from the L.S.E. as a teaching institution was a characteristic tactical move by Sidney Webb: it enabled him to raise funds specifically for the Library, without confusing the money with the School's general account; and by making the School the nominal tenant of premises occupied by the Library he was able to profit from a reduction on rates offered to library premises. After unsuccessful attempts to secure a large sum to launch the Library from a single benefactor the Webbs, Beatrice observed (BWD 20 March 96), sent out a series of personal begging-letters: 'Sidney wrote to all the politicians, I raked up my old ball partners'. A printed appeal with eminent sponsors was issued at the beginning of April.

41 Grosvenor Road, Westminster Embankment<br>January 13 1896

Dear Miss Payne-Townshend

I enclose you a memorandum on the duties of the Librarian at the proposed Library of Political and Economic Science. Of course we have not yet got our Library! But we shall have to make some sort of start this spring, as our present offices and classrooms are really too small and inconvenient to go on with, for another year. I need not say how grateful we should be for *any* help towards making this start. I rather despair of the ordinary wealthy persons – they have no faith in knowledge and have, in fact, a feeling that a state of ignorance is safest. I think therefore that we

40

shall have to raise what money we can among those who really desire to apply scientific methods to social and political questions with a view of getting a more satisfactory state of things for the whole community. I believe that, in this London School and this Library, there is a great opportunity of getting together a body of students who will have a real influence on 'the condition of the people' by raising the standard of efficiency of Public administration; and showing, by careful investigation, how much we can do by public administration and what must be left to Private enterprise, tempered by a healthy public opinion.

Will you think over both matters: whether you would feel inclined to throw in your energies into the Librarianship and whether you would be prepared to contribute towards the first start? – either or both!

I should not make these bold requests if I did not feel that you had somewhat encouraged me to think of you as a possible fellow-worker.

I shall be at The Grand Hotel, Birmingham until Saturday. Could you come to lunch here 1.30 Wednesday or next week and meet Mr Hewins, the Director of the School?

Yours sincerely

Beatrice Webb

### 311 PP BEATRICE TO SIDNEY

Herbert Spencer had settled at Percival Terrace, Brighton, where Beatrice occasionally visited him. She was distressed to find him degenerating into a 'noble wreck', tetchy and egotistical. She had spent part of January at the Miners Federation conference in Birmingham. The unhappy story of Carrie Darling after her marriage to a teacher named Brown is mentioned several times in Beatrice's diary and she summarised her 'servitude' to a worthless husband in the entry for 17 January 1896.

[Percival Terrace, Brighton]
Thursday evening [January or February 1896]

My own dear darling one

We have had peaceful day – a walk in the morning – a drive in the afternoon – and disjointed chats with the old man. The party consists of ourselves, the secretary and a Miss [?Lingnard] – a quite harmless and very musical young woman who is keeping house for Mr Spencer. The house is comfortable – not quite enough meat in the diet for my taste – the rooms large and an absolutely quiet situation – the last row of houses with the Downs easily accessible. I have been neuralgic today but that is no doubt the reaction from the bustle of London. I think a few days here – tho' not extraordinarily enlivening will do me good and put fresh vigour into my work. Now I am sitting by the fire in my own room writing to you and thinking of you lecturing. Dear Darling – how happy we are in our perfect union of hearts and heads! I wonder whether you are getting on with your

41

work – whether the thought of your Bee's face keeps you from dawdling over that paper in the morning. I should like that chapter on Arbitration finished before I return.

Carrie Brown is settling down and is losing her exciteability. She has very much changed, *superficially*. Living so long with inferiors she has lost a good deal of her old charm – more than I would have believed possible. On the other hand she is still a brave energetic woman, in a most uncomfortable plight. Her marriage is a ghastly failure – a counterpart to poor Alice Green's desire to be married. Why do women long for marriage *for its own sake* – quite apart from the man! Evidently Carrie married Brown in order to be married whilst Brown married her to get an assistant mistress and a housekeeper. Both have been 'done' because there was no love between them. If she could only get her little bit of money back again, I should recommend her to cut the connection and get work in Australia or elsewhere. She is evidently a good organiser and teacher and is now thoroughly acclimatised to the low level of colonial and Anglo-Indian life! With that husband she will always be wretched even if there is no catastrophe.

My own dear darling one – I should so like to have just one kiss – it seems so long now to be without you. I was melancholy at Brighton and I am melancholy here – in spite of feeling that it is doing me good and that I am fulfilling a double-rite of friendship. I fell fast asleep when I was sitting with Mr Spencer this afternoon much to his amusement!

Ever your devoted wifey

Beatrice

P.S. I shall post this tomorrow afternoon. I like you to get it in the morning to cheer you for your classwork.

BW

312 FP  BEATRICE WEBB TO EDWARD PEASE

On 29 January 1896 the Webbs introduced Charlotte Payne-Townshend to Bernard Shaw. She was elected to the Fabian Society in March: at that time the conditions of membership included attendance at two meetings of the Society.

41 Grosvenor Road, Westminster Embankment

Feb. 18th 1896

Dear Mr Pease

I enclose the nomination of Miss Payne-Townshend with cheque for £5 as an entrance subscription. She is a good Socialist and I think will prove an acquisition to the Society – the amount of her cheque showing the degree of her convictions.

She was prevented from attending the second meeting of the Society by a severe cold, but she will attend a second meeting directly her medical man allows her to go out in the evening.

Ever yours

Beatrice Webb

## 313 AP/BLPES SIDNEY WEBB TO WILLIAM MITCHELL ACWORTH

William Acworth (1850–1925) was an international expert on the relationships of governments and railways. The railway department of the L.S.E., which catered for students sponsored by the private railway companies, was an important part of the L.S.E. in its early years, providing both income and enrolments. As an outstanding authority on railway economics Acworth was a considerable asset to the teaching staff. Arthur Lyon Bowley (1869–1957) a specialist in income distribution was appointed to the staff of L.S.E. in 1895 and became professor of statistics in 1915.

41 Grosvenor Road, Westminster Embankment

7 March/96

My dear Acworth

1) Hewins is delighted at the idea of making the 'London School' the Centre for 'Higher Technical Education' for the railway world, and of making a good course by you the central feature next October. Could we not add to this some lectures by Bowley (or another) on *statistical methods* as applied to railway figures, with specimens? Possibly even some lectures on Railway Law! If you could, in consultation with the magnates, sketch out any kind of curriculum of this sort, to be worked more or less under your direction, or in consultation with you, and in co-operation with your own lectures, we might possibly be able to manage it. Let the magnates say what they want taught, and send us the students, and the 'London School' shall rise to the occasion! We can't quite designate you 'Professor of Railway Economics and Dean of the Faculty of Railways' – but that is what I should like to see it grow into.

2) Will you not let me add your name to the enclosed first proof list of supporters of the Library of Political Science? I do not ask for cash: there are others in the list, Bishops and such like, who give only sympathy. But your *name* would be very useful.

3) The Library ought to furnish what I know you have always pleaded for, a special collection on Railway matters. But this needs cash. I wonder whether you could ever find it possible to mention it in high circles from this point of view! There might be a special 'Railway Room', equipped with all that can be got on the subject from all parts of the world. If the idea should commend itself to anyone, he might stipulate that his donation should be applied specifically for that purpose. I am in hopes of getting a rich Bimetallist to equip a Currency Room under Foxwell's direction.

Yours very truly

Sidney Webb

Beatrice's sister Laurencina and her husband loaned the Webbs their holiday house in the Lake District for an Easter vacation. While there the Webbs received 'furious letters' from Ramsay MacDonald. He was, Beatrice decided, 'discontented because we refused to have him as a lecturer for the London School. He is not good enough for that work – he has never had the time to do any sound original work or even learn the old stuff well. Moreover, he objects altogether to diverting "socialist funds" to education. Even his own lectures, he declares, are too educational "to make socialists" . . . the truth is that we and MacDonald are opposed on a radical issue of policy . . . do we want to organise the *un*thinking persons into socialist societies or to make the *thinking* persons socialistic? We believe in the latter policy'. (BWD 18 April 96)

A long battle on educational strategy, which was to have a profound effect upon the political affiliations of the Webbs and to strain their personal relations with other Fabians, was now beginning. After the 1895 election the Conservatives had asked Sir John Gorst to prepare an educational Bill to reorganise the chaotic structure of elementary education and to establish a national scheme for the scarcely-developed secondary system. The original intention was to replace the local school boards (nominally restricted to elementary provision but already beginning to stake claims to secondary and technical classes) by combined education authorities, to provide aid from public funds to the 'voluntary' or Church schools, and to abolish the 'Cowper-Temple clause' in the 1870 Act which prohibited denominational teaching. Most Fabians (especially Graham Wallas and Stewart Headlam, who were members of the powerful London School Board) allied themselves with Nonconformist and Liberal opinion against the proposed measure.

High Borrans, Windermere<br>8.4.96

Dear Wallas

Thank you for your renewed invitation. But we are not wanted for either funeral, and have decided to stay here – probably until Tuesday next. We should have been glad to have been with you and Shaw, but this place is very healthy and envigorating, 700 feet high, in the midst of moors, and quite apart from other habitations, 4 miles from the Lake. We went to Rusland yesterday, (the Potters' old house) and bicycled some 20 miles on terrific hills, down which we come unhesitatingly – the Argoed hill is nothing to what we now accomplish.

I think your articles on Gorst's bill are excellent by way of agitation. What will be more important, however, will be good Committee amendments. The Government will not drop the bill now, and it must therefore pass, but we may be able to improve it. I can't make out what is intended as to London: nor yet as to private secondary schools. The Technical Instruction Acts are not repealed. It seems to me you would do well to consider the whole matter in the light of the teachers – it is clear that the N.U.T. [National Union of Teachers] cannot oppose the bill as a whole, but it might be a very useful ally for particular amendments, if properly worked. There ought to be about two points, carefully thought out in advance from a House of Commons standpoint, on which every teacher writes up to his M.P. at exactly the right moment.

If you don't mind 'widening your sphere', I should think Sir C. Dilke's advice would be very useful as to what amendments should be pressed.

Come in Wednesday afternoon (15th).

Sidney Webb

### 315 BL BEATRICE WEBB TO CHARLOTTE PAYNE-TOWNSHEND

Charlotte Payne-Townshend had gone back to Rome, where she had lived for some time and formed a close friendship with the Swedish doctor Axel Munthe, the author of *The Story of San Michele*.

41 Grosvenor Road, Westminster Embankment<br>[?20 April 1896]

My dear Miss Townshend

We are back from our holiday – a delightful fortnight in the Lakes – feeling ever so much stronger for the change.

The appeal for the Library Fund in the Papers has produced nothing. As it happened the immense excitement caused by Gorst's revolutionary Education Bill has sickened the public of every educational institution. Moreover, the idea tho' it appeals so markedly to the enlightened man who knows and cares for Public Administration does not recommend itself to the mere Plutocrat. We have had various subscriptions coming in from those we have written to privately and the Clothworkers Company have promised £100 – altogether the fund now amounts to £3,000. I am afraid we must be content to start with that. That means either a very small house in the Charing Cross neighbourhood or a house in Bloomsbury; and a very modest beginning in the way of books. I have suggested to Sidney that the scholars should be expected to collect and catalogue the books and papers connected with the subject they undertake to investigate – the Library of course defraying the cost of postage and purchase. Small special collections similar to our collection of trade union reports are so much more valuable to future students than a mass of stuff sent in haphazard.

Mr Hewins reports well of the School – there are more enquiries about it than at any previous time – there is no doubt that the appeal for the Library has advertised it immensely.

Shaw and Wallas are still at the Cottage – but the latter has been up and down to London writing all the articles for the *Daily Chronicle* on Gorst's Bill. The last time that I saw him was immediately after it was introduced, when he and Massingham (the Editor, *Daily Chronicle*) dined with us – both were boiling over with rage at the Bill. Sidney takes a more moderate view and sees some good in it – but on the whole he thinks it will be mischievous and if it remains as drafted hopes it will not pass.

How do you find Rome and your Italian friends? Do you not find that London and the Fabians and such sordid subjects as Economics and Public Administration seem an ugly and distasteful memory, under the blue Italian sky! We shall be very glad to see you back to consult about the Library etc.

Ever yours

Beatrice Webb

P.S. By the way do you not think we might adopt the shorter address of the Christian name?

### 316 PP  SIDNEY WEBB TO WILLIAM CLARKE

William Clarke, one of the original Fabian essayists, was dropping out of sympathy with the Fabian Society but he remained one of the Hutchinson trustees. The decision to lease the premises at Adelphi Terrace was eased by Charlotte Payne-Townshend's agreement to occupy the residential upper floors of the building as her personal apartment.

41 Grosvenor Road, s.w.<br>5/5/96

Dear Clarke

Nothing that I can write will give you any adequate idea of the worry and anxiety I have had during the last few weeks – in the attempt to find suitable premises for the 'London School' and its Library. I do not know whether I have told you that the fund now stands at over £3600 (that is, £2100 over our own £1500) – no insignificant sum to have got given us without reservation or condition – but not enough to buy much of a place near Charing Cross. It is no use bothering you with the various places Hewins and I have looked at, and I was getting into a state of despair – for Bloomsbury seemed as difficult as the Strand – when this morning Hewins found what seemed to be a solution.

The ideal has always appeared to me to be Adelphi Terrace, but there was nothing to be had. Now the Crichton Club has burst up, and 10 Adelphi Terrace, *next door to the Statistical Society* is vacant. There is 7 years lease – rent £360 a year, premises in good sanitary condition, and not needing much repair. Premium of £100 is asked, but can probably be cut off.

It is exactly the house we want. I should have preferred to *buy* a house (and thus use our money, and reduce maintenance charges) – but, after all, to take a place at a rent is less of a committal than buying it. In 7 years time all the Adelphi property falls in together, and the owner (Drummond, the banker) will not commit himself for the future: but unless there is some unforeseen big scheme the property will simply be relet then.

Hewins is making further enquiry, but I thought I had better let you know at once that a likely property is available.

It seems to me that the chance is an admirable one for *minimizing* our future commitments. If we were to buy a place now, and the School failed, we might lose a good deal of capital. If, on the other hand, we bank the money, and merely rent a place, we stand to lose very little in the worst event.

I have every hope that the Technical Education Board will grant £100 this year. I lecture tonight to the 'Municipal Officers Association', who will resolve that they will attend the classes, and that it is just what they want, and that the T.E.B. should go on assisting.

I feel we must not miss this chance, and I may therefore have to summon a Trustees meeting at short notice. Meanwhile would you mind sending this on to Pease when you have read it, and sending me a line, if you can, as to how it strikes you.

Sidney Webb

317 BL   BEATRICE WEBB TO CHARLOTTE PAYNE-TOWNSHEND

There had been a plan to organise an L.S.E. summer school but the effort was more than the infant institution could make at the end of its first year. Arthur Dyson Williams, the husband of Beatrice's sister Rosalind, died after a long and distressing illness. She later married George Dobbs (1869–1946), employed in the travel business: in 1927 their daughter Kitty married the journalist Malcolm Muggeridge, son of the active Fabian, Harry T. Muggeridge.

41 Grosvenor Road, Westminster Embankment<br>Sunday 28th [June 1896]

My dear Charlotte

Your offer of another £500 is very generous. I am afraid you must not ask me to give you an opinion – not at least an *unbiased* opinion on the worthwhile of subscribing further to the Library and the School. All I can say, is that if I had a surplus income I should be much inclined to 'concentrate' on the endowment of a school of Public Administration and the endowment of Economic Research – and that therefore I should probably do what you propose to do and give another £500. But then I am a bit of a fanatic on the subject! For the last 20 years I have had a fixed idea that if we are to progress quickly and *safely we must apply the scientific method to social questions.* At present politicians of all parties are Quacks – sometimes they hit on the right idea and sometimes they do not. No business man would build a railway or an ironclad on a 'rule of thumb' philosophy! Latterly physicians and surgeons have taken to scientific methods of enquiry and training much to the advantage of their patients! Of course it it is a stupendous task to convert politics into a science – it is possible we may only succeed in laying the foundations. But then, on the whole, it is better to try to do a big thing than to fritter one's brains or one's money away in accomplishing small things. Moreover, *intellectual enterprise* is least likely of all good objects to gain support either from the democracy or the plutocracy and depends entirely for its existence on a small and very select class of persons who believe in knowledge for its own sake. These persons are unfortunately not usually endowed with means. If one happens both to have this faith and also the means to carry it out, then it seems that the 'Call' is clear.

I hope that you are having a good time. I sometimes feel inclined to envy you your opportunities of cultivation and enjoyment – then I console myself with the thought that I am exceedingly happy in the routine of my life in spite of feeling sometimes rather worn and fagged out. I am too much of a bourgeois for any life but one of daily routine. Still I should enjoy a few months among beautiful sights and a complete change of thought, if only we could get this volume off our hands!

When do you return? The summer meeting has been given up; it was obvious that if Mr Hewins was to spend time over getting the new premises, to preparing the syllabus for next session and then carrying on his own research he would be completely knocked up by the additional work of a summer meeting which would break into the holiday. So that there will be nothing to prevent our going to the country the end of July if that would suit your plans.

We shall be away for a fortnight or three weeks at Whitsun at The Argoed and are taking the Hewins' down with us, also my little sister and her child. My brother-in-law is dead; which on the whole is a relief – as his life had become one long agony.

Yours affectionately<br>Beatrice Webb

P.S. I will certainly not mention to any but the 'inner ring' your proposals about the London School. I quite understand your dislike of gossip. I always felt it keenly and therefore prefer my own counsel.

BW

### 318 FP  SIDNEY WEBB TO EDWARD PEASE

In the summer of 1896 Webb wrote a number of omitted letters to Pease on Fabian business, especially about the Fabian book-box scheme, which supplied small circulating collections of books on economics and politics to local Fabian groups, I.L.P. branches and Co-operative societies. Sidney was being drawn into the debate on education – a development, Beatrice noted at Whitsun, which would 'force us more into political society'. There were dinners and lunches, with both eminent Liberals and Tories, and much private consultation. 'I do not hide from myself that I am pleased and flattered that my Boy is recognised as a distinguished man!', she added, though she regretted the distraction this caused to their work on their book: they had to toil hard during their two-month recess that summer. The Bill which Gorst had drafted was withdrawn after Arthur Balfour had casually accepted an amendment in the House of Commons which would have made it unworkable.

The Webbs rented a rectory at Stratford St Andrew, near Saxmundham in Suffolk, for their holiday, going down after they had attended the International Socialist Congress in London. Charlotte Payne-Townshend, now regarded as one of what Beatrice called 'the Bo family', went to stay with them. Beatrice had thought she might make a suitable match for Graham Wallas but in the course of the summer, while the Webbs worked, she became the constant companion of Bernard Shaw, who also stayed at the rectory.

Beatrice was already recovering her old skills as a hostess and much of her time in the autumn was taken up with entertaining to support the various interests of the Webbs. The opening of the L.S.E. at Adelphi Terrace in October added to the strain of these social demands. Tract 70, *Report on Fabian Policy*, was drafted by Shaw for the International Socialist Congress. A stout defence of permeation against the elements in the Fabian Society which sympathised with the I.L.P., it was the last substantial statement of the Fabian position for many years.

41 Grosvenor Road, Westminster Embankment<br>18.7.96

Dear Pease

(1) It occurs to me to suggest that the book-box circular should be sent to the press (especially the Labor press) *at once*. In view of the congress, editors will possibly be disposed to notice it, if sent during this next week. It would be well, also, if it could be got out to local Fabian Societies and all I.L.P. and S.D.F. branches *this next week*, so as to remind them of our educational work, at the moment that the *Clarion* and *Justice* will be abusing our Report on Policy.

I do not think we need fear being overwhelmed with applications. It is a pious thing to spend money on.

(2) If you would send me the list of books already in the Boxes (which I would return promptly), I would give you suggestions for additions.

Could you get Howell to mark in 'What to Read' those books already in the Boxes?

Yours

Sidney Webb

### 319 SHSW   SIDNEY WEBB TO H. D. LLOYD

Henry Demarest Lloyd (1847–1903) was the author of a number of reformist books, notably *Wealth Against Commonwealth*. He was an American friend of William Clarke. Charles Zueblin (1866–1924) was a sociologist at the University of Chicago from 1892 to 1908. He subsequently gave up his academic career to become an advocate of municipal reform. On one of his visits to England he had met the Webbs and joined the Fabian Society. William Jennings Bryan (1866–1925), was the Democratic candidate for President of the United States in 1896 and at two subsequent elections. He became Secretary of State 1913–15.

'Trade-Union Democracy' by Sidney and Beatrice Webb was published in the *Political Science Quarterly* for September and December 1896.

41 Grosvenor Road, Westminster Embankment, London, Eng.

21 Dec. 1896

Dear Mr Lloyd

Many thanks for your letter of the 30 November to which I now snatch just enough time to reply briefly.

My lectures to the Fabian Society are not published, but the gist of them is in two articles in the *Political Science Quarterly* for September and December 1896. I send herewith a brief report of some of them.

The 'International University of Political Science' we are striving to create in our 'London School'. I wish you could come over and give us some lectures. Mr Zueblin will tell you more of it.

Foxwell, by the way, is an ardent Bimetallist – so are nearly all the economists here. Even Leonard Courtney has just delivered a striking lecture to the School, in favor of Bryan! (See *Nineteenth Century* for January 97).

As regards the Fabian position hereon, let me say that our differences from American friends are perhaps to be accounted for by circumstances. We are all heartily and unanimously for exclusively Government money – coin *and* notes. But that issue is past for England. The Bank of England is to all intents and purposes a Govt Dept (as regards note issues): no private note issues are allowed in London; no new ones in England; and existing private issues are limited and are rapidly dying out (*not* so in Scotland, but this is a trifle). Hence Bimetallism *to us* is neither Collectivist nor Individualist. We should be heartily with you in demanding *Govt Money. Our* bankers do not control the currency at all.

I cannot now stop to enter into your most interesting remarks on Democracy and Politics, on which England and U.S. have much to learn from each other. I have said something in the articles referred to, and shall say more in the book Mrs Webb and I are now engaged on, of which these articles are a small part. We both believe it to be the *least bad* system, but its machinery needs the most careful study.

It is to aid such study that we are trying to build up a Library of Political Science, chiefly for official documents, reports etc. of all kinds of public administration. I wonder whether you would help us in this by sending us anything you can. We should like campaign literature, pamphlets, specimen ballots as well as any sort of public report or document.

I read with the greatest interest the article in the *Progressive Review* on the Presidential Election, which I identified as yours.

Yours very truly

Sidney Webb

320 HL   SIDNEY WEBB TO HERBERT SAMUEL

By this time Webb had clearly broken all ties to the Liberal Party and, socially and politically, was beginning to build significant links to Balfour and other

Conservatives. The state of the Liberal Party was confused and a source of confusion to all groups on the left. It did not offer a coherent alternative to the Tories; its leadership was still committed to *laissez-faire* economics and obsessed by the Irish question; and yet it was too large and too important to permit the emergence of any other significant reformist party. This problem was intensified by the slump in the fortunes of the I.L.P. which, after a promising start, had proved unable to organise its recruits effectively and its survival at least seemed questionable. Harry Snell (1865–1944), later Lord Snell, was an active Fabian and ethical propagandist who was taken on as an assistant to Hewins at the L.S.E.: at this time he considered that the whole socialist movement had suffered a moral disaster and that its members were disillusioned by the paucity of results for their aimless enthusiasm. There was indeed a widespread collapse of morale and great uncertainty what line to take. Webb's letter shows the extent to which he too was affected by the failure either to radicalise the Liberal Party or to create an effective alternative to it.

> 41 Grosvenor Road, Westminster Embankment
> 25th Jan. '97

My dear Samuel

I would gladly do anything for you, and gladly for Woods, but I cannot possibly manage even one evening for the Walthamstow Election. I am very hard at work, and should in any case find it almost impossible to spare the time. Moreover, I cannot bring myself to take part in a fight for the Liberal Party at this moment. I feel absolutely no assurance which side it is going to take on any question whatsoever. On one crucial point after another, it seems just as likely to be against me as for me. Under these circumstances I cannot try to make the Party any stronger – it may be, only to see its strength used against all I care for. Until it is settled *what* the Liberal leaders mean – what reforms they have really at heart, and in what direction their intellectual convictions impel them to lead – I can only wish to see the Party weaker. There is no calamity in politics *against* which I would work harder than a return of the Liberal leaders to office without a definite programme. Every weakness of the Conservative Government, *every success of a Liberal candidate at a bye-election*, makes me tremble lest the Liberal Leaders should be thereby encouraged to 'wait', and rely on the return of the tide.

This feeling would not be worth troubling you with, if it were not shared by many others besides myself. (Only last Saturday, a prominent and active Radical candidate, who in 1892 was full of zeal and trust told me that he had definitely decided to give up politics, and to concentrate himself entirely in non-political social work.) How intense is this feeling among London Radicals you know as well as I do. Are the leaders kept in ignorance of these things, or do they imagine that they can ignore them?

> Yours very truly
>
> Sidney Webb

51

At the beginning of April the Webbs rented a cottage near Dorking for three months to finish *Industrial Democracy*. They took Charlotte Payne-Townshend with them and Shaw also came for much of the time. They watched the developing relationship 'with concern and curiosity'. Beatrice felt that Charlotte was 'deeply attached' to Shaw but that there were 'ominous signs' that GBS was drifting away from her. In any case, she believed, Shaw was 'too high-minded and too conventionally honourable' to marry Charlotte for her money, or even to appear to do so. His plays were at last giving him something of a reputation but not an adequate income on which to propose to a rich woman. (BWD 1 May 97)

The Webbs were both tired and somewhat disillusioned with current politics: they had already begun to plan a tour round the world once *Industrial Democracy* was published.

Sidney's plan to secure rate-exemption for the Library had now succeeded.

[*Note at top of letter*: *Cancel* notice of Committee Meeting of London School for Monday *next*: that was a mistake.]

Lotus, Tower Hill, Dorking
15.5.97

Dear Pease

I forgot to ask you to arrange a Hutchinson Trust meeting – say Monday 24 May at 4.30 p.m. at 10 Adelphi Terrace, when we will have London School Committee at 5. Usual agenda. The School needs a cheque – it has had nothing since November. I estimate that £300 will cover total deficit up to 30 September next. It had better have £200 now.

F.S. will want a cheque too, I suppose.

I think we must give Hewins a rise (from £300 to £400). He slaves incessantly, and gives up all chance of increasing his income. His position, I can see, entails constant little expenses on him – inviting students to his house, lunching foreign professors, always dining away from home, visiting Oxford and Cambridge etc. His father-in-law has, I gather, rather 'dried up' lately for various reasons, and I am convinced that though Mrs H. is a most careful housekeeper, they are pinched. (1½ babies)

Would you therefore put on agenda

'Report as to London School of Economics'

(a) Grant of £250 to Library from City Parochial Trustees

(b) Probable exemption of premises from local rates (saving £90 a year)

(c) Suggested increase of Director's salary.

Yours

Sidney Webb

A number of Fabians objected strongly when Pease let the Society's office as a viewpoint for the Queen's diamond jubilee procession to St Paul's cathedral; they also protested at the suggestion that the Society should contribute a modest sum towards the street decorations in the Strand. Advised that the Society could not cancel the contract to let its windows to spectators, the critics found ironic satisfaction in the fact that the letting agent absconded without payment of the fee.

Lotus, Tower Hill, Dorking
22/6/97

We leave here tomorrow, and shall be bicycling until Saturday next when we reach 41 Grosvenor Road. (Lion and Lamb, Farnham, Surrey, for Wednesday night, White Horse, Romsey, Hants for Thurs. night). I assume there can be no doubt we must *not* give that subscription for street decoration, after such a vote etc. Sorry we have never been able to reach Limpsfield, but it is too far for us there and back.

Yours

Sidney Webb

## 323 PP  BEATRICE WEBB TO GRAHAM WALLAS

Wallas had just become engaged to Audrey (Ada) Radford (1859–1934), described by Beatrice as a 'cultivated, public-spirited, somewhat aesthetic' Girton graduate. Beatrice did not care for her, dismissing her as 'a woman who carried rigid principles into the smallest concerns of life . . . my distaste is really to her clothes. I could forgive them if they were not worn *on principle*'. (BWD 21 January 98)

In August and September Charlotte and Shaw stayed with the Webbs at The Argoed. Beatrice hoped that GBS would make up his mind but 'as he has always advertised his views of marriage and philandering from the house-tops, every woman ought to be prepared for his logical carrying-out of these principles'. (BWD 27 September 97) Earlier in the year Beatrice had gone through a distressing interview with the artist Bertha Newcombe, who had taken Shaw's flirtatious advances too seriously and had hoped to marry him.

41 Grosvenor Road, Westminster Embankment
[?13 July 1897]

My dear Graham
   *re engagement*
   We are both of us delighted – indeed that is far too conventional a term to express our warm feelings of satisfaction. You seem to be making an ideal marriage – just such another as our own! (the highest compliment we can pay you).
   We shall welcome Miss Radford with the 'Bo' family, if she will consent to join such a humble crew. All we know of her family and above all your

53

admiration for her convince us that she must have high qualities of character and intellect as well as the necessary personal charm.

Will you bring her to lunch Wednesday 1.30? Sidney is out every evening this week. Of course she will come with you to The Argoed on the 12th – it is just the place for two lovers and who knows whether your example may not be contagious and that our Benedict [Shaw] may not feel constrained to follow suit!

Ever yours affectionately<br>Beatrice Webb

### 324 FP   SIDNEY WEBB TO EDWARD PEASE

Webb was already considering the relation of the L.S.E. to the University of London and the future organisation of the university as a whole. He was working closely in this respect with R. B. Haldane who, in turn, had close ties – cutting across party lines – with Arthur Balfour, now the Conservative leader in the House of Commons, who had a special interest in the work of the Commission planning the reorganisation of the university.

41 Grosvenor Road, s.w.<br>[14.7.97]

Dear Pease

You may have noticed that Hewins has been appointed Professor of Political Economy at Kings College. This means only an income of £30 a year, for nominal duties, but it is a great score for the School, as it gives Hewins the right to call himself Professor – increasing his claim to the future Professorship in the new University – and also ensures what we have been playing for, viz. the inclusion of the School in the future University and thus our virtual command of the economic faculty.

He spoke to me about the *possibility* of this coming off last year, but it came at the last moment with a rush. It will be reported to the next Committee (Thursday 28th inst.)

Yours<br>Sidney Webb

I have settled the dilapidation claim on 9 John Street for £8.15.0.

### 325   BEATRICE WEBB TO GRAHAM WALLAS

The 'three great works' were Shaw's play *The Devil's Disciple*, the Wallas biography of Francis Place and *Industrial Democracy*. The dinner was cancelled as Beatrice had to go to see Alfred Cripps at Parmoor on her way to The Argoed. Writing to Ada Radford to apologise on 1 August she said that Wallas had no doubt prepared his fiancée 'for all my deficiencies – perhaps even for my abominable handwriting!'

My dear Graham

What day next week can you and your beloved come to dine? Would Thursday or Friday suit you?

You will find us back on the 28th if you would look in for a chat in the evening, or on Wednesday afternoon. We have had a terrific hard pull at our chapter on Economic Characteristics of Trade Unions which now extends to 100 pages of 370 words! parcelled out into 4 sections. I am so exhausted that I have given over working for the last three days. Sidney is at present writing a ten-guinea article for the *New York World* on municipal administration. Shaw has been working ever so hard at his plays – altogether we feel, as a party, extremely virtuous and rather tired. Miss P-T helps Shaw – we two sit in one room, they in another, meeting at meals and in the evening. They have taken to scouring the country on a tandem. She is a charming woman and Shaw is a fool not to make it up with her.

We are in the middle of the last chapter – a short one – Trade Unions and Democracy. But all the virtue has gone out of me. I look at Sidney writing away and feel the essential inferiority of the woman. The German translation is being admirably done – far better than *The History of Trade Unionism*. How is Place? Can we have a dinner celebrating the birth of the three great works delivered by the Bo family? I have three bottles of '34 Port which Arthur Playne gave me – as Shaw does not take wine it would be sufficient for the enlarged Bo family! My prospective 'Love' to your beloved.

Ever yours affectionately
Beatrice Webb

### 326 FP  SIDNEY WEBB TO EDWARD PEASE

The Webbs always handled the production of their books themselves, using the printing firm of R. and R. Clark, Ltd. of Edinburgh and fixing both the prices and other details. They normally distributed the books through Longman's, Green, though they frequently arranged private or reduced-price editions to reach special markets. This system, which gave them total control over the content, size and appearance of their books, meant that they always had part of their capital tied up in printed stock: they made a steady but not spectacular income from publication – enough to serve as a revolving fund to underwrite the printing of new books but insufficient to recoup the money they spent on research assistants or pay for their own efforts as authors.

41 Grosvenor Road, Westminster Embankment
14 Nov/97

Dear Pease

*Industrial Democracy* will be 25/- net retail which (considering that it is 2 vols) is 2/- cheaper than *The History of Trade Unionism*. The trade price is, I understand, 20s/10d less, I suppose, 5%, but without any thirteenth or twenty-fifth copy. It would not do to negotiate any reduction; and of course the issue in Book Boxes does tend to affect the sales somewhat, if only by lessening the pressure on the Libraries to get it.

I suppose that by the time this book is issued, we shall have actually sunk some £2000 capital in this work, in actual cash outlay, (quite apart from our own living expenses, or any payment for our time). I only mention this to make it clear that we are not making a profit out of the Society. What I can do is to give a donation of £5 to the Book Box fund, to help equip these new boxes. I doubt whether the book will be ready quite by 1 December: there may be a few days delay, so you might equip some. You can certainly get the £100 cheque on the 22nd.

Yours

Sidney Webb

It will be uniform in size with the *History*, and I expect not quite so thick, as the paper will be thinner.

### 327 PRO SIDNEY WEBB TO JAMES RAMSAY MACDONALD

A strike called by the Amalgamated Society of Engineers in support of the Eight Hour Day had begun in London in May and become a national dispute by July, after the engineering employers had discharged a quarter of their workmen as a tactic to burden the union's unemployment fund. Led by George Barnes (1859–1940), the secretary of the A.S.E., the largest union in the country held out for months. In late November negotiations led to a compromise formula but, on a ballot of the members, its terms were decisively rejected. On 15 January 1898 the men capitulated. The Fabians actively supported the union's case but Beatrice concluded that the 'hopelessly incompetent' officials 'gave us away completely' by their proposed compromise. (BWD 21 January 98)

41 Grosvenor Road, Westminster Embankment<br>13.12.97

Dear MacDonald

From what I hear and learn, I believe that F.S. declaration on the Engineers ought to be a more important matter than I contemplated on Friday, or than the Executive then authorised. The time seems to be ripe for a definite lead, which the Parliamentary Committee of the T.U. Congress is evidently incapable of giving. I sent Shaw some suggestions on Saturday, which he has improved and worked up. He has carried off the MS to complete, and sent tonight to Pease. Will you go to 276 Strand and see this tomorrow morning early – if you agree when you see it, or if you cannot go, we have asked Pease to get it into proof at once.

Our view is that the F.S. should spend a little money in issuing this 'Call to Arms' to trade union branches and the press, *at once* i.e. at the end of this week. But this would be an important step, and though I believe the Exec. left it to the Committee to act, we suggest that a Special Exec.

should be called, say for Wednesday evening when we shall know the exact situation, to consider it.

Yours

Sidney Webb

## 328  FP  SIDNEY WEBB TO EDWARD PEASE

Sellick was an official of the A.S.E. Francis W. Chandler (1849–1938) was general secretary of the Amalgamated Society of Carpenters and Joiners. He was a member of the Royal Commission on the Poor Law in 1905–08.

41 Grosvenor Road, Westminster Embankment<br>21.12.97

Dear Pease

(1) I enclose the transfers etc. only signed by Miss P-T and myself. I have kept the deed of appointment which is complete.

(2) MacDonald (whom I saw last night), and Shaw (whom I saw on Sunday), both agree with me in thinking

(a) That our Manifesto ought to be at once got ready to issue.

(b) That *instantly* the men's vote is known – even unofficially and approximately – it should be issued broadcast (assuming the vote to be for refusal).

(c) I assume that the result of the vote won't be known until the 20th December, but I think you had better send over to Sellick's and ask him (a) how soon he can let [me] have a private indication of the result, (b) to let you have this as early as possible.

(d) We suggest that you should take care to put the whole thing in order before Xmas if you can – e.g. you could have envelopes addressed to the *press* (with covering cyclostyled letter?); to leading workmen's clubs and societies, and T.U. secretaries; and so on. You could then, if need be, 'fire the mine' by telegraph, if you are going to be away.

(3) Our view of the situation is that it is 'touch and go'. The A.S.E. officials have greatly spoilt their case by their last Manifesto, signifying that they would be willing to give way on Collective Bargaining (with which the public sympathises), in return for the smallest mess of potage in the way of Hours (with which the public does not sympathise). But the rank and file will probably vote for rejection, and thus *stiffen* their leaders again.

If they do, the result all depends on whether the T.U. will play up; and we must do our very best to make them. It may be a matter of a few days only, so we must strike instantly.

We have induced the Amalgamated Carpenters to issue the enclosed to all T.U. officials – with the intention of publishing it next week as widely signed as possible. If you can easily get any signatures of T.U. officials, please do, and return it direct to F. Chandler, at Manchester by end of this week. But I send it mainly for your information.

57

(4) I return proof of the Manifesto in the shape in which I think it should be issued. You should certainly manage to print off enough to send out with the *News*, and supply freely at once. I hope you will manage to get it out *next week* if the men vote 'no'.

Yours

Sidney Webb

## 329 PP   BEATRICE WEBB TO FREDERIC HARRISON

Harrison had been one of the first intellectuals publicly to assist the trade union movement in the 1870s, helping to establish some legal security for it. Though he never became a socialist he remained sympathetic to organised labour.

41 Grosvenor Road, Westminster Embankment<br>[mid-December 1897]

Dear Mr Harrison

We send you herewith an advance copy of our work on *Industrial Democracy* as a token of our regard for all your work on behalf of trade unionism. If you have time to look at it, you will find a quite unintentional explanation of the failure of the A.S.E. to maintain its position as one of the leading unions. It is really heartrending to see a great body of men – well-off and intelligent – being so badly led and giving away the whole position – point by point. It seems to us that their long drawn out disputes will end in both employers and men being badly beaten – the employers utterly failing to secure increased output per machine and the men losing ground on the central position of trade unionism – the substitutes of collective for individual bargaining. And all for lack of some shrewd person who understands the requirements of both sides! However one can easily exaggerate the importance of single events?

Should you have time we should, someday, much like to have your opinion on our work. But we are fully conscious of its unreadable character and we do not expect our friends to do more than refer to it occasionally when they discuss information on some current labour question. It is appearing simultaneously in Germany – in fact the first volume is already published in German.

I need hardly ask you to keep the work out of the way of indiscreet journalists as it is not to be *published until January 4th.*

Ever yours

Beatrice Webb

## 330 PP   BEATRICE WEBB TO FREDERIC HARRISON

Welcombe, Stratford on Avon<br>Dec. 28th 1897

Dear Mr Harrison

Very many thanks for your kind words about our book.

We do not take so gloomy a view of the prospects of trade unionism as you do. The A.S.E. has been for the last ten years one of the worst led and worst organised of societies. Until last year they had a hopeless drunkard as general secretary and the present man, tho' able, is young and untrained. Consequently the Union has been most exasperating in its policy and the employers were justified in making some kind of stand against it. Unfortunately by the character of their terms they are playing into the hands of the obstructive and violent section of the society and losing their chance of laying down the lines of a reasonable and satisfactory arrangement with regard to piece work and machinery. On the other hand the decisive public opinion in favour of Collective Bargaining which these terms have elicited is all to the good and represents a clear advance on the trade unionism of William Allan. Part of the difficulty has been that the A.S.E. unlike the Cotton Unions and Miners Unions have *never had collective bargaining recognised* throughout the country and the employers – if they knew this one case – might show that Allan never intended it! The fact is that the A.S.E. instead of being the advance guard of trade unionism is at its very rear. Of course one does not wish to explain this to the Public! But if this dispute should end in the A.S.E. getting any kind of collective agreement for the whole of the Federation workshops it will be a real victory for them, and as I believe a real advantage for the employers who have been suffering all the disadvantages of trade unionism with none of the advantages.

It is quite true that the whole of our Book as it now stands has been written by one pen – as I have become hopelessly parasitic on my husband's greater capacity for writing 'clear copy'. But every statement and every argument has been thought out by two minds and we have spent whole days in discussion and argument – a most delightful occupation! Indeed if the Book falls dead we shall have been amply rewarded by the extreme happiness of working together – day by day – a sort of eternal honeymoon!

We are looking forward to a similar work on Local Government (we realise this will take us 6 years) when we come back from a long holiday visiting the Anglo-Saxon Democracies of America and Australasia. We go directly after the L.C.C. election in March (not to be mentioned in 'Moderate' circles), but I hope we shall see you and Mrs Harrison before then.

My husband was deeply grieved to see Mr Charles Harrison's sudden death; he leaves a magnificent record as a public servant and as one of the makers of London.

Believe me
Yours very sincerely
Beatrice Webb

# 3. A fresh start

## April – November 1898

By March 1898 the Webbs came to the end of the first phase of their partnership. The decision to take a sabbatical leave and go round the world meant, Beatrice said, 'a complete break in our life'. In six years of marriage they had completed two substantial books on trade unionism: they deposited the residue of their material at the L.S.E. to be sifted by future researchers. The L.S.E. itself was 'growing silently tho' surely into a centre of collectivist-tempered research'; and with their books making a mark, with the School as a teaching body, the Fabians as a propagandist group and the Progressives returned with a decent majority at the 1898 elections, as 'an object lesson in electoral success', Beatrice felt that 'no young man or woman who is anxious to study or to work in public affairs can fail to come under our influence'. She contrasted such progress with the failure of the Liberals to make any headway under their inadequate leaders who 'are either following their own professions or dancing attendance on London Society'. (BWD March 1898)

Sidney had done well in Deptford again, bringing in as his running-mate a wealthy young friend, Robert Charles Phillimore (1871–1919) who, with his wife Lucy ('Lion'), had been an active Fabian for the past five years and served with Shaw on the St Pancras vestry.

The Webbs were now about to make a fresh start. As a prelude to a huge new research project on the development of English local government, they were off to the United States and the Antipodes, visiting about forty legislative assemblies on the way. Apart from the run-up to the L.C.C. elections they spent the Spring of 1898 preparing for their journey. Beatrice permitted herself the rare indulgence of having 'a really good "go" at clothes' for her travels, buying a trousseau with 'everything a sober-minded woman of forty can want to inspire Americans and colonials with a true respect for the refinements of collectivism'. Thus harmonising extravagance and conscience as 'a sort of rebound for the hard drudgery' of recent years she consoled herself that she did not 'feel a bit old' to start on a new stage of life. (BWD February 1898) Galton was found another appointment; the two servants went to work for Margaret Hobhouse; and new homes were found for the two Webb cats. 'All will have to be new and strange when we return – Work, Secretary, Servants', Beatrice noted in a valedictory entry in her diary. 'We may easily, on all points, change for the worse. Meanwhile we intend to enjoy ourselves and let the future look out for itself.' (BWD March 1898)

331 BL   SIDNEY WEBB TO GEORGE BERNARD SHAW

Landing in New York on 30 March the Webbs found the United States on the brink of war with Spain and politicians in a feverish mood which made it difficult to conduct academic discussions on legislative procedures.

Frank Harris (1856–1931) was then editing the *Saturday Review*, for which Shaw worked as drama critic from 1895 to 1898. Richard Mansfield (1859–1907) was a successful actor–manager who had given Shaw his first real success with the American production of *Arms and the Man* in 1895; his production of *The Devil's Disciple* at Albany on 2 October 1897 was the play's world premiere. Mansfield then took the play on tour. The royalties, soon running into several thousand pounds, gave Shaw his first substantial income as a playwright. Sydney Olivier crossed the Atlantic with the Webbs and Charles Trevelyan (who went as their travelling companion), on his way to an official meeting in Washington to discuss U.S. tariffs on West Indian products.

| until 3 May | Westminster Hotel, New York |
| until 21 May | Post Office, Boston, Mass. |
| until 7 June | c/o Prof. Zueblin, 6052 Kimbark Avenue, Chicago, Illinois |
| about 1–7 July | Post Office, San Francisco, Cal. |

26.4.98

Dear Shaw

Your letters are delightful: please write whenever you can, without expecting many answers, for we find ourselves overwhelmed with engagements and local letters of acceptance and refusal.

We had a fair passage over, notwithstanding the gale we left behind us. I was ill for three days, Beatrice much less so. The Holt influence at Liverpool got us a magnificent upper deck cabin – absolutely the best on the ship, used for millionaires and princes! At New York we found plenty of friends, and lived for three days in a whirl of excitement. We insisted on going on to Washington, which we found seething with war fever. There we spent a fortnight, attending Congress, interviewing politicians and dining out. Then we gave a week to Baltimore and Philadelphia, and are now back in New York for ten days or so. We have already inspected seven universities, and addressed the students in three of them (not bad advertisement of the book!); we have had discussions with about 30 professors of economics etc.; we have spent hours in the Senate and the House, had long private talks with the Speaker, the leading Senators and Representatives, and the most important officials; attended two City Councils and met a half-dozen Mayors and Ex-Mayors, and as many leading municipal officers; and we have got together a huge pile of things for the British Library of Political Science. And so far we have survived it all, even the ice-cream!

This people, in all that concerns the *machinery* of government, is infantile. I suspect the St Pancras Vestry is a finished product – a masterpiece – by comparison. All good people bemoan the evil state of their government machinery, but we have found hardly any glimmering of an idea as to how to get it any better. The 'Reform' party are feeble folk as a rule, with no more knowledge than an S.D.F. branch, and no more energy than a mothers' meeting. If the American Nation would sell all it has, and buy with the price the Fabian Executive, it would make a good bargain in the sphere of government. Our sympathies really are tempted to go with Tammany and the other 'machines', which are at any rate efficient in what they set out to do. However, we are just about to investigate these, and they may turn out no better than the rest.

As far as we can make out, every city here contains a few enthusiasts who read everything signed G.B.S., and take the *Saturday Review* for that purpose. So the news of your projected secession is grave – for Harris. No doubt you are right, but stick to those investments and make them up to £5000 as soon as you can – you will have seen that we were lucky enough to catch Mansfield at Washington and see *The Devil's Disciple*, the *first* Act went splendidly: afterwards we thought Richard had cut out too much, and rattled it off as if it *had* been an Adelphi piece, slurring all the intellectual points. But the audience liked it. The house (a small one) was nearly all full (I think *all* but the boxes, of which 3 out of 8 were taken) – and this notwithstanding many Washington people had already seen it. We sent our cards in to Mansfield after the first Act, inscribed that we were friends of yours who had heard the play read but had never before seen it – an enterprise which brought the enclosed note next day.

You have, I assume, the photographs of the play, a set of six. If not, we would get them for you.

Olivier has just left us, and if no Spanish fleet searches his vessel, and impresses him as a Spaniard, he will give you our news. We go next to Boston and then to Chicago – Trevelyan has gone on ahead as projected. You might pass this on to Wallas, whom everyone asks after, and give a report on us to the Fabian Executive and other friends who have any curiosity for we really cannot do our duty in the way of letters.

Best love

Sidney Webb

## 332 PP   BEATRICE WEBB TO CATHERINE COURTNEY

The City Solicitor in Baltimore was John E. Semmes; the Republican Mayor was William T. Malster. Daniel Coit Gilman (1831–1908) was President of Johns Hopkins University from 1875 to 1902, establishing there the first important graduate school in the United States. Talcott Williams (1849–1928) was assistant editor of the Philadelphia *Press*; the Mayor of Philadelphia was Charles F. Warwick (1852–1913). William James (1842–1910) the Harvard philosopher, was the brother of the novelist Henry James. Woodrow Wilson (1856–1924) was then professor of political science at Princeton University, later President of the United States 1912–20.

In New York the Webbs were impressed by the organisation of Tammany Hall, which they described as 'government by a firm of contractors, who are given the job of governing the city for so many years by the electors and quite naturally govern it entirely through their own men'. (BWD 31 March 98) Edwin Lawrence Godkin (1831–1902) was the editor of *The Nation* and a leader of the Reform Party in New York City politics. Joseph H. Choate (1832–1917) was a prominent Republican lawyer and Minister to the United Kingdom from 1899 to 1905. Robert Anderson Van Wyck (1849–1918) was elected as the first Mayor of greater New York in 1898, defeating the municipal reformer and President of Columbia University Seth Low (1850–1916). Richard Croker (1841–1922) was the boss of Tammany Hall.

William James Ashley was currently professor of economic history at Harvard University. The Webbs stayed three days in Boston with the Ashleys and then visited Mrs Fairchild, a socially prominent lady in Boston with an interest in reform, and her daughter Sally, with whom they maintained a casual connection for many years. Jane Addams (1860–1935) was a pioneer social worker in Chicago who established her notable Hull House for settlement work in 1889.

Westminster Hotel, N.Y.
April 29 [1898]

My dear Kate

We were delighted on our arrival here to find your letter forwarded through Galton: it was the first news we had of England since our departure, even the newspapers giving no indication of what was happening, except extracts from the anti-American Press (*St James* and *Saturday*) about Cuba.

Since we left Washington 10 days ago we have lived in a whirl. At Baltimore we saw something of the city government – meeting the city solicitor, Mayor, Director of P. [Public] Works and attending meetings of both branches of the City Council – something also of Johns Hopkins University – addressing the students of Political and Economic Faculties, attending a reception for the President of the University etc. At Philadelphia we stayed with the assistant editor of the principal paper (strong supporter of the Republican machine – the Editor having been appointed last week Postmaster-General of McKinley's Govt.), had long talks with the Mayor and ex-Mayor, attended Council meetings and interviewed principal officials of the City. Here again the University (Pennsylvania) claimed part of our time – there being a group of clever young professors who insisted on our addressing some 200 students, and one of the professors taking me for a long ride in the beautiful country roundabout the town. Then we spent Sunday with the Dean of Brynmawr (the Women's University) at her luxurious 'Deanery' – a charming place some 15 miles out of Philadelphia – Professor James (the psychologist and brother of Henry James) being the other guest. On Monday we stopped to lunch with Woodrow Wilson (author of *Congressional Government* – the book that Bryce made so much use of) at Princeton University. Mr Wilson is quite the most intellectual man we have met – has none of the *literalness* of most Americans – resembles a young and alert John Morley in appearance and temperament. And here we are back in New York – spending our days with Tammany and our evenings in good society!

Our tour is turning out far more instructive than we expected – rather more of an investigation and less of a lounge than we planned. The city government here is the most amazing instance of topsy-turvy land that I ever came across. Altogether American municipal institutions, both in their rapidly changing constitutions and their infantile procedure make one think that we must be Alice in Wonderland witnessing a huge and somewhat grimy joke. The only remedy I can see for the kink into which American Democracy has got into is the supply of 1,000 Leonard Courtneys to act as Governors, Presidents of State Legislatures and City Councils and Financial Comptrollers of all American institutions, with, perhaps, an occasional Sidney Webb to invent ways of dodging their silly constitutions – of course with the moral approval of the Leonard Courtneys!

For all that they are an attractive people – clean-living, bright and pleasant-tempered and wonderfully hospitable – intelligent too in their hospitality; they really try to find out what you want to be at and to help you to get at it. We have been most kindly treated here – we dined last night at the Godkins (Editor of *Nation*) who had a dinner and reception to meet us, we lunch with George Howell tomorrow and dine with Joseph Choate the great N.Y. lawyer, and have all sorts of other social engagements for the next few days. Mayor Van Wyck – Croker's man – has been very friendly and introduced us to all his officials (owing to an introduction from Michael Davitt). We had a long talk this morning with a Tammany lawyer of big position and practice. Tammany has a 'moderate' policy in all municipal matters, objects to expenditure on schools, parks, street cleaning and other services, insists on doing all its work by contractors etc. Otherwise it is based on human fellowship (carried to an almost inconceivable extent in highly-organised neighbourly help) tempered by blackmail, corruption and extensive subsidies from the Corporation who hold, or wish to acquire, franchises (i.e. rights to run tramways, gas, etc.). Apparently it gets its hold on the affections of the people, not only by its systematic philanthropy and personal friendship, its blackmail and favoritism, but also by appealing to the economical ratepayer and by resisting the attempt of the Republican State Legislature to regulate here, there and everywhere.

We go to Cornell University on Thursday, where Sidney has promised to lecture; then to Vassar (Women's University) then on to Harvard (staying with Professor Ashley) then to Boston where we stay with the Fairchilds. Address us Post Office, Boston, until the 20th May (the date we leave for the West). Address c/o Miss Addams, Hull House, 335 South Halsted Street, Chicago, until the 10th June when we go to Denver.

We pick up Trevelyan on the 1st July in San Francisco, arriving in New Zealand the middle of August. Let us hear from you: political news most acceptable.

Ever yours

B Webb

Gustav von Schmoller (1838–1917) was one of the younger leaders of the 'historical school' of economics in Germany, which significantly influenced Webb's approach to economic history. Robert James Sprague (1868–1929) was an American professor of ecocomics who in 1898 was visiting London to do research.

> We shall be at Post Office, Boston, Mass.
> until 21 May
> c/o Prof. Zueblin, 6052 Kimbark Avenue,
> Chicago, Ill. until 7 June
> Post Office, San Francisco, Cal.
> 1–7 July
> Boston
> 14/5/98

Dear Hewins

I have now discussed the London School more or less at half a dozen Universities, with a score of professors, including W. J. Ashley, and I am moved to send you some hints.

We shall not get many American students for any long stay until they can get a degree by it. The next best thing is to make it clear and public that they can combine a stay at the School with getting their Ph.D. degree in Germany. Can you ascertain, (so as to publish) whether it is permitted to a student at a German university to count time spent at the London School? Schmoller or Brentano might tell you, or you might consult someone in London. The attraction of Germany is very much on the wane here, and we *can* win them to England gradually, but it is a necessity for the young man to get his Ph.D. A *certificate* of study and research at the London School would be useful to some extent.

What the advanced students value and appreciate is *individual* attention. They say they *usually* fail to get this in Germany, and when I describe (my idea of) what they get from you – guide to sources, letters of introduction, suggestion, criticism etc. – they are delighted. It occurs to me (and this is why I write *now*) that it might be useful to get out something with this intent before next October – a sort of prospectus of the research department describing what we do for the research student. I have said that, among other things, we provide him with introductions to persons on all sides of his subject in all parts of the kingdom – employers, trade union secretaries, factory inspectors, etc. etc.

Ashley, who is very sympathetic and friendly, adds the hint that in view of the state of opinion here, we ought not to let it be imagined that the School is especially for study of *Labor* questions. The aspirant for a professorship is always afraid of being compromised in the eyes of trustees and other capitalists in authority. The School should bring to the front its

Municipal, Banking, Railroading sides, more prominently than its Trade Union side, though of course, not to the exclusion of the latter.

Ashley goes to England next month for 15 months. He promises to send a miscellaneous parcel of pamphlets and other things for the Library. (It will be shipped with the rest from New York in July.) He read out pretty things about you and the School, from Sprague (who, however, added that the 'academic atmosphere' was 'sadly to seek'). I think you will find Ashley helpful to consult.

Your cheery letter reporting the steady progress of the School, and your other news was very welcome to us.

I am posting you herewith the Harvard syllabus. In their larger volume (Calendar) they have a list of American Universities of which they accept the B.A. degree as *admitting* to their Law School, (exclusively a graduate school); and of course they add that anyone else can be admitted on satisfying the professors etc.! Would it be pretentious for you in any research department circular to say that it would be confined to graduates, etc. etc., and to others who satisfy etc. You know what I mean. I am inclined to think this might be a good line to take.

If you cannot authoritatively say that a term spent at the London School would be 'counted' as time spent at a German University (for the Ph.D. of the latter) it would be well to emphasise the possibility of students coming to London for a few months on their way to Germany. (The trouble is of course to fit in with College courses, and I do not see how this can be done without giving up a year to London, either before or after Germany.)

The School lacks a little in *status* on this side. (Of course this is inevitable in so new a thing, and the marvel is we have done as well as we have.) We should do well to push forward our publications (keeping up the standard.) Your own book will help us not a little. If we could get out anything in the nature of a list of the staff; record of original publications by them and the students; an elaborate 'Calendar' and so on, it would do us good.

I think that, after our touring around here, *all* the American economic professors, economists and historians ought to receive your next session's prospectus; and I think you would do well to address it also to '*The President*' of as many universities here as you can get the names of.

Now with regard to the Library – we are getting piles of municipal and other such things, which Longman will ship in July. (By the way, if you ask him to post the letters I suggested to States and Cities, he suggests that all you need do is to send the parcel of letters addressed to him – i.e. C. J. Mills Esq., 91 Fifth Avenue, New York – *to Longman's in Paternoster Row*, asking them to enclose it in their next forwarding.) I enclose a list of learned societies' journals and proceedings, all of which I think we ought to acquire. I have not bought them (as you can always buy them from London); and because you may get some for nothing. But I think you had better take action at once, without further waiting, about the 5 University series on page I, and the 'Annals' at foot of page IV in enclosed list.

These contain most of the monographs of value, and any serious student of pretty well any subject must refer to one or more of them. We, for instance, need a dozen or more of them ourselves.

I do not know whether you have the 'cheek' to ask the Universities to give you them, offering our publications in exchange, and putting it on the ground of a youthful institution inviting the aid of older ones. If not, I suggest that you should *order* them – perhaps asking whether second-hand sets can be got – through your American agent or P. S. King and Son – the latter, by the way, publish in London the 'Annals' of the American Academy.

All kindly greetings to yourself and Mrs Hewins. This is a business letter!

Yours

Sidney Webb

334 PP   BEATRICE WEBB TO CATHERINE COURTNEY

Mr McCrew was a senior executive in the Carnegie enterprise: Beatrice described him as 'a shrewd young man with a devouring zeal to get rich'. (BWD 24 May 98) Andrew Carnegie (1835–1919) was about to retire from the steel industry to devote himself to the distribution of his huge wealth to endowments for education and the pursuit of peace. M. E. Ingalls was a railway promoter in the Middle West. Edward Colston was a lawyer who developed the technique of using court injunctions to break strikes. The 'coarse-grained' individual who controlled the book trust was about to move to Maine as a means of tax evasion. (BWD 29 May 98) The Republican boss of Cincinnati was George B. Cox (1853–1916). He did not himself hold office. After he had been exposed for selling posts in the city judiciary his nominees were ousted by a reform coalition and its new city constitution was being challenged in the Supreme Court.

John Peter Altgeld (1847–1902) was a radical Democrat who, as Governor of Illinois, had shown sympathy for organised labour and pardoned the surviving anarchists sentenced after the notorious Haymarket bomb explosion in 1887.

Professor Zueblin's, Chicago<br>May 29 [1898]

My dear Kate

Your letter, with its news, was most welcome: you can imagine that never seeing the English papers it is pleasant to have any kind of political gossip as well as family news.

We have had a busy 6 days since we left the pretty little conventional university of Yale last Sunday. Pittsburg is a veritable Hell of a place: a city which combines the smoke and dirt of the worst part of the Black Country with the filthy drainage system of the more archaic Italian city.

The people are a God-forsaken lot: rents about half as much again as the most crowded slums of London, tenements built back to back – craggy wooden structures crammed in between offices 20 stories high, streets narrow and crowded with electric trams rushing through at 20 miles an hour – altogether a most diabolic place with the corruptest of corrupt American governments. Carnegie's Works dominate the City. One of the smart young partners was sent to escort us over. The 11 millions of capital is exclusively owned by the 25 persons actively interested in the concern, Carnegie being the only one on the retired list, and the policy of the firm being to bring in all their managers and superintendents, not only as stockholders but as a council of management. We saw quite a number of these managers – they are all young men working at the top of their [ ?speed] full of zeal to get rich enough at 45 to retire to Paris or London and have a 'fine time', like their beau-ideal Mr Carnegie. The firm simply shovels in capital into the plant and machinery and reckons to replace all their machinery once in three years, writing off the old as dead. Hence in walking over the acres of ground covered by the workshops we found half the place in confusion – boilers, railway-tracks, converters being torn up for new ones to be inserted whilst in the other half the huge engines and cranes and blasting furnaces were grinding away at a furious pace. There was a strange and almost uncanny absence of labour – the firm having trebled its production in a few years and diminished its labour about 13%. Everyone works 12 hours with no Saturday half-holiday. One wonders what is the economic effect on the national prosperity of this shovelling-in of capital out of surplus income into one industry (in order to gain a complete monopoly of American production) whilst other national industries are being starved – shipbuilders having to pay extravagant interest for the capital with which to make the most necessary improvements. But to my mind even worse than the sweated labour crowded in indescribable slums was the spectacle of these 20 energetic vulgar young men, all pushing and striving and utterly uninterested in any public concern!

At Cincinatti we were entertained by Mr Ingalls, the President of the Big Four Railway (introduction from Robert Holt – please send this letter on to Lallie with our grateful thanks for the introduction). He was the best type of American Capitalist – a really enlightened man (from our point of view) who had done his level best – reformed Cincinatti municipal government, was strongly in favour of an income tax and disapproved, as likely to breed trouble, of the Carnegie policy towards labour. He invited us to lunch to meet the city officials, and the following day took us with a select body of the business and legal swells of Cincinatti for a 4-hours special 'Trolly' ride round about the electric tram system of Cincinatti, ending up with a gorgeous dinner at his country house. He also presented us with a pass over his railway and gave us introductions to other Railway Kings further west with a kindly 'they will look after you'. We met on this party the Railway attorney who first introduced 'Government by Injunction', also the Boss of the great School-Book Trust which supplies 5/8 of the school books of America and is supposed to have half the school boards of the U.S. in its pay. As they all talked their own 'shop' to us we enjoyed ourselves vastly. The next morning we spent with the Republican machine Boss, whose administration of the city had just been ousted by a brave new charter, the legality of which is being disputed in the State Supreme Court. The State Legislature meets every two years and usually passes a new Charter for Cincinatti in order to turn out some particular ring of administrators. We also attended the meeting of the new Boards of City Affairs and watched them ousting all the officials of the old Board and dividing up the spoils between the [?other] Republicans and State Democrats who had made a deal in order to get a new Charter. Then in the afternoon we came on here after a stiflingly hot journey and are resting in a charming American home. We shall see ex-Governor Altgeld next week and others to whom we have introductions. My last letter to Maggie will have given our address at various dates. Do write – we are delighted to get your letters.

Ever yours affectionately<br>Beatrice Webb

### 335 BL  SIDNEY WEBB TO GEORGE BERNARD SHAW

*Plays Pleasant and Unpleasant* was published in the Spring of 1898. George Birkbeck Hill (1835–1903) was editor of Boswell's *Life* of Samuel Johnson.

We shall be at  Post Office, Denver, Colorado until 23 June
Post Office, San Francisco, Cal. until 7 July
Post Office, Auckland, New Zealand until 24 Aug.
Post Office, Sydney, New South Wales until 7 Sept.

Hull House, Chicago<br>5.6.98

Dear Shaw

Here we are in the middle of the Continent, both of us rather overcome with the American weather. I have just recovered from a mild attack of influenza, and now Beatrice is down with it. This has decided us to 'chuck' the rest of these overgrown, ugly cities, each more corrupt and misgoverned than the last, and to take a bee-line for Colorado. There we shall try to get into the Rocky Mountains for a week or so, going probably to a certain high valley (which by the way, is said to be owned by Lord Dunraven, L.C.C.) where we can lie on our backs and be quiet.

Your published plays made a brief sensation here in the newspapers, but the latter have their eyes too firmly fixed on the war, and the reading public is too impatient, to care for anything very long. We find your portrait, now and again, in houses; your plays occasionally; and quite frequently, people who take the *Saturday* to read you. [?Yarros] says the *Saturday* announced your projected retirement, with the information that you had made £10,000 out of America.

We are wondering how and where you are going to spend the summer. Let us have a letter whenever you can. By the way, Prof. W. J. Ashley, author of the two volumes on Economic History, now Professor at Harvard, returns to England this month for a year. He is quite friendly to 'us' (he is more or less a 'Christian Social Union' man); and as he holds a leading position in American economics, he could help the London School greatly. Mrs Ashley is a daughter of Dr Birkbeck Hill, the writer on Johnson and Boswell. Would you kindly tell Miss Payne-Townshend that the Ashleys are coming, and that it is important that they should get a favorable idea of the School. Hewins knows that they are coming, but if Miss Townshend were to be nice to them it would, I am sure, be a good thing – besides being only a return for their very great hospitality to us.

I can't tell you of our doings – which are the same in one city as in another – interviews, lunches, dinners, speeches, collecting documents and so forth. Just now we are utterly fagged out and we gaze helplessly at Chicago – an 'unspeakable' city, viler than tongue can tell, and as hopeless as the Inferno. It has undone our two months holiday and we will now begin again in the purer air of Colorado.

Yours

Sidney Webb

### 336 PP   BEATRICE WEBB TO MARY PLAYNE

Charles Trevelyan travelled ahead of the Webbs across the United States, rejoining them in California. The Webbs themselves spent a week recuperating at Estes Park in the Rocky Mountains near Denver. In Denver Beatrice attended the biennial convention of the Federated Women's Clubs and spoke on 'How to do away with the Sweating System'.

Denver, Colorado<br>[?10 June 1898]

My dear Mary

I was very glad to get your cheery letter from Ems. I am sorry there is no prospect of continuing a good family but the R.P.s have contributed a goodly number to the Anglo-Saxon population and what with your public work and your innumerable nephews and nieces you will find your life continue full of interest and variety.

Our stay at Chicago was rather unfortunate: Sidney was ill, with the Chicago grippe (a diabolically bad throat with fever) for the first 4 days and I for the last of our visit there and I am still suffering from the remnants of the disease. So we gave up the other great cities we had intended to visit and came straight on here and go on Tuesday right into the mountains for a week's complete rest 8000 feet high. Chicago is an unlovely place: but as we stayed half the time in the University and half in the famous Hull House Settlement we heard and saw a good deal to instruct us. Tell the Courtneys that we saw a good deal of ex-Governor Peter Altgeld. He is an attractive man with a strong independent will and visionary intellect – with neither traditions nor any great knowledge of men or affairs. I am not sure that I do not think him a *dangerous* fellow: he reasons from abstract principles of the Jeffersonian type with little consideration for either present facts or past experience. He was keen on the Supreme Court Judges being elected for 8-year periods and being ineligible for re-election! on the grounds that all men were corrupted by power and that only a 'sense of justice' was needed in the administration of law! But he has all the charm of the absolutely fearless man who has little or no sentiment and is prepared to carry out his somewhat crude ideas to their logical end. We also lunched with Robert Lincoln President of the Pullman Co. and formerly ambassador to England (son of Abraham). He was an objectionable philistine and his womenkind snobbish Anglo-Indians. They desired to be remembered to the Courtneys. Miss Adams the Head of Hull House is a remarkable woman who has been waging an unsuccessful administration out of the rut.

This little western city is just the same as the Eastern cities in its tangle of bad government. We have made friends with Governor Adams – a sensible and upright little fellow fighting all he know against the peculations of his elected officials and the absurdities of their system of taxation. The Governors are the recruiters and he tells us that all the finest youths in Colorado are volunteering for the war. Trevelyan, whom we hear from constantly, sends glowing accounts of the 'stuff' of the newly-manufactured American army. He has been visiting the camps.

We are reading hard at American History and have taken out some twenty books from the Public Library to take with us to the mountains. We return here on June 4th as I have promised to speak to the great biennial conference of Women's Clubs – from all parts of the States – the Club movement is one of organised movements to promote civil good government. By the way there is universal woman's suffrage here: the general opinion being that it has made little or no difference except that the women *have* turned out some of the more notorious 'Boodlers' (corrupt politicians) from the municipal government. They seem to have brought a fresh addition of conscience but no addition of wisdom. Still that is to the good.

If you come back *before* June 20th we should be delighted to get a letter at *Post Office, San Francisco*; if later and before July 14 to Auckland, New Zealand; after that to Sydney, Australia.

Please let Rosie see this letter: thanks for hers which was full of news.

B.W.

The achievements of the Mormon administration in Utah greatly impressed Beatrice – especially the combination of parsimony and freedom from corruption. She was intrigued by the notion of polygamy, which she thought raised the possibility of 'scientific breeding' and of a rather different role for women: 'it is the childless woman who makes the best wife for the professional man . . . it is a loss to the world that the experiment of polygamy was not continued by a sect exceptionally well-fitted to give it a fair and full trial'. (BWD 29 June 98)

The Mayor of Salt Lake City was John Clarke; the Governor of Utah was Heber M. Wells. Brigham Young (1801–77) was the leader of the Mormon emigration to Utah. He had seventeen wives and fifty-six children.

San Francisco
July 2nd 1898

My dear Kate

I believe I have written more letters home than I have received from all my sisters combined! – do remember how much pleasure a nice chat like that we found awaiting us here gives to poor exiles.

We had a most entertaining time at Salt Lake City. Since you and I were there 25 years ago, it has changed from a garden with houses into streets lined with trees and breaking now and again into gardens. But the Mormons, after having lost control for some years, have just come in again with power in the State and in the City. We attended the city council – by far the most orderly we have seen in America – we interviewed the Mayor, a shrewd and wealthy elder: we had a friendly chat with the young Governor – an able wholesome young fellow, one of the many children of [?Squire] Wells, a great name amongst the Mormons. Apparently the Mormons have regained their control, by ceasing to form *one* party; the word having gone out from the Heads of the Church that they were to divide themselves between the two national parties. Thus the Governor is a Republican, the Mayor a Democrat – and the Mormons' overwhelming majority in the city and State legislature being made out of both parties. But by far the most interesting talk was with 'Senator' Cannan – (State Senate) a lady, a plural wife, who opposed and beat her husband (an elder of the Church), who is on excellent terms with him and who combines a fervent faith in woman's rights with a serene belief in polygamy as the best and happiest of social institutions. She really was a delightful little woman, alert and self-respectful; a medical practitioner and active politician, and though she appeared very indiscreet about the affairs of the Church she managed to give us a most agreeable impression of Mormon society. She declared that polygamy enabled the woman to select really fine men as the fathers of their children instead of having to put up with any person who had been 'left over', that it rested on the truth that whilst women in the main wanted children and a kind protector, men required the constant and unremitting attention of a woman for every day of the year – an attention that no one woman could give without neglecting her children or sacrificing her profession! She deplored the U.S. Law which had forced the Church to abjure plural marriages not only because it had broken up many 'happy' families but because it had stopped one of the most interesting experiments the world had ever seen in the deliberate breeding of a fine and healthy race from specially selected fathers. She wanted to take us to see her defeated husband – 'a splendid old man' and also some of Brigham Young's widows and children but alas! we had engaged our compartment and had to whisk off to San Francisco.

We found a warm welcome here. The Chairman of the 4th of July celebrations has arranged that we shall ride in the great procession in which the 10,000 troops now stationed here are to take part. The war-fervour here is very hot – the volunteers are really a splendid set of young fellows – quite the pick from all classes. As for the American–English alliance I don't gather the feeling that it amounts to much – all it has done is to put a temporary stop on some of the American Irish abuse of us, but I don't believe the ordinary American looks upon it as a real factor – he is far too full of exploits of his own nation and its perfect self-sufficiency. At present he sees no necessity for an alliance with England; stowed away in this great continent he firmly believes that all Europe combined cannot touch him and that if he chooses to fight he will always be offensive and never defensive. C.P.T. [Trevelyan] joins us tomorrow and we sail on the 7th. Address Sydney Post Office. We shall certainly run over for a day to Dunedin if only to see the Olivers and exchange notes of you.

Ever yours affectionately

B. Webb

338 PP   BEATRICE WEBB TO SALLY FAIRCHILD

Bernard Shaw and Charlotte Payne-Townshend were married on 1 June 1898. Shaw had become seriously ill with a tubercular or gangrenous infection of the foot – a condition which made him convalescent for a year. On their marriage the Shaws moved to a rented house in the country near Hindhead.

In Boston the Webbs had taken a strong liking to Josiah Quincy (1859–1919), the Democratic Mayor of Boston from 1895 to 1899. Quincy was a patrician New Englander who combined aristocratic manners with great competence as a municipal administrator: the Webbs thought his goal was 'Fabian collectivism'.

San Francisco
July 8th 1898

My dear Miss Fairchild

Before we leave this big country of yours I must write you a line thanking you for all your kindness to us whilst we were at Boston. Our visit to you will remain as one of the pleasantest and most useful experiences of our extremely agreeable and suggestive tour.

73

You all have heard of Bernard Shaw's marriage to our friend Charlotte Townshend. He apparently broke down utterly in health and was reduced to such a state that he felt the need of a devoted and charming woman. They have settled in a house at Haslemere. I believe they will be extremely well-suited, certainly they delight in each other's companionship, which is after all the main matter in marriage. It has only been a deeprooted prejudice against an old-fashioned institution which has kept them apart. When you come and stay with us in London you must examine the results.

We were obliged to skip some of the big towns and to take refuge earlier than we intended in the mountains, as we broke down in Chicago with the 'grippe'. But we have added extensively to our collection of American municipal institutions: up to now Mayor Quincy has not found a rival in our affections! – not even the Mormon mayor of Salt Lake City – a shrewd old autocrat. We leave U.S. next Thursday. We shall be in Auckland, New Zealand, until the end of August, thence to Australia, back to Europe in December, in London from January. Come over to London: you will always find a welcome at 41 Grosvenor Road.

With kind regards to Mrs Fairchild<br>Ever yours affectionately<br>Beatrice Webb

339 PP   BEATRICE WEBB TO CATHERINE COURTNEY

The *Echo* was the first halfpenny newspaper in London: after it was reorganised in 1896 the Webbs took a modest shareholding in it. It subsequently ran into financial difficulties. Graham and Ada Wallas temporarily occupied the Shaw flat above the L.S.E.

Honolulu<br>July 12th 1898

My dear Kate

We arrived here in fine style – with flying colours, signalling to the expectant inhabitants the Annexation of the Islands to the United States. We were therefore accorded, by the crowd of American settlers gathered on the quay, a magnificent reception – military band floral wreaths and the firing of cannon from the Executive buildings. We had had a delightful voyage across a really pacific ocean in a good ship with a pleasant captain and [?fairly agreeable] passengers so that we were in a good mood to enjoy tropical vegetation and tropical climate. If it were not for mosquitos, which Captain Cook, of damnable memory, introduced with other abominations! We find the little place in an uproar of excitement. The self-elected oligarchy of respectable American capitalists and lawyers who have been governing since 1893 are in triumphant mood. With a handful of supporters they have been sitting tight on some 115,000 inhabitants of all races (only about 6,000 European and American) and have never known from day to day whether there might not be a successful revolution: unsuccessful 'conspiracies' have been a monthly occurrence. I fancy, from all accounts, the so-called Republic has done well by the natives: the President and officials being the substantial men of the place – sons of the original American missionaries who, most of them, held office under the monarchy in its palmy days of constitutional behaviour. But the natives have never accepted the government, and having refused to take the oath of allegiance, have not had the franchise, so that the legislature which begged for the annexation represented at most some 3,000 out of the 120,000 inhabitants. The natives are an attractive race – soft-hearted mild-mannered Maoris – who have intermarried freely with the 'foreigners' and produced a large half-caste population. There is a large Chinese–Japanese population – some 30,000 – who have always been denied representation.

We had very good introductions; have visited the President, the Chief Justice and other leading American citizens. Yesterday afternoon we spent with Princess Kaiulani – the niece and heir-apparent of the deposed Queen – a charming girl, half-Scotch, half-native whose father (a wealthy Scotch merchant) has a lovely place some three miles out. This afternoon Trevelyan and we are going 'surf-riding' with her – which consists of going out to sea in a canoe (in your bathing costume!) and riding over the coral reef, on the crest of a breaker, at the rate of 40 miles an hour! two natives guiding the enterprise. Bathing here is heavenly – the water is warm and inside the reef absolutely calm and just the right depth for hundrum people like ourselves. Sidney is firing off an article to the *Echo*; if you send a card to Mr S. Crooks, 22 Katherine Street, Strand W.C. he will send you a copy with it in. I hear the *Echo* is doing very well: and paid at the rate of 10% the first quarter with a handsome balance over! Trevelyan joined us in San Francisco in first-rate spirits: he has been seeing scenery while we have been studying institutions. We have attended 20 American representative assemblies of one sort or another and have picked [up] all sorts of odds and ends of facts and suggestions for those notes of our future work on British local government which will deal with American institutions – their likeness to and divergence from the British pattern. I have kept a most elaborate diary – but I find it will be both too technical and too indiscreet for publication – so it must be buried with the other volumes for some enterprising great-grand-niece to decipher and edit in the last half of the 20th century! Address Post Office Sydney until end of August, Melbourne until end of September; Adelaide until about the 10th October (we sail from there 15 November). Would you please send this letter on to Ada Wallas at 10 Adelphi Terrace and then to any sisters who care to read this scrawl?

Ever yours affectionately

BW

The Webbs enjoyed their stay in New Zealand. They stayed first with Leonard Courtney's sister Louise, the second wife of Richard Oliver (1830–1910), who had extensive business and agricultural interests. He was a member of the House of Representatives for Dunedin 1878–81 and of the Legislative Council 1881–1901, holding several Cabinet posts. The Olivers returned to settle in England in 1901. Richard Seddon (1845–1906) was the Lancashire-born premier from 1893 to 1906 and under his administration the country pioneered many reforms, including the vote for women and some experiments in nationalisation. Beatrice's comparison was to Benjamin Pickard (1842–1904), leader of the Yorkshire miners and a Liberal M.P. from 1885 to 1904; and to William Sproston Caine, the Radical M.P. and temperance campaigner. George Hutchinson (1846–1930) was a lawyer who sat for the Patea seat as an Independent. Sir Joshua Strange Williams (1837–1915) was the first president of the Arbitration Court.

Wellington<br>Aug. 24 1898

My dear Kate

We have had a most pleasant week with the Olivers, who insisted directly we arrived in Wellington that we should stay with them. Their comfortable house has been a delightful change from hotels and we have found talks with them and their friends most instructive. As all our introductions were to members of the present government it has been a great advantage to us to spend our leisure hours with the opposition: to interview the radicals and dine with the Conservatives has, I am certain, been the most profitable and certainly the most agreeable way of spending our time!

We enjoyed our ten-days drive through the Hot Lake district, inspite of being kept two days and two nights on the wrong side of a roaring torrent in a little inn, the ferryman absolutely refusing to take us over until the flood subsided. As we had to eat and sit with 4 sheep drovers (also delayed) two swaggers (tramps) a station manager and a varying number of station hands, we heard a good deal more of the details of station life than if we had stayed a week with a respectable station holder. Politics were of course the one subject of general conversation, the station manager and head drover being Conservatives and all the rest of the company ardent 'Seddonites'. You probably know as much as we do about New Zealand politics; anyway it is too complicated to write about. We are impressed with Seddon's force, he towers over every one else in the House – he is like an idealised Pickard with Caine's good temper and a huge capacity for work; he is abominably vulgar in the worst sense, does not mind telling a lie with the certainty that it will be found out(!) So long as it gets him over a difficulty he is absolutely shameless in all questions of manners. But inspite of general charges of corruption we cannot discover anything that approaches to American spoils systems or the taking of bribes, and he seems to go out of his way to get the best men he can find for permanent appointments and to use capacity wherever he can find it, in many cases with sublime disregard for the person's political opinion. He is intensely susceptible to popular desires and thinks nothing impossible, so that the ordinary man in the street feels that he has a servant with zeal and force and industry and forgives him his vulgarities. Of course if there was anyone in the front opposition who 'outclassed' him in knowledge and manners he might be deposed: but Capt. Russell is a gentlemanly officer far more ignorant than Seddon, and Hutchinson (the so-called Jo Chamberlain of New Zealand) is even more vulgar and unscrupulous than Seddon himself.

We have seen something of the working of the Compulsory Arbitration Act: have attended meetings of the Conciliation Board and the Arbitration Court and talked to the present Judge and the assessors of both sides. There are very grave defects in its working, some the result of bad drafting, others we think inherent in the scheme. The present Judge (Judge Williams is in England) is going to make a mess of it; he has no notion of any general principles upon which to base his awards, and he has no talent for grasping the technical circumstances of the different trades. I am afraid his awards will prove to be a caricature of judge-made law; and will prove that if you are to have legal regulations, its main principles must be determined by Parliament; even if the application of these principles be left to a Court of Technical Experts.

Altogether we are delighted with New Zealand. The climate and country are ideal: and there is a splendidly healthy public spirit with very little corruption. There is any amount to criticise: but unlike America one feels that there is nothing to prevent it being put right – the people have control of their government and they themselves mean well.

The Olivers seem extremely happy: Mr Oliver is evidently looked up to in the Legislative Council and Louise seems quite a personage in 'good society'. Trevelyan is staying at Government House: we have not been introduced to that highest point of Wellington Society, but we understand that the present Governor is not of much account. This afternoon we go to Christchurch, then to Dunedin and back again here this day week.

It is an age since we have heard from any sister – not for 2 months I think! Write to P.O. Melbourne up to end of September, and P.O. Adelaide up to middle of October.

Ever yours affectionately<br>Beatrice Webb

341 NLNZ   SIDNEY WEBB TO WILLIAM PEMBER REEVES

The inner group of Fabians had taken in William Pember Reeves (1857–1932) and his wife Magdalen (Maude) as personal friends as well as political allies. Reeves, who had served as Minister of Labour, Education and Justice in New Zealand, had moved to London as Agent-General. He became the third Director of the L.S.E. in 1908. Maude Reeves played a leading role in the Fabian Society, serving on its executive and taking a prominent part in its Women's Group.

William Whitehouse Collins (1855–1923), a Liberal who sat for Christchurch 1893–96, was currently out of office; he was elected again in December 1899. He was an acquaintance of Annie Besant and a leading socialist. George Warren Russell (1854–1937), a journalist who sat as Liberal for Riccarton until 1896, was also re-elected for Avon in 1899. Mrs Reeves was the mother of W. P. Reeves: Mrs Robinson was his mother-in-law.

Captain William Russell (1838–1913) was Leader of the Opposition from 1893 to 1903; William Rolleston (1831–1903), an outstanding provincial administrator, was briefly Leader of the Opposition from 1891 to 1893; Mackay John Scobie Mackenzie (1845–1901), a sheep-run owner with literary aspirations, sat for Dunedin; Thomas Edward Taylor (1862–1911), a temperance reformer and supporter of female emancipation, sat for Christchurch until 1899, losing his seat as a result of his opposition to the Boer War; Arthur Richmond Atkinson (1863–1935) was a lawyer and journalist, the son of a former prime minister, and sat for South Wellington. Charles Louisson was mayor of Christchurch; John Merriman Booth, who owned a sawmill in Canterbury, was a member of the School Committee; Henry George Ell (1862–1934) sat for Christchurch. Sir Wesley Bassett Edwards (1850–1927) was president of the Arbitration Court 1898–1900; Edward Tregear (1846–1931) was a socialist, civil servant, author and friend of Pember Reeves and, as head of the Department of Labour, had collaborated with him in the programme of advanced social legislation. He was later called the 'Grand Old Man of New Zealand Labour'.

In the Dunedin Express(!)
27 Aug/98

Dear Reeves

We have had no time to write anything since an impertinent postcard from Rotorua. That railway was really awful: we happened on a day when there was no 'birdcage' carriage on, and we had to sit for 11 hours in that queer side-seated cell. We all applauded Capt. Russell's vote of censure about more rolling stock. However, we have since forgiven you, as we consider the 'birdcage' compartments the height of luxury; Seddon has given us a free pass; and this reckless train is actually going across the plain at the rate of 25 miles an hour! Moreover, Mrs Webb has started the theory that the N.Z. trains are really only coaches, pretending to be trains, and once you realise that, the speed is wonderful, and there is very little time wasted in changing horses.

We had a good time between Rotorua and Napier on the whole, finishing up with four days rain, and 48 hours detention at the Mohaca River – bridge down, and the Seddonian official – combining innkeeping with ferrying – refused to cross, not unnaturally preferring to keep us 2 days before venturing on the flood in the dug-out canoe. So we had 2 days political and economic discussion with a station-manager, 4 sheepdrovers, a swagger, and some stationhands – delayed with us. At Napier (a charming toy town) Mrs Webb's spirits rose on seeing the great stretch of fertile land on which she levies her harbour bond interest. But I don't think much of the harbour.

We have had a high time at Wellington, dining with the Tories and discussing with the Whigs. We stayed with the Olivers – the Hon. R. by the way, is 'coming along very nicely' for an M.L.C. [member of the Legislative Council] and saw a good deal of Russell, Rolleston, Scobie Mackenzie, 'Tommy Taylor', young Atkinson etc., as well as the Govt. and Labor; and all the Govt. departments. Everybody has been most cordial and helpful. We chanced on the heated personal row in the Financial Statement debate, and we did not think the 'gentlemanly party' were any better than their opponents.

We have just had $2\frac{1}{2}$ brilliant days at Christchurch – bright sun and still frost, with a constant stream of persons calling to see us. We had a very pleasant time at Mrs Reeves', and another at Mrs Robinson's – long talks with ex-M.P.s Collins and Russell – the Mayor (Louisson) – employers like Booth and Beaver, Ell – and all the trade unionists. Now we are off to Dunedin for 2 days in brilliant weather; returning to Wellington to catch the *Monowai* for Sydney on 2 September.

We have 'investigated' all the time, and have formed lots of emphatic generalisations, which we look forward to discussing with you. I can only give here a few impressions.

We very soon decided, and we grew more and more convinced as we came southward, that the Seddon Government is still very strong electorally, and that it seems fully likely that it will weather at least the next election. Public opinion thinks that the Opposition has no policy of its own, and that it is *very* weakly led – an opinion which the Opposition itself shares, and frankly admitted to us. Seddon, with all his faults, towers like a giant over the rest of the House, and is evidently an 'old Parliamentary hand'. The 'Left Wing', followed by the Opposition, does its best to make a row about 'corruption' and so forth. We hunted down its principal charges, and found that it had no sense of proportion: that it shrieked alike about everything; and that the customary government favouritism and genial tolerance of fallen human nature among constables and charwomen were accounted to Seddon as heinous crimes. To us, fresh from the Augean Stables of America, these seemed peccadilloes, which would certainly never arouse the working-man to revolt. And, unfortunately for the Opposition, Seddon's vulgar brutalities are being paralleled by Tommy Taylor and George Hutchinson in their several ways. Our inference is that Seddon won't be a candidate for the Agent-Generalship for 2 or 3 years at any rate.

Our other principal subject of investigation has been the Arbitration Act. We have attended meetings of the Board and Court in Wellington, and we cross-examined everybody everywhere, from Judge Edwards down to the Deputy Registrars, and employers and workmen members, plaintiffs and defendants. Public opinion continues to approve the Act in principle in a wonderful way – even the employers who have been worried and brought into court on 'got up' cases not denouncing it otherwise than as to details. Frankly, we are still unconvinced of its excellence. It is, in effect, *not* arbitration to end an actual war, but a means of securing the legal enactment of the conditions of employment. To that we have of course no objection, but then we are much afraid of leaving those important 'extensions of the Factory Act' to the uncontrolled discretion of a judge. It seems to us – in the realms of Labor Law – rather like the state of things in English Equity long ago, when each judge gave relief as he chose, before a rigid code of precedents had been elaborated. You were evidently very lucky in Judge Williams – he might have been the Lord Eldon of your Labor Equity and have worked out a system. But Judge Edwards will make a hopeless mess of it – not because he is (consciously) biassed, but because he knows nothing about Labor, and won't learn. He has no idea what assumptions he intends to proceed on, and is clearly unaware that anything but 'commonsense' is needed. His late award in the Christchurch engineers case is significant – especially as *we* know now, on the best authority, that the employers could quite well have afforded a rise in wages. The most hopeful thing is that he hates the work, and wants to give it up. The sooner he is 'promoted' the better for your Arbitration Court. Meanwhile the workmen, fortunately, will be slower than heretofore in bringing cases. Unfortunately the employers, relying on him, are beginning to break their past agreements and awards.

With regard to procedure, and especially as to enforcement, we have much to discuss with you, but this I defer.

Tregear has been most kind and helpful in all ways. I have done no speaking in public in N.Z. as I don't want to criticise the Seddon Government and yet I can't altogether approve its present Labor bills. We are *delighted* with N.Z., it is immeasurably *nicer* than America.

By the way, Education has gone to sleep, from the bottom to the top, and N.Z. is clearly behind the best now. 'Charitable Aid' too, needs reforming, or the outdoor relief will ruin the Colony. These two departments require urgent attention and drastic changes.

Goodbye

Sidney Webb

342 PP  BEATRICE WEBB TO CATHERINE COURTNEY

The Webbs arrived in Sydney on 8 September and then travelled up to Queensland. Sir George Reid (1845–1918) became Premier of New South Wales in 1894: he was a strong advocate of the federation of the Australian colonies. B. R. Wise (1858–1916) had been attorney-general in the Parkes government. Sir Edmund Barton (1849–1920) became the first Prime Minister of Australia in 1901, retiring in 1903 to the High Court. Sir Joseph Abbott (1842–1901) became Speaker of the New South Wales Legislative Assembly in 1890. Viscount Hampden (1841–1906) was Governor of New South Wales 1895–99. The Earl of Jersey (1845–1915) was Governor of New South Wales 1891–93; his wife Margaret, notable for her fashionable entertaining, was a founder and president of the Victoria League.

Brisbane, Queensland<br>
[17 September 1898]

My dear Kate

To think that you will not get this letter until the end of October and I have only just received yours written before starting your holiday!

We have gone through 10 days at Sydney – a busy time of seeing and being seen – chiefly by politicians of all parties. We struck on a political crisis: a vote of censure on the Reid ministry for half-heartedness in carrying Federation – the newly elected house being all nominal Federationists and almost equally divided between Reidites and Anti-Reidites. Premier Reid we have seen much of – spent a whole day with him steaming about the beautiful Sydney Harbour, visited the university with him and chatted with him in the House almost every day as well as heard him make his big speech in reply to the Vote of censure. He is the finest type of 'place-man': with no particular convictions of his own, but with a shrewd jovial appreciation of human nature, watching public opinion as closely and keenly as a stockjobber watches the market, but concerned to discover the permanent as distinguished from the temporary changes in public opinion, so that his policy should be tolerably continuous and consistent. He is an extremely agreeable companion because he has no prejudices and opponents and friends are all alike circumstances with which he has to deal; and has besides this philosophy of indifference a fine sense of humour and a really kind heart. But his enemies of course think him cunning and unscrupulous. One of the leaders of opposition is B. R. Wise, a cultivated Oxford man, the son of a judge of the N.S.W. Supreme Court and himself a rising barrister. He is the exact opposite to Reid – refined, scrupulous, dogmatic and academic, with the one idea of transplanting into colonial politics the English theory of two parties basing their respective policies on definite intellectual principles. He speaks remarkably well and uses high constitutional arguments and the House including Reid is amusingly proud of him as an example of what N.S.W. can do when it chooses to be high-principled and refined. Barton, the actual leader of the Opposition, is now fighting a constituency so we did not see him: Wise has promised to ask us to meet him when we return. We have also arranged to meet the Labour party (20 out of a House of 125) privately to hear their view of the situation. They are not overkeen for Federation and form part of Reid's uncertain majority. But I think that

Reid has made up his mind that N.S.W. is now in favour of Federation and that he really means to carry it through. We sat through three or four days debate in the House: the level of speaking is low and the House tho' good-humoured is disorderly, the speech constantly becoming a series of rapid and rowdy interjections and retorts. The poor old Speaker – Sir J. Abbott – is most conscientious but deplorably weak and will allow the members to debate a point of order whilst he is buried in books of procedure trying to make up his mind what ruling he shall give. He usually ends by reading to the House a long paragraph out of Sir Erskine May about the conduct of the House of Commons – the relevance of which no-one quite perceives; by that time, however, the House being made up of Englishmen has got tired of the point of order and proceeds of its own accord to business. Notwithstanding this the House seems to represent what is best in N.S.W. and from all accounts the Ministers work hard and do not steal, directly or indirectly; and the Civil Service tho' not extremely efficient is absolutely honest.

We do not like Sydney people nearly so much as New Zealanders: it is a lower middleclass civilization suddenly got rich – the rich people having no public spirit and no cultivation and spending their time and money on racing. The little set of professors and cultivated professional men are depressed and somewhat soured by the contempt of the rich people and the insolence of the rest of the population towards any attempt to raise the tone. Government House seems to drift with the tide and to entertain almost exclusively members of the Jockey Club. We dined there one night and met a wholly uninteresting party of racing and dancing idiots. It shows how strong the tendency is because Lord Hampden is a cultivated pedantic sort of person and Lady Hampden a gentle-natured aristocrat. It is sad that Lady Jersey tried to pick and choose and to make the rich racing set 'know their proper place', but that they were utterly impervious to her sarcasm and made it so unpleasant for her that the Jerseys left after two-years' residence. We stay here for a week, visit some stations on our way back, then go with Mr Wise and another young politician for a tour in the Blue Mountains, return to Sydney for a few days, then on to Melbourne staying at stations on our way. We are having glorious weather – brilliant sunshine and not too hot for exercise. We are finding any amount to interest us: it is extraordinarily interesting to watch one's own race making the old kind of civilisation under quite new conditions; and the question of Federation and the constitution of the Federal government gives to Australia politics just now wider issues than heretofore. Coming from America the colonial politicians of all parties seem honest and public-spirited; even the municipalities, which are a byeword for inefficiency and petty jobbery (elected by a plural property franchise), are highly respectable judged by the American standard. Altogether the British genius for democratic self-government shines out in the colonies, partly in contrast to America and partly in contrast to the low level of manners and general cultivation in all other departments of colonial life. *It would be intolerable to live here except as a politician* – then I think one might have a rather good time: there is a big field here in public life for men of ability and conviction.

We sail by the *Ormuz* from Adelaide on the 17th November, reaching Colombo about the 27th November. Do write to us there, passengers on the *Ormuz*, c/o Orient S.S. Company and send us any papers with Leonard's speeches: we shall be most anxious for news.

It will be very pleasant to see you all again.

Ever yours affectionately

Beatrice Webb

## 343 PP   SIDNEY WEBB TO GRAHAM WALLAS

During Webb's absence an attempt was made by his critics on the L.C.C., stimulated by Ramsay MacDonald, to withhold or at least to reduce the grant to the L.S.E. from the Technical Education Board. In the first years of the School this money was vital to its survival and Webb remained anxious about the maintenance of this annual subsidy. T. A. Organ (1859–1911) was a teacher, then barrister, who was standing counsel to the National Union of Teachers. He was a member of the L.C.C. and succeeded Webb as chairman of the Technical Education Board.

Brisbane
18.9.98

Dear Wallas

Here we are on the edge of a Colony as large as France, Germany and Austria put together, as the local politicians inform us – but with only half a million people. We were glad to get your letter in Sydney, and hope that when you get this you will be a happy father. Don't experiment too much with the infant!

I am glad that the London School will get its grant, and am surprised at the opposition to it. I don't very well see how a Political Science Faculty could be got any cheaper, and of course the number of students in the higher subjects can never be large. As a matter of fact Bowley's classes don't cost more per head than many of the T.E.B. trade classes in bricklaying. Compare for instance what results from the £1000 grant to the Wandsworth Technical Institute, with its merely elementary evening classes.

But what I want to say most especially is to urge you most strenuously to prevent any prejudicing of the question of the future of this School or its grant until I return (I shall be present at the very first meeting after Xmas.) I urge this, not only for the sake of the School, but for the sake of the T.E.B.'s influence in the whole organisation of London University; and also in the interests of Organ's pet scheme of Commercial Education. You can easily play for delay in one way or another. It ought to be borne in mind that the School is steadily forming a most useful nucleus for a Higher Commercial College such as exists at Paris, and that if the T.E.B. eventually decides to establish anything of that sort, it will be worth a great deal to be able to have certain classes transferred to it as a going concern, instead of having to begin *de novo*.

We start for home from Adelaide on 17 November in the Orient steamer *Ormuz*, calling at Colombo (28 November) Aden, Suez and Naples (18 December). We shall be *very* grateful for any letters and news-papers addressed to these places ('On board S.S. *Ormuz*, care of Orient Steamship Company, Colombo' – or any port.)

We are learning a lot about Democracy, and our conclusions are very hopeful indeed as regards England and these Colonies, which present a remarkable contrast to America. We pass our days with Premiers and attending debates, taking side-glances at town councils, and including 'Government House' by the way. Did you know Bernard Wise at Oxford – he is one of the best speakers and ablest leaders in New South Wales.

With best love

Sidney Webb

344 PP  BEATRICE WEBB TO CATHERINE COURTNEY

Thomas Glassey (1844–1936) had been a labour organiser in England before emigrating to Queensland, where he became leader of the opposition in the colonial legislature in 1898, going on to the first federal Parliament. Sir Samuel Griffith (1845–1920), Premier of Queensland, became Chief Justice of the High Court of Australia. Lord Lamington (1860–1940), formerly a Conservative M.P. in North St Pancras, was Governor of Queensland 1895–1901. R. H. Roe (1850–1926), headmaster of the Brisbane grammar school for boys, did much to promote the University of Queensland and was its Vice-Chancellor from 1910 to 1916. Bishop W. T. T. Webster (1837–1903), who became Bishop of Brisbane in 1885, established the Bush Brotherhood to serve the outback population. Maud Sellers (1862–1939) was a Newnham graduate who was second mistress of the Brisbane grammar school for girls.

The Webbs stayed at Coomburra with the Queensland pastoralist F. W. Donkin. They visited Katoomba in the Blue Mountains with James Ashton (1864–1932), journalist, pastoralist and politician, who sat in the New South Wales legislature continuously from 1894 to 1934. Sir Samuel McCaughey (1835–1919) of Coonong, N.S.W. was reputed to be the first man to own more than one million sheep.

Sydney

Oct. 7th 1898

My dear Kate

We were so glad to get your cheery letter from the mountains and hope that others are on their way.

We are back again in Sydney on our way South. We found a good deal to interest us in Brisbane: very little to please us! Queensland has for the

84

last 8 years had a 'continuous government' one leader after another retiring but the same party remaining in power. The ministers are an unsavoury lot of ruined financiers and impecunious lawyers, at the head of a large majority – a motley lot of nondescript politicians with little thought but a desire for public money to be spent in their respective constituencies and bound up into one party by their common horror of the Labour Party. This latter numbers 22 out of a House of 72, and has recently accepted the position of 'H.M. Opposition', the little knot of 7 Liberals being too feeble and too disunited to get on the front opposition bench. For 4 years the Front Opposition Bench was *untenanted!*, the Labour party refusing to occupy it. The Labour party (whom we met collectively and individually) have many honest men among them, but beyond attending most assiduously to their parliamentary duties are hopelessly incompetent as critics of their opponents and have shackled themselves with a quite impossible programme – a violent affirmation of Abstract Socialism. As their leader they have a well-intentioned vain person – an inferior edition of Keir Hardie – while some of their stronger men are rough angry bushmen who are always giving themselves away by defying the standing orders. We saw a good deal of Sir Samuel Griffiths, now the Chief Justice – formerly the leader of the Old Liberal party – a remarkably able man – too fine an instrument for colonial politics – or rather too much intellect and too little character – allowed himself to get financially entangled in the speculations of his political opponents and frightened out of his progressive convictions by the revolutionary sayings of the Labour party. The net result has been a period of real reaction – the suffrage restricted by technicalities, direct taxation repealed, regulation of industry relaxed and one gathers rather gross irregularities in the way of patronage and contracts. It adds to the unpleasant social atmosphere of Brisbane that the present governor – Lord Lamington – is a cynical Tory clubman of very doubtful reputation in his private life. His wife is an insignificant gentle-natured little thing without expression or dignity; I felt sorry for her, for she seemed to find her life out there among a shady set of people in a semi-tropical climate rather a nightmare – poor little thing. Of course there are some nice people: there is a refined Oxford man, the Headmaster of the Boys Grammar School, a muscular Christian with athletic [?tastes] who has been struggling to make the Brisbane boys into English gentlemen: there is a nice old Bishop (Webber of St Johns, London) who was delighted to talk over colonial life with us and somewhat downcast at its gross materialism, and there was a Miss Sellers (friend of Katy Holts) a vigorous determined young woman who was pushing herself to the front (as a mistress of the girls grammar school) of the educated world of Brisbane.

On our way back we stayed with a squatter's family on the Darling Downs – then we went to the Blue Mountains for 5 days – very beautiful but monotonous with their great stretches of gum forests. With us we took

85

a young N.S.W. politician – Ashton by name – whom we think is going to be one of the big men in the colony and whom we duly impregnated with our kind of collectivism! He is the best type of colonial – a great big open-faced fellow, with a fine public spirit and an alert intelligence. He refused a portfolio from Reid because he disagreed with him about Federation, but will join him presently if he remains in power and the country supports his attitude on Federation. Tomorrow we spend the whole day with Reid – who interests us immensely and who seems to find us equally interesting! On Sunday Barton, the leader of the Opposition, lunches with us and in the evening we leave for the Reserve – to stay with a succession of squatters – ending up probably with a visit to the great millionaire – McCaughey the King of Squatters – owning 3 million acres and 1 million sheep! We have been a great deal to the N.S.W. House: and as we have been accommodated with seats on the floor of the House, we have chatted with a good many of the members of all sides. We are on the whole impressed with honesty and efficiency of the machinery of government in N.S. Wales – there are, for so small a population – a quite unusual number of able and public-spirited men both as politicians and as civil servants. I still think that the only tolerable life in N.S.W. would be that of a politician or a leading civil servant!

This is a long scrawl: but I know you and Leonard are interested in public men and public affairs. I am just off to dine at the Women's College of the University.

Ever yours affectionately<br>Beatrice Webb

345 PP   BEATRICE WEBB TO CATHERINE COURTNEY

Sir George Turner (1851–1916) was Premier of Victoria from 1894; his low-keyed administration followed the financial crises of the early 1890s. Sir Isaac Isaacs (1855–1948) was a strong federalist, becoming Attorney-General of Australia in 1905, then Chief Justice of Australia and the first Australian-born Governor-General in 1931. Professor Sir David Masson (1858–1937), whose family were close friends of Herbert Spencer, emigrated to Melbourne as professor of chemistry in 1886.

Melbourne<br>Oct. 20th 1898

My dear Kate

We have rejoiced in your letters from abroad and hope that you have kept up sending them; by this time you will have got my letters from New Zealand and N.S. Wales and I hope you are posting some news to Colombo. When you get this there will be just time to reach us at Port Said, (due to arrive December 12) if you delay a day or two at Naples (due to arrive December 16) where we disembark, probably meeting the Bernard Shaws for a lounge through Italy reaching London early in January. How pleasant it will be to see you all again!

Melbourne is a city of magnificent buildings, run up in the Great Boom time, cut in squares, like an American city, by parallel streets, only they are wide and admirably paved with an excellent service of trams. But the inhabitants are still in the depths of depression and seem to have learnt little by adversity, are in fact longing for another gamble. We have as yet met no one as entertaining as Reid, or as able and public spirited as Ashton! Premier Turner is a modest unassuming county-solicitor sort of person, apparently a businesslike administrator but with no ideas or convictions; it is said, by some of the more astute of his critics, that he has destroyed 'responsible government' (we should call it party government) by bringing in bills and accepting amendment or rejection with perfect equinimity. 'Take it, alter it, or reject it just as you please gentlemen' he says practically in the House, 'whatever your policy may be I shall carry it out with equal zeal and industry.' And he *does* work hard, always at his office and practically doing the work of a permanent civil servant endowed with an extra amount of devoted zeal. His colleagues are all of them excellent persons, against whom there is not a word with regard to honesty or industry, but all of them mediocre in capacity except the Attorney-General – Isaacs – a clever, pushing young Jew of whom I think, more will be heard. The Labour Party (numbering some 20 out of a House of 95) supports the government, as in N.S.W., and the Legislative Council (upper House) opposes it. The only legislation of importance of late years has been the establishment of Wages Boards in some of the sweated industries which actually prescribe a *legal minimum wage*, which is enforced by a Factory Inspector. We are enquiring with interest into the working of these Boards. Of course everyone here is proletarian except the single-taxers, who are strong free-traders and anti-regulation, and the Squatters, but it is difficult for the single-taxers to coalese with the landed-proprietors and form a party! Victorians are also almost unanimously in favour of Federation and are hotly abusive of our friend Reid, who only wants Federation on certain conditions favourable to N.S.W. But that is only natural since poor Victoria has been steadily losing ground to prosperous New South Wales during the last 5 years.

Proportional Representation is quite a live question out in the Colonies and there is now a proposal before the Victorian Legislative Council to introduce it in the large counties of population as an alternative to the present system of plural property votes. It is said to be actually in force in the Church Assembly here and we shall ask how it works. I daresay Leonard knows that in Queensland there is the system of an 'alternative' vote, *whenever there are more than two candidates*; practically a second ballot in advance. It has not been much taken advantage of – the only alteration it has made in electoral results being the rejection of the man who 'proposed it'. A warning to Leonard! Professor Masson (formerly of Cambridge) now mathematical professor at the Melbourne University is an enthusiastic promulgator of a scheme – more complicated than the 'single-transferable vote' – a scheme by which the man who gets the largest number of votes is the most completely out of it! No doubt Leonard will recognise it! Woman's Suffrage will soon be here: it has passed the lower house and was only rejected by the upper by 4 votes – altogether things are oddly mixed and I cannot make out whether the colony is more or less advanced in its ideas, than the old country. I think it is a degree more muddle-headed! Write to Port Said.

B. Webb

### 346 PP  SIDNEY WEBB TO GRAHAM WALLAS

Alexander Hamilton (1757–1804), the author of *The Federalist* papers, greatly influenced American constitutional theory and practice. The attitude of the Webbs to the growing debate in England about state and church schools was sharpened by their Australian visit. Sidney became convinced that the denial of public funds to denominational schools penalised the children in those schools who received poorer accommodation and inferior teaching. Believing that national efficiency, rather than dogmatic principle, should be the criterion for educational policy, Webb found himself opposed to the position taken by secularists such as Wallas and their political allies in the powerful Nonconformist lobby who objected, as the cant phrase went, to 'putting Rome on the Rates'.

The diary entries (much of the diary during this journey was written by Sidney rather than Beatrice) do not shed any light on the 'new drawback' to the payment of members. Beatrice noted after their return (BWD 5 February 99) that this period of keeping a joint diary inhibited her for some time because she had thus 'lost the habit of intimate confidences'. The diary entries for 1899 are scrappy and stilted.

[Melbourne]<br>26/10/98

Dear Wallas

I just snatch a few minutes before the mail to write a much delayed letter. We are flying around among Premiers and Civil Servants, Mayors and Socialists, picking up many hints. I am afraid we shall not be able to bring you back any new or complete theory of Democracy – things here are cut in much the same mould as in England, and why, after all, should there *be* any completely rounded and systematically perfect theory of anything whatsoever?

One practical observation is interesting. Australia is utterly and completely unlike America in every respect. From top to bottom there is absolutely no likeness or analogy. So whatever discouragement you derived from America – in the quite unfounded belief that the U.S. is a Democratic country – this place would restore your spirits, and persuade you that what is wrong in the U.S. is the peculiar copy of 18th century Toryism that Hamilton fastened on America 120 years ago. Not that this place is 'advanced' – it is very much what England was in 1870. But owing to their having copied the real English Constitution of 1850–60, instead of the nominal English Constitution of 1789, you have here a genuine Democracy, the people really getting what it wishes to get. The politicians and the newspapers are in fact, the *best* product of Australia; and they are very good indeed. The trouble is that the people are an exceptionally Individualist graft from our Individualist epoch (1840–70); and they are all of them gambling profitmakers keen on realising the Individualist ideals of the lower middle class of 1840–70.

We shall bring you back a new crop of reasons why you should be satisfied with our Voluntary School compromise – refusal of aid to the Denominations, exclusion of Religion *and History* from the State Schools, consequent isolation of 1/5th of the children in *uninspected* R.C. schools, and terror of every Education Minister at 're-opening' the question preventing any improvement in the State School system.

Our experience of Payment of Members leads us to attach *less and less* importance to all the objections yet urged against it. (We have discovered however a new drawback of some force – yet on the whole not outweighing its advantages, or their practical necessity.)

We have just seen the new School prospectus and in it the paragraph as to your lectures, which will be very interesting. But I don't find that the Australian Democracy was or is based on any abstract ideas, or arbitrary psychology. We are interested to find it really an admirable success in all essentials – purity, public spirit and results – what it lacks is intellectual leadership, but this is lacking in the Colony as a whole. What there is goes into politics, and certainly no conceivable other system or government would have produced anything like such good results.

With love

Sidney Webb

347 PP   BEATRICE WEBB TO CATHERINE COURTNEY [*incomplete*]

Lord Brassey (1836–1918), son of the great railway contractor Thomas Brassey, had been a Liberal M.P. and went to Victoria as Governor in 1895–1900.

Melbourne, NW<br>Nov. 1st [1898]

My dear Kate

Somehow or other I always find myself writing to you: I suppose because I imagine that you and Leonard will be more interested in scrawls about colonial institutions than my less political sisters.

We have been working hard in Melbourne: indeed the longer we stay away the more we find ourselves drifting into full investigation and spending our whole time talking shop with politicians, civil servants, employees and trade unionists and attending the meetings of Parliament and municipal bodies. It is a case of 'the old craving' with us; tracking facts is like any other sport to which one has devoted the best portion of one's life, one is restless unless one is indulging in it! But it has the incidental advantage of bringing one in close contact with an extraordinary variety of classes from 'Government House to the Trades Hall' and from the office of the Greek shipowner to the meeting place of the riff-raff of the socialists.

The most interesting experiment here are the Wages Boards which have been established in the separate industries. These are composed of representatives of the employers and workpeople, elected by ballot from a role compiled in the Factory Department, with an impartial chairman, either elected or nominated and with a civil servant acting as secretary. These Boards have power to fix wages (also hours and number of apprentices in some of the trades), whether time or piece, their 'Determination' becoming law by proclamation in the Government *Gazette* and being enforced like any other part of the Factory Act. On the whole the experiment has succeeded and the Act will certainly be extended from trade to trade with the above until it covers all industries. But the detailed experience of these Boards, with regard to the exact level of the minimum wage is extremely interesting and some of the results are throwing light on economic theories. The Boards have certainly not lacked audacity; for instance the Clothing Board has fixed 20/- a week as the minimum wage for a woman, whereas prior to the determination of the Board, women were paid as low as 7/- for a week's work. The piecework list has unintentionally been fixed on a higher basis and as all outworkers are paid piecework, it has driven all the operatives into the factories and contributed to the employment of better machinery and to a more perfect organisation of labour. On the other hand it is asserted that the women have been forced to work harder during the legal hours and that the employers are stricter in their supervision and more particular in their selection. I had this morning a long interview with the largest employer: he has been converted to the principle of a legal minimum, but says that the minimum fixed is a trifle too high and that the piecework list should be lowered to the level of the time work in order to permit some work to be given out – into the homes of 'poor widows and spinsters'.

We have also looked carefully into the working of the State education both here and in N.S.W. and Queensland. Our conversion to our English compromise has been completed. The education here is in a deplorable state; owing to the hostility of the Catholics and Anglicans to the system as it exists, no ministry dare touch the subject and the State Education remains where it was 20 years ago. On the other hand over 1/5 of the children are growing up in denominational schools which are not inspected or regulated. 'Higher-grade' state schools do not exist and the establishment of them would be bitterly opposed by the denominational secondary schools which at present hold the field. Altogether the colonies have bought their secular education very dear!

These colonies too are extraordinarily interesting in their various attempts to discover some perfect way of recruiting their civil service which will, at once, ensure efficiency and destroy all vestige of favouritism. Just now Victoria, in a reaction from political appointments, has bound itself up in a system of strictly mechanical promotion according to seniority which is rapidly destroying efficiency; N.S.W., owing to Reid's capacity, seems to have struck up a sensible compromise, whilst Queensland is still wallowing in favouritism and competition. But the strenuous struggle in these colonies after an almost ideal priority in administration is very hopeful; and the public spirit and industry of the ministers is beyond praise. It seems to us here, as in N.S.W., that the best brains go into parliamentary government in Victoria.

Melbourne is just now full to overflowing for the great Race Week. The Melbourne Cup takes place tomorrow. You will be amused to hear that Sidney and I have been made honorary members of the 'Victorian Racing Club' and are lunching tomorrow with the crack racing set! We have seen a good deal of the University folk, a remarkably able and pleasant set of young English and Scotch professors: I am bringing Leonard back papers about the proposals for proportional representation and the working of the system in Tasmania. It is quite on the cards that the single transferable vote will be adopted here for the 2 or 3 large towns. The Brasseys have been very civil to us: Lord Brassey is not popular, he delivers dull lectures when he ought to make graceful speeches, and hurts colonial feelings by giving bad champagne, and supplying oranges and bananas when grapes and strawberries are expected! Also it has got about that he himself was a miner! Do write to me at Port Said, December 12; Naples December 16th.

Ever yours affectionately

Beatrice Webb

348 PP  BEATRICE WEBB TO MARY PLAYNE

Sir Edward Wallington, who had been Beatrice's partner at balls in her youth, became private secretary to Queen Mary; he also was appointed as a governor of the L.S.E. Sir Fowell Buxton (1837–1915), formerly a Liberal M.P., was Governor of South Australia 1895–98. In 1921 Beatrice added a footnote to her diary entry for 12 November 1898 to say that he and his wife were 'too refined for the job . . . public-spirited puritans, teetotallers and rigid in their attitude to immorality'. Sir Samuel Way (1836–1916), Chief Justice of South Australia from 1876, was also lieutenant-governor and the first Australian judge to serve on the Judicial Committee of the Privy Council. He was Chancellor of the University of Adelaide. Charles Kingston (1850–1908) was the Premier of South Australia 1893–99, and responsible for reforming legislation. Arthur Wolfe Chomley (1837–1914) was a county court judge and sometime chairman of the Public Service Reclassification Board.

Adelaide

Nov. 7th 1898

My dear Mary

This will be the last time of writing before we leave for England, and I feel that I owe you the letter.

We finished up at Melbourne with the great racing carnival – the Melbourne Cup – the meeting place of all the rich folk of the Australian colonies. There must have been over 200,000 present, but the arrangements were so perfect that there was no sense of hurry or crowding; the three sections of the community – the working-folk who go without payment on the 'Flat', the middle-class who pay 2/6 and go on the 'Hill', and the well-to-do who pay 10/6 for the 'grand stand', being kept *absolutely separate*, with separate trains and separate stations and separate entrances – a most undemocratic arrangement! (but then Australia is the most *un*democratic as it is the most *un*aristocratic nation in the world – unadulterated bourgeois!) Sidney and I went off tolerably early and wandered about the Flat and the Hill, watching the bookmakers, the pedlars and the 'Comic men' before we joined our friends in the grandstand. We had been provided with four tickets as honorary members of the Victorian Racing Club – (the organisation which runs the whole of the colonies' racing) – and the secretary had been deputed to show us round the saddling paddock, the jockeys' quarters and the Ring. All the rich women of Australia put on their best dresses for the Cup: I never saw an uglier crowd – a predominance of cheap silks and satins (Sidney says the result of our ad valorem duties!) elaborately made: figures like those of town-bred servants and no notion of how to walk or hold themselves. We lunched with the leading members of the club: a nondescript body including past Conservative premiers, judges and dignitaries. The present radical government was conspicuous by its absence. We were placed in the 'Governor's stand' for the race – the vice-regal party including four of the Australian Governors, their wives, daughters, and A.D.C.'s – the latter small-headed youths of aristocratic family and tame-cat manner. (The A.D.C.'s are the weak point at the 'Government Houses' and are productive of much evil – passive and active.) Altogether the whole business interested us; but the crowd of over-dressed ugly people who were betting heavily because they thought betting the 'right thing' was somewhat depressing and we were glad to get away and spend the evening with one of the university professors and talk 'shop' with Judge Chomley who is now engaged in reorganising the Victorian Civil Service.

From Melbourne we payed a flying visit to the two goldmining towns – Bendigo and Ballarat and thence to Adelaide – the last stage on our journey. Here we found your old friend Edward Wallington in command of Government House, (the Governor, Sir Fowell Buxton, having gone to England.) Curiously enough we had heard of him throughout Australia as the ideal *aide de camp* – always instanced to us, by thoughtful observers, as a proof that a permanent professional official would be far better than the flighty young aristocrats brought over by governors; but I had never connected him with the Wallington we used to know. He, on his side, had been instructed by the Governor before he left to look after us without in the least knowing who we were except that we were 'literary people'. So you can imagine how pleased we both were to find that we were old friends! He came to dine with us yesterday and talked to us very freely of the three or four 'Government Houses' he had served in, and the different excellencies or defects of the various governors.

He is just the same pleasant discreet man as of old, quick at understanding a suggestion and with a wily shrewd judgement of whether it is practicable. He is vastly superior to any of the '*aides*' or governor's secretaries we have met and ought to be taken on as the permanent 'Society' official when a 'Governor-General' is appointed for 'Federated Australia'. He has grown distinctly 'old-maidish' and his mental attitude towards all creeds and political views has been emphasised by his 15 years service at the Government Houses of various colonies. He enquired after you and Arthur, Bill and Mary Pollock most affectionately.

The Acting-Governor – Chief Justice Way – is a fussy little Methodist who is violently hostile to the present Premier – Kingston – a burly ruffian who works tremendously hard and is an unsavoury combination of the demagogue and a London vestryman of the old type – he is also somewhat disreputable in his private life. The Bishop and his wife are said to be charming people and we dine with them tomorrow. Otherwise I don't think we shall find such interesting folk here as at Sydney and Melbourne.

We arrive Naples December 16th. *Rome* December 20th and remain there over Xmas. Do write Poste Restante.

Ever yours

BW

# 4. Making the most of talent
## December 1898 – November 1899

Shaw's continued ill-health made it impossible for him and Charlotte to meet the Webbs in Naples for a planned joint holiday. His illness, in fact, had kept him as isolated as the distant Webbs from current Fabian activity, though Charlotte had become a member of the Society's executive. She, however, found herself 'out of patience' with 'a parcel of boys and old women thinking they are making history and really making themselves ridiculous'. (To BW 6 November 98 PP) On their return the Webbs went at once to stay at Hindhead. Beatrice thought that in this prolonged period of seclusion Shaw's work 'seems to be getting unreal: he leads a hot-house life; he cannot walk or get about among his equals', although she noted that he was 'as witty and cheerful as of old'. (BWD January 1899)

Beatrice and Sidney themselves had come back to face a formidable agenda. In the next phase of their partnership they had three aims. First, to press on with a history of local government which proved to be an almost unmanageable task, taking many more years to complete than they originally anticipated. Secondly, they had to put the L.S.E. on a firm footing. Thirdly, they were bound to play a leading part in the impending reorganisation of London education – the sphere of work which had become Sidney's specialty in the L.C.C. Reviewing their plans later in the year Beatrice noted that their finances were sound and their health good. 'We are fast becoming elderly, we have not so many years left, we must make the most of our talents and leave the future to take care of itself. And it is useless to be down-hearted because of the indifference and stupidity of the world even as regards its own true interests. And it is childish to yearn after some sanction to the worthwhileness of human effort . . . We can but follow the still small voice of moral instinct which insists that we shall seek truth and love one another.' (BWD 10 October 99)

349 FP  SIDNEY WEBB TO EDWARD PEASE

> Blen-Cathra, Hindhead,
> Haslemere, Surrey
> 26/12/98

Dear Pease

(1) Make my title for 27 January 'Some Impressions of Australasia'. Please forego a syllabus; it is not needed, and I can't do one at the moment.

(2) I have no suggestions for N.Z. book boxes. Of course they should be all four different, and I think you need not put any *opponents'* books in – make them chiefly standard economic and political works, with the best Socialist works.

(3) I will see you later as to letter to N.Z. labor members. This can wait.

(4) Similarly, as to American things. I have forgotten what I advised, and must re-survey the whole before making any more suggestions.

(5) School and Library finance I will see you about later. What you suggest seems all right temporarily.

(6) Shaw progresses satisfactorily but very slowly.

(7) We shall be in London from Tuesday to Friday next week – 3rd to 5th – then at Parmoor, Henley-on-Thames, until Monday, 9th January and then definitely at home.

With kindest regards,
Yours

Sidney Webb

350 FP   SIDNEY WEBB TO EDWARD PEASE

Since the Webbs had been away when Shaw married they had yet to give their wedding presents. They sent this first collection of Shaw's work to the notable binder Joseph William Zähnsdorf.

While they were staying at Hindhead Sidney asked Charlotte for a further donation of one thousand pounds to shore up the shaky finances of the L.S.E. Shaw objected to providing what he called outdoor relief for stuttering nincompoops and ironically retorted that Sidney should underwrite a production of the as-yet-unstaged *Candida*. Nevertheless, out of affection for the Webbs, the gift was made: Shaw was always meticulous in distinguishing between his own earnings and Charlotte's personal fortune.

41 Grosvenor Road, Westminster Embankment

4.1.99

Dear Pease

I want to buy copies of *all* Shaw's works.

1. *An Unsocial Socialist.*
2. *Cashel Byron's Profession.*
3. *Love among the Artists.*
4. *The Irrational Knot.*
5. *The Quintessence of Ibsenism.*
6. *Plays Pleasant and Unpleasant.*
7. *The Perfect Wagnerite.*
8. *Fabian Essays and Tracts.*

(a) *Economic Basis* ⎫ in *Fabian Essays*
(b) *Transition* ⎭

(c) *The Fabian Society*
(d) *Impossibilities of Anarchism*

Are there any more in his name?

Of the above I can buy Nos. 5, 6 and 7 new.

No. 2 I have in a cheap edition. I should like a better edition if obtainable.

No. 1 I want.

Nos. 3 and 4 are in *Our Corner*. Do you know where I could buy the necessary set?

No. 8 you can supply me with.

Any help towards getting these complete would be gratefully received.

Yours

Sidney Webb

N.B. We want these to get artistically bound in a set, and present to Mrs Shaw as our (belated) wedding gift.

### 351 FP  SIDNEY WEBB TO EDWARD PEASE

The suggested book club was not established. The idea, however, was typical of Sidney's attention to detail in Fabian affairs. Though he and Pease were never on close personal terms they had a good working relationship in which Sidney's initiatives were conscientiously implemented by the somewhat unimaginative and bureaucratic Pease.

The Webbs had now taken on a new personal assistant, Frederick Herbert Spencer (1871–1946), a former elementary school-teacher who had been among the first part-time students at the L.S.E. Spencer, Beatrice wrote, was 'trustworthy and devoted . . . a sound tho' not brilliant judgement'. (BWD 7 March 99) In the summer of 1899 she added that he had 'evidently the right sort of manners for the clerk class, impresses them without making them feel he is above them in any way'. (To S.W. n.d. PP) Spencer married Amy Harrison, another of their assistants who was a research student at the L.S.E. She became a specialist on factory legislation. Spencer left their employment after six years and became an inspector of schools.

41 Grosvenor Road,<br>
Westminster Embankment<br>
13.3.99

Dear Pease

Why should not F.S. propose to start a *Book Club* for country Fabians, to buy and circulate new books among themselves, on the plan so common in provincial towns?

This plan is that a dozen or twenty people join, each one can suggest one new book to be bought per annum, these are bought and sent circulating according to a printed list of members, at member's own cost of transmission – finally sold to highest bidder to be kept.

My idea is to form such circles among country Fabians with this difference – *you* to buy the new books at F.S. expense, choosing such as are suitable for book box use eventually; and that they be withdrawn after six months and added to book box stock.

I would charge members a small fee – say 5/- a year – for 40 books and make them pay postage on their transmission of the book to the next person. *You* would merely buy the book, put the printed list of 'circulars' on it, and start it on its travels – in the sure and certain hope of its resurrection at the end of its journey! Perhaps each circle should be limited to 20, and a week each = 6 months (allowing 6 weeks leakage.)

Yours

Sidney Webb

## 352 FP SIDNEY WEBB TO EDWARD PEASE

At Easter the Webbs went to Leeds, where Sidney presided over a conference of socialists elected to municipal authorities – a field in which the I.L.P. was beginning to make significant headway and for which the Fabian tracts provided valuable guides. Beatrice and Spencer stayed on in Yorkshire for five weeks to begin their research into local government archives.

Frederick Whelen was an active Fabian, employed as a clerk in the Bank of England, who had strong interests in the theatre and was the founder of the Stage Society – devoted to single private performances of advanced plays – which presented several works by Fabians, including Shaw and Sydney Olivier.

Cromer Hall, Leeds.

7/4/99

Dear Pease

I enclose my Voting Paper.

I expect to be here until 20 April, returning that day to London: we are busy reading the old minutes of the Leeds Town Council

The Conference of Flected Persons was a great success, and I intend to propose that the F.S. take certain action arising out of it. How would it do to form a Local Government Joint Committee with the N.A.C. [National Administrative Committee] of the I.L.P. for the avowed purpose of giving information and answering enquiries? You do the work now, but a Joint Committee might widen the sphere of usefulness, increase our influence over these I.L.P. members, and perhaps – if e.g. Whelen was appointed Secretary of it – lighten your personal work. I think we should try to make increased use of the two or three hundred 'elected persons'. I have several things to suggest to such a Joint Committee.

I think the new Building for the London School is safely landed. My Solicitor is preparing the Trust Deed!

Yours

Sidney Webb

## 353 PP SIDNEY TO BEATRICE

Sir Edwin Chadwick (1800–90), the great sanitary reformer and public servant, played a leading part in the establishment of the new Poor Law after 1834 as secretary to the Commissioners. He was a member of the Board of Health from 1848 to 1854. A. W. W. King, of the publishing firm of P. S. King, was a member of the Library Committee of the British Library of Political Science. Charles Harrison had died in December 1897.

97

My own dearest

I was very very glad to get your letter this morning. I went to bed at 10, but woke up very early and wanted to turn to my B. and lay awake. But I got down to breakfast at 8.30, Now I have spent a long day on the Council's business, and shall not get away in time to write any worthy letter.

This Parliamentary Committee is going on still at 6.45 p.m.

Lord Hobhouse writes offering us 11 volumes of State Papers (print). Frederic Harrison writes placing Charles Harrison's papers at our disposal. There are 39 tickets taken for my Australian Course as yet. No further news about the University.

There are no letters for you.

I wonder how you have got on today at Wakefield. By the way, Kemp has presented to the Library about 30 bound volumes containing the reports of the General Board of Health (predecessor of L.G.B.) for 1848–50 etc. – some of them Edwin Chadwick's copies. This just completes the full *set*, *with those* I have ordered from King. This is very lucky – just what we want.

Goodbye, dearest

Sidney

---

### 354 PP   SIDNEY TO BEATRICE

Sidney was negotiating with John Passmore Edwards (1823–1911), a Radical philanthropist who edited the *Echo* from 1876 to 1896 and was president of the London Reform Union. Edwards was a generous benefactor to libraries and hospitals and Webb persuaded him to donate £10,000 to provide the L.S.E. with its first building on a site at Clare Market, made available on a long lease by the L.C.C. as a by-product of the new Aldwych clearance scheme. Beatrice's old friend, Dr Mandell Creighton, had become Bishop of London in 1897 and he was the first president of L.S.E. Freeman was an L.C.C. official.

41 Grosvenor Road, Westminster Embankment
22/4/99

My own dearest

I thought I was going to have a quiet day, but I have been much rushed.

First I got your nice letter, which I will attend to. I am glad to think of you as getting on well, because it seems more to justify our being apart this much – which I grudge.

Then I went off to Passmore Edwards to whom I had sent the draft trust deed. As I half feared, he would have nothing to do with the deed! Said it was nonsense and verbiage and unnecessary – took fright seemingly not at any material point or intention, but at little words and phrases of no consequence. He was very friendly and cordial – anxious not even to *seem* to be drawing back – but recalcitrant. So I had to stay with him a bit. Ultimately he agreed to write me a letter, which I drafted, which will, I think and hope, be a legally enforcible document, but I had to draft it on the spur of the moment and follow his whims.

He will make the Bishop, Haldane and me sole trustees, without himself; expressly undertake to pay up to £10,000 *as the building progresses*; and at once to deposit securities at the bank in our names. Freeman agrees to let us have new lease at present rent – offers in fact *25* years extension, to make it fit with his ground lease period of repairing.

[unsigned]

355 PP  SIDNEY TO BEATRICE

Blen-Cathra, Hindhead,
Haslemere, Surrey
22/4/99

My dearest

I *think* this may reach you on Monday morning so I write in haste to say that Shaw seems none the worse in general health. He was trying his bicycle! He fell off, and put out his foot to save himself – the wounded foot – and sprained it seriously – not the ankle again fortunately, but the fore part of the foot all round the wound. It is black and blue but they say the wound itself *seems* none the worse, though this cannot yet be stated definitely. They are in good spirits *now*, but it was evidently a dreadful shock. He had been walking about for a fortnight but of course since then he has been on crutches again.

Charlotte says she is in a *dreadful* way about where to go in June. But as apparently they can take this house on then from week to week, they will very likely stay on a bit.

They were delighted with the Zähnsdorf books.

Goodnight

Sidney

356 PP  BEATRICE TO SIDNEY

Downs was the cook at 41 Grosvenor Road. Edmund Wilson (1838–1914) was a prominent lawyer in Leeds, an active member of the Liberal Party and a city councillor 1881–90. He was a founder and honorary secretary to the Leeds Industrial Dwellings Society and most knowledgeable about slum conditions.

The Ford sisters were Quakers and cousins to Edward Pease; they had been in the group which originally formed the Fabian Society in 1884 and were involved in labour and reform activity in Leeds for many years. On her visit to York Beatrice stayed with Edwin Gray (1847–1929), a solicitor from an old and prominent York family, who was the city's Lord Mayor in 1898: both Gray and his wife were interested in housing and social problems.

B. Seebohm Rowntree (1871–1954) the chairman of the Rowntree confectionery firm in York, was much interested in social problems. His pioneering

*Poverty: A Study of Town Life* in 1901 had widespread influence. He later wrote on unemployment and industrial relations.

[Leeds]
Saturday evening [22 April 1899]

My own dearest

I have not posted a letter today as it would hardly reach you before Monday. The Meinertzhagens refused as they would be out of town. I must have forgotten to tell you I am unhappy about the Ashleys: could you not write to Mrs Ashley and tell her that I am away but ask her and Mr Ashley to come to middle day dinner with us on Sunday 7th [?May] 1.30, the first day that I shall be home; and meanwhile could you not ask Ashley to dine with you; he might like to attend the C.C. [County Council] Tuesday week and come back with you to dinner and you might ask a C.C. [County Councillor] in to meet him: *Costelloe* for instance. Tell Downs, if you do, to give you a nice little dinner. (I told her to give you a chicken once a week!)

I spent the whole morning with Spencer going carefully through the syllabus with regard to Leeds: we found many questions unanswered but I daresay we shall get most answers by the end of next week. This afternoon I spent with Mr Wilson – (a wealthy solicitor who has been a member of the Corporation and is now interested in house property) – wandering about the slums and getting a very clear vision of the Council's action or non-action with regard to Housing – all of which I have written out. The Back-to-Back *Slums* are indescribable: one of the parallel streets on to which the houses are supposed to open being closed up at both ends by interspersed cottages and filled with buildings – workshops, privies, pig-styes and any abomination – there being *no* entrance to these houses except by a narrow passage *tunnelled* under the cottages which closes up both end of the original 'street'. He showed me a survey of Leeds in 1849 and now, from which you can see the extent to which the streets have been covered with buildings and presented me with a plan of an area which has recently been bought up by the Corporation and cleared; but of 50 miserable cottages there was not *one occupying owner*, tho' there were 20 separate owners in all. He says this is typical of Leeds, and that as Solicitor to an Industrial Dwellings Co. he has spent months tracking out the owners of cottage property. Apparently the last 3 or 4 years the Council have been taking action under the Housing of Working Class 1893 Act and removing 'obstructive' buildings in the back streets and throwing them open. He also told me much that was interesting and promised to introduce me to the City accountant next week.

*Sunday morning*

It was delightful to see your dear handwriting this morning. I am sure it is right for me to remain on: we cannot hope to do this big work without considerable sacrifice and after all we are extraordinarily lucky in being able to do the work we believe in and enjoy, and in our health, love and wealth. This morning I shall spend writing out accounts of interviews and preparing questions for Harrison. This afternoon I bicycle to [*illegible*] to see the Fords. (I had a delightful ride the other day which did me much good.) We have had winter cold but today is sunny and smiling and still and I shall think of you with the Shaws, perhaps lying out under the bank enjoying the chat and the rest.

I have had a very nice letter from Mr Gray and the enclosed from Rowntree. I think I shall tell Spencer to meet me at York on Tuesday or Wednesday. We might as well get York done as we know an ex-Lord Mayor.

Ever your devoted wife

Beatrice Webb

### 357 PP SIDNEY TO BEATRICE

J. G. Godard, of the firm of solicitors J. N. Mason and Co., was a lifelong friend and legal adviser to the Webbs and to the Shaws. Sir Courtenay Ilbert (1841–1924) was a parliamentary draftsman and later Clerk to the House of Commons. He spent several years in the public service in India and in 1896–98 gave a series of lectures on Indian institutions at the L.S.E. Herbert Albert Laurens Fisher (1865–1940) taught modern history before turning to active politics and becoming a Cabinet Minister and then Warden of New College, Oxford. Sir George Prothero (1848–1922) had just resigned his chair of history at Edinburgh to edit the *Quarterly Review* and to co-edit the *Cambridge Modern History*.

41 Grosvenor Road, Westminster

24.4.99

My own dear one

I am rather afraid I am going to have another cold – I looked in at home this morning on my way to the Council, and found your very nice letter. There was also one from P. Edwards, very fully and completely *promising* and *undertaking* all he offered. Now the question is, does this letter amount to a legal trust that we could enforce? So I got away from the Council as soon as I could, and went to see Godard. From him I went to Haldane – and it rained hard all the time! The upshot of our confabulations is, so far, that Godard sees considerable dangers, *if we had to go to law*; but Haldane says he can get over the difficulties: and we are to have a formal consultation with him on Wednesday morning.

P. Edwards makes a point of beginning building *within a year* – wants, in fact, to lay the first stone in the Autumn! So I have had to run about all today from 12 to 4 in the pouring rain – cabs and omnibuses did not help very much.

I have therefore bought some quinine, and am presently going home to nurse myself for the evening.

I had a pleasant quiet day on Sunday, fine but a cold east wind. Charlotte came up with me this morning for a day's shopping. We got Shaw actually to send off the draft settlement to Godard (as *his* solicitor); and I think Charlotte will at once make a will as soon as the settlement is signed.

But Friday last was so wet that I rather felt like beginning a cold and I am afraid today has settled it. But I will fight against it.

We met Sir C. Ilbert at the station, and stoked him up about a School of History. But nothing will come of it, especially as Hewins tells me that Fisher will probably get the Professorship of History at Edinburgh, vacated by Prothero. What Ilbert is likely to effect is a small Royal Commission to inquire into what archives exist. This would be all to the good.

The *Morning Herald* has my article on Australian Federation in full form. It looks a good paper.

I do hope you are not overworking yourself. I quite agree as to beginning as much as you can, but take it easy.

Goodnight dearest

Sidney

358 PP   SIDNEY TO BEATRICE

All Webb's skill at committee work and negotiation was required to steer the L.S.E. through the difficult period when it had no assured status or income. The money from the Hutchinson bequest was insufficient to underwrite the increasing costs: in the ten years it lasted the donations to the School totalled only £5,388. The annual grant from the L.C.C. was always vulnerable to attack. Such financial uncertainties made the proposal to build on a new site even more risky than the original decision to start the L.S.E. Webb was in fact gambling on the provisions of the University of London Act of 1898, which reorganised the university to permit the inclusion of recognised teaching institutions such as the L.S.E. Both Webb and Haldane were much involved in the discussions which preceded and followed the Act. It was only on 16 March 1900 that Webb could report to the Hutchinson trustees that the L.S.E. application for university status had been accepted and that a majority of the new Faculty of Economics would be L.S.E. academic staff. The L.C.C., as part of the complex of agreements following the reorganisation of the university, guaranteed it an annual subvention of £10,000, of which £2,500 was earmarked for the L.S.E. Beatrice noted the 'continuous strain' of these negotiations, adding that 'no one outside our little group wants this new-fangled structure to stand, and there are many who would go a long way to undermine it'. (BWD 28 April 99)

41 Grosvenor Road, Westminster Embankment
28.4.99

My own dearest

I propose to come by the 1.30 train tomorrow, due at Bradford at 5.34 p.m. It is high time we were together again.

However I am glad to say my cold is much better – going away fast – and I hope to be quite well tomorrow.

I have the enclosed very nice letter from Charlotte this morning which is very satisfactory.

A very long row of blue books have come from King's – the Local Government Board reports right back to 1835, costing £13 odd. It is a splendid set, which I am very glad to have, but heaven knows how we shall get through it.

Today I have prepared my lecture for tonight and done a few things. But I am still waiting to be called as a witness in the Brighton Railway Bill as to Workmen's Trains, and so have had to look in at the House occasionally to see whether they are coming near me. This is a great bother, but I believe it is the last of these cases for this year, and I had to do it.

I was sorry to hear you had at last somewhat overdone it, and worked too hard. But perhaps this would induce you to take it easy yesterday, the ride was no doubt good, but too far! However you will be resting today and for the weekend I hope.

Wallas came and stayed till 11 last night, talking over things in general and the baby in particular very pleasantly. He is now clearly settled at Radlett altogether.

By the way, Phillimore is said to be worse again, and very ill with severe rheumatism.

I got nervous (being without my Bee) last night about the London School and the University, and all the complications, thinking that it would all collapse like a pack of cards. But Hewins today said he felt sure that the admission of the School to the University was all right (though we can hear nothing of the Commissioners.) If this is so, the £2,500 is all right, and we can do much on that.

And if it does collapse, well then it must. We shall have done our best.

But we have overcome so many difficulties that I dare say we can overcome the others. Sometimes I wish I had nothing else to do but work at the local government book with my Bee, without all these worries and distractions. But these, I suppose, are there because I am well and strong. One day when I break down, I can retire to be nothing but a student and amanuensis to my dear investigator.

Goodnight

Sidney

41 Grosvenor Road
Westminster Embankment
29.4.99

Dear Pease

I meant to have told you that Mrs Shaw yesterday sent £200 as her subscription towards the School. This eases matters for the time.

By the way, *don't* put anything in the published notice or agenda of Fabian Annual Meeting; as to my reporting on Hutchinson Trust. We have not done so before. I will report at the meeting as a matter of interest to the members.

Yours

Sidney Webb

360 PP  SIDNEY TO BEATRICE [*last sheet*]

On 15 August the Shaws went to Ruan Minor for a month: on 21 September they left for a six-week Mediterranean cruise on the *Lusitania*. They had not yet decided to settle in the apartment above the L.S.E., though this did remain their London home for some years: Shaw had previously lived with his mother in Fitzroy Square.

London County Council, Spring Gardens, s.w.
[?5 June 1899]

I spent a pleasant Sunday at the Shaws. His foot is nearly healed up, and he walks very well – the only trouble is the long-continuing weakness of the limb. But his general health is first-rate. They have taken on the house temporarily, and don't know what to do. He is restless to get back to Fitzroy Square! and show that his marriage has made no difference to his work. She wants to go abroad. Her present proposed compromise is to take a cottage in Cornwall (the Lizard) for August, for seabathing; and to go on a Mediterranean Orient Line trip for September and October – to let him work in London for November; and perhaps go to Rome for Christmas. He has not yet agreed. Fitzroy Square will be in the painter's hands, which will be an argument.

Godard writes that he has finally re-settled the Trust Deed! This seems to indicate that Haldane has agreed.

Goodbye, dearest

Sidney

361 PP  SIDNEY TO BEATRICE [*incomplete*]

The original appeal for the British Library of Political Science was not very successful, producing little over two thousand pounds. Yet Webb was indefatigable in securing gifts, tapping political friends for copies of official publications and soliciting papers from city councils as far apart as Bombay and Elmira,

New York. By 1898 the library already had over 25,000 items: by 1904 the total had risen to over 100,000. The method of stocking by accession date subsequently led to a major problem of cataloguing and access. The library was renamed the British Library of Political and Economic Science (BLPES) in 1925.

At this time Haldane suggested an approach to Andrew Carnegie, who had begun to endow free libraries in Britain. 'We loathe what we saw of Pittsburgh', Beatrice replied; 'we could not possibly approach "the reptile".' (BWD 16 May 99)

National Liberal Club<br>
Whitehall Place, s.w.<br>
[?June 1899]

I have had rather a successful afternoon at committees – getting the Higher Education Sub-Committee to agree to *recommend* to the T.E.B. to charge the G.R. [Ground Rent] on the proposed grant, without demur. The School Committee included Sir C. Ilbert, full of interest, Pease and Oakeshott. The School is hard up as usual, but not unduly. I think the aggregate accumulated deficit up to 30 September will be only £150. Next year will add a little to that, but I don't think we shall be £500 to the bad up to 30 Sept/1900 anyhow, and probably much less. We must beg or borrow this somehow.

Hewins had a long talk with me this morning. He is firmly resolved to postpone issuing any Library appeal at present, and must have his way – he wants to appeal as a University institution, he says. The Commissioners have not yet reached the recognition of Teachers or Schools, but all *seems* well.

By the way his brother-in-law died this afternoon, so he has gone away until Tuesday.

Goodnight, dearest, I miss you terribly – it prevents me working so steadily, and I wander off into dreaming about my B and what she is doing in Manchester.

Sidney

362 PP  SIDNEY TO BEATRICE

Beatrice was away in Manchester, where Sidney had just spent two weeks assisting her in the research. They were, Beatrice noted, feeling somewhat discouraged at the size of the task they had set themselves.

National Liberal Club<br>
13/6/99

My own dear one

I have just time to send a few words of greeting for breakfast time. I have had a very full afternoon. The T.E. Board was long and disputatious over matters of no interest, and then I had many arrangements to make before and after it. Dr Garnett is still away, reported not getting on very fast, and the Board insisted on voting a resolution urging him to stay away until October.

Our house looked all right – a mass of letters etc. of no interest or importance, but I had scarcely time to open them.

The Council tomorrow has before it (it will be adjourned) a definite proposal from the Improvements Committee to widen Millbank St to Lambeth Bridge, extend the Victoria Tower Gardens all the way to Lambeth Bridge; and to take for recoupment and rebuilding in grand style practically all up Horseferry Road. If this is passed, it will make a fine district. The wharves remain untouched, I believe.

The Valuer reported to the Corporation Property Committee and they acquiesced, that the ground rent for our new site should be £430 a year! I asked the Committee on the spur of the moment to let it stand over for the T.E.B. to secure the freehold in trust, which the Committee did not object to. The Valuer said that this might involve a payment *for 60 years* of £500 for interest and sinking fund, instead of £430 Ground Rent. But then we should have (virtually) the freehold: and nothing to pay after 60 years.

I had a stuffy journey up – the train crowded with flash bookmakers going up for Ascot. But I read half through the thick volume of Extension Inquiry. I send the *Westminster Gazette*.

Now I must stop to catch the 7 p.m. post. Goodnight my own dearest. It is a great hardship to be separated, but we have so much in the world that we must not resent this. But I do miss my B.

Sidney

### 363 PP  SIDNEY TO BEATRICE

Sir Cornelius Warmington was a barrister who was a member of the Senate of the University of London. The Earl of Aberdeen (1847–1934) was a Liberal statesman interested in social welfare who had recently returned from five years as Governor-General of Canada. Sir Weetman Pearson (1856–1927), later Viscount Cowdray, was a rich contractor whose many large-scale projects included the building of the first dam on the Blue Nile. He was a Liberal M.P. and a substantial benefactor.

During their Australian visit the Webbs had encouraged the New South Wales politician and journalist James Ashton to contribute articles on Australian affairs to British newspapers. Herbert John Tozer, who was on the council of the Passmore Edwards settlement, was a Progressive who wanted Shaw as a candidate in South St Pancras in the 1904 L.C.C. election. Clara Collett had worked on Charles Booth's survey of London poverty.

41 Grosvenor Road, Westminster Embankment<br>16.6.99

My own dear one

I am nearly as tired this morning as if I had bicycled to Clacton and back, instead of going in a luxurious saloon carriage! It was a brilliant sunny day. I started off about a quarter to nine and got home just twelve hours later. A whole party of the Sunday School Union went down, a hundred or more, but Mr and Mrs P. Edwards, Warmington, Galton, one Cuthbertson a city shopkeeper (whose name reminded me of the English architect who sought us out in San Francisco, and who turned out to be the cousin he spoke of to me), and so on – went in a special saloon carriage. Lord Aberdeen and Sir W. Pearson M.P. came by a later train, and were too late for the actual ceremony, so Edwards himself declared the Home open and I made a little speech. The whole thing was admirably organised, *and the day yielded for the Home altogether £2,100 in donations*, Edwards giving another £1,000 in addition to his original £5,000. I gave nothing as I had made up my mind beforehand, and was not asked to give. Then there was big lunch and more speeches, and a fatiguing journey back in the saloon with Edwards and the others. He was extremely cordial and flattering to me, privately and publicly. I had a few minutes quiet talk with him at the station – *not* raising Haldane's point, as I did not know how that stood, and as I feel sure I can easily get a safeguarding letter or memo. if need be – but telling him of my project for charging the ground rent on the Grant, at which he was delighted; and about architects, as to which he was quite compliant.

I *think* this will go all right now, at which I am glad as I don't like 'worrying' about it – what with this affair and other things I have not been able to give a single moment to the Book in any way: and now I am so tired with the strain of that 12 hours with the Sunday Schoolers that I am fit for nothing this morning! I could not sleep last night much, and I missed my B to console me.

But it was on the whole very good business; among the crowd were at least half-a-dozen prominent Deptford people whom I spoke to usefully. I even laid the foundation of organising closer relations with the Chartered Accountants Society, as to its students for the School.

Lord Aberdeen was very anxious to have met *you* there, as he wanted telling about the Tennants bill as to Outworkers. He took me off for ten minutes walk along the front, and I told him all I could about Responsibility of the Giver Out.

Sir Weetman Pearson, by the way, (the contractor who built the Blackwall Tunnel) said that the Americans were far and away *inferior* to English contractors in all sorts of ways: he said they simply had not begun to learn how to do great engineering operations with any sort of technical efficiency. Of course they got through somehow, but at frightful cost in life and money.

You don't say, by the way, whether the *Guardian* accepted Ashton's article. I have therefore done nothing with it yet. I could still doctor it up for *next* week's *Speaker*, if you say it has not been printed in the M.G. [*Manchester Guardian*].

I enclose some more print as to the International Congress.

I can see no reason why I should not come to Manchester on *Wednesday, 26th July*: so you might arrange to take the house from that day.

By the way, Galton said that he was informed by Tozer that the Economic Club had had an evening over *Industrial Democracy*, with short papers on it. This was at Miss Collett's suggestion, 'in order to make the members read it'. Tozer's account seems to be that the authors of the papers found very little to object to. One read out our publisher's advertisement as a tremendous list of subjects claimed to be dealt with, and observed that the 'etc.' with which the list concluded was unnecessary and unmeaning, as *everything* was in the list. There was some general discontent as to our application of the Theory of International Trade, though no one could pick any hole. Schloss and Miss Collett both doubted the truth of a small incidental assertion, viz. that overtime tends to be [?*word omitted*] much work in times of depression.

Goodbye dear one I must now go off to meetings.

Sidney

364 PP  SIDNEY TO BEATRICE

The Commission responsible for the reorganisation of the University of London held regular and protracted discussions. Sir George Young (1837–1930) served on a number of official committees. He was a strong protagonist of the higher education of women and actively supported their admission at Cambridge. Lord Reay (1839–1921), the first President of the British Academy, had been Governor of Bombay and was a specialist in international law.

After the Jameson Raid in 1895 the relationship between Britain and the two Boer republics had been deteriorating to the point where war seemed likely in the near future.

Blen-Cathra, Hindhead,
Haslemere, Surrey
17.6.99

My own dearest

I send a few lines on the chance of their reaching you on Monday morning. Shaw seems quite well – went out for a long walk with Wicksteed this afternoon.

The brothers Trevelyan and Mrs Reeves were here today to lunch – Shaw is reported to have rebuked C. P. Trevelyan effectively for his betrayal of the children – George is reported as insufferable!

Massingham has gone away to Norway, seriously affected with 'clonic spasms' – a sort of convulsive cramps, which may become serious epilepsy. His house is up to let furnished.

At University College meeting today, Sir George Young strongly objected to the Economics Faculty, and in spite of Lord Reay's defence of it, the Council decided to petition against it. But this will not influence the Commissioners.

I met C. P. Lucas of the Colonial Office on the way down and travelled half an hour with him. He says the South African situation is most grave. He is still unmarried; has grown much handsomer.

I am glad to be able just to chatter to my B – it seems less lonely; and there is only another week.

Goodnight, love

Sidney

**365 PP   SIDNEY TO BEATRICE**

Lord Tweedmouth (1849–1909) was a leading Liberal politician who had been Chief Whip under Gladstone in 1892 and Chancellor of the Duchy of Lancaster in Rosebery's Cabinet in 1894. His wife Fanny, the sister of Lord Randolph Churchill, was a notable hostess. Sir Henry Campbell-Bannerman (1836–1908) who became prime minister in 1905, was leader of the Liberal Party in the House of Commons in 1899. He strongly opposed the imperialist policies of Salisbury and Chamberlain and supported Irish Home Rule. Sir William Job Collins (1859–1946), a leading surgeon, was Chairman of the L.C.C. in 1897–8 and twice Vice-Chancellor of the University of London. W. Dickinson (1859–1924) was a Liberal M.P. and during his period on the L.C.C. served as its chairman. Richard Knight Causton (1843–1929), later Lord Southwark, was a Gladstonian Liberal M.P. 1888–1910. Thomas Bateman Napier (1854–1933) sat on the L.C.C. from 1893 to 1906. Harry Lawson Webster Levy-Lawson, was the proprietor of the *Daily Telegraph*, a member of the L.C.C. and a Liberal M.P. Lord Welby (1832–1915) was permanent secretary to the Board of Trade 1885–94 and L.C.C. alderman 1894–1907. In 1899 he was Chairman of the influential Cobden Club.

The official Liberals were clearly unaware of the degree to which Webb now felt alienated from them. Herbert Gladstone, the Chief Whip, had already made an approach to Webb through Haldane in the middle of May offering to back him as a parliamentary candidate in Deptford or any other London seat and to meet all his expenses. Sidney, Beatrice noted, had a 'growing disinclination to push himself forward for any position desired by anyone else . . . He is as energetic and persistent as ever, but his energy in perpetually seeking the line of least resistance for his cause is the line of least advancement for himself'. (BWD 16 May 99)

Technical Education Board<br>116 St Martin's Lane, w.c.<br>21.6.1899

My dearest

I feel better today – I say this lest my rather melancholy letters should have grieved you. I *have* missed you very badly.

Last night's dinner was curious and interesting. Lord Tweedmouth had 40 to dinner, in his gorgeous house, on gorgeous plate. There were present Campbell-Bannerman, all the London Liberal M.P.'s except Stuart and Burns, Herbert Gladstone, and all the chosen Liberal candidates and probable candidates for London – including 24 County Councillors. I was given a very high place – put next to Sir H. Campbell-Bannerman at the main table! There was a most gorgeous dinner, and after it, to my surprise, and I think unexpectedly to others, Lord Tweedmouth invited us all to make suggestions how to win London. In response to cries Dr Collins and Dickinson spoke, and then there were cries for me. So I rose, and being quite unprepared, rather missed my opportunity I am afraid. It was difficult to say what one should have said. But I managed very politely to express my feeling that the leaders would have to make it clear that they meant business on London questions, especially Taxation of Ground Rents and Water; and that I was not myself a candidate. This led to rather a funny result – Causton, and Herbert Gladstone and Bannerman, in speaking later, all insisted with ludicrous iteration, that I *must* become a candidate. It became the 'note' of the evening, to everybody's amusement. Steadman, Dr Napier, Lawson also spoke, saying not much. The fact is we were all unprepared to speak, and of course rather hampered by our position as guests. I am sorry now that I did not say more 'for their good', but I felt bound to try to be extra-courteous.

Of course I told Causton and H. Gladstone afterwards very decidedly that I quite certainly would *not* stand – and I don't feel in the least inclined to do so. But it was evident that last night they meant to make a dead set at me.

Bannerman talked only small talk at dinner – he is a most *unintellectual* man.

Today we have had a conference with the School Board as to overlapping in evening classes, which Organ conducted very well. We were all conciliatory, and perhaps some good will come of it.

A parcel has come from Manchester with the Municipal Code (11 vols.)

Goodnight, dearest, I must leave off now as I must dress for Lord Welby's dinner – quite a burst of dissipation for me.

Sidney

### 366 PP   BEATRICE TO SIDNEY

Sidney was to go to Manchester where Beatrice had found a house to rent for several weeks while they continued their research. Before he went up Beatrice felt it necessary as 'an act of piety' to visit Joseph Chamberlain's two sisters, Clara Ryland and Lina James. In April Mrs Ryland had lost her husband after a long illness; Mrs James had been widowed longer but had recently lost her brother Richard for whom she cared in his last months of life. Beatrice was depressed by the combination of meaningless luxury and dull despair in which the two women lived. (BWD 25 June 99) Beatrice was due to speak at the International Women's Congress in London in July, where she had been asked to represent New Zealand. She noted some tension between the genteel British delegates, 'parochial and religious' and the 'screeching sisterhood' of the Americans. (BWD 3 July 99)

Dear One

I have a few minutes before going down to see the City Engineer and I will just send a line to chance getting you tonight.

I am so glad that the Liberal leaders made much of my boy – I like him to be appreciated. But of course we can't expect them to be pressingly polite and yet have the privilege of refusing their attention. I think you are right in not going into Parliament. I am sure that for you the work you are doing is more effective. We shall do better to go on 'in our own modest way', being kindly and courteous but firm in our opinions. It is useless being aggravated and bitter: one gets more for the cause by being persistent but agreeable. On the whole I am glad that you were *courteous* even if by being it you were less effective.

I went over the house again and liked it much: it was so beautifully clean and fresh and situation is quite excellent, quiet and shady. We will have a good time together.

Remember to write one nice long letter to Clara Ryland: I regret the visit will be rather dolesome with them, the sad widows! But it will at least be restful. I am getting nervous about my speech: which [*illegible*] are thought about.

Ever your devoted wifey

Beatrice Webb

367 PP  SIDNEY TO BEATRICE [*incomplete*]

Beatrice wrote to Sidney (n.d. PP) that 'we must try not to be too much separated not only because of our unhappiness but because we are so much less effective apart than together. I feel that I do not get the full value out of myself because I am so bad at the writing out; I am *part* of the machine not the whole, even of an inferior one!' Most of her letters to Sidney in this period are routine notes of her schedule of interviews with local government officials.

41 Grosvenor Road, Westminster

22/6/99

My own dear one

It was very nice of you to send me an extra letter, which came very pleasantly.

It is good that we shall soon be together again. The apparent advantage of dividing our forces is delusive, as I am afraid my work falls off to nearly as much as the gain. I have been able to do *nothing* towards the book this evil fortnight. *Partly* this must have been the case, owing to the arrears of other business. But partly, (and I am afraid in no small degree) it has been due to my own failure. I have been strangely incapable. It has been almost a failure of will-power. Of course it is not easy to be sure this is not idleness. But, after all, if idleness is so strong as to incapacitate, it does not much matter what you call it. What is annoying is that it is a miserable state. If one is idle, one ought at any rate to enjoy the idleness!

I am afraid, therefore, we must not count on being able to increase our output by working apart. I am sure the very opposite is the case – a much more agreeable prospect!

The 'young men' don't get command of the *Speaker* until October and the present Editor has returned Ashton's article. It is now too late to use it anywhere, as it comes flat *after* the announcement of Reid's sweeping victory. I have written to Ashton explaining, and saying he had better not send anymore mss on spec., but that we will look out for him.

Lord Welby's dinner last night was a great function – 150 present – but naturally rather dull. Leonard [Courtney] made a most 'wise' speech, excellently delivered, and naturally quite the best of the evening. I sat *next* to Baker, our new Tramway Manager, whom we took from Nottingham Corporation – seemingly an able man, but of the 'practical', not intellectual, type. He either could or would not say much about municipal structure. He was of course 'dumbfounded' by my paradox as to the tram fare itself having economically the same effects as a tax on the fare. I told him what we were doing, and said we should want his help later.

I am quite willing to go to Lancaster from 26 July to 2 August but would it not be just as well to have that week as *holiday*? You will be very tired, and we shall perhaps get more real value by resting that week than by trying to begin a new local authority.

The Shaws would probably gladly have us; or we might go off *alone*(!) together and really rest for a few days. Consider this. I am afraid that August and September in Manchester and Liverpool may exhaust you so that you will be unfit to 'think' in the Autumn. Perhaps my own sheer incapacity at this moment is temporary, but we ought to be careful not to take the edge off our brainpower.

### 368 PP SIDNEY TO BEATRICE

After a spell of work in Manchester the Webbs took their summer holiday at the Holt summer house on Windermere, returning to London in early October. Visiting the Holts at Liverpool on their way back Beatrice noted signs of stress: her sister Lallie becoming disillusioned with domestic life, her husband Robert, small-minded and vain, pleased with his unique achievement of having refused a baronetcy after it had been publicly announced, the children commonplace in outlook and mediocre in ability – 'hardly a credit to plutocratic environment'. They arrived back on the eve of the Boer War, Beatrice noting that the whole series of intrigues which preceded it being 'an underbred business' and feeling equally upset by the unsavoury proceedings of the Dreyfus case in France. (BWD 10 October 99)

The grant of £500 was in fact the only direct gift from the Hutchinson trustees to the British Library of Political Science.

24 June/99

My own dearest

Your portmanteau and bicycle have arrived safe and sound – soon you will be here also!

It is very weak of me to have suffered so without you, but I am afraid it is as you say – we have grown parasitic on each other! At any rate, it is clear that I cannot possibly get along without my Bee. Of course it has been hot, and I have had many 'worries', but I should have got over them much better if you had been there to comfort me.

I am worried chiefly about the School – wondering whether I shall be able to carry it through all its complications. A new difficulty has started up about the site – namely a curious legal complication. Garnett says that the County Council has no general power to hold land for technical education. This was given by an Act smuggled through in 1892, but given in such a way that it provides only for cases in which the Council is itself the governing body of the institution. This seems at present a barrier to my plan of leaving the Council the freehold, and giving the School and the University a lease at a peppercorn.

Of course, we could fall back on an ordinary 80 years lease at £430 a year, but then someone has got to be responsible for paying that. It may be necessary to get the School incorporated in some way, and let the School take the lease, but this is troublesome and might be objected to.

However, I dare say I shall find a way out of it presently. I cannot believe that the Council has not power to hold the freehold, and grant the lease I want. Dr Garnett is very friendly to the project, and will do what he can to find a way.

I enclose letter from Mrs MacDonald. You won't have any difficulty in writing a 15-minutes paper on Tuesday morning – it is necessarily very short, and I shall be able to help you.

We had a Hutchinson Trustees meeting yesterday – present Pease, Charlotte and I – and they were very cordial about the School and Library, voting £500 as a grant to the latter; and willing to vote more. So far so good, but this is not everything.

Goodbye dearest. I shall try to write tomorrow, though whether the letter will reach you on Monday morning I know not. Soon we shall be together again.

Sidney

369 PRO   SIDNEY WEBB TO JAMES RAMSAY MACDONALD

MacDonald was proposing to edit a series of books: the scheme evolved into a 'Socialist Library' which began to appear about 1905.

41 Grosvenor Road, Westminster Embankment
18 July/99

Dear MacDonald

The scheme of 12 or 13 volumes that you suggest is certainly a taking one – but it is a very 'large order', and I do not understand how you propose the expense to be found. I fear that the sale of the volumes would not pay for their printing, so that the cost of this must be added. An even more serious difficulty would be to find competent people to do them all.

What *I* had in view was a more modest idea, which might however, serve as a beginning of your larger scheme, without committing you or anyone else to that larger scheme. That was *one* volume on women in skilled handicrafts, especially in London. I think Hewins has had some talk with the W.I. [Women's Institute] Council people on this – the investigators to work more or less under the direction of himself and his colleagues (e.g. the statistical work to be supervised by Bowley, and so on), and the volume possibly published in the School series – though I don't know that this is essential, if the W.I. Council prefers itself to pay for the publication.

Would it not be well to do one volume first, and then consider your larger scheme?

If you are contemplating *paying* contributors (even a little); paying an editor (as you certainly must); and producing a dozen volumes which will not have a remunerative sale – at any rate not at first – your scheme would cost something of the order of a couple of thousand pounds.

I don't say that it would not be worth doing at this, but the Hutchinson Trustees would naturally hesitate about embarking on so large an undertaking on a single topic. More serious is my doubt whether you could get the investigators, even if you had £2000.

If I were a woman millionaire I would certainly set on foot such a scheme as yours – putting £5000 into it; hiring a first-rate editor and superintendent to give his whole time; and gradually *training* a staff of investigators.

But in the meantime I should be very glad if we could get one competent volume done. If you could help to get that one under weigh and actually done, it might help towards attracting money for the rest. I should be glad if you would find out how this volume stands, and whether it now waits only for a definite promise of money, and how much.

Yours

Sidney Webb

370 SHSW   SIDNEY WEBB TO H. D. LLOYD

Lloyd's book, *Newest England*, was published in 1900.

41 Grosvenor Road, Westminster Embankment, London

12 Aug/99

Dear Mr Lloyd

In reply to yours of the 27th ult., I am sorry to say I cannot refer you to any separate publication by me on New Zealand. My wife and I made up our minds before we started out that we would not write about America or Australasia, as we felt we could not adequately study them. All that I have written on New Zealand arbitration is to be found in our *Industrial Democracy*, and was written before we had visited the country. I have not been able to escape giving a few lectures on particular points but these have been neither written nor published. I am afraid that any newspaper paragraphs that may have appeared are most unreliable. I take the opportunity of saying this to you, as I have been told that pars have appeared in the American press, purporting to give opinions and utterances of mine on the United States – these are *quite unauthentic*, and must not be debited to me!

I am glad you are going to write on New Zealand. We were *delighted* with the country and the people, and on the whole we approved of its legislative experiments for *New Zealand*. There is the right spirit about the laws and the politicians. But much of the legislation struck us as very far behind England (such as all relating to local government, education, charities etc.)

With kindest regards,
Yours very truly

Sidney Webb

371 PP    SIDNEY WEBB TO WILLIAM SMART

As the note appended by Beatrice indicates the letter to Professor Smart was not sent: it is included here for the same reason that led her to preserve it in her diary. Smart's book was *The Distribution of Income*, published in 1899.

41 Grosvenor Road, Westminster Embankment

8 Nov. 1899

Dear Professor Smart

Mrs Webb and I have to thank you very sincerely for your kindly thought in having a copy of your new book sent to us. We shall value it not only for its own interest, but as having come from you. And we are both of us so much absorbed in our own narrow work, that, unless books are actually sent to us, we usually do not manage to see even those on the subjects most interesting to us, that are not actually within our present sphere.

But having your book actually at hand, I have read it through – much of it more than once – with great interest, and much appreciation of its lucidity and charm. As I cannot give the time or space for a balanced judgment, I will venture to comment on some points in which I feel critical.

Naturally, I appreciate the full and friendly references to *Industrial Democracy*. But pardon me a few words as to the way you have dealt with our book. You more than once enquire whether the trade unions act as we suggest they act, or will 'homologate' our explanation of their action. Now, we tried our very best to observe, dissect and record the *facts* of trade unionism: and the aspirations or theories of the trade unionists are relevant to this inquiry only as being themselves facts. The effect of a given regulation is as it is, and will be as it will be – whatever the workmen intend or believe it to be.

Clearly, we may be inaccurate as to the existence of the facts – indeed, perfect accuracy is obviously impossible to anyone. What we hope for, therefore, is that other observers will test our facts, and correct our errors.

Consider what happens when a biologist publishes a monograph on a complicated and obscure species. Other biologists immediately 'verify' his observations – find some incorrect, others accurate. So physical science advances. I can't help thinking that Economics advances only in the same way. It seems to me not very pertinent to ask whether we have found principles for action *unconscious* of a principle – what Science is concerned with is the plain issue of fact. Does or does not the action in question embody and imply those principles? Much that actually exists is outside our individual consciousness.

You will see I think, that this criticism goes to the root of economic method. What economic science is concerned with, I assume, are the *facts* as they are – quite irrespective of what anyone says they are.

You raise, for instance, an interesting point when you ask how far labor is, here and now, geographically mobile. But forgive me if I say that I don't think that casual statements in the House of Commons by Asquith, Chamberlain or Burns, are evidence – unless one assumes that such statements were the careful outcome of a scientific study of the subject – which no one would suggest! If they had made similar assertions on a point of biology, no biologist would have dreamt of referring to them as significant.

The fact, and even the extent, of mobility of workmen in any particular trade, town or street is not difficult of approximate ascertainment – for instance, in any well-organised constituency it is known what percentage of electors move inside and outside the constituency in a year – and until we *do* ascertain this fact, our 'science' can proceed but slowly.

[*Note by B.W.*] This letter, I advised Sidney not to send: Professor Smart is too old to alter his methods; our criticism would only offend. I keep the letter as it shows Sidney's vision of Social Science.

# 5. New antagonists and allies
## December 1899 – December 1905

The Boer War divided and embittered opinion in Britain as sharply as the long-drawn out issue of Irish Home Rule – the political alignments in fact following much the same line of cleavage. It put a particular strain upon the Webbs, who found themselves with conflicting loyalties. On the one hand they had ties to the Fabians, many of whom were anti-imperialist and sympathised with the I.L.P. and the 'Little Englanders' (pacifist Nonconformists in the Liberal Party) in opposition to the war. On the other hand the closest political associates of the Webbs were the Liberal Imperialists such as Haldane, Grey, Asquith and Rosebery. The 'Limps' believed in Britain's 'civilising mission' and had close personal ties to the pro-consul Lord Milner (1854–1925), who was High Commissioner in South Africa and coloured his provocative policy with an ideology of social advance in the colonies. The Liberal Imperialists, Beatrice noted on 20 February 1900, were forced openly to condemn the methods by which the war was waged 'whilst they secretly approved of the policy of the Government.' The Webbs had also been drawn into the fringes of the Conservative Party, discerning sympathy for their collectivist ideas in the group around Arthur Balfour.

The conflict of loyalties thus confronting the Webbs was intensified by the fact that, despite Sidney's years in the Colonial Office, they had taken little interest in either imperial or foreign politics: the Fabian Society, moreover, had never concerned itself with such matters. The first Fabian lectures ever to discuss the Empire had only been planned in the autumn of 1899.

For Beatrice personally the war raised the still-painful question of her attitude to Joseph Chamberlain; she felt that, whatever the broader merits of his policy, he had been as 'vulgar and tricky' in his dealings with the Boers as in his 'coarse-grained indifference' to her feelings. Realising that she was 'a prey to an involved combination of bias and counter-bias' she confessed that she was relieved that 'we are so far removed from political influence that it is not necessary for Sidney to express any opinion'. (BWD n.d. mid-October 1899)

As the first weeks of the war brought a series of British defeats the antagonism of pro-war and pro-Boer factions increased. 'No one knows', Beatrice wrote sadly in December, 'who is friend and who is enemy'. Sidney, she noted, 'does not take either side and is therefore suspected by both. He is against the policy that led to the war, but that issue being past he believes in a policy of thoroughly dealing with the Boers.' Beatrice herself thought the war was inevitable, probably brought about by 'the impossible combination in British policy of Gladstonian sentimental Christianity with the blackguardism of Rhodes and Jameson'.

The reaction within the Fabian Society was immediate and fierce. Among the leaders Shaw, Bland and Wallas were in favour of the war, Ramsay MacDonald and Sydney Olivier bitterly opposed to it – an attitude which Olivier managed to reconcile with holding a senior post in the Colonial Service. Webb's main concern was to prevent the storm of emotion sweeping the Society into ruinous disagreement.

117

The trouble started soon after the war broke out, when the anti-war faction sought to commit the Society to an immediate denunciation of imperialism. Webb's immediate reaction was to find some tactical device which would put off any divisive vote. Shaw, who had been on the way back from the Mediterranean when the war started and was now restored to full health and vigour, was more provocative: he was prepared to argue a case for the war on the grounds of efficiency, believing that small nations were a bothersome impediment to progress and that the conquest of the Boers might offer an opportunity to apply collectivist policies in Africa, especially in the mining industry. Nevertheless he supported Webb's proposal that the whole Fabian membership should be consulted by a postal ballot – not on the substantive question of support for or opposition to the war but on the tactical matter of whether the Society should or should not form-ally express an opinion. By the relatively narrow margin of 259 to 217 votes Webb got his way, at the price of the angry resignation of some thirty prominent members, led by Ramsay MacDonald: the episode intensified his animosity to the Webbs, and widened the gap between the moderate Fabian leaders and those who thought the Society should throw in its lot with the I.L.P. The majority of the pro-Boers, however, remained in the Society: both Webb and Shaw were at pains in the elections for the Fabian executive in April 1900 to ensure that there was a reasonable balance between the two factions and to prevent the disagree-ment on this issue inhibiting the main work of the Society on matters of social policy.

Unfortunately few letters from either of the Webbs bear directly upon this important dispute or upon its continuing political consequences for them both. It certainly was a factor in isolating them from the growing movement for a Labour Party. They had never been sympathetic to the I.L.P. and, unlike MacDonald, they were not drawn into closer relations with the Liberal Party as a result of common opposition to the war. Neither their letters nor Beatrice's diary show any interest in the successive steps which led in February 1900 to the forma-tion of the Labour Representation Committee. This development, which followed a resolution of the Trades Union Congress in 1899 in favour of the return 'of an increased number of Labour Members to the next Parliament', did not seem particularly dramatic at the time. Similar motions had been passed at various times and each attempt to convert such decisions into an effective political force had petered out without notable results. The I.L.P., however, had painfully built up the nucleus of a constituency organisation and its standing formula of an alliance between local socialist enthusiasts and the funds of the trade unions was at last beginning to seem viable.

At the meeting which set up the L.R.C. as a federal body, including affiliated trade unions and socialist societies such as the I.L.P., the S.D.F. (which soon withdrew) and the Fabians, Edward Pease represented the Society. Shaw, nominated as one of its delegates, did not bother to attend. Pease, elected to the Committee, contented himself with a watching brief. Since Ramsay MacDonald had been chosen as the secretary of the new organisation it was not likely that the Fabian 'Old Guard' would concern itself unduly with an organisation which he was soon to control.

The Webbs, it soon became clear, had misjudged the situation, alienating themselves off from independent Labour politics at the very moment that the new party was effectively founded. They did indeed believe that the realignment of British politics at the end of Victoria's reign might produce a new collectivist party in which they could possibly play a significant role; but they thought this party would be predominantly middle-class, led by intellectuals and experts, and that it would draw its strength from Chamberlain's Liberal Unionists and Rosebery's Liberal Imperialists – a party of national efficiency at home and social imperialism abroad. Despite the ties with the trade union movement they had built up during their research they had little confidence in organised labour as the basis for a party. Since, moreover, the main political links of the unions at this time were with the 'Little Englander' wing of the Liberal Party which the Webbs distrusted and despised they were opposed to MacDonald's successful attempt to reach a private accommodation with the Liberals. His covert agreement with Herbert Gladstone, the Liberal Chief Whip, enabled the L.R.C. to establish itself as the electoral ally of the Liberals.

Both the Webbs seem to have drifted into this position without any moment of deliberate choice, though it was the sum of a series of political attitudes and experiences in the years since their marriage. It led them, first, to press continually for the neutrality (in party terms) of the Fabian Society, for this was the only reliable political base for their activities. For the next ten years they and Shaw were engaged in a running fight with the elements in the Society which wished to ally it more closely with the I.L.P. and the emerging Labour Party. Secondly, it led them into a posture of manipulation, seeking to use whatever allies came to hand to promote their ideas – a posture which earned them a reputation for intrigue and wirepulling. Thirdly, they were drawn as a consequence into the salons and country-houses of London's smart political Society: Beatrice had known this milieu as a young woman, renounced it, and on reverting to it found herself torn between the attractions of intimacy with the fashionable and powerful and the dedication to disinterested public service which had originally made her abandon her old style of life. Many entries in her diary in the Edwardian years testify to the agonies of spirit induced by this ambivalence.

## 372 PP  BEATRICE WEBB TO MARY PLAYNE

The Boers invaded Cape Colony on 11 October. Mary Playne's son Bill enlisted soon afterward: he was crippled for life in the 1914–18 war. Mamie was his wife.

Cecil Rhodes (1853–1902), the dominant figure in South African politics, was considered by many to have provoked the war by his imperialist intrigues. Frank Costelloe died on 23 December 1899. William Lawrence Harrison Cripps was the eldest son of Blanche and William Cripps.

> 41 Grosvenor Road, Westminster Embankment
> [mid-December 1899]

Dearest Mary

I wonder how you are and whether you are in any anxiety about Bill and possible volunteering?

What a ghastly business it is – what a fiasco of ignorance. Of course we have got to beat them, but I imagine we shall be pretty sick of it before we have finished. Letting them get the start and be on the defensive in our own territory seem to have been a mad mistake; apparently in that sort of country defence is easy and attack difficult – to wit Mafeking and

Kimberley. It is rather humiliating for the whole Empire to be engaged in fighting a population not larger than Brighton! Everybody in London is very sick; even the newsboys have lost their lungs from crying 'British defeat' and the streets seem mournfully silent. Sidney says Chamberlain may prove to be a North, and not a Pitt! Personally I think the folly was in ever allowing the Boers to arm so thoroughly – and that was due to some extent to that criminally idiotic raid. Gladstone's christianity and Rhodes' blackguardism have not made a happy mixture and have been altogether outclassed by the shrewd bigotry of 17-century Puritanism.

We go to Plymouth tomorrow – to 21 Leigham Street, The Hoe – and shall be there the best part of a month investigating local government. We think of spending Easter vacation at Bristol and Gloucester, and I will, if you happen to be at Longfords, come and look you up between Easter and Whitsuntide and do the Stroud Board of Guardians and anything else I can lay my hands on. We shall be glad to get away from London, it has been so dark, mentally and physically and Sidney's old friend F. Costelloe, our next door neighbour, is dying of cancer – a depressing thought. I hear bad accounts of Lawrence Cripps: Standish, who was dining here the other day, says that he has got a fixed idea that he has Locomotor Ataxia. I fancy matters at Stratford Place are not over cheerful – but Willie chooses to be offended with me – I know not why, so I have not been there lately.

How is Mamie? has she recovered her senses?

Ever yours

Beatrice Webb

373 FP   SIDNEY WEBB TO UNKNOWN ADDRESSEE

Both the Webbs had been uneasy about the attitude of many Co-operative societies to trade unionism. The consumer societies had not always been good employers or observed 'fair' conditions of hours and wages. The Webbs felt that attempts to make Co-operative employees participate in doubtful bonus or profit-sharing schemes, instead of paying trade union rates, was a hangover from the less desirable features of the old producer Co-operatives which had collapsed in the past and left the field to the Rochdale consumer model.

Dear Sir

Your letter of the 1st instant, has been forwarded to me, in which you ask advice upon the proposal of the Woolwich Co-operative Society, in building its own houses, not to pay any profit-sharing bonus to the operatives, but to engage them on the trade union conditions of the district, plus a halfpenny per hour addition to the Standard Rate.

I may say at once that I think the proposal a wise, and even a generous one, which should, in my judgment, receive the support of the trade unionist members of the society. It is calculated to do more for the real interests of the operatives employed, and of their class as a whole, than a scheme of 'Bonus on Profit', or profit sharing.

To put it briefly, I consider that any scheme which makes the payment of the workmen vary with the profits of the undertaking as a commercial concern is inconsistent with fundamental principles of trade unionism. The trade unionist demand for a Standard Rate is based on the principle of 'identical pay for identical work' for all the operatives of the district. If those engaged by one employer expect something in excess of the standard rate because he is making profits, those engaged by another employer must anticipate something being taken off the Standard Rate because he is making losses. Even the same employer would soon assume that his employees, having shared his profits in the good times, must, in the inevitably alternating bad times, also share his losses by submitting to a lowering of their wages. Thus, the whole idea of a Standard Rate, securing 'identical pay for identical work', becomes lost. Once destroy the dyke of the Standard Rate, and all possibility of effective collective bargaining disappears. Every weakening of the dyke increases the danger of a descent into individual bargaining, with its inevitable accompaniment of sweating.

No less fundamental to trade unionism is the claim that the principal conditions of employment (the Standard Rate, the Normal Day, the customary requirements in the way of sanitation and safety etc.) expressing, as these do, the workmen's standard of life – should be regarded as a fixed charge – and a first charge – upon the community, independent of the profits of particular employers or particular years. An employer does not reduce the rations of his horses or overcrowd them in their stables, because his business is temporarily unprofitable. Why should he be allowed, and even encouraged in bad times to lower the standard of life of his workmen, whose continued efficiency at the highest possible point is as important to the nation (though often not to the individual employer) as that of the horses?

Once the workman makes his pay, and therefore his expenditure, vary according to profits, he inevitably exposes himself and his family, whenever bad times come round, to a cutting-down in food, clothing and house-room, which seriously affects their comfort and the nation's efficiency.

It must be remembered that, in the actual organisation of commercial undertakings, the amount of the profit, or indeed, the question whether there will be loss instead of profit, depends to an enormous extent, not on the workmen, but on the wisdom of the management, the skill in buying materials and selling the product, the ups and downs of the money market, the vagaries of demand, and a thousand and one contingencies with which the workman has, and can have, nothing to do. The workmen employed on the job do not, and should not, choose the foreman and the manager, the architect and the board of directors. Why should the amount of the workmen's weekly housekeeping depend upon the chances of the undertaking being, in a commercial sense, wisely conducted?

I do not mean that the workman who is, as we all are, a hired servant of the community, ought to be content with being nothing but a hired servant of the community. But it is as a citizen, not as a bricklayer or a carpenter, that he should claim his right to share in the administration of industry and in its results. So long as the workman is employed by a private capitalist or joint stock company, any sharing in the administration of industry is impracticable for him. But in the building operations about to be undertaken by the Woolwich Co-operative Society, the individual workman can take his proper place as a citizen. The whole administration will be in the hands of the members of the Society, in which every bricklayer or carpenter employed can and should enrol himself. He will then exercise his legitimate share of power in the management, electing the executive; and he will, in this way, also enjoy his legitimate share in the commercial profits (or losses) of the undertaking, in a form not affecting his weekly housekeeping.

                    I am, Dear Sir,
                    Yours very truly
                                        Sidney Webb

P.S. You will find the whole subject of Profit-Sharing in relation to trade unionism discussed in the following works, which probably find a place in every Co-operative Library. *Industrial Democracy*, by S. and B. Webb, Vol. II, p. 551, and the chapter on 'The Standard Rate', Vol. I, p. 279; *History of Trade Unionism*, pp 323–326; *The Co-operative Movement in Great Britain* and 'The Relation between Co-operatives and Trade Unionism' by Beatrice Potter (Mrs Sidney Webb); *The Methods of Industrial Remuneration* by D. F. Schloss; and *The Labour Movement* by Leonard Hobhouse.

374 FP   SIDNEY WEBB TO EDWARD PEASE

During a month-long visit to Plymouth Beatrice reflected on the 'gloomy' prospect of British politics. 'The middle classes are materialist', she noted on 31 January 1900, 'the workingmen class stupid and, in large sections, brutish . . . whilst the government of the country is firmly in the hands of little cliques of landlords and great capitalists and the hangers-on. The social enthusiasm that inspired the intellectual proletariat of ten years ago has died down and given place to a wave of scepticism about the desirability or possibility of any substantial change in society as we know it . . . If we found ourselves faced with a real disaster should we as a nation have the nerve and persistency to stand up against it? That is the question that haunts me.' Fabian tracts and leaflets, often used by I.L.P. branches in the absence of other suitable material for the political education of their members, had been the main form of influence exerted by the Fabians on the labour movement. A tract on workmen's compensation (No 82), for instance, sold over 120,000 copies in six months. But after 1899, as the I.L.P. fell out with the Fabian leadership, both the sales of tracts and the supply of Fabian lecturers to the provinces dwindled to a mere trickle.

The enquiry started by Pease resulted in Tract 105, *Five Years' Fruit of the Parish Councils*, written by Webb and published in 1901.

21 Leigham St, Plymouth
8.1.0

Dear Pease

(1) I can't do a further correspondence class paper for a fortnight *unless you can send me here* a copy of the text book, Blake Odgers *Local Government*, a cheap and always useful book.

(2) I shall *not* be at Exec. on 12 January, nor in London until 17th instant.

(3) It occurs to me to remind you and the Publicity Committee of the Act just passed making Parish Council Elections triennial only; hence the next election will be specially important. I don't know whether it is in the Spring of this year or next. I think this should be considered, with a view to revising our tract, and perhaps making a special effort.

My idea is to send out a form of enquiry to all Fabians and other suitable persons, asking for exact particulars of what their Parish Council is, and has done, since its formation. We could then compile a useful penny tract, giving actual *achievements* with names and dates, as examples to other parishes. I enclose rough form of circular as a beginning.

Sidney Webb

### 375 FP  SIDNEY WEBB TO EDWARD PEASE

Shaw eventually ran an eccentric campaign for an L.C.C. seat in St Pancras, polling 1,460 votes against the lowest of the two Moderate opponents, who was elected with 1,808 votes. Frederick Ernest Green published a number of books on farming and the countryside: the reference is probably to a pamphlet.

41 Grosvenor Road, s.w.
30.1.0

Dear Pease

(1) Please add to the Housing Bibliography, or rather remind Peddie,
'The Cottage Question' published by the Land Law Reform Association.
'English Country Cottages' by Green, published by the Rural World Office; also anything else he can find on the *Rural* Housing Question (e.g. by Herbert Samuel).

(2) You know that Shaw is willing, and Mrs Shaw desirous, that he should get on the L.C.C. Now, Freak, the member for North-East Bethnal Green, has removed permanently to Leicester, and must resign. The official desire is to put off his resignation until October, which will avoid a bye-

election. But I hear there is a move in the local workingmen's clubs to insist that he should resign at once. I believe Shaw's only chance is to get himself nominated locally by the proper authority. Can you suggest him as a willing candidate to some influential person locally? – preferably a leading man in the Workmen's Clubs?

Sidney Webb

### 376 PP   BEATRICE WEBB TO SALLY FAIRCHILD

Many families were unhappily divided by the war. Beatrice reckoned up the score for her eight brothers-in-law and observed that their opinions ranged from outright jingoism to the fervent pacifism of Leonard Courtney.

41 Grosvenor Road, Westminster Embankment<br>
[?January 1900]

My dear Sally

I was very glad to get your bright letter and amused with your description of a Southern legislature. Sidney will send you an agenda of the L.C.C.: as for the parliamentary papers of the Transvaal Wars, these are voluminous: you had better order them through an American friend otherwise you will have to pay a fortune in postage and duty.

My husband and I find ourselves occupying very middle-ground and have hitherto found it possible to be sympathetic on both sides! My own family is rent asunder: some of my sisters are raging imperialists, others are pro-Boers of the most ultra character: brothers-in-law to match! Frankly we feel that this War is not our business and as we are not called upon to run the show we do not care to indulge in [?definitive] views; moreover we don't *quite* agree. Sidney is on the anti-war side of the line, I am on the 'war was inevitable' side: but we are both of us so close to the dividing line, that we can still go on holding hands! our habitual attitude!

We are still hard at work collecting material: spent August in Manchester, September in Liverpool, and Xmas in Plymouth. I am longing for the time when we can retire to the country with cases of material and write at our leisure. Give my affectionate regards to Mrs Fairchild. So Mayor Quincy is married! We hope to see him and his wife in May. I am sorry you are not coming over.

Ever yours affectionately<br>
Beatrice Webb

### 377 PP   SIDNEY TO BEATRICE

At the beginning of March Beatrice combined a visit to Herbert Spencer at Brighton with research into local records. She was distressed at his deterioration, 'to see a nature to transparently sincere, so eager to attain truth, warped . . . into the character of a complete egotist, pedantic and narrow-minded'. (BWD 8 March 1900)

My own dearest

I could not possibly write yesterday – I was completely busy every minute until midnight. But though I shall see my B. tomorrow, I will write her a morning's greeting.

The Housing Conference was dull but successful. There were 100 people at the opening and several hundreds later. The papers were good, and as we cut all speakers down to 5 minutes, no-one was very oppressive. The resolutions were all passed; and Pease sold over £2 worth of literature. The Conference, however, coming on the Relief of Ladysmith, failed to get much reported, though the *Daily News* gave it 2 columns and a leader.

In the afternoon we chose at L.C.C., Miss Durham as our archivist, unquestionably the ablest of the lot, but not Hewins' first pick, and though an occasional pupil at the School, not really or chiefly its product. I think she is too good for the place, and will not care for its drudgery.

In the evening what with dining with the Shaws, giving my lecture, and then going to Lord Welby's, I was full up! The streets were a sight! I never saw anything like it. All day long, in the City, there appears to have been a pandemonium of joy and shouting; and *all the evening*, from about 7 till past midnight, one heard cheers and shouting in all directions. Bands of young men paraded up and down singing and cheering and waving flags. The tops of omnibuses shouted cheers to the pavement, and the inmates of hansom cabs wildly waved hats and sticks to all and sundry. This went on in *all* the West End streets for six hours or more, never ceasing.

Today I have spent entirely on various Technical Education Board and School things that I had to do. The School and Library aggregate deficit at the end of next Michaelmas will not come to much over £100 (*plus* £300 of the T.E.B. grant that we have perhaps no right to use, as it is paid in advance on 1 October – but this is not clear, and anyhow does not matter so long as it continues).

But we shall be horribly short next session, as the Library money will be exhausted. This makes a gap of £400 in the School receipts – we must cut down some, and try to collect some.

I enclose a rather uncomfortable letter from the Railway Signal Company, *deferring* any dividend at all! This looks very ominous.

Goodnight dear one. I arrive tomorrow at 5.15.

Yours

Sidney Webb

## 378 PP  SIDNEY TO BEATRICE

Bertrand Russell was working hard on *The Principles of Mathematics*. After five years of marriage his relationship with Alys was under increasing strain. The

Russells briefly shared the house of Professor F. W. Maitland (1850–1906) in Downing College, Cambridge, with Professor Alfred North Whitehead (1861–1947) and his wife Evelyn.

The London University commissioners had just issued the list of teachers recognised as qualified to teach for the university's degree – a device which enabled degree-level courses to be offered in a variety of colleges and institutes. About half the recognised teachers were accepted as members of the various faculties. Edward Bond was a Moderate member of the L.C.C. and a Conservative M.P. William Bousfield, a prominent member of the Clothworkers Company, served on the London School Board 1882–88 and the Technical Education Board 1895–1904.

41 Grosvenor Road,
Westminster Embankment
7.3.0

My own dear one

Last night as I sat alone, reading to relieve my loneliness, there came in Bertie Russell and his wife, who had seen the windows light when passing by. They were only up for a short visit, returning to Cambridge today. They asked me to breakfast with them this morning at no. 44, which I did. They were in the best of spirits, keen about the war, and eager to get on foot a sane theory of Imperialism; anxious to federate the Empire and so on.

They have taken Maitland's house at Cambridge.

The list of teachers for the London University includes about 490 names, net, omitting duplicates – including about 32 in the Polytechnics, which is all we asked for. The Faculties comprise about 280 names, including 9 in the Polytechnics, which secures the principle of their admission. The largest section is of course Medicine with nearly 300 teachers, of whom 150 are in the Faculty. Willie Cripps is recognised at Barts, and put on the Faculty.

This morning I had to give up to School and T.E.B. business, so that the day will pass without a line of the book.

I am afraid that I ought not to come to meet you tomorrow, as I must go to my Parliamentary Committee in the afternoon, and look after some Bills, which will be on about 5. I have of course to lecture in the evening at 8, and I suppose we are to dine with the Shaws at 6.45 as usual – so I will go straight there, and meet you there.

I hoped to have got through today in sub-committee the terms on which the School is to have the Clare Market site; but Bond and Bousfield quibbled so much over a preceding matter, that we had to adjourn it. I *think* they will all agree to a peppercorn rent, but I cannot be sure.

Miss Honor Morten has been the cause of a silly dispute in Hackney, with Dr Garnett, in which he seems to have been altogether in the right; and she very angry about nothing. I mention it as one more piece of evidence of her strange perversity of nature.

Goodnight, dear one. Tomorrow you will be back!

Sidney

May Morris (1862–1938) was the daughter of William Morris: she was separated from and later divorced her husband H. Halliday Sparling (1860–1924), an unimpressive Fabian and free-lance journalist. The house in question was 17 Fleet Street, which in 1898 the owner proposed to demolish. After long negotiations the L.C.C. purchased the house in April 1900. The lower part was set back as part of the widening of Fleet Street; the upper part is still open to the public as 'Prince Henry's Room'.

41 Grosvenor Road, Westminster Embankment<br>7.4.0

Dear Miss Morris

You will have seen that the L.C.C. decided, after much hesitation, to buy the Fleet Street house, in order to preserve its interior. So far, I suppose, we have done well from the artistic point of view. *How* we shall preserve the house is a difficult question, and I fancy few will eventually agree about it – because the exact architectural and constructional facts are not accurately and fully known to people.

Personally I am entirely in agreement with the idea and spirit of your letter, and will use any influence I can in that direction. Whether the house *can* remain just as it is, with its false front of 1820 workmanship, I don't know. *If* the 1610 front is practically intact underneath, would you not prefer the 1820 fraud to be taken off?

The poor L.C.C. has no malign or Philistine intentions. It is deadly anxious to do the right thing in these art matters, but is bewildered by the *diversity* of the artistic advice pressed upon it. And no artist person will come forward to take his share in London government, by becoming a member. We have authors, and men of science (whose work is just as personal and unique as that of the artist), as well as the business person, but no sort of artist. I fancy the artists of the 16th century would not have thought the L.C.C. work alien to or beneath them. I speak feelingly, because the L.C.C. means well in art, necessarily exercises great influence on art education and production, is always very adversely criticised by the art world – but no art person comes forward to fight a seat.

Unfortunately, the law won't allow *you* to stand, but I write this so that you may, if you think fit, pass it on to anyone who denounces the L.C.C. from this point of view.

Yours

Sidney Webb

## 380 PP SIDNEY TO BEATRICE

Hubert Bland and his wife Edith Nesbit had recently moved to Well Hall, near Eltham, Kent, a large and attractive old house, where they entertained the more bohemian Fabians and Edwardian writers and artists at memorable weekend parties. The money to maintain this style of life came from Mrs Bland's successful books for children, rather than Bland's journalism.

41 Grosvenor Road, Westminster Embankment

9.4.0

My own dear one

I had a quite successful ride yesterday, 10 miles each way, but it was lonely! The Blands are living in a queer and ramshackle old house, somewhat baronial in 18th-century style, right out in the country, with a moat, swans, wild ducks and rabbits on their own $4\frac{1}{2}$ acres of ground. It is an odd but attractive rough place, which they have on 5 years lease, by which time they will be built up to. I found them very cordial and pleasant. Bland quite acquiescent in everything etc.

Then I rode home comfortably, but the result of it all, and of my loneliness was that I could not sleep a bit; and am accordingly not doing much this morning. Spencer has been here, but the electricians have now invaded his room, so I have sent him to the Fabian office.

I have today a long and quite confident letter from Mauger (the Melbourne hatter, Anti-Sweating League) just elected to the Victorian legislature, as to Factory Acts – he is quite confident as to the Royal Commission, says the opposition *to the principle* has quite died out.

Goodbye dearest – only two days more!

Sidney

381 PP   SIDNEY TO BEATRICE

As the elections to the Fabian executive proceeded Webb and Shaw became anxious; they wished to ensure a majority for their supporters but feared a total defeat for their anti-war opponents. Webb's circular letter of 13 April was preceded by a fuller and more lively appeal by Shaw. (CL 11 April 1900)

41 Grosvenor Road, Westminster

10.4.0

My own dearest

I shall be glad to see you tomorrow at Stroud station, by the train leaving about 3 p.m.; and we can bicycle round together.

Everything went perfectly at the T.E.B. yesterday, grants to the University and the Schools voted without a word. Also the Corporation Property Committee approved the porch at Clare Market, and agreed to bear the cost of the sewers, gas and water pipes on the site – so this is all right.

About 175 Fabians have voted up to now – all those to whom I have written and who have replied, answer most cordially. Shaw, Bland and I will issue our own letters this week to the non-voters. I *think* it will be all right, but it is worthwhile making sure.

The Library Sub-Committee has decided to buy for the L.C.C., our *History of Trade Unionism*. I offered to present it, but the Committee said I must not set that precedent.

Goodnight, dear one – till tomorrow.

Sidney

## 382 FP SIDNEY WEBB TO FABIAN SOCIETY MEMBERS

Two-thirds of the Fabian membership voted in the executive elections, returning all but one of the candidates who supported the Webb policy of non-commitment on the war issue. Four anti-war candidates were elected. Three of them, the actor Charles Charrington, the dentist Dr Frederick Lawson Dodd (1868–1962) and R. Wherry Anderson, were retiring members. The last place went to Samuel G. Hobson (1864–1940), a perennial leader of revolts against Webb's leadership in the next twelve years.

41 Grosvenor Road, Westminster
13 April 1900

As I do not think that you have yet voted in the election of the Fabian Executive now pending, I venture to ask you to fill up and return your Ballot paper at once. (You will find it enclosed with the April *Fabian News*. The last day for receiving votes is 20 April.)

On this occasion a vigorous attempt is being made by certain new candidates to get themselves and their friends elected; and the unusual step has in some instances been taken of asking members to vote *only* for these 8 candidates. This may have the unfortunate result of excluding from the Executive two or three very useful workers, whose silent service of the Society is less well known to the members. On their account, in particular, I venture on this occasion to importune you to record your vote – whomsoever you prefer to vote for.

If you wish a continuance of the Society on the same general lines as heretofore, I advise you to vote for the 11 candidates named below.

Yours very truly

Sidney Webb

| | |
|---|---|
| Bland | Pease |
| Bell | Shaw |
| Macrosty | Mrs Shaw |
| Oakeshott | Standring |
| Miss O'Brien | Webb |
| Whelan | |

## 383 PP BEATRICE TO SIDNEY

Beatrice, away on a research trip, stopped at Marlborough where, in a diary entry for 22 May, she expanded on her elliptic reference in this letter to 'little panics'. She had been feeling mentally distressed since the beginning of the year –

a combination of hypochondria, anxiety and physical debility afflicted her severely for most of 1900 and 1901. She felt that her work was not going well and that she was a prey to 'foolish daydreams based on self-consciousness and personal vanity'. She was, in fact, still obsessed by her old passion for Joseph Chamberlain, now much in the public eye as the leading figure in the controversies arising from the war. She allowed herself to compare Chamberlain and Sidney. 'Just as it was the best part of my nature which led me to accept Sidney after so much doubt and delay . . . yet notwithstanding this conviction I find my thoughts constantly wandering to the great man and his family, watching his career with sympathy and interest and desiring his welfare.'

Early in July this juxtaposition was dramatised in the flesh by a casual encounter. The Webbs, invited to dine with Haldane at the House of Commons, met Chamberlain on the terrace. Chamberlain later joined the dinner party and talked amiably to Beatrice for an hour. Embarrassed by a gaucherie on Sidney's part and by the fact that this meeting after so long was taking place under 'the eye of London Society', Beatrice was nevertheless glad to talk to Chamberlain again: 'there is a bond of sentiment between us – I for the man I loved – loved but could not follow'. (BWD 4 July 1900)

During these summer weeks Beatrice was busy entertaining: though she regarded lunches and dinners as a distraction from 'profitable brooding over the problems of local government' she felt that 'social connections are essential . . . In the England of to-day success in establishing new undertakings for public purposes depends on your influence over the various governing cliques: the more cliques you have access to the broader the foundations of your power to get things done'. (BWD 19 July 1900)

The Webbs spent much of the summer staying at a vicarage in Newcastle-upon-Tyne while they did their research, taking three weeks on the Northumberland coast at Bamburgh. In October, after they had returned to London, H. W. Massingham told Beatrice of a rumour that Chamberlain and his third wife were estranged. She was 'terribly depressed' at 'the thought of the misery of the man I once loved'. (BWD 19 October 1900) A month later she wrote of her 'miserable suspense' while waiting confirmation of the news and of her 'morbid consciousness' that some gossips were blaming her for the separation. Wishing that all would prove to be well, she could not help reflecting on the might-have-been: at this time in her life she let her fantasy run freely over imaginary relationships. (BWD 16 November 1900) In a note inserted years later into the typed version of her diary, she wrote: 'And to think that I am over forty and he is over sixty! What an absurdity!'

She continued to brood over the past for several months. This train of thought led her on New Year's Day 1901 to conclude her diary with a long and frank comparison of her relationships with her former love and her husband. She contrasted the manner in which Chamberlain had 'absorbed the whole of my sexual feeling' with the fact that 'neither my physical passion nor my social ambition' were stimulated by Sidney, whom she had agreed to marry from a combination of pity and 'altruistic utilitarianism'. She now consoled herself with the thought that their joint work had prospered and that after nine years of married life 'we are still on our honeymoon and every year makes our relationship more tender and complete'. (1 January 01)

My own dear Love

I cannot expect a letter from you this morning, so that the next best thing is to write one to you.

Spencer turned up last evening: he was thoroughly satisfied with his time in Bristol, said he had seen more fully into the life of the place than anywhere else: was much impressed with Pearson and amused and interested by Wood. I had a pleasant journey down in the company with a Jew trainer who had stables on the Downs and amused me with 'Shop'. The Hotel is fairly comfortable except for lack of fires, however I indulged myself with one in my bedroom, to smoke by. I propose to come up by the 12.40 train, about 2.40 Paddington. We will have a quiet evening together.

I don't like being away from my boy, but I lie awake and think how much I love him and how glad I am to have married him.

These next 8 years of our lives will be decisive of our usefulness to our generation: we have got to carry through two big undertakings, the School and our own work on Local Government. I quite agree to risking a good deal to make these two undertakings thoroughly successful. But we shall need energy and courage and the best kind of judgement. My boy must forgive me if I get sometimes into little panics. I do not think that I shall in anything that regards the School or our work; because to risk for objects that one believes in is always worthwhile. And the building up of a science of society *is* the object that I have believed in persistently through all the phases of my life and character. To have found a comrade who also believes in it is extraordinary good luck.

Ever your devoted wifey<br>Beatrice Webb

### 384 FP  SIDNEY WEBB TO EDWARD PEASE

The manifesto was Shaw's provocative pamphlet *Fabianism and the Empire* (published by Grant Richards, not as a Fabian tract) in which he argued that the division of the world by the imperialist powers was part of an historical trend to larger and more efficient units of government and that the elimination of small or ramshackle states was a means to modernisation. More than half the pamphlet of one hundred pages was devoted to domestic politics, restating the Fabian doctrine of municipal socialism. Originally intended to offer an unofficial Fabian comment on the war, since the Society had voted to make no pronouncement either way, Shaw's argument seems in the event to have been directed less at the Fabian membership than at Rosebery and the Liberal Imperialists, setting out the basis of a possible platform on which the Fabian moderates and the 'Limps' might come together. The pamphlet was, however, conscientiously circulated to the Fabian members in proof and carefully discussed before publication.

Sidney Ball had been the leader of the Fabian group at Oxford as a student and remained its president after becoming a don. He was the author of Tract 72, *The Moral Aspects of Socialism*, published in 1896. Will Crooks (1852–1921), had emerged as one of the leaders of the 'New' Unionism after the 1889 dock strike and joined the Fabian Society. He was the first Labour mayor in London and became Labour M.P. for Poplar from 1903. C. P. Sanger, a barrister and a lecturer at L.S.E. from 1896 to 1900, married the sister of Edward Pease.

Until 26 Sept ⎰ Victoria Lodge, Bamburgh,
⎱ Northumberland

11.9.0

Dear Pease

Thanks for yours with enclosures and news – will send back the former presently when I can find time and energy to comment.

As regards Manifesto I cannot help thinking your suggestion of dispensing with sending members proofs is *not prudent*. Many good and sensible members will certainly be rather upset by the document – and will therefore be *much aggrieved* if they have not been consulted in advance, and asked to send in criticisms – such a man as Sidney Ball for instance, whom we could ill spare. I would rather omit the members' meeting, explaining the impossibility of treating a book like a mere tract. But I would *certainly* send out proofs in *galley slips* not paged – this both for economy in making up, and to prevent them being kept. The galley slips should *each* be headed 'Private and Confidential' but should bear nowhere any title, or mention of its being a Fabian Society document, or other description.

There should be a separate request (? in *News*), asking everyone to return his proof with criticisms and suggestions, which we should promise to attend to.

*Finances* I have for some time wanted a special appeal to members to increase their subscription – we want some standard. I suggest that we should urge people to pay as a minimum, 10/- per £100 of income or earnings.

*Parish Council* I will see to this in October. Keep.

*£100 Compensation Essay at School* Nothing formally settled so far as I know. Hewins has been corresponding with the donor, who inclines to Sanger.

*Musicians Union* Crooks is quite right (and you). L.C.C. can do nothing.

Sidney Webb


385 PP  BEATRICE TO SIDNEY

Alfred Cripps had been very ill with influenza and become 'a hypochondriacal wreck' in the course of the summer. (BWD 1 January 01): his depression had been intensified when the Conservatives did not appoint him Solicitor-General; Beatrice noted that his 'kindly and moderate temperament' was outraged by the 'rampant Imperialism' of the Government. He had also lost his seat at Stroud.

Beatrice went down to Parmoor and carried her brother-in-law off to Margate for a rest-cure: though she was fond of him she criticised his 'pettish mortification at a personal reverse', contrasting it to Leonard Courtney's 'sublime indifference' at the wreck of his political fortunes and the social ostracism which followed from his outspoken support for the Boers. (BWD 16 November 00)

Margate
[? October 1900]

My own dear darling one

It was a horrid gloomy afternoon, but I kept Alfred out for 1½ hours and he had a quite comfortable evening. Last night he did not sleep quite so well, but from his own account there is not much to complain of. If he will only stay here for a fortnight or three weeks I believe he will be quite fit.

Dearest, I am sorry to think of you as a bit depressed and with a head-ache. We cannot expect that things will always go right with us: but at any rate looking back at the last 8 years we have accomplished a good deal: you have organised Technical Education, started the Economic Faculty, and to a large extent guided the L.C.C., and we together have written a really first-rate book! I have been reading the last part of *Industrial Democracy* and am lost in admiration for it! It is so much abler than either of us! And if we get turned out of the L.C.C. we will write a still more magnificent work on local government. We have this great advantage, that it is a toss up whether it is most useful to do a great deal of administration work and little scientific work, or a great deal of scientific work and little administrative work. But we will try and not lose the L.C.C. election. Think of writing a series of signed articles on London Education for the *Daily Mail*? I should be inclined to write and propose to the Editor to contribute 3 articles dealing with the *Educational Ladder*: you might say that it was desirable to popularise the educational facilities open to the lower-middle-class or working-man's child and that you thought the *Daily Mail* the best avenue. You might get an advertisement for the London School, University and Scholarships. Think over this. They ought to appear about December, after the School Board Election. It would not be waste labour, since they could be reprinted as a pamphlet, with a few alterations for the L.C.C. election. We must do something different from last time, and articles in the *Daily Mail* seem to me a new feature. It would be no use waiting until the L.C.C. election is in full swing as it is doubtful that the *D.M.* could take them. The *Evening News* might be dealt with nearer the election. A little thought now may save a good deal of worry and disappointment later.

I will be back by the 10.13 train Thursday.

Ever your devoted wifey
Beatrice Webb

133

Queen Victoria died on 22 January 1901 and was interred at Frogmore on 4 February.

Rosebery had been pleased by *Fabianism and the Empire* and sent congratulatory messages to both Webb and Shaw through Haldane. The unnamed guests at the dinner were Hewins, Reeves and John Massie (1842–1925), a leading Congregationalist and Liberal, Professor of New Testament Exegesis at Mansfield College, Oxford. The purpose of the dinner was to discuss plans for a large meeting at the Mansion House, chaired by the Lord Mayor and addressed by Rosebery, to promote 'commercial education in the abstract and the School in the concrete' – that is, to launch a building fund for the L.S.E. (BWD 9 February 01) This hobnobbing with the eminent, Beatrice observed, 'has its unpleasant side'. She felt that it was 'much more wholesome to win by hard work than by these capricious gusts of fancy in great folk. I feel that I am skating on rotten ice which might suddenly give way under me'. She was worried about her 'incapacity to keep my intellect and heart set on our own work, undistracted by personal vanity or love of admiration'. The meeting was planned for 21 March.

Beatrice was upset by the death of two old friends – Carrie Darling at the end of 1900 and Mandell Creighton in January 1901. The loss made her reflect upon the way in which the Webbs were losing contact with their old circle of intimates, even with Wallas and Shaw. They had taken up with new acquaintances, some such as Hewins and senior members of the L.S.E. staff being much involved with university affairs, some such as Phillimore being connected to Sidney's L.C.C. interests, and others coming from the clique of Liberal Imperialists with whom they were on dining terms. They had also come to know Edward Stuart Talbot (1844–1934), then Bishop of Rochester, whose concern for social and educational reforms was of some assistance to Webb in his complicated operations over the Education Bills.

Massey was probably a servant from the Playne house at Longfords who had enlisted with Bill Playne. Earl Grey (1851–1917) was a Liberal statesman who strongly advocated imperial unity. He was a member of the board of the British South Africa Company and became Governor-General of Canada 1904–11. Noel Edward Noel-Buxton (1869–1948), later Lord Noel-Buxton, became a Liberal and afterwards a Labour M.P. He was an energetic pacifist and philanthropist. Miss Talbot was the daughter of the Bishop of Rochester. Joseph Frederick Green (1855–1932) was secretary of the International Arbitration and Peace Association 1886–1917: a member of the Fabian executive who resigned in 1900 as one of the pro-Boer faction, he became a militant patriot during the Great War.

41 Grosvenor Road
Feb. 10 1901

Dearest Mary

You gave me no address on your postcard or I would have written to you before. We are at last free of the funeral. It has been a true national 'wake', a real debauch of sentiment and loyalty – a most impressive demonstration of the whole people in favor of the monarchical principle. The streets are still black with the multitude in mourning from the great ladies in their carriages to the flower girls, who are furnished with rags of crepe. The King is hugely popular and evidently intends to play his part well. As for the German Emperor, we all adore him!

You will be sorry to hear that the Courtneys have been in trouble – having discovered that Leonard has a somewhat serious affliction of the heart. He is forbidden to walk uphill, or frequently, upstairs, has been told to avoid public meetings and other excitement. But the doctors do not think there is any danger to life at present, but he will have to accept existence on a lower level. The complaint showed itself quite suddenly like the eyes: one can only hope that like his eyesight it may remain stationary. It is curious that it has come so soon after his exclusion from public life, like his blindness came after missing the Speakership.

Sidney is hard at work at L.C.C. election. For the first time we have a really strong opponent – a local Tory lawyer, whose family have been Vestry Clerks for 100 years and who has just retired from the office himself. I think Sidney is safe tho' he will lose some of his majority, but we rather expect to drop the second seat, as Phillimore will not bestir himself.

We dined at Haldane's rooms last night and met Lord Rosebery, Mr Asquith and 3 other men – I being the only lady! The great man was more gracious and less self-conscious than last time, but he is a most confirmed *'Poseur'* and it is impossible to get on natural terms with him. It certainly would not do to count on him, as he has no sooner undertaken to do something, than he wants to get out of it, and by the time one has acquiesced in that, he suddenly re-appears again on the scene! He will never be a leader of men and I should imagine that he would do far better to join the Unionists on Lord Salisbury's death or retirement and become a brilliant [?Item] of the Conservative Cabinet. He is far too capricious and aristocratic to re-form a great Popular party. We had a somewhat futile but amusing evening with a great deal of repartee and chaff and very little businesslike discussion.

I have written today for some flowers for next Saturday. I have a little party to meet the Hobhouses – the Daveys, Lord Grey, Noel-Buxton (a most eligible and charming young man) Miss Talbot and Mr F. J. Green. Your flowers will be a great addition to my entertainment.

Mrs Creighton has been very ill with appendicitis – and will not be out of bed for some weeks. They are to have apartments at Hampton Court – that being one of last commands of the Queen and one of the first of the King. I have been down once or twice and seen the girls: it is very melancholy for them with their mother – their great stay and comforter – seriously ill. The more I think of Dr Creighton's death, the sadder it makes me. His image and charming personality seems to shine out in one's memory; and one regrets one did not manage to see more of him during the first weeks of his illness. The 'Profession' generally are firmly convinced that he died of cancer of the stomach like his mother 5 years ago.

Do write and tell me your news. I hear Bill is very flourishing and has Massey with him!

Ever yours affectionately

Beatrice Webb

### 387 BL SIDNEY WEBB TO JOHN BURNS

Dr Frederick George McCleary (1867–1962) was married to Hilda Cox, sister of Olivier's wife Margaret. He became medical officer of health for Battersea and later Deputy Senior Medical Officer of the Ministry of Health. He was a pioneer in the field of maternity and child welfare. At this time he was preparing Tract 94, *Municipal Bakeries*, and Tract 95, *Municipal Hospitals*, for the Fabian Society. As the Webb influence grew they acted as patrons for many promising young men, serving almost as an unofficial employment agency for entrants to the public service.

41 Grosvenor Road, Westminster Embankment

4/3/1

Dear Burns

McCleary is the candidate for the Medical Officership of Battersea Borough Council that I spoke to you about. They decide it on March 12. He is, on his record, about the best qualified candidate for such a post that I have ever known.

But what I wish to add is that he is a staunch Fabian, a convinced teetotaller, the brother-in-law of Sydney Olivier, and a first-rate chap! Pray put in a word in season for him with the Borough Councillors.

Yours

Sidney Webb

### 388 NLS BEATRICE WEBB TO R. B. HALDANE

Rosebery's speech on behalf of L.S.E. at the Mansion House was something of a disappointment; Hewins complained that little money came in apart from £5,000 from Lord Rothschild and seemed to blame the lack of support on the Webbs' connection with the Fabian Society. Beatrice, however, was satisfied. 'I feel that now we have done our utmost to give the School an independent life, it is true that it toddled out of our nursery and to some extent took its own line.' (BWD 22 March 01) Lord Rothschild (1840–1915), banker and philanthropist, was the first professing Jew to become a member of the House of Lords. He succeeded Mandell Creighton as honorary president of L.S.E.

41 Grosvenor Road, Westminster Embankment

March 21 1901

Dear Mr Haldane

Do remember to tell Lord Rosebery how deeply grateful we are for his speech this afternoon. He said exactly what was most useful and most effective.

136

Our gratitude is not only for the material help that it may bring to the School, but also for the stimulus to our own effort – we shall work all the harder and the better for this recognition and sympathy.

You need no assurance of our appreciation of your help – we regard you as an aider and abettor, if not, as a fellow conspirator, in our small attempts to outflank some of the stupidity and unenlightened self-interest of this troublesome world. (If self-interest *had* been 'enlightened' would we have ever turned Collectivist?)

We shall look forward to seeing you on Thursday.

Ever yours sincerely

Beatrice Webb

### 389 DN  SIDNEY WEBB TO ÉLIE HALÉVY

The distinguished French historian Elie Halévy (1870–1937) with whom the Webbs maintained a lifelong connection, was the author of *The History of the English People in the Nineteenth Century*, which appeared in several volumes between 1912 and 1932.

The few surviving letters for the middle months of 1901 deal with minor matters, such as a deficit in the Fabian finances and the possible purchase of Foxwell's library for the L.S.E. They do not refer to the unexpected recovery of the Progressive Party to a substantial victory in the L.C.C. elections in March – on which Sidney spent much effort in the first four months of the year.

Beatrice was still in poor mental and physical health. After an Easter visit to Lulworth Cove with Sidney she spent much of the summer out of London, staying with the Russells at Friday's Hill.

During these months the split in the Liberal Party between its leader, Campbell-Bannerman, and the 'Limps', Asquith, Haldane and Sir Edward Grey, became more serious. Sidney was in a dilemma, Beatrice suggested, because his emotional sympathies lay with the Boers while he agreed politically with the Liberal Imperialists. (BWD 9 July 01) Webb was also under pressure from Shaw to build up Rosebery as the one possible national leader who might be amenable to the old permeation tactic. Writing to Beatrice on 24 July and to Sidney two days later (PP), Shaw proposed that Webb should write the article, 'Lord Rosebery's Escape from Houndsditch' which was published in the *Nineteenth Century* in its September issue. The article, revised and polished by Shaw, praised Rosebery as the destroyer of Gladstonian shibboleths.

The Webbs, however, had not fallen in with very energetic or consistent allies. Rosebery vacillated, reluctant to abandon his ambitions and yet unwilling to make an overt bid for leadership, to collaborate with the other Liberal Imperialists or, because of his commitment to Free Trade and his dislike of Chamberlain personally, to make overtures to the Liberal Unionists. By 1 October Beatrice was forced to confess that she had 'no illusions' about the 'Limps' and that 'neither Rosebery nor Asquith mean to declare themselves in favour of our measures of collectivism. But they hold no views that are inconsistent with it . . . The time will come when, if they are to be a political force, they will have to "fill up" the political workers with some positive convictions. Then, we think, for the needful minimum of nourishment they will fall back on us!'

41 Grosvenor Road, Westminster Embankment

23 May 1901

Dear Monsieur Halévy,

I hasten to thank you for kindly sending me your two volumes on Bentham and Utilitarianism. I shall read them with great interest, especially as I shall want, presently, to make up my mind as to the extent to which the special ideas of Chadwick can be traced to Bentham. No doubt the main principles come from Bentham, but I am referring rather to Chadwick's various devices for good government.

Mrs Webb and I are now hard at work writing about the Vestry, and other local governing bodies at the beginning of the 19th Century.

Please call on us whenever you are in London.

Yours truly

Sidney Webb


### 390 FP  SIDNEY WEBB TO EDWARD PEASE

The income from the sales of Fabian publications had fallen sharply and Pease was pressing for a subsidy from the Hutchinson funds to ease the stressed Fabian budget.

*Twentieth Century Politics*, a redraft of the *Nineteenth Century* article, appeared as Tract 108. Hutchinson money was also used to underwrite Webb's Tract 106, *The Education Muddle and the Way Out*. This tract had been in preparation for more than two years, a draft having been discussed at a Fabian meeting in May 1899; Wallas and Headlam had led the opposition to Webb's readiness to abolish the local school boards, and Wallas had been an active member of a revision committee set up to produce a compromise version.

The position of the school boards had changed decisively after 20 December 1900 when Mr Justice Wills handed down the 'Cockerton Judgement'. William Garnett had encouraged two ratepayers to challenge the London School Board's expenditure on secondary and adult classes as *ultra vires*: this challenge was confirmed by the auditor, T. Barclay Cockerton, who surcharged the Board for making improper payments. After Justice Wills supported Cockerton the case was appealed and Wills was upheld in the higher court in April 1901. This case effectively blocked the attempt by the school boards to extend their jurisdiction beyond elementary education and made the need for new secondary education authorities more urgent. Webb saw it as an opportunity to start a full-scale reorganisation, creating a new coherent structure which would run through from elementary to secondary and advanced institutions.

Webb was now working closely with Robert Laurie Morant (1863–1920), a remarkably able and single-minded educational administrator, who had returned from several years as tutor to the Siamese royal family to become the architect of the Conservative reforms in 1902 and 1903, in the latter year being appointed permanent secretary to the Board of Education. The Webbs thought highly of Morant, who exemplified their view of the highly-qualified expert. In 1898, reporting on the Swiss educational system, Morant had revealed how close his ideas were to those of the Webbs. He wrote of the 'increasing need of voluntarily submitting the impulse of the many ignorant to the guidance and control of the few wise . . . special expert governors or guides'. (*Reports on Educational Subjects*, Volume III).

41 Grosvenor Road, Westminster Embankment

3.10.01

Dear Pease

How would it do to suggest – leaving out of account present deficit for the moment – that a separate account should henceforth be kept for the Publishing Committee – including Book Box items and Advertisements – and that they be required to limit themselves to their receipts.

This would leave the members subs. to pay for the office work, meetings and news – the £50 from Hutchinson Trust being considered a full equivalent for incidental expenses to the country lecturing.

Then, any further contribution from Hutchinson Trust, if and when needed, *could take the form of buying tracts.*

Now, as to existing deficit. I am not disposed to make a grant, simpliciter, from Hutchinson Trust. I should prefer to take off the Society's hands part of the stock of tracts, and distribute them. What stock have you? Could you sell 20,000 assorted tracts – including what you can strike off cheaply from stereo – without denuding stock unduly?

I am much inclined to a great issue of tracts *by post* to selected lists. I should like to have the positive part of my *XIXth Century* article turned into a tract entitled *Twentieth Century Politics* – perhaps over my name – and sent out very broadly with such as Education, Temperance, Factory Act and other tracts. If this could be done, might it not be the best way (a) to help the F.S. over its deficit; (b) to take a new start in politics; (c) to get a good advertisement for the Society's other tracts etc.

Suppose we could get lists of 10,000 good people – e.g. the doctor, preacher or teacher graduates of London University, all over the country, your Liberal Association secretaries, etc. – postage to them would cost £25.

20,000 tracts (2 to each) at 50/- = £50

or　30,000 (3 to each) = £75

This is the best way I can think of to spend £100.

I may be a little late tomorrow but will come.

Yours

Sidney Webb

## 391 PP BEATRICE TO SIDNEY

Still in poor health Beatrice had gone down to stay at Freshwater in the Isle of Wight with Mary Playne. She noted her 'bad state of physical health and a rotten state of mind'; in fact she was suffering from eczema, chronic anxiety and morbid fear of death. She felt that 1901 had been a bad year. (BWD 9 December 01)

In this private entry, inserted into the manuscript volume much later, she was suggestive but opaque. She wrote of sentimental day-dreaming, of believing herself to be admired by 'some eminent personages' and succumbing to vanity. The individual or individuals were not named, but Beatrice commented that only a sense of humour, a code of conduct and a realisation that she was 'grizzled, wrinkled and over forty' checked 'the morbid growth of feeling'. She may still have been indulging fantasies about Joseph Chamberlain.

On the way back from the north in October she met a food faddist on the train who convinced her that she was suffering toxicity through excessive eating. From this time she began – and normally maintained – an austere diet. In the first instance it led to a marked loss of weight, though she attributed her recovery to this regimen. The habit of frugal eating, which in any case appealed to Beatrice's dislike of self-indulgence, remained for the rest of her life, being imposed in part upon a somewhat reluctant Sidney. One young relative recalled that he ate more when dinner-table flowers concealed his plate from Beatrice.

[Freshwater, Isle of Wight]
Nov. 5 1901

My own darling boy

I am grieved that there was no letter from you yesterday: the fog must have prevented the transit, as it did turn to one. We are enveloped in white mist tho' it is better today but still gloomy. Mary hired a bicycle and we went out together for an 8-mile ride. I am getting much better: I really think I shall be well tho' not strong by the time I get back to you. The soreness of the mouth is clearing off, the eczema has not returned, I sleep well and thoroughly enjoy my allowance of food. All I feel now is rather tired and stupid and unequal to much exercise.

I have refused the Sangers' invitation as the less I go out now the better. I do so want to get back to work. Rosebery is apparently coming back to politics: depend upon it, he is stirred up by Asquith making the running for leadership. It is quite possible that he is going to raise his flag and see how many organizations will invite him to address them. In that case he will be practically bidding for independent leadership as against C.B. [Campbell-Bannerman]. A curious situation, since the H. of C. Liberals may find the ground cut from under them.

Ever your devoted wifey

Beatrice

392 FP    SIDNEY WEBB TO EDWARD PEASE

41 Grosvenor Road,
Westminster Embankment
12.11.1

Dear Pease

I quite dissent from the principle on which you propose to exclude. My idea of the object of this distribution is intellectual and political propaganda,

140

among people of influence, belonging either to the 'centre' or to the non-political class. It is not an attempt to get money for the F.S. If it were the latter, I don't think university graduates a good class at all.

I suggest the following lines. Choose (1) men, not women; (2) residents in England and Wales, not elsewhere – Scotch politics and administration being so diverse, and oversea residents being no good, I should first go through the London list on these lines, omitting no one else.

Then I would take any Welsh university list that you had – with the same exclusions. Then I would take the Glasgow list, with the same exclusions (thus taking only residents in England).

But by no means omit ministers, lawyers and doctors. These are just the very people I want to influence (with the teachers) – just the great non-political, locally influential, finally decisive, folk whom we have to get at.

If you doubt, consult the Publication Committee, reading them this letter. What we are aiming at is intellectual influence and thus power, not money.

Yours

Sidney Webb

### 393 PP   SIDNEY TO BEATRICE

Joseph Gregory was a member of the Operative Stonemasons and one of the small group of workingmen on the L.C.C. who had little sympathy for Webb and distrusted his concern with higher education. Ramsay MacDonald was able to enlist the support of this group for his attacks on Webb after he had entered the L.C.C. unopposed at a bye-election in 1901.

41 Grosvenor Road, Westminster Embankment<br>26.11.1

My own dear one

Your cheery letter was specially welcome.

Yesterday, at the T.E.B. I failed in temper rather grievously – much worse inwardly than outwardly, but badly outwardly I fear. And it related to the School. It was this way. Over another, quite unimportant matter. Organ made a sudden attack on a Committee proposal, without previously speaking to me, or giving any notice. It was about a proposed expense of 100 guineas to get assistance in a Special Inquiry on Higher Scientific Education. I was very vexed at this, because some of the workmen made very nasty statements about Garnett's salary etc. etc. – and the proposal had to be withdrawn, which will rather upset things.

This put me out. Then next came School Equipment vote, for which Garnett had drafted the resolution rather clumsily, though the preceding explanation was full and good. On this Dr Collins raised a question, quite without malice, but incidentally saying that I had taken good care of Economics. Then these same workmen chimed in – especially Gregory

141

(Stonemasons) who remembered the attack on the School in 1898 while I was away; and made some scoffing remark, implying as I understood my favoritism.

Then I fired up rather – said that I would not have the vote passed unless the Board was fully satisfied – explained how we had given the County Council the building and so on. The Board was, I think, quite with me, and rather penitent (except that Beachcroft was a little captious in point of form), and of course the resolution passed. But I was nettled and visibly so – which was a mistake – and I can see that – owing largely to the Vice-Chairman's lack of skill in administration and his obstinacy, from 1898 onward – the Board will no longer work quite so smoothly. I am specially annoyed at the workmen's constant insults to Garnett – doubtless more incisive than their authors mean them to be – and Organ's bullying tone with the officials.

The result to me was, curiously enough, a really severe 'emotional perturbation' which would not be allayed and which prevented me sleeping. Anger is certainly what upsets me most.

There. I have told you all my trouble, just as if you were here to counsel and console me. After all, one is judged by one's totality. And I dare say it was not so bad outwardly as I felt it myself. But I shall have trouble with that Board yet. However, I can let the Chairmanship pass in three months' time.

Lord Grey came in unexpectedly at 6.30. He is in the big American scheme for a great office building on the new street – a two-million building on the Strand site – and he came to beg me to get it favorably considered.

What a frivolous person he really is.

This morning, sleepless, and with a lecture tonight, I have done nothing but correspondence. Yesterday and today there are orders for some 50 or 60 copies altogether. This makes about 220 volumes ordered altogether, I think – say 120 of the *History* and 100 of *Industrial Democracy*.

Goodbye dear one – I must now go. It is when you are away that I am 'betrayed by what is false within' as Meredith says. Come back well and fat!

Sidney

### 394 PP SIDNEY TO BEATRICE

On 13 October Beatrice noted that Sidney was now the dominant figure in the politics of London education: 'the whole process of moulding events falls into the hands of the little *clique* who happen to be in the centre of things'. She observed that he effectively controlled the award of grants by the L.C.C., was (as chairman of its Administrative Committee) the head of the L.S.E. and, as a member of the Senate, a power in the University of London. He also 'knows every rope and has quick and immediate access to every person of influence'.

The L.C.C. grant to the L.S.E. remained the crucial balancing item in its still-precarious budget.

Sir Walter Prideaux was the Clerk to the Goldsmith's Company. Sir Michael Foster F.R.S. (1836–1907), professor of physiology at Cambridge, was the Liberal Unionist M.P. for the University of London 1900–06. Maud Parry, the wife of the composer Sir Charles Hubert Parry (1848–1918), was an active supporter of advanced causes.

41 Grosvenor Road, Westminster

29.11.1

My own dearest

I have asked Sir W. Prideaux and Sir M. Foster for the 12th December, and posted the letter to Lady M. Parry.

Yesterday's lecture to the Deptford clergy was rather a frost. It was at Blackheath and only 7 clergy attended who happened not to belong to Deptford. But the others sent most regretful letters, and it was good as far as it went.

Three pheasants have come from Parmoor.

I have again struggled with the preface, but had to stop to discuss with Hewins the budget for the new building. We need, it appears, £2,000 a year over the University grant. We can get, in fees, anything between £500 and £1,000, we cannot yet tell: £300 or £400 from subscriptions, and perhaps a little from lettings.

Thus, we must get the grant of £1,200 continued, and shall then be all right. If not, we shall have a struggle to live.

Two or three orders only today.

I have no time to add more. Tomorrow we shall be together again.

Sidney

## 395 UI SIDNEY WEBB TO H. G. WELLS

Herbert George Wells (1866–1946) was introduced to Shaw and Webb by Graham Wallas, whose sister-in-law was a neighbour to Wells at Sandgate, on the Kent coast. After making a sudden success with his science-fiction stories, especially *The Time Machine* and *The War of the Worlds*, Wells turned to social forecasting, contributing a series of articles to the *Fortnightly Review* in the course of 1901. These were published in book form at the end of the year under the title *Anticipations of the Reaction of Mechanical and Scientific Progress Upon Human Life and Thought*. What Beatrice called on publication 'the most remarkable book of the year' at once made Wells a second reputation. His concept of a technocratic elite – which he named 'the New Republicans' – evoked a sympathetic response from the Webbs, who saw him as a potential ally in their developing campaign for a government of national efficiency, based upon collectivist principles. Wells was flattered to be taken up by the Webbs, responding to this letter from Sidney with an invitation for the Webbs to visit him at Sandgate. After the Webbs had left he wrote to Pease on 29 January to say that they were 'wonderful people and they leave me ashamed of my indolence and mental dissipation and awfully afraid of Mrs Webb'. Beatrice thought Wells 'an interesting though somewhat unattractive personality . . . a good instrument for popularising ideas'. (BWD 29

February 01) The Comte de Buffon (1707–88) produced an immense *Histoire Naturelle* 1749–67; Goethe wasted much energy on research on optics.

41 Grosvenor Road, Westminster Embankment
8 Dec. 1901

Dear Mr Wells

I venture to write to you – not only as an immensely interested reader of your *Anticipations*, but also as a friend of Graham Wallas and Bernard Shaw whom you know. It is, indeed, possible that we may have met at Kelmscott House, in the old Hammersmith Socialist Society days.

Well, as I say, I admire *Anticipations* greatly, and find myself in sympathy with many of your feelings and criticisms and suggestions. I do not intend to refer to all these points of agreement.

I want rather to take the liberty of inviting your attention to a side of your own 'anticipation' that you seem to undervalue, if not to ignore. I agree with your feeling about the coming predominance of the man of science, the trained professional expert. But you see him – may I suggest? – too exclusively as an engineer, a chemist or an electrician. In the extremely complicated, densely-peopled world on a large scale that you foretell, there must inevitably be a great deal of what is called 'administration'. I do not mean the amateur business that is now called government – still less do I mean politics. But all experience shows that men need organising as much as machines, or rather, much more; that the making of such arrangements, and constant readjustments, as will ensure order, general health and comfort, and maximum productivity, among human beings, is a professional art in itself – not consciously studied in England, where we do much instinctively, but recognised in India, and deliberately studied in Germany.

Now, I believe that along with your engineers and chemists in the dominant class of the future will be the trained administrator, the expert in organising men – equipped with an Economics or a Sociology which will be as scientific, and as respected by his colleagues of other professions, as Chemistry or Mechanics. You seem to ignore this class. Its inclusion, and the influence of its studies on the other men of science, perhaps alters the colour of your picture at this place. It takes, for instance, more imagination to organize men than machines – even more poetry!

A second point to which I venture to ask your attention is your Abyss – indeed, your whole vision of 'the Grey'. I cannot help thinking that you altogether underrate the capacity of the wage-earning class to differentiate itself, and the extent to which it will segregate. The 'People of the Abyss', in this country at any rate, need not be any large mass – more probably a constantly dying 'residium', always kept in existence as such by individuals dropping from above – not a class.

The English wage-earning class, for instance, is rapidly putting on 'bourgeois' characteristics, developing any number of markedly different classes and strata, segregating with great rapidity into streaks of bright colour, which are becoming more intense. These segregations are quickly coming to play a great and intelligent part in the world – they contribute what is, in its way, a real governing class. This will play no small part in that administration, that organization of men to which I have referred. Moreover, this class has stopped its rabbit-like multiplication. Altogether, I plead for a widening of your bands of colour – a considerable restriction of what you see as the Abyss.

Now all this, and much else to the same effect, you cannot find, I fully admit, in the ordinary books on Political Economy, if you have ever looked at them. They are as much out of date as Buffon's *Natural History* or Goethe's *Theory of Colours*. But for all that, the facts must be taken into account, even though the Economists won't either record, classify or systematise them.

I wonder whether you would care to look through *Industrial Democracy*, in which my wife and I have tried to deal in a scientific way with the structure and function of English industrial organization. I send the book (2 vols) herewith on the chance that you may be willing to look through it. Begin with the last *three* chapters, which give our conclusions.

Yours very truly

Sidney Webb

396 FP  SIDNEY WEBB TO EDWARD PEASE

14 Eastern Esplanade, Margate
13.1.2

Dear Pease

I can't come next Friday, as I shall be staying with Wells at Spade House, Sandgate from Thursday to Saturday – when I return for good.

Could we have a meeting on Thursday week, just before the Publication Committee Meeting?

I am quite willing for one or two evenings discussion of Imperialism – or as I would call it – Principles of Foreign Policy for the British Empire – provided the object is bona fide that we should learn from each other, and not seek to pass foolish and useless resolutions. It will be remembered that the so-called Imperialists in the Society have been against votes and resolutions all through. They prove nothing, and they effect nothing – whilst a vote at a London meeting does not even represent the Society.

Yours

Sidney Webb

Though the Webbs kept up their close social and political association with Haldane and his colleagues they were becoming more dubious about the 'Limps'. 'Why are we in this galley?', Beatrice wrote in her diary on 28 February. 'Partly because we have drifted into it. These men have helped us in our undertakings, they have been appreciative of our ideas, and socially pleasant to us . . . Moreover, the leaders of the other school of Liberalism are extremely distasteful to us: we disagree with them on almost every point of home and foreign policy . . . if Sidney is inside the *clique*, he will have a better chance of permeating its activities than by standing aloof as a superior person and scolding at them.' By 19 March she had concluded that Asquith was 'deplorably slack', Grey 'a mere dilettante', that Haldane loved playing at 'political intrigue' and that Rosebery, for all his talents, was 'an enigma'. She was relieved that they were about to be relieved from the pressures of salon politics for the next three months. They went first to stay at Crowborough, in Sussex, where they drafted the chapter on sewers for their local government book, and Sidney wrote a long article on 'London University', published in the *Nineteenth Century* in June 1902. They then went on to stay with the Russells at Friday's Hill for nine weeks.

Samuel's *Liberalism* was published in 1902.

41 Grosvenor Road, Westminster Embankment
20.3.2

Dear Samuel

I have never had time to thank you for sending me your *Liberalism*. I have, however, managed to read it, and with much appreciation. It seems to me *far*, far better than the bits you read to me years ago. You have really done it with great skill – and let me say, too, no little courage. I like the book from end to end, and it cannot fail to be useful. It comes at a very favorable moment, and ought to sell well.

Now for criticism. Of course my main one is that you are weak and vague in the *connection* between your fundamental principle of Liberalism, and some of your particular projects – you need more accepted 'axiomata media'. Thus, without such, Factory Acts and Housing schemes are apt to be *merely* empirical.

The sort of middle axioms you need, I think, are such as To Raise Compulsorily the Standard of Life, To Enforce a National Minimum in each important point, Collective Regulation of all matters of Common Concern, and so on. These are the instruments by which your fundamental principle can be applied – the lathes in which particular reforms are but the cutting tools to be changed from time to time as the task requires.

I wonder whether you see what I mean. The reply to your projects, by a reasoning Liberal of the old School, would be, 'I do not see that the proposed remedy would not be worse than the evil to be cured.' He says this because he is unconsciously assuming quite a different set of 'axiomata media' from yours, thus he believes that The Standard of Life can only be raised by Individual Action, that the enforcement of any National Minimum is bad as Infringing Liberty, that Individual Freedom is the basis of any healthy state; and so on. We have got to drag these hidden assumptions out, and replace them by others.

However, this is not a criticism of what you have done – only a comment on what seems an additional need. I wonder what John Morley says of your idea of Liberalism!

Yours

Sidney Webb

## 398 PP SIDNEY WEBB TO GRAHAM WALLAS

The personal intrigues and political manoeuvres behind the Conservative Education Acts of 1902 and 1903 were extremely complex. The Government itself was divided in attitude and uncertain about policy. Lord Salisbury (1830–1903) was in his last months as Prime Minister; he was pro-Church and felt a political debt to the Anglican church for support at the 1900 election. The Duke of Devonshire (1833–1908) was at the end of a long public career and caring more for his sporting interests than for his complicated task as minister responsible for the educational measures. He was a Liberal Unionist and objected to rate-aiding the church schools. Joseph Chamberlain, the dominant figure in the Cabinet, still accepted the Nonconformist objection to denominational teaching. Sir John Gorst was out of favour and Sir George Kekewich (1841–1921), the senior civil servant in the Board of Education, was opposed to the Government's policy and favoured the retention of the old school boards.

In this muddled situation Morant was instructed to draft a Bill acceptable to the Cabinet. He visited Webb in April to concert tactics with him. After much discussion Morant began his draft and Sidney threw his energies into covert lobbying, taking particular trouble to make contact with Anglican and Roman Catholic churchmen of influence. The original plan was to set up new comprehensive education authorities which would take over elementary education from the old boards and develop a new secondary system; to provide public money to assist the voluntary schools and to repeal the Cowper–Temple compromise of 1870 which excluded denominational teaching. Disagreement within the Government, powerful pressure from affected interests and parliamentary tactics secured a substantial modification of the Bill before it was passed on 20 December 1902. The Act set up local education authorities as part of the local government structure; the Cowper–Temple policy was allowed to stand but religious instruction was placed in the hands of the managers of each school, of whom one-third were to be appointed by the local authority; and voluntary schools were given support from the rates for their maintenance.

This Act, bitterly opposed by the Nonconformists and disliked by progressive opinion as a capitulation to clericalism and reaction, led to the campaign of 'passive resistance' in which objectors refused to pay their rates; a few authorities in Nonconformist strongholds declined to implement the Act for some years. The campaign helped to swing middle-class Nonconformist voters, who had been sliding to the Liberal Unionists and Conservatives, back to the official Liberals and prepared the way for the Liberal victory in 1906. It also saw the

147

emergence of David Lloyd George (1863–1945) as a national figure and leader of the Radical wing of the Liberal Party.

Webb used the Fabian Society as a means of promoting a number of amendments to the Education Bill: by passing them through a members' meeting for transmission to the press and interested parties he protected his own political base and gave a certain public status to the proposals.

> 41 Grosvenor Road
> Westminster Embankment
> 26.4.2

Dear Wallas

I am sorry we had so little time to discuss the Education Bill resolutions yesterday. I have today in revising them done my best to add your points, as forcibly as I can. Of course, all our proposed amendments do not amount to a Second Reading objection – and so far I suppose, you will not care to stand in with us. But a Second Reading rejection is out of the question – the Bill will pass Second Reading by a majority of, I reckon, 275 – and indeed, barring accidents, the Bill *is* to become law. What we can best do is to put forcibly every amendment that we should wish to see adopted.

I can't adopt your condemnation of the machinery, as it is almost word for word what we agreed to in *The Education Muddle* – the statutory committee, the outside members, the Education Department scheme, the delegation to managers, the Voluntary School managers etc. You, I think, concurred in that then as inevitable, and I don't see any alternative now. I have put in provisions to improve it so far as possible.

I fear there is no getting over the fact that Church and R.C. schools will insist on Church and R.C. teachers. Have you any practicable alternative to this?

Don't trouble to reply, but *formulate* any additional amendments you think should be pressed, and let Pease have them before Friday.

> Sidney Webb

### 399 PP   SIDNEY TO BEATRICE

Haldane had enlisted Webb's support for what was loosely called the 'Charlottenburg Scheme' to build an advanced technical institute in London on the model of the German institution at Charlottenburg, near Berlin. The superiority of German secondary and technical education – emphasised by the fact that it was necessary to employ a significant number of Germans in London commercial offices – was a cause of envy and anxiety on the part of advocates of national efficiency. The plan was to assimilate the Royal College of Science and the School of Mines at South Kensington with the City and Guilds Institute to form what became the Imperial College of Science and Technology. Haldane had interested several wealthy South Africans, especially Sir Julius Wernher (1850–1922) of Wernher, Beit and Co. The Webbs became friendly with Wernher, who provided financial support for several of their social and educational activities.

By midsummer, it had become clear that the Education Bill would not apply to London and that the same ground would have to be fought over again in the following year. Webb wished to make the L.C.C. the comprehensive authority for education in the capital. The Progressives, controlling the L.C.C., were mostly disposed to retain the London School Board, which was dominated by Liberals and Nonconformists. The Conservative government, reluctant to strengthen the powers of the L.C.C. which was in the hands of its opponents, toyed with the idea of handing education over to the much smaller metropolitan borough councils. Webb's strategy was to persuade the Conservatives to accept the L.C.C. as the authority and, at the same time, to induce the hesitant Progressives to abandon the London School Board. This intricate operation was probably Webb's most successful intervention in practical politics.

County Hall, Spring Gardens,
London s.w.
17.6.2

My own dearest

Haldane sent for me to say he thought he had really secured *three* towards the first *five* hundred thousands, and one hundred thousand towards the second half million. In fact Beit and Co. would give this second hundred thousand. Lord R. wants a little meeting next week to discuss it, which I am to attend.

By the way, Rothschild consents to take the presidency of the School.

I have sent off a few of the memos. this morning. Haldane had seen Balfour at length, and he said the latter was quite aware of our 'clericalism', and had fully recognised that a Borough Councils body was out of the question. But he was not hopeful as to anything positive.

I went alone to Reeves' reception, as Mary was tired – there was a dense crowd, but I had a hasty word of greeting from Seddon in the crush. Mrs Reeves, in despair of someone to talk to Mrs Chamberlain, turned me on! J.C. was not there himself.

The indiarubber bath has arrived.

Alas, I shall have to come up on Saturday next, by the 1.30 train, just for one meeting – to return by the 5 train. But I shall be able to have from Thursday evening to Saturday middle day with you.

Goodnight

Sidney

400 PP SIDNEY TO BEATRICE

Beatrice had left for a three-week holiday in the Italian Lakes and the Engadine. While staying at the Russells' she had noticed that relations between them were strained and that Bertrand Russell was away part of the time. Suspecting that the marriage was in difficulties and realising that Alys was on the point of breakdown she took her away for a holiday: Beatrice herself, still suffering from eczema and debility, felt the need for fresh air and relaxation.

Arthur Winnington-Ingram (1858–1946) succeeded Mandell Creighton as Bishop of London in 1901. Sir Charles Algernon Whitmore (1851–1908),

Conservative M.P. for Chelsea 1886–1906, was leader of the London group of Tory M.P.s and an L.C.C. alderman. William Frederick Smith (1868–1908), philanthropist and Conservative M.P. for the Strand division of Westminster 1891–1910, took over the firm of W. H. Smith and Co. from his father. Cosmo Gordon Lang (1864–1945), formerly chaplain to Queen Victoria, was suffragan bishop of Stepney 1901–09. On the following day, after seeing Cosmo Lang, Sidney described him as 'a most fascinating, handsome, young courtier, of extreme good looks and good manners . . . Really, I am capable of being jealous of such a man' and thought him 'destined to rise still further'. Lang became in turn Archbishop of York and Archbishop of Canterbury.

The Olivers had returned from New Zealand to settle in London. The revised edition of the Webbs' *Problems of Modern Industry*, published in 1898, appeared in 1902.

41 Grosvenor Road,
London s.w.
4/7/2

My own dearest

Your postcard came late last night, and gave me the joy of knowing that you were safe at Basle. By now, you will be looking out on the splendid panorama of the Alps, and I hope, in the bright Italian weather.

I have seen this morning the Bishop of London, who was very cordial and cheery, saying he had always upheld the L.C.C. But he had not thought about London under the Bill, being busied with an attempt to arrive at a compromise with the Nonconformists generally. He took in my ideas, and promised to see Whitmore and Smith, but said he must defer to the advice as to the Parliamentary situation. Tomorrow I am to see the Bishop of Stepney. But I have not much exercise. The drawing room at Fulham is, on all the walls, covered with *illuminated addresses* to Ingram! of the ordinary common type, from Schools and Church Societies. I came out by the garden gate, through the grounds we have been in so often, thinking of the change.

The Olivers came to see the Playnes, and asked me to dine with them tonight, which I am doing, and shall try to tell Oliver about London University, so as to be able to send him my article.

Longmans write that their American house will take 100 copies of 'Problems', to begin with, in sheets, at 1/8, being the usual third of the net price. This will be £8 at once towards our total outlay of £25 or £30, and we shall have 400 more on sale. I sent the M.S. of the new Introduction and ordered the printing on Wednesday.

I have invited the School lecturers for the 10th (and ordered a waitress!) With myself, we are 14 in all, and up to now all have accepted! But there will certainly be one or two unable to come. Hewins writes that he has put in the School courses for the University Calendar – some 1200 lectures for the year, being about three times what we have offered hitherto; and quite certainly the best programme of any university in the world in the subject. He says that (except his own course at King's), *no other* Economic faculty courses had been put in yet – not even Foxwell's at University College, though University College Arts, Science, Medicine and Engineering were in. Poor Foxwell, he evidently does not know how to meet the situation. But University College can really make a sort of a show, by the aid of its history, statistics and law; and will probably do so later.

Now, we must contrive to get audiences to these 1,200 lectures!

Goodbye dear one

Sidney

### 401 PP  BEATRICE TO SIDNEY

Russell did not reveal the name of the woman with whom he had fallen in love as his relationship with Alys deteriorated. His biographer identifies her as Evelyn Whitehead, the wife of Russell's collaborator and friend Alfred North Whitehead. Beatrice's comments confirm the identification. Mrs Whitehead was ill with heart trouble, concerned about her husband's mental stability and worried about his irresponsibility in money matters. Russell covertly subsidised the Whiteheads at this time. While Alys was away Russell was staying with the Whiteheads in Cambridge and completing *The Principles of Mathematics.*

Hotel Monte Generosa,
Bella Vista, Switzerland
Friday [?4 July 1902]

My own dearest one

Here I am basking in the sun, looking over wooded hills and mountains – resting between early coffee and *dejeuner* at 12 o'clock. The right name of the Hotel is not *Bella Vista* (which is the working-class cabaret near to the station of that name) but Monte Generosa. It is clean, roomy, cool and plain – with good but not super excellent food and a lovely entourage of woods and hills and views of the Italian plain. Altogether the exact place for us, at any rate at first.

Alys is a delightful companion – all the more attractive because she has evidently suffered acutely these last months. Her nerves are still in a very weak state – and one can see that she finds it difficult to keep from breaking down in tears. Physically she is quite fit – stronger than I am, eating and sleeping well and quite able to endure fatigue. She speaks warmly of the Whiteheads and shows no outward sign of jealousy or grudge about the lady – but clearly her thoughts and feelings are revolving round Bertrand in a pathetic way. She seems much happier and says that my love makes her feel stronger in body and mind. I imagine she will get quite well while she is abroad – but the breakdown of nervous strength has evidently been serious and may, I fear, return. But I hope gradually to instill some useful mental hygiene and a calmer way of looking at life. I

151

think she clings to us and wants Bertrand to be with us as much as possible. They have almost decided to spend the winter in London – as she says B. is dead against Cambridge, at any rate at present. What she would like would be for him to get a Professorship at Cambridge or elsewhere so that he might be brought in contact with all the young men. I cannot make out that there has been any great trouble recently – she speaks quite philo-sophically of the young lady's tragic affairs – Bertrand must have trans-ferred his feeling about it to her. Altogether I am inclined to think that the *mental* hygiene of the husband is more at fault than that of the wife!

I am wondering whether I shall get a letter from my boy this afternoon – hardly I fear!

Ever your devoted wifey

Beatrice Webb

402 PP  BEATRICE TO SIDNEY

Mary Emma Buxton, the wife of Francis Buxton and an old friend of Beatrice, was staying higher up the mountain. George Gilbert Aimée Murray (1866–1957), was the outstanding classical scholar who became professor of Greek at Cambridge University. The volume by Charles Seignobos was probably his *Political History of Contemporary Europe since 1814* published in English in 1901.

[Monte Generosa]

Monday [?7 July 1902]

My own dearest

Your letters are a great delight to me – every little scrap of news about your doings interest me. Last night I felt quite homesick – a longing for my boy's face and voice and a foolish fancy that he might not be well. How-ever I consoled myself with the thought that you would be with the Shaws and that they would be chatting to you. And now I am thinking how you will get over this afternoon and if that grant of £1200 will go smoothly.

Yesterday was a very hot day – and I did little but lie under the trees. I am in a most unenergetic humour and have up to today felt 'heady' with the inevitable woman's troubles coming on. But today I feel distinctly brighter. Mrs Buxton came down late in the afternoon and wanted me to come up to dinner – but we did not fancy a steep descent of 1000 ft in the late evening. She has evidently been quite glad to renew the old friendly intimacy.

I find Alys a most pleasant companion and today we are starting reading Seignobos aloud to each other between 10 to 12 o'clock. She has certainly showed none of the characteristics which Bertrand warned me of – her references to Mrs Whitehead are most generous and appreciative tho' she evidently intends *not* to live there again. They are debating whether they will take a house in London for the winter or a cottage near to Murrays –

B. seems set on London tho' he says he always has headaches there. I favour the cottage near to Murrays as otherwise I think privately B. will go to Cambridge with the excuse that London disagrees with him. Alys is leaving it entirely to him to decide. If they do go to London they will take the small house next to the Courtneys for 3½g. furnished – and we must try to see something of them. Alys ejaculated half unconsciously – 'You are the only *woman* I shall ask: I shall cultivate men friends for Bertie'. So you see what a reputation I have as a 'safe' female friend for attractive young men!

There are an elderly female with an aged father – genteel English folk – who very much object to my smoking on the terrace. Last evening they remarked loud enough for me to hear and repeated several times. 'I am ashamed of my countrywoman' 'Disgusting' and 'She brings her case and matchbox' 'Quite disgusting'. The old gentleman was smoking a cigar! I smiled goodnaturedly at them and they collapsed!

Ever yours

BW

### 403 PP  SIDNEY TO BEATRICE

The Shaws had taken a house at Maybury Knoll, near Woking, where G.B.S. was finishing *Man and Superman*. On the same day as this letter Shaw wrote to the publisher Grant Richards (SCL) to say that he might publish the book himself on a commission basis – a practice he subsequently adopted for all his work. After the revised draft was completed early in 1903 Shaw arranged for R. and R. Clark to print it.

41 Grosvenor Road, Westminster

7/7/2

My own dear one

I got your two postcards and your letter all together this morning, Monday, as they had not arrived on Saturday afternoon when I started for the Shaws. I began to get quite anxious about my B. and was relieved to hear from her up to Saturday. But now I hope she has got *three* letters from me, and four packets of newspapers, all addressed to 'Hotel Bella Vista'.

The Shaws were very pleasant and their house very restful in the intense heat. But I am convinced that Woking is a specially *hot* place, the dry sand acting as reverberator, and containing no moisture to cool the air. I am confirmed in my dislike of the place. Shaw has done nothing on our chapter yet. His Don Juan play is finished *in the rough*, and I read it – without any admiration at all! The brilliant and lengthy preface that we heard has little to do with the play, which frankly did not interest me.

They are quite uncertain where to go for August. I suggested Bamborough, *or* Jersey, as they want to bathe.

I did not write to you yesterday Sunday; but I posted the *Westminster Gazette and Pilot*.

This afternoon will settle the question of grant to the School, and I shall try to keep cool and be candid, as you advise. I will post you a late post-card with the result. We have done very well anyhow.

I am delighted to hear so good an account of your companion: but the psychology seems more obscure than ever. Anyway, have a good time together now.

Goodbye dear one – write often.

Sidney

<br>

404 PP SIDNEY TO BEATRICE

A. L. Leon was Progressive member of the L.C.C. between 1889 and 1919. Edward Lyulph Stanley as a member of the London School Board from 1876 to 1904, supported attempts to extend the authority of the school boards into secondary and technical education and opposed aid to denominational schools. MacDonald was about to leave on a visit to South Africa.

'The English Parish' was published in the *Political Science Quarterly* in June and September 1902.

41 Grosvenor Road, Westminster

8.7.2

My own dearest

Your Sunday letter came this morning, showing that it is just two days post – hence I hope this will reach you on Thursday morning before you leave. On second thoughts, I doubt it, and I shall address it therefore to Sils Maria, though this means that you will not hear from me for a day or two, I suppose.

Yesterday at the T.E.B. meeting, as I informed you by postcard, we got through the grants to all four schools of the University, for one year subject to re-examination of the whole position next year. It went almost too successfully, as MacDonald found himself, by his own lack of alertness, shut out from an attack of the School, which I saw he had prepared. Leon and Stanley began by demurring mildly to the grants at all, now that we aided the University, and after an explanation from me, Stanley moved as an amendment or rider, to grant them this year, subject to a report on the whole position next year. I said this would do, and the Board passed it straight away. Then MacDonald jumped up and said he had wanted to say something on the London School of Economics, but he was clearly too late, and with a little grumble he subsided.

Apparently, his objection was going to be to the number of Fabians on the governing body: this I heard him expounding afterwards to others. But it is only his way of making one objection after another, and unless he opens it to me, I shall let him persist in that as it is a point on which the answer is good. He will, moreover, have at least two opportunities of raising the point at the Board this month. Then we shall be relieved of him for six months!

We must make a success of this session, without committing ourselves too deeply for the after future.

Maggie [Hobhouse] writes she would like to stay here for Monday–Wednesday next, 14th–16th, when she will be up servant-hunting; as Harriet declined the place after all (I should like Harriet's version!). So of course, I have invited her.

The heat is terrible, but my health is first rate; and I am merely uncomfortable and incapable of mental effort. It is quite right that you should be away, and I am glad for your sake, though I shall be glad when this month of worry is over.

Glad you find acquaintances about – no doubt there will be others, so look out for them.

*Political Science Quarterly* has come with our Parish article – first part, which looks well. Bank book shows good balance.

Goodbye dear one.

Sidney

405 PP  SIDNEY TO BEATRICE

Joseph Chamberlain had been badly cut in an accident to his cab on the way to his club.

41 Grosvenor Road, Westminster

9.7.2

My own dear one

I may as well write to you each day though you may possibly receive the letters all together, on your arrival; and be puzzled which to open first!

The heat continues, and I feel it very trying to be alone and worried, but I am in good health and do not sleep badly.

MacDonald has blown off steam by a long letter to Ward, as Chairman, asking that he may have an opportunity of saying what he has to say against the School. Ward told me this, but had not the letter by him. I gather that MacDonald admits that it is a good institution, but complains that it is too much the F.S., that Fabians are admitted at half fees (not explaining that the other half is paid us), and proposing that the T.E.B. should nominate three-fourths of the governing body. Ward made light of the letter to me. I explained to him and suggested he should promise Mac-Donald a full hearing at next T.E.B. meeting, when an occasion will present itself.

This is all right – we must have a full explanation – and it will enable me to refute calumnies. But it is a worry to have it in mind for the next fortnight and my B. not here to comfort me. I propose to be calm and frank and explicit; and to say the T.E.B. must make up its mind whether it wants such work done or not. I propose to say that we have striven constantly to make a governing body in which the City and the public, as well as the Board, would have confidence and we would welcome any members, but we begged for Conservatives, Moderates or Individualists – to redress any possible bias.

Chamberlain's accident (you will see it in the papers) is a nasty one, but he seems going on all right, and out of danger.

I shall spend next Sunday and perhaps Saturday night at Hewins', to discuss all the School business.

Morant writes that he thinks a Borough Councils Board quite out of the question now, but that nothing can be done about London until the autumn. The London secondary headmasters are writing to their M.P.s in favor of a modified T.E.B. and strongly against Borough Councils.

Goodbye dear one – I like to think of you in the good air and hills.

Sidney

### 406 PP  BEATRICE TO SIDNEY

The Webbs had recently learned that MacDonald was the source of the untrue gossip that both Sidney and Beatrice were receiving salaries from L.S.E. out of the grant from the L.C.C.

[Monte Generosa]

[10 July 1902]

We start this morning for Engadine and I send you this line of greeting.

Delighted at passing of grant, which is now safe if the School lives up to its opportunities and really *does* provide first rate training for administrative officials. Accountancy and railways ought to be especially seen to, and local government clerks provided with training and examinations. How glad Hewins will be. Be pleasant to J.R.M. if you get a chance: now that he has been beaten a friendly word might give him a chance of an explanation and a change of policy on his side and a new start when he comes back from S.A. It is a pity Pease cannot give him a fatherly talking to with regard to his somewhat shortsighted hostility to you!

BW

### 407 PP  SIDNEY TO BEATRICE

When Beatrice and Alys Russell arrived at Sils Maria they found Goldsworthy Lowes Dickinson (1862–1932) and his friend Nathaniel Wedd (1864–1940) staying there. Both were fellows of King's College, Cambridge, and associated later with the Bloomsbury group. Dickinson taught political science and Wedd was the classics tutor to E. M. Forster and encouraged him to write. Sidney was giving a dinner to L.S.E. staff. Halford J. Mackinder (1861–1947) was reader in

156

geography at Oxford and London universities: he became Director of the L.S.E. in 1903. He was noted for his strong imperialist opinions.

Emily Wordley was the maid at Grosvenor Road until the Webbs left London more than twenty years later.

Thomas Bailey Saunders (1860–1928) was the secretary to the Commissioners for the Reorganisation of the University of London 1898–1901. James Hope (1870–1949), later Lord Rankeillour, was Conservative M.P. for Sheffield. He was one of the main Catholic spokesmen on educational politics.

41 Grosvenor Road<br>
Westminster<br>
10.7.2

My own dearest

Your Monday's letter arrived late last night (Wednesday), and it was very sweet to me. I am glad to think you are resting and recuperating. Today you will be arriving at Sils Maria, after a pleasant journey, I hope. Tell Lowes Dickinson he is the only absentee from the School dinner tonight. Mackinder telegraphed *yesterday* that he would come, and Bowley wrote to same effect – after a week's silence. I had assumed they were abroad. We shall therefore be 13, if all are faithful: this will make a crowd, but Emily and Downs say they can manage – a waitress and Mrs Milton are coming.

Hewins is in good spirits and very well.

The weather keeps hot and thundery, with heavy showers, and I have a headache, a little, this morning with my worries and I did not sleep very well. MacDonald is causing me to 'worry'. I know this is irrational, as he is not really affecting anything, and at the moment is aiming only at increasing the Board's representation on the School Governors, which is not vital and would be harmless, unless he nominates himself – even this would be no more than annoyance. I will try to forget it until Monday week.

I am going off now to lunch with Bailey Saunders at the Savile Club, and then to see the Bishop of Islington at the Atheneum, and then *perhaps* to see James Hope M.P., the Roman Catholic, at the House, as to London education.

Maggie and I are to dine with the Courtneys on Tuesday. I have sent Georgie £2. Chamberlain has gone home (from Charing Cross Hospital) practically well. I mention this, because *you* don't always see things in the papers!

Goodbye dear one. I hope soon to hear from you from Sils Maria – perhaps a hasty postcard *en route* is on its way. You have now been away 9 nights, nearly half the time! Courage.

Sidney

Hotel Margna, Sils Baseglia,
Engadine
Friday evening [11 July 1902]

My own dearest

It was delightful to get your two letters on arrival here. We had the most delightful drive up the Maloja pass – starting at 6 and arriving here about 1.30 – the most beautiful valley I have ever seen – a real dream of vineyards, rocks, campenalla and snow mountains. We are delighted with our first impression of the Engadine with its lakes and meadows and fir-cones and endless walks on flat or hilly ground as you choose. The air is like champagne and all the fatigue and inertia has left me – one feels almost too excited and anxious to take exercise.

The Alpen Rose proved to be a large Hotel, chock full of Germans with all the rooms engaged after Monday. So after I had rested and had a cup of tea I strolled out to the neighbouring hamlet (both are tiny places on the Lake) and discovered an extremely comfortable Swiss pension – much more quiet and select than this. There were only 2 rooms there – one good one which with pension was 11f.50 a day and another queer-shaped room in the roof 9.50. Alys preferred economy and I preferred extra comfort so we move there tomorrow.

Alys wants to go back one day sooner so we shall be in London on Thursday afternoon 23rd. We shall leave this address on Tuesday morning (21st) sleep at *Hotel Via Mala Thusis* on Tuesday night and travel right through by Bâle to London arriving (I think) about 5 o'clock on Thursday afternoon. So post to me here until *Saturday* morning next and to Thusis on Monday morning.

It will be most satisfactory to have the whole position of the L.S. of E. cleared up definitely at the T.E.B. without seeming to be too much personally concerned. I should insist on making a somewhat lengthy explanation giving all the details as to starting the School by a group of friends who believed both in research and the discovery of new truth, and also in the education of officials; and remarking that these objects had a sort of indirect connection with faith in governmental action and public administration: then pointing out the sacrifices this group had made in money and time; and ending with a demonstration of the way the originators had done their best to draw in all schools of thought – how Hewins was *not* a Fabian and was a strong Churchman, how many of the lecturers were Conservatives and Individualists, how each new addition to the governing body had been belonging to other interests – ending with the Rothschilds and the general managers of the railways. I should end it all up by remarking that difference of opinion on social and economic questions was being rapidly merged in one cry for efficiency – that *we* were anxious for the efficiency of private enterprise (railway companies) and the Rothschilds were anxious for efficiency in municipal enterprise. That when we had by lectures and education made all officials efficient we might leave the future generations the task of deciding which form of organisation was *most* convenient. But my boy will know best what to say and do – but do be explicit and accept the occasion gratefully.

Darling, when you get this, it will be hardly more than a week before I am back by your side to love you – love is the best counsellor.

Ever your devoted

Beatrice

**409 PP** SIDNEY TO BEATRICE

41 Grosvenor Road, Westminster<br>12/7/2

My own dearest

Your Thursday's card came late Friday night, stating you were just starting. I cannot help thinking of you as on the journey, but you will be by now at Sils Maria, where you will find new and pleasant company. I do miss you. I am quite well, but I 'worry' about things, and am unhappy, and last night I could not sleep much. The weather continues hot and close, and I count the days till you come back.

I have made an analysis of the accounts of the School and Library from the beginning. Its income has been – for the whole 7 years – including everything – about £44,000. Of that, the T.E.B. will have contributed £10,160, or less than a quarter. Fees, sub-letting and sundries account for £4,000. The other £30,000 has come in subscriptions and donations. It is really marvellous.

Roughly, the £30,000 is made up of

| | |
|---:|---|
| £11,000 | Passmore Edwards |
| 5,000 | Rothschild |
| 3,500 | Charlotte Shaw |
| 3,500 | Hutchinson Trustees |
| 1,500 | Other Fabians |
| 5,500 | Other people |
| 30,000 | |

Which is pretty good. As I know (though no one else does) that J.R.M. will attack the finances on Monday week, I am putting these figures about, quietly, so that they may fill minds.

I have asked Organ to become one of the Governors, in the interests of insurance, taking the opportunity of telling him the above figures.

Now I am going off to spend tonight and tomorrow with Hewins settling the programme for next Session; and resting in a different atmosphere, so as not to be alone. But it will be nice to have my B. back again, in another 13 days – it is now nearly half way.

159

I grieve to think that I have so far done absolutely nothing at the Book – have never even looked at the MS. But I have had a great deal to think about, and it has necessarily had to wait until my B. can go at it again with me. We must let it take its own time – after all, a year more or less does not matter in such a case. I am afraid Shaw has not yet looked at the municipal chapter.

Goodbye dear one. I am glad to think of you at the charming Sils Maria.

Sidney

## 410 PP   BEATRICE TO SIDNEY

Frederick Canning Scott Schiller (1864–1937) was a Fellow of Corpus Christi College, Oxford, and a leading exponent of pragmatic philosophy.

Hotel Margna
[13 July 1902]

My own darling

By the time you get this it will be not much more than a week before we are together again and I am listening to all your news and consoling you in all your troubles and encouraging you in all your successes.

We are very happy here: the air is wonderfully invigorating – bitterly cold at night and tho' sunny and dry, not too warm in the day to get out with winter underclothing tho'. Our pension is a roomy private house and we have rooms in a strange kind of loft overlooking the lake – most original and attractive. There are only 5 or 6 other boarders – Germans – and very quiet – the food is passable for two females!

We had a pleasant walk and talk with Lowes Dickinson and Wedd and this afternoon we go to tea with the Schillers who have a house here. This is excellent for Alys and fills up the day without over much exertion. I got up only for a walk and we continue our reading every morning for 2 hours.

I am so glad you are energetic about London Education Bill – it is a great thing to create a consensus of opinion and pressure, it may just make the vital difference to the government's action.

I have written a long and I hope, a wise letter to Bertrand, giving him a detailed report about Alys and adding some indirectly worded advice. Her attitude to him is a good deal more sensible and more devoted than his to her. She continues to talk enthusiastically of the Whiteheads and their fine characteristics – especially of the lady's. I close this to catch the post in case we should not be back in time.

Your devoted wifey

Beatrice

## 411 PP   BEATRICE TO SIDNEY

Frederick Schiller was the younger son mentioned. Sir Frederick Lacy Robinson (1840–1911), a Moderate member of the L.C.C., had just ceased to be deputy chairman of the Inland Revenue Commission. Sir Melville Beachcroft was the chairman of the L.C.C. in 1909–10.

Sunday evening [?13 July 1902]

My own dearest Boy

I wrote you a shabby letter this afternoon because I would be certain of catching the post and we had the unexpected invitation to tea with the Schillers. Old Mrs Schiller – an able German woman – has taken a pleasant house here and has her two sons and Lowes Dickinson staying with her. The oldest is one of the 'friends' in L.D. meaning of the [?good] – an Oxford man settled in some business in India, cultivated, and pessimistic but extremely pleasant to talk to. The younger son is a Don at Oxford, heavy and common. Little Wedd from Cambridge is also constantly here.

This place is much better value from the point of view of health than Generosa, but not nearly so beautiful and attractive. Certainly that Italian plain with the Alps ending abruptly and the Lakes winding in and out of mountains and plain was extraordinarily charming and suggestive. The Swiss scenery is conventional and lacking in associations and all the buildings are ugly and commercial.

Monday

It has turned quite hot – and we are discarding all our winter clothes and feel no longer so keen for exercise!

The financial statement with regard to the School is excellent: if you have induced your friends to contribute £30,000 you and they have not been over-represented. Moreover the suggestion of the T.E.B. being so large a part of the governing body as J.R.M. proposes, would be a reversal of its own policy – it has never asked for more than a mere representation in the institutions it has aided – if it had to provide $\frac{1}{3}$ of the governing body of all the Schools of the University and the Polytechnics, it would be hard put to do it! I think you will be able to show that J.R.M. is asking for most exceptional treatment of the L.S. of E. Still, you are wise to end up with a request for Conservative Individualist and Moderate members and the representatives of the big business interests and to instance your invitation to Robinson, Barnes (and Longstaff and Beachcroft) and the general managers and Rothschild as a bona fide attempt to get it. Lord Rothschild as President is a good card to end up with. J.R.M. by his accusation of too many socialists in the governing body has given you a first-rate reason for opposing his nomination at any future time. *Rub that in*: it will help you in the future – we do not want him on the governing body. Preface your reply very carefully so as to get it as explicit, impressive without being too long or windy. It is worth while quashing J.R.M. once for all over this attack. It is a blessing that he has chosen that particular line – he has really delivered himself into your hands and I think made it impossible for himself to get on to the School governing body; which would be an infernal nuisance.

I don't believe that after this he will be much bother to you or the T.E.B. and he will have damaged himself with the members and the heads of the Progressive party.

Keep up your courage, dearest comrade, in less than a week now I shall be by your side. Remember to write to me Monday night a full account – addressed to Hotel Via Mala, Thusis. We shall be there Wednesday morning, leaving for Bâle sometime during the day to catch the night express.

Beatrice

### 412 PP SIDNEY TO BEATRICE

Arthur Balfour had just succeeded his uncle the Marquess of Salisbury as Prime Minister.

41 Grosvenor Road, Westminster
14.7.2

My own dearest

Very glad to hear that you are safely at Sils, and have found a comfortable hotel. And it is particularly good to hear that you will be home on Thursday, 24th. I will *try* to be at Charing Cross to meet you, but do not count on it. You will bring back a fund of strength and energy to fortify me, as I feel a bit tired and dispirited.

I spent Saturday night and Sunday with Hewins, who seems very well and happy – his three children flourishing. We talked about [the] School for several hours on end, arranging programmes and discussing details of all sorts. We shall have to draw in a quite fresh set of students, to reinforce our few score of really hard workers, and our few hundreds of lecture attenders. We propose to leave the fees for separate courses much as they now are, viz. 1/- or 9d a lecture. But as the full student will have the run of over 1,200 lectures(!), and will need to attend 270 to satisfy the University, we shall put the full fee at £10 a year, or £3.10.0 a term.

We can see our way to about 25 such students, paying £10 a year each, among scholarship holders alone, who will be forced to pay it – but this full number will not be reached for 3 years. It seems hard lines if we cannot get 75 more – and this would give us £1,000 in fees, without counting the desultory people, who are good for a few hundreds more; and the possibility of a few hundreds from the railway (to whom we intend to charge £1 per term).

Salisbury's resignation and Balfour's succession come at a smooth time, and will I think make no ripple of change.

I send you a 'Great Thoughts', with portrait of me, and a (faked-up) interview on London University. Note the praise of *your* article.

I hear that the Medicals entirely approve of it. But nothing has been said or done about it.

Now I am off to see the Bishop of Rochester about Education, and then to various committees, and then to Deptford to preside at a Salvation Army meeting. Goodbye dear one – it is now only 10 days till I meet you at Charing Cross.

Sidney

413 PP  BEATRICE TO SIDNEY

The Russells spent six months in Chelsea and then moved to a new house, Lower Copse, Bagley Wood, near Oxford. The Webbs stayed for nearly two months at Chipping Camden in the Cotswolds working on the Poor Law chapter of their local government book.

[?Hotel Margna]
Wednesday [?16 July 1902]

My own dearest

Don't *think* of coming to Charing Cross: Mrs Smith is meeting Alys with the fourwheeler and Alys says she will bring my portmanteau so that I shall come straight away with my bag and be at Grosvenor Road ready to receive you when you are free from the Senate. It is much pleasanter to meet in one's own house, cleaned and refreshed with a cup of tea, than in a crowded railway station.

I think the expedition has been a great success for Alys, tho' I hardly think she is out of the wood. Her nerves are in a very shaky condition and she has from time to time difficulty in not breaking down – either when she talks of Bertrand or herself or when any untoward agitation occurs like a dispute with an innkeeper (which we had at the Alpen Rose over the bill). I hardly think therefore that the notion of an American [?investigation] would be a wise proposal. They have made up their minds to take 14 Cheyne Walk for the winter and perhaps that will be the wisest compromise. We must try to see them often as I think we are a bond of union between them, Alys feeling that I am on her side and Bertrand really liking and respecting both of us. I am far more concerned about the man's mental conditions than about the woman's! Bertrand is going to have trouble with his own nature, of that I am convinced. His work is too abstract and inhuman to satisfy his somewhat uncontrolled emotional nature and strong tendency to introspection of his own and other's natures.

We drove right through the Engadine to Pontresina. St Moritz and all the intermediate places are most unattractive, compared either to this place or Pontresina. This little village is in the midst of a broad valley swept by winds both from Italy and the north; on either side of the narrow belt of land, on which it is built, there are shallow lakes skirted with fir woods, and easily-climbed snow mountains of undistinguished shapes. Pontresina is right in among mountains and glaciers with rushing torrents, rocks and pine-covered valleys. Yesterday was sultry and hot and Pontresina with its closed-up valley, and large hotels, did not compare favourably with this more open country. But I should imagine for winter it was far better – this would be almost intolerably exposed to the north wind. For summer I should certainly suggest Sils Maria as the ideal Engadine resort.

Would you like to ask anyone to dinner between the 24 and the 1st? (August) If so, do so now. It will be the last chance before the autumn session, which may decide the Education Bill.

Are you going to the Limps [Liberal Imperialists] dinner? As you have thrown in your lot with them it might be desirable to turn up. If so ask Haldane to get me a seat in the gallery: I should be interested to see the show.

I have been looking out on a magnificent thunder storm sweeping up the Maloja Pass – no doubt the result of the terrific heat they have been having in Italy – and thinking of my own dear boy and our meeting in another week. We will get on with the book when I come home and we will have a quiet happy time at Chipping Camden.

Your devoted wifey

Beatrice Webb

### 414 PP SIDNEY TO BEATRICE

James Henry Yoxall (1857–1925) was general secretary of the National Union of Teachers from 1892 to 1924 and a Liberal M.P. from 1895 to 1918. Thomas James Macnamara (1861–1931) was Liberal M.P. for North Camberwell from 1900 to 1924. Joseph Austen Chamberlain (1863–1937) was a Liberal Unionist M.P. from 1892 to 1937. In 1902 he was appointed Postmaster-General: he subsequently became Chancellor of the Exchequer and Foreign Secretary. The negotiation with the Commissioners of the 1851 Exhibition were for the land on which to build Imperial College.

41 Grosvenor Road, Westminster

16.7.2

My own dear darling

I am glad to think you are comfortable and with friends. Another 8 days, and we shall be together again. It is still terribly hot here, but I keep quite well – only a great weariness of spirit comes over me, and I feel inclined to throw it all up, and retire to a purely studious life. But you will comfort me, and this month of trials is half over.

Things do not go badly – on the contrary, they seem going well. We have various T.E.B. complications and difficulties, not specially concerning me, but we shall struggle through them somehow. The Council is slowly getting the idea that it will have to be the Education authority – Burns said it would inevitably be so – by a Bill next year. Yoxall whom I met accidentally asked me why London should not be included straight away. On the other hand Macnamara meeting me next day protested hotly against the idea which he said he found prevailing and declared it would be a breach of faith. I answered that *Yoxall* had propounded the idea to me the day before! and that there seemed something in it now that the School Board had voted suicide, and I didn't know what pledges the Government had given him (Macnamara).

I failed to see the Bishop of Rochester – he had forgotten his appointment, and now writes apologising. I am offering to go any morning.

Haldane telegraphed for me last night, and I saw him at the House late. (We walked up and down Westminster Hall, and Burns came past us, and dramatically warned me, jestingly, that on this spot Strafford was condemned for conspiring against the people!) Haldane's news was that he had at last arranged with Rosebery that he, the Duke and Balfour should sign a letter to the Exhibition Commissioners asking for the land. He wanted me to draft it, which of course I am doing. He thinks we shall get no forwarder until the autumn, but by that time there will be more money. He has got the Prince of Wales interested, and has sent him our article to read.

Collins, by the way, after not attending any meetings, refused to sign the T.E.B. report on Science and Industry; and will probably oppose it. We shall have trouble with him: though he is on friendly terms personally.

Last night at the Courtneys, all was friendly and pleasant, they not talking S. Africa. Leonard said he heard that Austen Chamberlain would certainly be given Cabinet Office – all other changes quite uncertain.

Coronation *is* to be Saturday 9 August – Parliament resumes *middle* of October.

Maggie goes home this afternoon. She has been very pleasant – as far as I can make out, she came up entirely to attend sales!

Goodbye now, dear one, come back full of love and *patience* for your loving but tired husband.

Sidney

415 PP BEATRICE TO SIDNEY

[?Hotel Margna]
Friday afternoon [18 July 1902]

My own dear Boy

Your letter this morning was full of news, but your feelings of weariness distresses me – perhaps you need a complete change. We will, or rather you shall, take it easy at Chipping Camden – but I would like to have you out here lying in the meadows in this high air. Really I think we ought to have arranged for you and Bertrand to have joined us and had a delightful fortnight all together. This morning I was up by ¼ past 5 o'clock and climbed some 1500 feet and lay in the sun looking over the whole of the Engadine valley. My description of the delights of the early morning air and sights has fired Alys with a desire to venture out tomorrow for a long excursion. The fine weather has returned – it is quite delicious – never too hot and yet dry and sunny. This afternoon I am resting and Alys has gone off with Wedd to coffee at a neighbouring village on the lake. Presently I shall saunter out when the evening lights are over lake and mountains, I need not be back so soon, as I have hot milk and eggs at 8 o'clock instead of table d'hote at 7. (I have kept the no breakfast plan and eat nothing before 12.30!)

Saturday morning

A rain storm, with thunder and lightning came on in the night and it is still pouring so the expedition is off and we shall spend the morning reading Seignobos instead. I find 2 hours reading aloud is good for Alys, as it passes the mornings and gives us something to talk about.

It will be Monday morning when you get this and you will be thinking of your little encounter with J.R.M. Don't exaggerate the importance of it but *use* the occasion for a real elucidation of your position towards the School and of the objects of the School – research and the production of a really efficient staff of officials for private and public enterprise. It is a great advantage to be able to convert fellow administrators to your own views of public policy and in the hurry scurry of administrative detail the opportunity of enlightening bodies such as the T.E.B. seldom occurs – or is at least seldom thoroughly desirable. But when anyone makes a systematic attack, the advantages, however great, of slipping things through with the minimum of opposition are thereby lost; and the alternative advantages of real intellectual conversion of the Board to a given policy should be accepted and made full use of it. So treat the Board to a little lecture on the subject – clear, calm and explicit. The tendency of the Board will, I think, be to push past the whole attack as they trust you and don't think much of J.R.M. But in spite of this, *use the opportunity*. Some day the attack may come in a more formidable form, and then it will be an advantage to have filled up their minds with the truth of the position.

If you have time to write me a letter Monday morning send it and *The Times* to Hotel Via Mala, Thusis; if posted early it will arrive by Tuesday evening – but send me a nice long account of the encounter by Monday evening post to Hotel Victoria, Basle – it will be a great pleasure to get it and the *Westminster* to read when we arrive there Wednesday evening. Our train does not leave Basle till 11.40 and we arrive (via Boulogne) at Charing Cross at 3.45 on Thursday. So if you are at the T.E.B. you might run over and we could go back to a cup of tea at Grosvenor Road before you go to the Senate, or even get a cup of tea at Charing Cross. Alys will bring all the luggage which will be together except my bundle of rags which we can carry.

My own darling Boy, how glad I shall be to see you.

Ever your devoted wifey<br>Beatrice Webb

Hotel Margna, Engadine
20 July 1902

My own dear Husband

I am posting this letter early tomorrow in the hope that it will reach you on the morning of our wedding day [23 July 1892] ten years ago when you and I united 'till death do us part'. We have had a wonderfully close comradeship, day and night, in work and in rest, in ways and ends – much more intimate and joyful and far more fruitful in output of thought and actions than either one of us expected, or had a right to expect. I see no reason why we should not look forward to another 20 or even 30 years of happiness and work. We must try to keep our health by temperance, and guard our minds against any vulgar striving for personal prominence, or disappointment that we do not get what we are really not aiming at. Fortunately you are not troubled with personal vanity or ambition and we both of us honestly prefer a modest existence of regular work and simple regimen. Still the temptation to play an *acknowledged part* is apt to come on one unawares – at least it is so with me – and with that desire come all the demons of competition and intrigue and humiliated vanity. So we must just go on loving one another, rejoicing in our extraordinary privilege of health and means, freedom to choose our own line of effort and above all our love for one another. Yet there is something sad in feeling that one's good fortune *is* so exceptional, and I confess to a certain background of permanent melancholy – the dark consciousness of the meaninglessness of the struggle for life on the miserable little planet. If only one had some good reason for faith in a wise and loving scheme of things; in which all the pain and strife would be ultimately merged and compensated in a greater good!

I shall come back much refreshed and ready I hope for a good spell of work. I fear I cannot look for any great vigour during the next few years and must be content to go slow. The last three weeks I have hardly once thought of local government or indeed of anything else intellectual. Alys and I have read Seignobos aloud to each other, but this I have done for her sake and quite mechanically, dreaming through my own thoughts or rather sensations of warmth and beauty and repose of body and mind. And I have not felt inclined for much physical exercise – perhaps because my monthly period is about due – a fortnight overdue! (This time it cannot be an inconsiderate arrival!) But barring a certain physical inertia I am remarkably free from minor ailments and if I wanted to use my brain I think I should find it clear and strong. It will be delightful to be back at our own little home and I feel eager to get to work again on the Poor Law Chapters. We will make a first-rate book before we have done.

This afternoon is the first time we have been kept in by a downpour of

167

rain: if it had come at the beginning of our holiday I should have been dispirited. But I have spent an hour in packing (there is a joy in putting all my things in to a cabin trunk for the last time before getting back to my boy!) and I am now contentedly sitting at my window watching the rain beating down on the Lake and the clouds covering and uncovering the mountains – wondering how my dear husband is spending Sunday afternoon, whether he has simply tucked himself up on the sofa, dozing and reading whilst Emily brings his tea, or whether he is talking to some casual visitor. When he gets this I hope he will be about and enjoying a very modest breakfast – I wonder whether he will already have remembered that this is the Wedding Day of himself and his old B? We will keep it tomorrow. By the way I shall want some dinner – a roast chicken, some nice stewed fruit, would be most acceptable.

Your devoted wifsey

Bee

### 417 PP  SIDNEY TO BEATRICE

James MacDonald was a prominent member of the Social Democratic Federation and secretary to the London Trades Council.

41 Grosvenor Road, Westminster

21.7.2

My own dearest

This is the last letter you will receive this journey: and it should reach you on the very anniversary of our wedding ten years ago. The new life that we began then has been a success for you – has it not? Whilst for me it has been a real new creation. I should not have been anything if you had not guided and inspired me. All that we have done since has been almost wholly due to your influence. By supreme good fortune, I won happiness as well as power. I shall never forget all that you have done for me. This is the first time that we have separated on our wedding day – the first time that I have written to you about it. And you will be spending it in the train. Yet you will be coming home – only three days more, and we shall be together.

Haldane writes that Mrs Wernher is coming to his dinner on Friday, 25th with her husband and Beit, and he wants *you* very much to come. I have told him you were already on the move, and I could not get an answer from you. But that I felt sure you *would* come. I have therefore written the Courtneys again *definitely* putting off their coming to us on that day, but hoping they would come Monday or Tuesday next week.

Spencer is still hunting up London Vestries, which take longer than he expected. He reports progress by letter about once a week. He proposes to go through their printed Annual Reports 1855–1888 which are mostly at the L.C.C.

Notice Balfour's speech on Saturday at Fulham, in today's (Monday) *Times* which I sent to Hotel Victoria. Towards the end he refers to the Education Bill, *and goes out of his way*, quite unnecessarily, to promise there shall be a Bill for London *on the same lines next session*. This is Whitmore's hand, and is his answer to me, I think.

On the other hand, it may be merely Balfour's way of trying what London will say about it, preparatory to including it in the autumn. If the Bill is really to be on the same lines, why not include it at once?

But I think it is an answer to me, or to those to whom I have talked. It is anyhow so much to the good.

I will put in another sheet this evening.

The attack did not come off! He [MacDonald] had made preparations, sent for balance sheets etc. – and when the item came, he asked whether any of it was for the Library fittings. On being informed that it was, he moved that the grant be referred back, on the ground that the Library was a separate institution, and that it had paid rent to the School(!); [No more! *inserted*] that it was not a 'College Library', and that he thought it very objectionable to make a grant for a Library which was a separate institution. *No one* seconded it – until Gregory did so. Then I made a brief explanation, taking the occasion to give the facts of the receipts of the School. The matter went to a vote, and only four voted for J.R.M. (Gregory, J.E. Macdonald, and *I think* Crooks).

We have various difficulties at the T.E.B. but they don't concern me in particular.

I am glad that this stile has been got over. It shows that there is no strength in the opposition.

Goodbye dear one.

Sidney

418 UI  SIDNEY WEBB TO H. G. WELLS

The idea of promoting 'national efficiency' was much in vogue, partly as a reaction to commercial competition, partly as a response to the growing military and naval power of Germany, and partly as a means of redressing the deficiencies in the physical wellbeing of the male population revealed by the rejection of many volunteers for the Boer War on medical grounds. The Webbs, mixing socially with a group which took the notion of an imperial destiny very seriously, saw an obvious link between the imperialist vision of a civilising mission abroad and their hopes of raising living standards and improving industrial capacity at home. On Beatrice's initiative they decided to form a dining club, calling it 'The Co-efficients' to reflect the notion set out by Sidney the previous year in 'Lord Rosebery's Escape from Houndsditch'. In this article Sidney had suggested that Rosebery might come forward as leader of 'a group of men of diverse temperaments and varied talents, imbued with a common faith and a common purpose, and eager to work out, and severally to expound, how each department of national life can be raised to its highest possible efficiency'.

In this select group Wells was to represent the literary interest, Haldane the law, Grey foreign policy, Hewins economics, Russell science, Reeves the colonies and Webb municipal affairs. The other members were H. J. Mackinder; Sir Clinton Dawkins (1859–1905) a financier and Morgan partner; a naval officer and Liberal M.P. named Carlyon Bellairs (1871–1955); Leopold Amery (1873–1955), who had distinguished himself as *The Times* war correspondent in South Africa and later became an eminent Tory politician; and Leopold James Maxse (1864–1932), a militant imperialist and Germanophobe, who edited the *National Review* from 1893 to 1932. The membership changed, both Shaw and Lord Milner belonging for a time, and the meetings were uneven in quality. Though the Webbs saw it as something like a shadow cabinet or 'brains trust' for a new party, standing for strong national leadership, military readiness and a raising of industrial and educational standards, the club was never much more than a forum for rather general after-dinner discussion and it declined within a few years.

Hulland House, Campden, Glos.
12.9.2

Dear Wells

The 'dining club' takes shape; and I am asked by the half a dozen who have nominated themselves the first members to invite you pressingly to join. It is proposed to restrict the number to ten or twelve; to arrange for about 8 dinners a year, mostly at a restaurant at the members' own expense; that the subject of all discussions should be 'the aims, policy and methods of Imperial Efficiency at home and abroad'; that the club is to be carefully kept unconnected with any person's name or party allegiance; and, in particular, it is not to be talked about – prematurely!

The first step is to meet at dinner at 41 Grosvenor Road on Thursday 6 *November* at 7.45 p.m., to discuss final membership and all arrangements. Kindly book this date at once, and fail not. We shall be a party of 8 or 9 and the project will be then finally shaped and decided.

Sidney Webb


419 NCUL SIDNEY WEBB TO WALTER RUNCIMAN

Walter Runciman (1870–1949) was a member of a wealthy shipowning family and a Liberal M.P. from 1899 to 1937, when he became Viscount Runciman.

41 Grosvenor Square, Westminster Embankment
9 November 1902

Dear Runciman

The London School of Economics is flattered by your enquiry for a secretary, but I find we have no one to recommend. There have been four requests to us to find able young men, for business or secretaryships within the last fortnight; and we are swept bare. Professor Hewins does not know the circumstances of all the students – most of them are in regular careers – and he has, for the moment, no more able young men ready to take situations, of whom he knows enough to recommend them.

He does not like to make the post known, because so long as it is a private matter, he feels he might be put in an awkward position if asked by some aspirant to recommend him to you.

If, however, you are driven to advertise, he would be glad to know, as we could put up a notice of it in the School, and possibly thereby lead some unknown genius to apply direct, who wants to change his work.

Yours

Sidney Webb

Mrs Webb begs me to add that we are asking a small party of progressively-minded people on Thursday, 27th November, to meet Sir Edward Grey; and we should be very glad if Mrs Runciman and you would come in about 9.30 p.m.

### 420 LSE   SIDNEY WEBB TO J. D. MCKILLOP

J. D. McKillop was secretary and librarian of L.S.E. in its first years. Sidney hoped that the British Library of Political Science would acquire the library of the economist H. S. Foxwell. Eventually it was purchased by the Goldsmiths' Company and presented to the University of London; a subsequent agreement led L.S.E. to concentrate on books published after 1850 while the University of London acquired those of earlier date.

41 Grosvenor Road, Westminster Embankment

14.11.2

Dear Mr McKillop

1) Enclosed seems just worth a letter, addressed to the Clerk of the South Metropolitan P.S. School District, whose address will be in Directory – say we would like to preserve a set of printed documents, and any M.S. Minute Books.

2) Prospects of getting the great collection of books *good* – but must be kept *quite secret*. Hence see that no English books on banking or ordinary economics are ordered.

Sidney Webb

Let me know if and when any reprint of *Calendar* is ordered – so that I may see for corrections.

### 421 PP   SIDNEY WEBB TO GRAHAM WALLAS

Wallas remained as a lecturer at the L.S.E., being appointed professor of political science in 1914. The School was now well-established with over five hundred students.

Haldane had been under strong criticism for refusing to follow the Liberal

Party's opposition to the Education Bill and engaging in private intrigues to assist the passage of this Conservative measure.

The Webbs were leading a very active social life, giving dinner parties to L.S.E. staff, to Moderate members of the L.C.C. and to their political associates among the Liberal Imperialist group. On one recent occasion John Burns, the Shaws, Wells and Asquith had been invited to meet Lady Elcho. They also dined out frequently in London political society,

For their New Year recess they went to Overstrand, near Sheringham in Norfolk, with the Shaws and the Wallases: Shaw read *Man and Superman* to the party. Beatrice liked the way in which Shaw's 'audacious genius' had tackled 'the most important of all questions, this breeding of the right sort of man'. (BWD 16 January 03) She noted that personal relations with Wallas remained 'affectionate and appreciative' but felt that 'frank co-operation' was impossible because the Webbs were 'prepared for a working agreement with the mammon of ecclesiasticism' while Wallas always saw 'the priest behind the policy'.

Sir Owen Roberts (1835–1915) was secretary to the Worshipful Company of Clothworkers.

41 Grosvenor Road, Westminster Embankment
30 November 1902

Dear Wallas

We are, at the F.S., going to propose resolutions on London Education, on *December 12* on the lines of an L.C.C. Committee, with strengthened local managers, some of which should be appointed by the Borough Councils.

The resolutions will be settled by Executive next Friday. I will try to send you early draft for your suggestions.

I *hear* that the London Unionist members are now prepared to accept an L.C.C. Committee (of sorts?); but cannot vouch for this. I believe that all the forces in the field, except the Borough Councils themselves, and your own Stanley–Macnamara–Headlam faction, are now in line for L.C.C.

About the Clerkship, Headlam said you were going to make the appointment at £1,400 a year. I can't help repeating my very strong feeling that the School Board will make a great mistake in doing this. Whatever good reasons there may be for it, it is one of those things which the public will not stand. I believe there will be a howl of execration. You will be compared to the M.B. [Metropolitan Board of] Works, which had to be summarily extinguished by hurrying on the appointed day. Of course I may be wrong – but *take advice*. Go to some cool outsider, like Asquith or Leonard Courtney or Sir Owen Roberts, and ask him how it will strike public opinion. If I am right in my forecast, such an appointment would seriously prejudice the influence of the new officer, and of the School Board members, *on the new body*; and thus really do considerable harm to the children in the schools. Do not throw away the feeling of sympathy for the School Board, and the Elementary side of things, which now exists, and which would be an asset to you in the future.

By the way, Headlam evidently hopes to induce *you*, after all, to stand for the post; and is going about saying so. Pray take some trouble to stop this, and make it quite clear that you won't. The mere rumour will do you harm – just as J. R. Macdonald's malicious statement that I was drawing a large salary from the London School of Economics did me harm, until I took pains to have it contradicted.

Sidney Webb

P.S. Do try to come to us at Sheringham.

41 Grosvenor Road, Westminster

3.12.1902

Dear Mr McKillop

Will you please let me know, before the 11th,

How many students have joined the Common Room?

How many have hired lockers? (and how many lockers we have in all?)

How many have joined the Union?

Sidney Webb

41 Grosvenor Road,

Westminster Embankment

4.12.2

Dear Wallas

I am really surprised and grieved that you should detect so much 'malice' in my draft resolutions. I am totally innocent of any such meanings as you imagine.

We have today done what we could to make clear that nothing of the sort is meant, and the [Fabian] Executive can further revise tomorrow if desired.

I quite realise that the mass of children, having to go to work at 14 or 15, can get no other day-schooling than what is provided in the 'primary' schools; and I want *all*, whether denominational or not, these to be made as perfect as possible. What the perfect curriculum for them is I don't assume to know – whatever it is decided to be by you and the other educationists, let us by all means have it. Then to that let us add the best possible evening opportunities by the best teachers, whether A or B I care not.

(As a mere matter of administration I should have thought that we

173

ought not to require or allow any teacher to teach more than so many hours in the week, whether day or evening (I don't know how many) – but this is another story.)

The children picked out to have both maintenance and 'higher education' paid for must always be a relatively small minority. But if there *is* any other way, by which higher education in day schools can be really made accessible to the children of the wage earners, than maintenance scholarships, I should be glad to hear of it.

Surely, we want *both*. I can hardly calculate which is the more valuable to the community.

What I want is

(a) The best possible primary schools available to all.

(b) The largest possible scholarship system.

(c) The best possible evening instruction.

(d) The most efficient secondary schools and University colleges.

(e) The most thorough provision for post-graduate study and research.

It is because the Bill *enables* the new authority to pay for all this, without limit, that I think it a great stride onward.

Sidney Webb

424 WP/BLPES   SIDNEY WEBB TO GRAHAM WALLAS

The sixth Marquess of Londonderry (1852–1915) was appointed President of the Board of Education in 1902. Sir William Anson, Unionist M.P. for the University of Oxford, was the Parliamentary Secretary to the Board.

The political manoeuvres over the creation of the Metropolitan Water Board were closely related to shifts in Conservative policy towards the L.C.C., which the Conservatives regarded as a hotbed of municipal socialism. They had for several years blocked an attempt by the L.C.C. to municipalise the private water companies serving London; their own solution was an independent public board with strong representation from the borough councils. There was strong Conservative support for organising the education service on a similar model. When the Liberals dropped their opposition to the Water Bill it seemed that the position of the L.C.C. Progressives had been weakened and that of the Conservatives who wished to withhold education from the L.C.C. had been correspondingly strengthened.

41 Grosvenor Road
Westminster Embankment
14.12.2

*Very private*

Dear Wallas

If you will act, and act promptly, and unquestioning, you can do a good stroke.

I have certain information that the London Bill is in very serious jeopardy. The collapse of the Liberal opposition to the Water Bill has greatly increased, all of a sudden, the power of those who want Borough Councils etc. Lord Londonderry is unconvinced, and can be impressed if you would go straight to see him, *tomorrow* Tuesday. It really is critical, as he leaves town in a day or two, and will have to make up his mind instantly. (Anson is of no use at this crisis.)

Now, will you trust my lead for once, and do as under. Go to see him tomorrow morning about noon. You will not then see him, but see Mr Davis his Private Secretary (whom you should not confide in, beyond that you very much want to see Lord L. that very day, as to London Education, *and that you will call again about 3 p.m.* on the chance of his being able to see you.) You must 'bluff' Davis to this extent, of *insisting* that you will so call, on the chance. Then come again about 3 p.m. and probably you will succeed.

Put to Lord L. two points, and two only. First, that *a* London Bill is imperatively urgent, and cannot be postponed without the gravest evil to education, and the gravest discontent among the ratepayers etc. Second, that there is no practical alternative (assuming ad hoc election out of the question) to an L.C.C. Committee; as Borough Councils are the devil, under the control of N.U.T. [National Union of Teachers], etc.

If you fail Tuesday, try Wednesday, but he may leave town early that morning. Do go, for Heaven's sake.

Sidney Webb

### 425 WSC   SIDNEY WEBB TO THE RT REV. ARCHIBALD ROBERTSON

Archibald Robertson (1853–1931) was Principal of King's College, London, and Vice-Chancellor of the University of London in 1902–03: he then became Bishop of Exeter. He had received some letters, one probably from Clara Collett, making complaints that the L.S.E. was under socialist influence; there may have been a connection between the letters and the attacks made by Ramsay Mac-Donald in the L.C.C. This letter, reproduced from a copy of the draft, was written by Webb as Chairman of the L.S.E.: a shorter letter, summarising the main points in publishable form, has been omitted.

Sir Arthur William Rücker (1848–1915) was a professor of physics and Principal of the University of London in 1902. Brian Hodgson (1800–94) was an Indian civil servant who became an expert on oriental languages and religions. He was a neighbour of the Potter family and his influence on Beatrice as a young girl, acknowledged in her autobiography, contributed she said to 'the sweeping away of my belief in the Christian Church and its Bible as the sole or even as the pre-eminent embodiment of the religious impulse in the mind of man'. (MA 86–88). It was possibly through Hodgson, who was a relative of Charlotte Payne-Townshend, that she became acquainted with the Webbs.

Dear Dr Robertson

Your letter telling me that allegations had been made against the London School of Economics was, in a sense, welcome to me, because I have been conscious, for some time past, of an atmosphere of slander; and when the statements come out into the open, they can be definitely contradicted. The School has, by its very success in doing what others thought impossible, aroused jealousy, if not enmity; and, of course, I have myself not failed to make enemies.

There are, I discover, other allegations, which I mention because you may hear of them. It has been said that I am making 'a good thing' out of it for myself, getting a handsome salary for my own lectures. It does not matter, but I may as well take the opportunity of stating that I have not received a penny from the School from the beginning – the whole of my lectures and teaching (and also such as have been given by my wife) having always been done gratuitously.

It has also been said that the School admits members of the Fabian Society at half fees. This is simply untrue. The School receives the full fees on all its students. What is true is that certain bodies – the Great Western Railway Coy., the Great Eastern Railway Coy., the Library Association and the Fabian Society – have, at one time or another, themselves offered their own members etc., special facilities or encouragement to attend – the body itself making up to the School the balance of fee.

With regard to the special point you ask me, I have written separately to you as Vice-Chancellor a letter which I hope you will show to Sir Arthur Rücker, and place on record, to be produced if required. It contains a detailed and categorical denial of the allegations made. But for your own information I now write more explicitly as to who were the founders of the School, where the money came from, and what were the ideas of the promoters. The people concerned would not like their names and bounties to be known or canvassed, so I have to give you this further information separately.

### Origin of the School

I think I must say that the School originated with my wife and myself. We had long been concerned at the lack of provision for (1) economic teaching and research, (2) training in administration, whether commercial or governmental. The London University Commissioners pointed out in their report in 1893 the need for creating in London an *Ecole Libre des Sciences Politiques*. The Economic Section of the British Association reported in 1894 strongly urging further provision. My wife and I discussed the matter for a long time, and resolved to make an attempt to start a centre of economic teaching and research in London on the lines of that in

Paris. During 1894–5 we gathered our resources together, opened up communications with friends, and we made a start in October 1895.

I remember going to Sir Owen Roberts in 1895 to try to interest him in the School, and telling him very candidly the ideas that I had on the subject. I said that, as he knew, I was a person of decided views, Radical and socialist, and that I wanted the policy that I believed in to prevail. But that I was also a profound believer in knowledge and science and truth. I thought that we were suffering much from lack of research in social matters, and that I wanted to promote it. I believed that research and new discoveries would prove some, at any rate, of my views of policy to be right, but that, if they proved the contrary I should count it all the more gain to have prevented error, and should cheerfully abandon my own policy. I think that is a fair attitude.

Now, the little group of people who really enabled the thing to get under weigh were the following:

(1) Miss Payne-Townshend, niece of Brian Hodgson the great oriental scholar, and an old friend of my wife's. She took to it from the first, and has been most generous; she must have given or spent on the School £5,000 during the first seven years; (2) Sir Hickman Bacon, Bart., a wealthy Lincolnshire landowner, who gave me a cheque whenever I asked for it, and must have subscribed £1,000 or more; (3) the Hon. Bertrand Russell, then a young Fellow of Trinity, who gave us nearly the whole proceeds of his fellowship, some £1,200 or more; (4) here I must name Hewins, whom I chose as the first Director of the School, and who did, at the start, all the organising and nearly all the teaching, throwing up all his Oxford and other connections, and putting inexhaustible energy and ability into the work of building up a new institution, for what was at first merely a nominal salary. (5) Finally, myself and my wife. We rendered some services and gave a little money, spending, however, much more, on anything that the School needed.

It is interesting to notice that, so far from these people being Socialists, they were of the most diverse opinions. Bacon was and is a Conservative – so was Miss Payne-Townshend, insofar as she had any politics at the time – Hewins was then as now a strong Imperialist and Churchman, and, at any rate, 'anti-Liberal' – Russell was, if anything, Liberal – and then there was myself.

Of course, we appealed to all and sundry for money, for the School itself, for scholarships, for a library, for a new building etc. etc. Politicians and economists of all shades of opinion subscribed and gradually money came in – Sir Owen Roberts got us £250 from the Clothworkers Company, and £250 from the City Parochial Trustees; eventually I got Mr Passmore Edwards to give £11,000, and others of our Governors got Lord Rothschild to give £5,000, and the Lord Mayor to preside at a Mansion House meeting, and so on. But those previously named were the people who really set the ball rolling, and were the spiritual and financial founders.

## The Hutchinson Trust

Part of the aid that I was able to bring the School – amounting, however, to not more than between three and four thousand pounds, out of the £45,000 which it received in its first seven years – was a series of donations from the Hutchinson Trustees. I want to tell you very candidly about this, because it is a matter which concerns me personally. Nearly nine years ago I got a letter from an unknown provincial solicitor to say that one Hutchinson, whom I had heard of but never seen, and never communicated with, had died, leaving all his property to me and four other trustees, designating me as the chairman of the trust, and leaving (by a quaint and almost illiterate will which he had drawn himself) to me, whom he had never seen, the widest discretion as to methods, but saying that the funds were to be applied 'to the propaganda and other purposes of the Fabian Society and its Socialism, and towards advancing its objects in any way that may seem advisable'. I had therefore to decide (for the other trustees largely accepted by views) what to do with this money. We might simply give it to the Fabian Society. We might retain the administration in our own hands and devote all of it to political propaganda. We might, on the other hand, devote some or all of it to any of the 'other purposes' of the Fabian Society, not being propaganda. Finally we might devote some or all of it to any other way of advancing the objects which that Society desired.

Rightly or wrongly, I decided that, if possible, I would neither hand it over to the Fabian Society, nor spend it in political propaganda. It has always been a special feature of the Fabian Society, since its establishment in 1884, that it has added to its work of propaganda, a great deal of purely educational work in economics. Moreover, it had for many years included among its functions, in its printed prospectuses, the promotion of economic investigation and research, and it has always done its best to foster this.

I therefore urged upon my co-trustees that it would be far better to devote some of the funds now at their disposal, not to propaganda of any sort, but to education, and, above all, to advancing one of the declared functions of the Fabian Society, namely economic investigation and research.

To make sure that this action was within our powers, we formally took the opinion of an eminent K.C., who said that it was. I also consulted the daughter and the principal friend of the testator, who both entirely approved. So cordially did they approve that the daughter thereupon made a will leaving her little fortune to me and my co-trustees, for general educational purposes; and the deceased's chief friend has, unsolicited, made donations to the London School of Economics. The daughter died almost immediately afterwards, and her will came into effect.

There are thus, *two* Hutchinson Trust funds, under different trusts, one wider than the other.

My co-trustees have so far agreed to my view that they decided to keep both trust funds in their own hands, and to use them as a fund from which to make donations from time to time to such societies as they chose, and to incur such other expenditure as they chose, within the very wide terms of their two trusts.

They have made repeated donations to the Fabian Society for its propaganda work, choosing to pay for that of really educational character. They have done various small things for education. They have directly paid for one or two little pieces of economic investigation. And they have made successive donations to the London School of Economics, for its own purposes, without stipulation or condition. They have still considerable funds in hand.

I venture to think that my own action in the matter as a Trustee was perfectly justified, and no one has demurred to it, but with this, of course, the University has nothing to do. The London School of Economics had to consider whether it would accept donations from the Hutchinson Trustees, as from any other body of trustees or other persons. The line which it has always taken has been to accept money from all sides, without question as to the donor's opinions, so long as the money was given bona fide for the declared purposes of the School, and without stipulation or condition affecting its impartiality or unfettered liberty of teaching and research. Thus, we have accepted two sums of money for investigation and teaching in the subject of liquor licensing – in one case from a brewer, and in the other case from a temperance society. We have had donations from monometallists and from bimetallists, free-traders and protectionists, individualists and collectivists. Frankly, the more diverse and varied are the views of our donors, the better I like it. But by far the largest gifts have, as a matter of fact, come from persons who are Unionist in politics, and individualistic, free-trading monometallists in economics.

After all, the test is in the character of the governing body of the School and its professors. No one can look at either the one or the other, without seeing that the aim has been to get the very best people irrespective of their political or economic views. And I believe that you, at any rate, will not need my personal assurance that the Governors, for their part, and Professor Hewins as Director, have all constantly maintained the School and its teaching and its investigations, on the lines of a University, with both *Lehrfreiheit* and *Lernfreiheit*, in their fullest and widest sense.

Yours very truly

Sidney Webb

In the afternoon of 26 January, before writing to Pease, Webb had seen Alfred Harmsworth (1865–1922), the owner of the *Daily Mail* and one of the founders of the new popular press. Webb had written to Harmsworth saying that he thought the Cabinet was about to come out for the 'Water Board' type of educational authority and suggesting that the *Daily Mail* should have the credit for making the government change its mind. When Harmsworth saw Webb he not only agreed to oppose the Tory scheme but also invited Webb to go each night to the *Daily Mail*, during the critical period, to supervise its news coverage and editorial comments on education matters. The 'attack' feared by Webb was the publication of the criticisms discussed in his letter to the Vice-Chancellor of London University.

41 Grosvenor Road,
Westminster Embankment
26.1.3

Dear Pease

I saw the great Editor, but found he knew nothing of any attack, and was very friendly! all the same, I believe my news; and I have probably merely got in ahead of the enemy.

I enclose my letter to the Vice-Chancellor for your guidance. I wrote him at the same time a private letter telling him frankly the whole story of the will, Miss Payne-Townshend etc. etc.

Yours

Sidney Webb

427 LSE  SIDNEY WEBB TO J. D. MCKILLOP

This letter, typical of a number dealing with L.S.E. business, shows the care which Webb took to promote the academic role and financial solvency of the School. No matter was too small for his attention in the critical early years.

41 Grosvenor Road, Westminster Embankment
2.2.3

Dear Mr McKillop

1) I shall need to draw that £500 in a week or so – hence please arrange the formalities as before.

2) As to Library classes, we shall get no special or extra grant, and must do it out of our £1,200. It may not be convenient for the T.E.B. to settle this until late. But we must proceed as if it were settled, just leaving a loophole in case it should not be granted, but referring to this as a *mere formality*.

If the Library Association leaders can promise the probability of 40 new students at 17/6; and 40 old students at 17/6, we could certainly double the courses.

Indeed, I think we must contemplate doing so – i.e. spending £60 on lectures, and making up again a course of 20 on Bibliography of Special Subjects (some repeated under new titles).

But we should *not* do this, unless there are students; and we must try to squeeze the L.A. to ensure enough students.

If all goes well, we can allot £10 or £20 for more reference books.

The L.A. must not ask for a grant to themselves. They won't get it, as it would be illegal.

Consult me further on any point.

Sidney Webb

## 428 FP  SIDNEY WEBB TO EDWARD PEASE

Webb's willingness to work privily with the Conservatives to secure an acceptable Education Bill was arousing much antagonism among Liberals, Progressives and Fabians. On 14 March Beatrice noted what she called 'the slump in Webbs' on the Progressive market. Sidney was criticised for his links with the Tories, for sacrificing primary to secondary education and for siding with the Anglicans against the Nonconformist interest. Dislike of the Conservative policy was making many Progressives blind to the potential of the L.C.C., which they controlled; they failed to see that Sidney's policy was to bring about a compromise in which the government would carry the substance of its educational policy – of which he broadly approved – while the L.C.C. gained by securing comprehensive powers over London education.

On 15 March Sidney was defeated in the Progressive caucus and lost his key position as chairman of the Technical Education Board. In noting this defeat Beatrice wrote: 'we are not in favour of ousting religion from the collective life of the state; we are not in favour of the cruder form of democracy. And we do believe in expenditure on services which will benefit other classes beside the working-class, and which will open the way to working-men to become fit to *govern*, not simply to represent their own class.'

On 25 March William Collins carried a resolution vaguely approving a directly-elected body as the educational authority for London (without naming the L.C.C.) and also attacking the government for subsidising voluntary schools. Feeling that this was a step forward Webb then went privately to see Balfour's private secretary and the Conservative Chief Whip. The best assurance he could get was a statement that the Cabinet would accept the L.C.C. as the educational authority if the L.C.C. in turn would cease to oppose the Bill. Even this assurance was shaky, for the Cabinet was divided: the Conservatives had just done badly at two bye-elections and they were concerned at the effect of the Nonconformist agitation on middle-class voters. To divert the government from any scheme to create an *ad hoc* educational authority Webb pointed out that direct elections would almost certainly ensure domination of such a body by Nonconformists and Radicals. On 27 March Beatrice concluded that the Cabinet felt so weak that its members would now 'throw themselves into the arms of the L.C.C. if this would give them "a rest from virulent opposition"'.

By the end of April the Progressives had begun to come round and the amended Bill gave the L.C.C. control of education, with some minor concessions to the borough councils on the appointment of school managers.

The Webbs thought that both the Progressives and the Moderates were stale and weary of the controversy: by the middle of the summer Beatrice was wondering whether there was any chance that they could 'produce a new party . . . held together by a broad, catholic and progressive educational policy'. (BWD 15 June 03)

Sidney's letter to London Fabians on the Education Bill was widely circulated.

41 Grosvenor Road, Westminster Embankment

5.2.3

Dear Pease

I cannot be at Executive tomorrow, as I have to go to Oxford that afternoon to speak (please note to my credit).

As to Education Bill my information is that the Cabinet is overwhelmingly in favour of the 'Water Board' plan, which would be most disastrous. But a fight is being made against it in the Cabinet, and the combination of forces against it outside is very strong – all grades of education, the church and the R.C.'s, all Liberals and Progressives, will unite against it – about $\frac{1}{3}$ of the London Conservative M.P.'s, are against it also.

It may yet be stopped – either now or later – but the moment is *now*, before the Government are publicly committed; and the method is to put pressure on the London Conservative M.P.'s, who are wobbling. Will the Executive authorise some such letter to London Fabians as the enclosed? Every *hour* is important.

Yours

Sidney Webb

### 429 FP SIDNEY WEBB TO EDWARD PEASE

41 Grosvenor Road, Westminster Embankment

13.2.3

Dear Pease

I am sorry I can't be at Executive as I have an important University Committee at South Kensington.

As regards London Education Bill, I have no news, but am a little more hopeful. The Unionist M.P.s are still obdurate and they are to meet immediately *after* Parliament meets, to discuss it formally – this having been put off as long as possible by the friends of L.C.C. to allow time for conversions. So writing to them is still good business, and the main thing to be done.

I think the clergy are being adequately looked after and stoked up by their own leaders.

I doubt whether we can do any more.

Yours

Sidney Webb

County Hall, Spring Gardens,
London, s.w.
8.4.3

Dear Mr McKillop

Here are three useful (though partial) bibliographies, which I have got for you.

I want to suggest that we ought (? in the summer holidays) to have a complete *Inventory* of all the furniture, fittings etc. in the School building. My idea is that we ought to take the opportunity of instructing all our Library Assistants in the art of making an inventory! – by getting them to do it. Could we (1) get the (volunteer?) services of some one who can put the professional touch to the commonsense business of making an inventory; (2) a cheap set of the professional style of note books.

Then I would suggest a brief preliminary exposition of 'what to do'; and then put the young women on, one to each room. Then let each *revise* another's room. Finally, a general revision and explanation.

It should be explained at the outset that making an Inventory is a necessary part of a Librarian's duty! Think of this.

Sidney Webb


431 FP   SIDNEY WEBB TO EDWARD PEASE

Joseph Chamberlain had returned from a visit to South Africa and come out strongly for a system of fiscal preferences as a means to imperial unity. On 15 May 1903 in a speech at Birmingham he abandoned Free Trade – a position he repeated in Parliament on 28 May. Though he had not yet committed himself to a thoroughgoing Protectionist position his rejection of Free Trade put an end to any prospect of a new alignment of Liberal Unionists and Liberal Imperialists: even if there had not been personal antagonism between Chamberlain and Rosebery the latter and his supporters could not abandon Free Trade. Chamberlain's decision, moreover, weakened the Balfour government, for several of its Liberal Unionist members were also unwilling to embrace any form of Protection.

41 Grosvenor Road,
Westminster Embankment
25.3.3

Dear Pease

(1) Yes: we had a squeeze, and just managed it, by 32 to 20, (inside the Party). The danger is not yet past, and I don't feel sure what is going to be the end result, with so weak a government. We are in for an era of crude upheaval, which will construct nothing, and lead to four-fold reaction. But I don't intend to budge, and I hope the F.S. will have the courage to hold on, and keep the faith.

I am a bit tired out, however.

(2) Glad to hear financial success – try to get down to balance clear.

Yours

Sidney

till 15 June   c/o Mr Hoddinott, Aston Magna,
Moreton-in-the-Marsh
30/5/3

Dear Pease

(1) Cheque signed herewith.

(2) Thanks for signing cheques. Miss M. should have put them before me.

(3) The speeches in the House on Thursday mean, to my thinking, a very early dissolution, probably before harvest, (middle of July), or at any rate October – a great Free Trade controversy; and probably a Liberal victory of some sort, though the Liberals will need to carry two out of three of all the British seats outside London to balance the Conservatives plus Irish.

I am disposed to stand by and say nothing myself, in view of the difficulties of my position over Education Bill etc. But I am dead against taxes on food; and also against protective tariffs – and I think the artisan in the North and the rural laborer will be also. (My impression is that it will hardly affect the political balance in London, where the Liberals will win half-a-dozen seats only, and win these anyhow.)

All the same I think Chamberlain (as with Old Age Pensions) has hit on a fundamentally right *idea*, which he ignorantly and rashly spoils by plunging on an impracticable *device*.

Ought we not to have a (private) members meeting early in July to consider it? We need not pass resolutions. If desired, I would '*open a discussion*' on 'The Fiscal Policy of the Empire'.

Yours truly

Sidney Webb

I have to run up for the day and night, Tuesday 9th June: so could consult then if desired.

Russell subsequently claimed that the cause of his resignation was a speech by Sir Edward Grey at a Co-efficient dinner advocating the Anglo-French alliance. Russell argued that this policy would inevitably lead to a European war. Moreover, after originally supporting the Boer War, Russell had become increasingly anti-imperialist, telling Wells that he would rather wreck the Empire than sacrifice freedom.

Aston Magna
[?late May] 1903
(we return on the 17th June)

My dear Bertrand

We have felt that you were out of sympathy with the Co-efficients and are prepared for your resignation. I doubt whether such a discussion society is of much value unless your business in life is mainly political – as it is with the majority of the C-E – in that case divergence of view is stimulating and enables one to understand one's opponents' objections. Sidney does not agree with the Protectionism of Maxse and Amery – but is in sympathy with the desirability of making the Empire the 'Unit of Consideration' rather than the 40 millions in this Island.

When shall we see you and Alys again? Is there any chance of your being down in June? Do let us know if you are.

We are having a lovely time here and getting on slowly but surely with the work.

Ever yours

Beatrice Webb

### 434 SUL  SIDNEY WEBB TO W. A. S. HEWINS

Balfour, opposed to an early election, chose to treat tariffs as an 'open question' within his Cabinet in the same way as the Tories had once handled the disputed issue of Catholic emancipation. In September he published his own compromise position in *Economic Notes on Insular Free Trade*, opposing taxes on food but proposing to use tariffs as a means of securing reciprocal concessions. In mid-September the Cabinet broke up, both Chamberlain and some committed Free Traders – such as the Duke of Devonshire – resigning from the government. Chamberlain then launched his own Tariff Reform campaign. The Conservatives remained divided, but the issue of Free Trade began to rally the Liberals, Asquith and other 'Limps' taking the orthodox party line on this issue.

c/o Mr Hoddinott
Aston Magna, Moreton-in-Marsh
30/5/3

Dear Hewins

I have now read Chamberlain's and Balfour's speeches – which, to my mind, mean an almost immediate dissolution i.e. middle of July, or at latest October; a great Free Trade controversy; and in all probability a Liberal victory of some sort, though they will need to balance the Conservative plus Irish. The irruption of this new steamboat into political waters will make a swell that is calculated to affect the smallest cockboat, and we must be careful. I intend myself to stand by and say nothing as to the Tariff issue except that I am against taxes on food.

I venture to suggest that it will be important to keep the School out of the stormy controversy that is going to arise; and as you and I are already both 'suspect' on the subject of Imperial protection, the less we say the better. The L.C.C. will be, and remain, Free Trade and Nonconformist Liberal.

Chamberlain, as usual, is going to spoil a good idea by rash and reckless adoption of an impossible device for carrying it out – just as he did about Old Age Pensions. It makes for the adoption of the idea by others, ten years hence; but fails at the outset.

Sidney Webb

### 435 PP  BEATRICE WEBB TO MARY PLAYNE

Before the Webbs left London for the summer Sidney was appointed to a Royal Commission on trade union law. The Trades Union Congress decided to boycott it. As the government did not want an early report the Commission, Beatrice said, 'went to sleep for a couple of years'. (OP 267) She hoped that it would have 'the incidental advantage of bringing us again into communication with the trade union world'. It did not do so. The Webbs had drifted so far into the shadow of the Balfour government that Sidney's appointment – together with a T.U.C. boycott of the Commission – reduced rather than improved his credit with the trade unions.

Sidney's relations with his own party were not much better. Beatrice commented on the Progressives whom she entertained that there was 'a good deal of rotten stuff; the rest upright and reasonable but coarse-grained in intellect and character. Even the best of them are a good deal below the standard of our intimate associates . . . and the ordinary Progressive member is either a bounder, a narrow-minded fanatic, or a mere piece of putty.' (BWD 8 July 03) A similar judgement was implicit in her description on 15 June of the means whereby she and Sidney proposed to promote their political ends. These were to be advanced not by 'stumping London' but by 'marshalling distinct forces, surely but silently . . . We have to aim at having the Church, the Catholics and the Moderates definitely working for the new policy . . . We hope to remain throughout on the Progressive side; but, if circumstances compelled, Sidney would come out in the open as the avowed organiser of a new party.'

This and some similar entries in Beatrice's diary not only show how far the Webbs had moved from the Radical wing of the Liberals and the growing labour movement: they also provide the essential key to the personal and political motives which drove the Webbs increasingly towards an attempt to create their own organisation during the next eight years. For a variety of reasons they misread the emerging pattern of British politics and, by a series of miscalculations, diminished their own potential influence over the development of policy and events.

Aston Magna, Moreton-in-Marsh,<br>Glos.<br>[June 1903]

Dearest Mary

We like our quarters immensely and shall look forward to seeing you here in August – it is a comfortable farmhouse and there is a nice room for you and we can get one 'out' for Arthur. The country is lovely and everything excellent.

It will be exciting to meet in a month or so – we think the adoption of Protection means a 'debacle' for the Conservatives – a small Liberal majority over Conservatives and nationalists. That is perhaps what B. and C. [Balfour and Chamberlain] are praying for, as they want to go out of office for a year or two and perhaps while in opposition they will elaborate a wiser scheme of an Imperial commercial policy than Preferential tariffs. Sidney thinks he could provide them with one! The Liberal party will come back on the stale old Liberal doctrines and will be powerless as a government. I only hope it won't be strong enough to repeal the Education Act for London before it comes into operation: that of course is a danger. We shall try to come to terms with Macnamara during the autumn.

Could you send me the recipe for Ice soufflé and for Ice pudding with hot sauce, also let me know the exact proportion of Ice and freezing salt for the Rice. I should be so grateful. I am entertaining my Progressives steadily. I am glad to say Sidney was re-elected to their little party committee which shows that the rank and file are not estranged. But we shall have to be careful the next months: one can't get one's way without arousing opposition.

Ever yours affectionately<br>Beatrice Webb

### 436 PP BEATRICE WEBB TO MARY PLAYNE

In this period of hectic entertaining Webb was worried because Hewins had become a passionate supporter of Chamberlain, writing a scarcely anonymous series of articles for *The Times* and resigning from the National Liberal Club. To maintain the public neutrality of the L.S.E. Webb found it tactically desirable to wave the Free Trade flag. Sir Michael Hicks-Beach (1837–1916) had been Chancellor of the Exchequer until 1902. After an early start in soldiering and journalism Winston Churchill (1874–1965) contested Oldham as a Conservative in 1899, and was elected in 1900. He switched to the Liberals in 1904 and was elected for N.W. Manchester in 1906 as a Liberal. He was Under-Secretary for the Colonies and promoted to be President of the Board of Trade in 1908. He lost the bye-election which followed his entry into the Cabinet, then won Dundee for which he sat as a Liberal until 1918. He then became a Coalition Liberal, a Constitutionalist and finally, in 1931, a Conservative again.

41 Grosvenor Road<br>[9 July 1903]

Dearest Mary

I had an amusing dinner at Maggie's yesterday – free trade Tories – Sir M. H. Beach, Winston Churchill, a Peer and some others, She put me between W.C. and Bryce. The former is a self-conscious and bumptious person with a certain personal magnetism, restless, shallow in knowledge, reactionary in opinions, but with courage and originality – more the American speculator in type than the English aristocrat. He talked the whole time of his electioneering and himself and seemed interested in other matters to a very minor degree. Sir M. H. Beach was dignified and calm as usual, but rather chuckling at being 'in revolt'.

We have been living in a veritable whirl – we had 25 persons to dinner or lunch last week, having others to see us in the afternoons. You see we launched the 'Charlottenburg Scheme' successfully in the Press and I hope the L.C.C. will be accommodating and that the City Magnates will 'pay up'. The Trustees are delaying appointing a secretary, but if and when they do, it will be Wellington. (Private)

I have a large gathering this evening of Progressives and students, L.C.C. and others. On the 21st (Tuesday week) I have the Prime Minister dining here and, to meet him, the Hubert Parrys, Charles Booths, Dean of Westminster, Sir J. W. Barry (a great engineer) and Haldane. It would be very kind if you could spare me some select flowers – I will send a P.C. nearer the time on the chance of it. He – the P.M. – seemed delighted to come.

We had a lovely party last week – Gorst, Alfred [Cripps], Beatrice Chamberlain, the Bishop of Rochester and wife, Sidney Low, (the leader writer on the *Standard* who is keeping at Free Trade) and Walter Hobhouse – the Editor of *The Guardian* – and Mr Crompton – the whole time, at, and after dinner, being a running discussion and chat about Free Trade and Protection. Alfred is going strong Chamberlainite, and had had the great man to dine the night before to meet 20 waverers – Gorst is vigorous Free Trade and means fighting, the Bishop a sentimental free trader, Low a reactionary old-fashioned Whig but an expert and cynical journalist. Sidney and I kept the balance in the Centre – a position in which we seemed determined to find ourselves in every issue that turns up. The next evening we had the Munro-Fergusons and a party of Liberals – L.C.C. Progressives and Limps, who also talked Free Trade and Protection – in fact you cannot turn round in any gathering without hearing the word Tariff echoed and re-echoed. It is somewhat tiresome.

Meanwhile we struggle on most mornings with our big task – at least I do, Sidney is distracted with other work. We shall be heartily glad to get into the country on the 28th.

We are expecting you and Arthur and can put you both up at Aston Magna. When will you come? You must bring your bicycles to run over to Campden [*illegible*] – it will be so pleasant.

Ever yours affectionately

Beatrice Webb

437 PP  BEATRICE WEBB TO MARY PLAYNE

Beatrice's suggestion that Balfour confused Charles Booth with William Booth (1829–1912), the founder of the Salvation Army, is presumably ironic. The grant to support the 'Charlottenburg' scheme was pushed through the L.C.C. with Rosebery's support and in the face of an attack by Ramsay MacDonald.

The 'beautiful Duchess' was possibly Millicent, Duchess of Sutherland, author, social worker and prominent hostess.

On 24 July Beatrice wondered rather wearily 'whether all this manipulating activity is worth while; whether one would not do just as much by cutting the whole business of human intercourse and devoting oneself to thinking and writing one's thoughts . . . with fewer liabilities for contraventions against personal dignity, veracity and kindliness'. (BWD)

41 Grosvenor Road, Westminster Embankment
[?26 July 1903]

Dearest Mary

Ever so many thanks for the lovely roses, carnations and sweet peas and grapes – a delicious combination exactly right for my peculiar style!

Our party went off brilliantly – the P.M. stayed until after 10 inspite of urgent messages from the Whips. He is certainly a fascinating person – extraordinarily graceful in mind and manner. But what a strange being to be at the head of a nation's affairs – regarding all questions as unsettled problems to be debated academic-wise, and cordially detesting social and economic issues as ugly and irrelevant to the life of a distinguished Soul. I put Charles Booth next him, but I am convinced he had never heard his name and was probably agreeably surprised that a 'Salvationist' could be so pleasantly unsettled in his opinions as Charlie seemed to be. On the other hand he knew every line of G.B.S.'s plays and regarded him as the 'first man of letters' of the present generation. As for the Tariff he was quite ready to talk about it – if only you would not expect him to think it out or listen to facts and figures. 'I am beginning to fear that even the Tariff won't turn us out' he said with graceful weariness. Philosophy, literature, music and the study of distinguished souls – especially if they happen to be clothed as charming women – refreshed with golf and motoring – are Balfour's real interests and tastes. I doubt whether even foreign politics really excite him and all the machinery for internal administration is a maze of complicated boredom.

You see we got the L.C.C. £20,000 a year grant and Sidney can feel that he has executed his part of the bargain. It will be delightful to get away and rest and get on with our work.

Do let me know exactly when you and Arthur will come to Aston Magna (Moreton-in-Marsh). It will be delightful having you.

The 'beautiful Duchess' turned up this afternoon – not so beautiful but much simpler than I expected.

Ever yours affectionately
Beatrice Webb

Forgive the mess. [ink-spots on pages]

Charles Gore (1853–1932), Bishop of Worcester 1902–05, was an Anglo-Catholic who had founded the Community of the Resurrection at Mirfield in 1898. He was active in the Christian Social Union and later a strong supporter of the Workers' Educational Association. The Cambridge professor was Sir Michael Foster, the Liberal Unionist M.P. for the University of London 1900–06 who was an opponent of the Education Act. Changing to the Liberal Party he lost his seat in 1906. Algernon Freeman-Mitford (1837–1916) was created Lord Redesdale in 1902. He had served in the diplomatic corps before becoming a Conservative M.P. and retiring to Batsford Park, Gloucestershire. Charles Robert Ashbee (1863–1942) was an architect and craftsman who founded the Guild of Handicraft in 1888 and removed its workshops to Chipping Campden in 1902. Beatrice Stella Campbell (1865–1940), known as 'Mrs Pat', was the actress with whom Shaw conducted a notable flirtatious correspondence.

At Aston Magna Beatrice felt so exhausted that she struggled to read one book on psychology while Sidney rushed through ten volumes on local government. She noted that his attitude to work was that of a natural examinee: 'unless he is downright ill he is never without a book or a pen in his hand . . . he cannot think, without reading or writing . . . if he has nothing before him more absorbing he finds himself counting the lines or spots on some object . . . If I would let him, he would read through meal times'. (BWD August 03)

Bishop's House, Worcester<br>25 Aug. 1903

My dear Kate

There is an hour before dinner. I am alone in this bachelor establishment, Sidney having gone for a walk with our host. Have you ever met Dr Gore? He is a saintly ecclesiastic of extremely simple heart – has put up his 'Palace' for sale and taken a large plain villa on the outskirts of the town – a delightfully open-minded and single-hearted man without guile or any great force of character or subtlety of mind. What a contrast to my old friend Dr Creighton with whom I used to stay here, when he was Canon. It is just 16 years ago about this time in August that I first came to Worcester and made friends with him and his family. I often think of him now – it is strange how deeply I felt his death – far more deeply than any death I have yet experienced. It seemed like Light going out of the World – and yet his nature was so complicated, so very far from transparently good. Perhaps it was just this sense of perpetual conflict between good and evil – with the good and the true always conquering, that gave him his extraordinary and enduring influence and makes one think of his spirit as still existing. But I did not mean to write about him!

The Playnes left us this morning in pouring rain – it was so pleasant having them for a couple of days in our little lodgings and I think they enjoyed themselves. S. has been hard at work – in fact we have both been hard at work – at the *XIX Century* article on London Education for October – he has definitely planted himself down on a Policy and it remains to be seen how his fellow Progressives receive it. Incidentally, writing the article has enabled him to master much of the detail of the School Board business and we have been deep in minutes and reports etc., making up his mind as to possible devolution to the Local Committee of Management. (This he will keep out of the article for future use.) What is surprising is the way the leading School Board members went out of their way to 'flout' the Department – fatuous it seems from the standpoint of an old civil servant who realises how much can be done by a little friendly chat and how little can be accomplished by bullying official letters. However when people's tempers are up it is difficult to be sensible – but with the checkmating policy of the School Board and the Education Department no wonder everything came to a standstill – higher grade schools, evening classes and teacher's training – even the Pupil Teacher's centres had been given their [?quietus] by a new 'Order' – excellent in itself but hopelessly out of gear with the School Board system of pupil teacher training. But enough of our Subject!

We lunched with the Elchos the other day (a lovely 13-mile ride across the Cotswolds) and met Mr Balfour. He again impressed me as the strangest mortal to be Prime Minister – a most attractive 'private gentleman' but with his mind really occupied in all the wrong things. However, he is delightful to talk to, because of the quality of irresponsible intellectual adventure in this readyness to listen to anyone about anything so long as the subject has no connection with anything of consequence. There was a clever Cambridge Professor of Physiology and the gentlemen all had a talk together about the degeneracy of the race whilst Lady Elcho and I were gossiping upstairs (the Professor apparently mentioned that we are being ruined by bad milk and syphilis!).

On Sunday we took the Playnes to lunch with Lord Redesdale – our near neighbour. It is a somewhat gloomy household, with the mother too mad to be kept at home and the father, an attractive autocrat, absorbed in his hobbies and disinclined to take his daughters out or invite anyone to see them. I was sorry for the girls; they looked so dreary and solitary in their great house in its beautiful garden – knowing no one, neither the gentry, nor the farmers nor the labourers – not even the clergyman's wife. They are coming to tea with me tomorrow to meet the Ashbees and Hewins and Beatrice Chamberlain (who is coming to discuss school management with Sidney.) Just before we left we had a telegram from Lady Elcho asking whether she might bring Mrs Pat Campbell to tea – so we shall be a large mixed party in our little pasture!

We pass through London on September 2nd and join the Russells in Normandy for a fortnight or 3 weeks cycling before settling into work. When do you come home? Best love to Lallie

Ever yours affectionately  B. Webb

Did Leonard get his portmanteau? Will you send this letter to Rosie?

*The London Education Act 1903: How to Make the Best Of It* was Fabian Tract 117, written by Webb and published early in 1904. Webb's position had become politically precarious. He was more in sympathy with the L.C.C. Moderates than with his own party, within which a strong faction distrusted and opposed him. In this situation, which could easily have led to his exclusion from the L.C.C. and the loss of his base in London politics, he and Beatrice were anxious lest the 1904 L.C.C. election should produce a large Progressive majority dominated by the Nonconformists. They hoped for a narrow win for the Progressives or, preferably, a small Moderate majority.

The Webbs, however, could not openly declare their hand. Having come to the idea of establishing a 'national minimum' as the social foundation upon which 'all forms of struggling upward' could be encouraged, they were devising specific policies which exemplified that principle. Sidney's 'scholarship ladder' in London was a case in point. 'We have in fact no party ties. It is open to us to use either or both parties', Beatrice remarked. (BWD 25 July 03) A few months later she revealed how far this form of permeation led the Webbs to work both sides of the street, for she covertly provided the Conservatives with a list of the Progressives who had most strongly opposed the Education Act and whom the Webbs would like to see defeated. These were, she wrote, 'the rotten part of the Progressive Party which would be best lopped off. Took care not to compromise Sidney'. (BWD 3 November 03) By an accident of the registration regulations Ramsay MacDonald found himself disqualified from standing at the coming election: this was, Beatrice noted on 18 November, 'an iniquitous flaw in the law, but not for us an ill wind'.

George Turner reviewed a book on *Rural England* by T. Rider Haggard in *Fabian News* for September 1903.

to 2 September   c/o Mr Hoddinott, Aston Magna,
Moreton-in-Marsh
28.8.3

Dear Pease

(1) Thanks for letter and news. We stay here to Wednesday and then return home for two days; starting Friday night for a fortnight's trip to Normandy etc. – first to the Bertrand Russells who are at Beaumont le Roger.

(2) As regards London Education tract, we will consider in October. In confidence at present, I may say that I have done an article for the *19th Century* for October 'enthusing' largely over the possible developments of Education in London – so as to get people's ideas out of the Elementary and Technical ruts, towards a complete system. I don't offer this as a tract, because I want to republish it in a slight volume, largely to give away in Deptford. But it may help the F.S. to a tract.

There is grave risk of the Progressives being captured by the Nonconformists; and all Progressive seats will be endangered, mine among others. Unless we can keep the Progressives sane, there will be a Moderate majority.

(3) *Please* induce Turner not to bring the School into his review at all. It might stand as I have corrected it, without harm, if you like.

Yours

Sidney Webb

440 WP/BLPES  SIDNEY WEBB TO GRAHAM WALLAS

*The History of Liquor Licensing in England, Principally from 1700 to 1830* was published by Longmans in 1903.

Some local authorities were holding out against the 1902 Education Act. In April 1904 the Education (Local Authorities Default) Bill was introduced to bring the recalcitrants into line. Though individuals continued the 'rate war' as a protest against public support of voluntary schools the resisting authorities then agreed to act.

Wallas was proposing to contest Haggerston in East London at the next L.C.C. election.

41 Grosvenor Road, Westminster Embankment<br>4.9.3

Dear Wallas

I suppose you are holiday-making somewhere. We are just back from our 5 weeks in the tiny Cotswold village, where we have been hard at work – preparing for separate publication a little *History of Liquor Licensing in England* – and diligently studying London Education. There is no doubt that we can make a very fine thing of it, with the enlarged powers, the extent of which no one yet adequately realises – if only the politicians and religionists and anti-religionists will let us. I have made up my mind that, *coûte que coûte*, I am going to fight this through as an educationist, having a 'conscientious objection', no less stubborn than anyone else's, to anything which stands in the way of giving the Londoner the most efficient educational system that I can devise.

I have written an article on 'London Education', to the order of the *Nineteenth Century*, for its October number, which I want you to be good enough to read very carefully and critically in MS., and advise me on. (It has *gone* to the printer, and will need to be *shortened* in proof, not lengthened.) A typewritten copy will reach you in a few days, and though I can't promise to adopt all suggestions in proof, I should be very grateful for them – as I cannot but believe that we both want the same thing.

The next six months are going to be a very difficult time. The ardent Nonconformists on the L.C.C. as elsewhere, want to *declare* for the Lloyd-George, Wales, Cambridgeshire policy of refusing aid to Voluntary Schools – though this is plainly premature for the L.C.C., which won't need to levy any increased rate until April 1905 at earliest.

If the Progressives do so declare, of course I shall oppose and denounce them; and the L.C.C. election will be fought on that issue (there happens

193

to be practically no other live issue municipally, now that the Labor policy is settled and Water disposed of).

On that issue, the Church and Roman Catholics will inevitably unite with the Moderates, and the Progressive vote will coincide with the Liberal vote – which means a Moderate majority in March next, free to work the Act in Church interests!

Of course I don't want that result, and I intend to use all possible influence with the Progressives to induce them to take a wiser line. But the Nonconformists on the Council mostly don't care a button about education as such; and many of them are standing for Parliament also!

Anyhow, I don't see how I can help going, in the strongest possible way, in favor of education as education, counting everything else as of secondary consequence.

I think the *Daily Mail*, and other 'non-political' papers will take this line also – which will make a Progressive defeat pretty certain if the Progressives are foolish.

On the other hand, by quietly accepting the Act as far as preliminary machinery goes, and *reserving all questions of policy* until they arise, the Progressives could keep all their forces together, and win their usual victory. We are, in the L.C.C., an administrative body – let the electors of London decide whether or not they want the Act amended at the proper place, namely the Parliamentary election!

I hope you are looking actively after Haggerston. No one can say how the Progressives will feel about co-opted members on the Education Committee – there will certainly be a strong feeling in favour of having none! (except women). I should *think* that the School Board would be given some, and if so, you would almost certainly be one. But shall we be able to get a 'scheme' through before March?

We are off tonight for a fortnight in Normandy. Letters here will be forwarded from time to time.

Sidney Webb

441 LSE   SIDNEY WEBB TO J. D. MACKILLOP

Through the summer of 1903 Hewins had been urging the Webbs to commit themselves to Tariff Reform and making his own commitment unmistakably clear. Webb's fear that the L.S.E. would thereby be gravely embarrassed was relieved when Hewins was replaced as Director by Halford J. Mackinder, also an imperialist in outlook, but less obviously partisan in his public opinions.

Beatrice was not sorry to see Hewins go, despite his 'audacity, enterprise, zeal and skill' which had helped to build up the L.S.E. But she thought him self-important and given to intrigue, though these defects of character, she decided, had been helpful when the School was young: 'for a cause that may be crushed in a weak infancy a certain secrecy of manouevre may be necessary and we have, in many cases, watched Hewins' duplicity with calm equanimity'. (BWD 18 November 03)

The letter to the Principal of London University explained that, to supplement Mackinder's salary of £400 p.a. as Director of the School it was desirable that he should also be appointed and paid another £400 p.a. as a Lecturer in Economic Geography.

41 Grosvenor Road,<br>
Westminster Embankment<br>
28.11.3

Dear Mr McKillop

I want this draft letter to the Principal completed by insertion of the resolution of regret passed at the last Governor's meeting; then typed by someone who will keep it quite secret; and *two* copies – one may be flimsy – sent to me for signature and prompt despatch.

I ought to have them by *midday* Monday. Without fail. Neatness not essential.

The enclosed letter from Mackinder should also be copied in duplicate, and the original put in the Minute Book, the copies being sent to me.

Sidney Webb

## 442 PP  BEATRICE WEBB TO GEORGINA MEINERTZHAGEN

Herbert Spencer, after years of hypochondriacal depression and invalidity, was now sinking. Beatrice had been to see him several times in the course of the autumn: he had expressed a desire to have her at his death-bed. Spencer died on 8 December. On the following day Beatrice reflected on her long association with 'the dear old man'. 'As a little child he was perhaps the only person who consistently cared for me – or rather who singled me out as one who was worthy of being trained and looked after . . . He taught me to look on all social institutions as if they were plants or animals – things that could be observed, classified and explained and the action of which could be to some extent foretold if one knew enough about them . . . And during those years it was mainly his intellectual influence that forced me, against my feelings and my intellect, to withstand the imperious demand for the submission of my intellect to another powerful personality . . . the philosopher beat the politician.' (BWD 9 December 03) Mrs Thompson had cared for Beatrice's father in his last years.

41 Grosvenor Road<br>
Monday [7 December 1903]

My dear Geo

I was quite disappointed to get your wire and note, I was looking forward to a nice chat with you; so remember that my spare room is always at your disposal. I hardly ever have a visitor except a sister. I was about to write to you to thank you ever so much for the pheasants – they are a most welcome addition to our fare; tho' I, personally, am a rigid anti-flesh-fish-egg-alcohol-coffee-and-sugar-eater. I have never in all my life had the good health I enjoy now – existence is quite different when one

195

never suffers from minor ailments and nearly always feels fit for work, exercise or society – and sleeps well into the bargain. Someday I mean to give up tea and tobacco – but as yet I have not the courage.

I was down three days at Brighton last week with that poor old man, who is sinking slowly out of life – very miserable and living on morphia and sweet champagne which disorders brain and stomach. I think I have been some comfort to him – or rather a ray of happiness every now and again. Now he is past the point when sympathy can be of much avail and wants only to be let die – so unless he sends for me I shall not go. He is being admirably nursed by a sort of Mrs Thompson woman to whom he has taken greatly and all his household are kindly and considerate of all his wishes. It is a pity that a shocking bad regimen and a somewhat crude philosophy has made the last 20 years of his existence so painful.

We are as busy as ever – working at our book every morning. Sidney is much perturbed at the outlook with regard to the Progressives and Education and I am not at all sure into which scale he will throw his weight next March. The Nonconformists talk of running a candidate against him and if there is a rift at Deptford there will be a rent throughout London – and we may yet see a Moderate majority! Politics are very topsy-turvy just now and one never knows who may be one's bedfellow!

Ever yours affectionately
Beatrice Webb

P.S. Take care of yourself and do come up for a chat!

443 PP   BEATRICE WEBB TO MARY PLAYNE

Spencer was cremated at Golders Green on Monday 14 December. William Jennings Bryan made his third bid as Democratic candidate for President of the United States in 1908. After he had dined with the Webbs on 26 November Beatrice described him as 'a most attractive personality, a large-bodied and large-brained man, with great simplicity and directness of nature, a delightful temper and kindly attitude towards life'. She thought he knew nothing of administration and 'was . . . dominated by abstractions – by words and not by things as they actually are'.

41 Grosvenor Road
[between 9 and 12 December 1903]

Dearest Mary

I was with the poor old man for three days the week of his death – until I saw that he really wanted to be left alone to die without further agitation of any kind. He was very miserable – poor old man – longing for his release, poisoned with morphia and sweet champagne which he insisted on taking in large quantities. But mentally he was clear and sane and much more tolerant and kindly than he used to be. Certainly my visits have been a pleasure to him – and given him the feeling that he was not completely forgotten and deserted and passing out of life without any kind of affection or regret. And in spite of all his defects – largely blank ignorance I believe – he lived his life according to a noble ideal of increasing knowledge and purifying motive. And now he is at rest.

The funeral is on Monday – the Courtneys, Georgie, Sidney and I go together. Leonard is addressing the little gathering in the Crematorium. It is rather melancholy to see how all parties accept the fact that his intellectual influence is dead – undoubtedly he realised this himself and I think at the very end the consciousness shook his faith in his own infallibility and made him more anxious to discover points of sympathy with other people's thought. Once or twice he said to me 'You and I don't really differ as to our ends, we are only disagreed as to the way of attaining them' and when I suggested that it might turn out that we were both wrong – and that there was a third alternative which neither of us foresaw he smiled benignly and answered 'It may well be so'. Probably the intelligent world ha. absorbed all that is valuable in his teaching and takes it as a matter of course without realising from whom it came.

It will be delightful to have a quiet time at Longfords before the L.C.C. fight – which I fear will be most disagreeable. The 'Noncons', if they win even moral victories at Lewisham and Dulwich, will become intolerable and it may well come about that Sidney will have to stand up alone against them in the Progressive ranks. But he is determined not to budge from his position of an impartial and energetic administration of the Act and if he is turned out it will be with his colours flying! He lunched with the Bishop of Stepney today to advise as to the Church manifesto (this is private) which will appear in a few days. Meanwhile he is quietly withdrawing himself – for the time – from the Progressive inner circles so that they cannot accuse him of treachery.

Ever yours

B. Webb

P.S. Photo of John Morley with Bryan, the late Democratic candidate for U.S. Presidency: a most fascinating man!


444 PP   BEATRICE WEBB TO LAURENCINA HOLT

Dr John Clifford (1836–1923), the eminent Baptist preacher and educationalist, led the passive resistance campaign to the Education Acts of 1902 and 1903. He had been the dominant figure on the London School Board and exercised substantial influence in the Progressive Party.

41 Grosvenor Road
Dec. 16th 1903

My dear Lallie

I am so glad you liked Leonard's address; Sidney and I thought it wonderfully good – so absolutely sincere and nobly felt, and with all, so unselfconscious and modest. I agree with your feeling that Leonard's utterance was more human than John Morley's would have been – who really never cared for Herbert Spencer and regarded him as a mere intellect. You would have liked the dignity, simplicity and almost stern absence of rite or ostentation of the funeral – right away in the small brick Chapel on the outskirts of London – with no one there who did not feel an immense respect for the old man. Even the odd look of some of the mourners – foreign enthusiasts and earnest-looking disciples, with no representatives of great personages and few from public bodies – all this seemed to add to the simple dignity of this last rite of affection and regard, and expressed the finest aspect of Herbert Spencer's life – its disinterestedness and freedom from the baser conventions of the world.

I am very glad that during these last months I have been able to be, now and again, with the dear old man – he seemed to feel the human tie so strongly – always called me his 'oldest and dearest friend' and delighted in my comings. What an old age he might have had, if he had followed a decent physical and mental hygiene!

Sidney and I are immersed in work, but we are both of us extremely fit. The next months are going to be extremely unpleasant for him, as he disagrees strongly with the attitude of the Progressives with regard to the London Act and will undoubtedly lose the support of the Nonconformists. But the question of London Education is one which he has made his own and he intends to take his stand for the Policy which he believes will bring about the best results into Educational Efficiency. But it is always an evil to have, more or less, to break with your party. However matters may right themselves before the election comes on. He is bringing out a little book early in the year, giving his policy in detail – which, at any rate, will be useful to those who will have, after March, the administration to act.

We think the Liberals will gain seats in London, tho' not so many as they expect. The Progressives will probably lose a good many – tho' they *may* keep their majority on the L.C.C. – but that will depend how far they are led by Dr Clifford and the N.U.T.

Yours affectionately<br>Beatrice Webb

## 445 FP SIDNEY WEBB TO EDWARD PEASE

Tract 116, *Fabianism and the Fiscal Question*, was written by Shaw. He had told John Burns on 11 September (SCL) that 'I am a Protectionist right down to my boots'. On 8 October (SCL) he had urged Beatrice to help him 'anaesthetize Sidney' while he extracted the remainder of Webb's classical Liberalism. In November Shaw told Webb that if he would agree to abandon Free Trade he might find himself in a future Chamberlain government.

Shaw's tract was as ingenious as his earlier pamphlet on the Boer War, employing the same device of arguing that collectivist gains might be wrung from an imperial policy. The deliberate interference of the state with trade would, he suggested, aid the socialist purpose of subordinating commercial enterprise to national ends. Wallas thought this a mischievous plea for a Chamberlain administration. When his attempt to move a Free Trade amendment at a Fabian meeting on 22 January 1904 was defeated Wallas resigned from the Society. Pease persuaded Wells not to resign in sympathy with Wallas, with whom he was then on close terms.

The Education Tract was No. 117, written by Webb.

41 Grosvenor Road, Westminster Embankment<br>5 Jan. 1904

Dear Pease

Please send me the third copy of draft on Education Act – I will return it if needed.

I am, personally, not over-anxious to have it issued, but have merely done it by order of the Executive. It is difficult to combine a permanent tract with an ephemeral situation.

Perhaps we might turn it into an avowed L.C.C. Election Manifesto. But this may be still more difficult. If Wallas and Headlam object with their usual violence – as they probably will – I should be disposed to let the thing drop.

By the way, I shall almost certainly have to be absent on 22 January – to attend an important meeting in Deptford, where I may need all possible help to save my seat. Shaw will get through his tract all right; and we could, in any case, hardly print and circulate the Education tract by then.

Yours<br>Sidney Webb

#### 446 PP SIDNEY WEBB TO GRAHAM WALLAS

Webb had produced a comprehensive statement of his opinions in *London Education*. He circulated copies of the book, especially to the press, as a form of personal election manifesto. He still hoped to influence the election campaign in a way which held back a swing to the Progressives and avoided strengthening of the Nonconformist lobby. Both he and Beatrice were now aware that the tide was setting against their 'Limp' friends and against the Balfour government, while Campbell-Bannerman – leading the Liberals with considerable tactical skill – was building up a coalition of 'Little Englanders' who had been against the war and imperialism, Nonconformists aroused by the Education Acts, Radicals, trade unionists and Free Traders. The old Radical shibboleths, the Webbs felt, were filling up the vacuum in Liberal policy.

41 Grosvenor Road, Westminster Embankment<br>10.I.4

Dear Wallas

I have read your criticisms on my draft Education tract, and am sorry you see nothing but insidious 'ecclesiasticism' in it and me. It is really a

199

mare's nest of your own finding, but of that nothing but time will convince you. Most of the paragraphs you object to are simply what the [Fabian] Society adopted (I thought with your acquiescence) in the provincial tract – which the Society directed us to adapt for London, and which I used the actual print of as M.S., altering a few words only (e.g. as to composition of the Education Committee, survey of the voluntary school buildings, salaries of teachers etc.).

So far as I remember the one *new* point is the subordinate machinery for London. I may be wrong, but you quite misapprehend me as to this so far as voluntary schools are concerned. It is just because I intend to secure to the Council absolute control over these, that I follow the Act in *not* placing them under the Borough Committees. My own view is to delegate *nothing* in the case of non-provided schools, and (on the contrary) to stretch to the uttermost the public control given by the Act – just because the non-provided managers are not, and cannot be made, entirely creatures of the Council.

But I do want to have a scheme of decentralisation of routine administration in the Board Schools by creating, out of the 'managers' required by the Act, an entirely subordinate set of local Committees, who are really to act under the guidance of the Councils' own officers.

You, apparently, are aiming at a different thing, viz., a perfectly centralised bureaucracy, in which there will be no more *local* power than at present, though there will be a larger and a more efficient staff organised and directed from the centre. If I can't get what I want, I can quite well accept your plan, which seems to me less good. But I don't think you can get your plan. Yours will, in practice, result (as it has for the past few years) only in continuing the present system – which, I gather, is what the 'School Board party' now counselling the Progressives really intend and desire.

What I want is to use the present revolution to make a new start, and set the whole of London Education on a much higher plane of efficiency – demanding a more complex organisation.

However, I am overruled and boycotted by the Progressives, and they will go their own way. You must take care that no harm happens to education in the widest sense – especially those parts of it, and those grades of it, which the School Board members do not habitually think about.

But, to come back to the tract, I strongly advised the Fabian Executive on Friday *to hang it up* – as introducing a new electoral complication, and especially as perhaps making you feel uncomfortable. If we issue a tract, it must follow the lines of our last one; and these I gather, you now object to. (It does not affect me, as I have planted myself down in the book that will be published in 10 days' time.) But the Executive, though it adjourned for a week to read the draft, seemed rather disposed to insist on a tract. Probably we can get them to delay it.

I may be wrong, but I think the Progressives are going to lose many seats. They might, if they had worked with a single eye for education, have kept their majority. But they seem now to be going to put against them the Catholics, the Church, the Educationists (other than School Boardites), the halfpenny newspapers, and I fear therefore, the non-political citizen. What this may mean at the polls I don't know.

Sidney Webb

## 447 FP  SIDNEY WEBB TO EDWARD PEASE

Shaw had been adopted as a Progressive to fight the L.C.C. seat of South St Pancras, with Sir William Geary (1850–1945) as his running-mate. Webb, who despite his fears of defeat was to be returned unopposed for Deptford, did what he could to help Shaw, taking charge of much of his organisation. Shaw, Beatrice noted on 7 March, was 'hopelessly intractable' as a candidate, irritating many of his potential supporters with his paradoxical wit and eccentric ideas of electioneering. In this, Beatrice complained, he showed the bad side of his character: 'vanity and lack of . . . respect for other people's prejudices'. Shaw was defeated but the Progressives did well. Though Sidney felt that he was to some extent rehabilitated he felt the need to proceed with caution and not to push himself forward for a prominent position in the new council.

41 Grosvenor Road, Westminster Embankment

18.2.4

Dear Pease

The Education Tract seems all right. I leave it confidently to you.

My notion would be to post copies at once to every Metropolitan Borough Councillor (about 1500); to members of Common Council of the City (240); and to L.C.C. candidates (about 200); and L.C.C. Aldermen (19) – say, 2000 to be distributed at once; the sooner the better.

Shaw's Election Address is an amusing and instructive 16 pp pamphlet. Why not ask him to give you 1000 copies to send out with *Fabian News*?

I think he may have a chance; and we ought to do all we can to get him in – especially as the official Progressives don't half like it!

Yours

Sidney Webb

## 448 PP  BEATRICE WEBB TO MARY PLAYNE

The Bishop of Stepney was Cosmo Lang. Frederic Thesiger (1868–1933) later Viscount Chelmsford, was a member of the London School Board 1900–04 and a Moderate on the L.C.C. 1904–05. He became Viceroy of India in 1916. Shaw's play *Candida* was given at a series of matinée performances in April.

Dearest Mary

So many thanks for the charming flowers and excellent vegetables.

My little party went off brilliantly – consisting of H. G. Wells and his wife, the Bernard Shaws, the Bishop of Stepney and Mrs Reeves, the P.M. and Mr Thesiger. Mr Balfour, finding the atmosphere at once sympathetic and irresponsibly non-political, let himself go and we had a most stimulating and sparkling discussion of the special function of the expert, hereditary monarchy – the Church, the Board School, the Public School and University, a 'Governing class' and the appropriate regimen (including diet!) to produce that class – training in Science, religion and athletics and the device of popular election – G.B.S., Wells, Mr Balfour and 'the Webbs' firing suggestions and counter-suggestions at each other, the astute ecclesiastic making sly remarks and Mr Thesiger (a new Moderate on the L.C.C., a clever young Tory lawyer) a son of Lord Chelmsford listening with bewilderment to our mingled dialectic and chaff. After dinner Sidney and the Bishop managed to implant in the great man's mind our scheme of the compulsory training (military and technical) of boys up to the age of 21. He stayed until 10.30, inspite of the Budget discussion, and said that he had had a most delightful evening – so that my vanity as hostess was fully satisfied. Oh! my 'Pictuer' dress did look so charming! He is much aged and looks out of health – I suggested the 'higher life' of restriction of food stuffs – quality and quantity – but he did not rise to it! He was, however, pleased with my suggestion that so far as we Fabians were concerned the distinction between himself and the Liberal leaders was, that whilst they said Why? to every new proposal, he said Why not?

I am looking forward much to seeing you on the 28th and have taken tickets for the afternoon of the 29th for G.B.S. play.

Tell Rosie I expect her on May 2nd. I have arranged a pleasant little party for her for the 5th May – I hope she will stay with us until the 11th or 12th – on the evening of the 12th I am full up. She must let me know whether she would like anyone asked to lunch or tea.

Ever yours affectionately

B Webb

### 449 UI  BEATRICE WEBB TO H. G. WELLS

The chapter on prisons from the Webb book on local government had been sent to Wells for comment. Before entertaining Wells in London the Webbs had spent two days visiting him at Sandgate: this was the period in which the relationship between Wells and the Webbs was most close. Even so, Beatrice sensed the distance between them. Wells, she noted on 15 April, was 'useful to gradgrinds like ourselves in supplying us with useful generalisations which we can use as an instrument of research'. Wells, for his part, criticised Sidney as 'foxey' and

Beatrice as a reactionary who pulled Sidney away from his natural radicalism. His criticism, Beatrice remarked, 'increases my inclination for a somewhat severe abstinence from trying "to run the show"'.

41 Grosvenor Road

[29 April 1904]

Dear Mr Wells

Ever so many thanks for your letter – the opening words of more than formal appreciation are grateful in the midst of the grind of a new chapter on Roads!

Your criticism is helpful – I agree that we must relate the conditions of the Prisons to the contemporary existence of the free citizen – to some extent this necessary background is given by our other chapters on Police and Municipal regulation. But we shall bear the suggestion in mind in our final chapter in which we hope to establish the perspective of each part of the social life of the period.

As to the *Psychology of Authority* – I am not sure I understand the whole of your suggestion – or that I should agree with it, if I did. I should like to discuss it with you some day. Would you apply the same assumptions to the relation between an institution nurse and her patient? I don't see any way out of a certain restraint on personal liberty for mentally and physically sick persons – and my view of the Prison is little more than a Mental Hospital. But then I have no objection to the principle of subordination – per se – it is a matter for delicate investigation the exact conditions under which it degenerates into tyranny. I should imagine that it did so in *all* Prisons – there I am with you.

Won't you turn up to lunch 1.15 tomorrow? Don't answer.

Yours

B. Webb

450 CCO   BEATRICE WEBB TO R. C. K. ENSOR

Robert Charles Kirkwood Ensor (1877–1958), who became a prominent journalist and historian, had been an active Fabian as a student at Oxford and served for some years on the Society executive. He was a member of the L.C.C. 1911–13. Beatrice included him as one of 'the new group of young men disposed to take our views seriously' whose support to some extent compensated for the estrangement from such old friends as Wallas, Llewellyn Smith, Vaughan Nash and Massingham. 'What is perhaps a less wholesome sign' of their current set of friendships, she added, 'is the accession of Society folk' such as the Asquiths, Elchos and Munro-Fergusons. They had, nevertheless, also acquired some new intellectual acquaintances, such as Wells and Mackinder and some educationalists – essentially people with a common interest in what she called 'Social Reconstruction'. She noted that what was 'utterly lacking' in their circle was an interest in art, literature for its own sake and music. She enjoyed the company of friends, such as Haldane and Russell, who thought about 'the relation of man's mind to the universe', but 'the subject bores Sidney as leading nowhere . . . he prefers reading a statistical abstract or L.C.C. agenda!' (BWD n.d. May 04)

My dear Mr Ensor

We have not thought out any definite proposals to talk over on the 18th – but I am sorry you cannot come – if you are coming up to London after June 5th and before the end of this month will you let me know.

I feel that we are to some extent responsible for not allowing the whole Progressive force in the country to slip back to mere destructive radicalism – that has now become a sort of idealisation of the *Status Quo*. At present the whole official Liberal party seems to glory in a stilted self-complacency with existing conditions and is wholly blind to the ghastly tragedies of the mental and physical decrease of the mass of our race. What I want to talk about with some select party is the possibility of making people realise this possible state of affairs and agree on some policy of a compulsory raising of the standard of health and conduct.

Will you be thinking 'at large' about it and the best way of getting some kind of co-operation on the basis of a national minimum?

Yours sincerely

Beatrice Webb

### 451 BLPES  SIDNEY WEBB TO EDWARD PEASE

Webb was now winding up the Hutchinson Trust. He signed the final report on 10 July 1904. The financial report showed how prudent and, for all MacDonald's criticism, fair Webb had proved in managing the money. The total income over the ten years was £10,390. Of this, just over £2,400 remained as a balance, which was divided equally between the Fabians and the L.S.E. The Fabian share of the fund amounted in all to £4,950. The L.S.E. received £4,889 and the British Library of Political Science had a single grant of £500. The money allocated to the Fabians had paid for over 1,000 provincial lectures, provided the stock for 140 book boxes circulated to more than 500 organisations, underwritten some Fabian tracts and paid part of the fees at L.S.E. for Fabians who enrolled at the School. The money granted to L.S.E. had gone largely to support its general account. Though the Hutchinson bequest had made it possible to start the School it had in the event only amounted to less than one-twentieth of its income in its first decade.

[41 Grosvenor Road]
17th June [1904]

Dear Pease

In closing up the business of the Hutchinson Trust, the Trustees desire to make provision for the continuance of the work which the Executive Committee of the Fabian Society has carried on by the aid of their grants, namely the provision of short courses of educational lectures, the circulation of book-boxes, and the special distribution of tracts (as a means among other things, of enabling new tracts to be published). With this object, the Trustees propose, if the Executive Committee will by resolution express its assent to the arrangement, to transfer to three trustees (to be appointed by the Executive Committee) Derby Corporation 3% stock of the nominal amount of £1,300, and £88. 17. 10 in cash, being the final balance of the Hutchinson Trust fund, in trust to apply both income and capital of the same in such amounts from time to time as they may think fit to continuing the work of the Fabian Society in the directions above referred to, and as near as may be, in the manner in which this work has been carried on during the past five years or more; it being expressly stipulated and agreed as a condition of the trust that the said trustees shall keep all said funds apart from the funds of the Fabian Society, and shall not use any part thereof for assisting work already being carried on by the Society out of its ordinary funds. The Hutchinson Trustees have always aimed at so administering their trust as not in effect to relieve the subscribers to the Fabian Society of the necessity of maintaining their subscriptions as heretofore and the present transfer is made in full reliance that this policy will be continued. But if at any time it is desired, by a majority not less than two-thirds in number of the Executive Committee for the time being, that the Trustees should assist by a grant from their trust-funds any new or extraordinary development of work of the Society, the Trustees may, if they think fit, in their uncontrolled discretion, accede to the request.

As soon as a vacancy occurs among the Trustees the Executive Committee of the Fabian Society for the time being should nominate a person to fill the vacancy, and the person so nominated should be formally appointed a trustee by deed executed by the two surviving trustees.

On receipt of a letter conveying an acceptance of this proposal by the Executive Committee, together with the names of the three trustees, the Hutchinson Trustees will transfer the fund.

Yours truly,

Sidney Webb
Administrator

## 452 LSE   SIDNEY WEBB TO J. D. MCKILLOP

The Webbs were often criticised for parsimony in the payment of their employees and in the supervision of both Fabian funds and the financial affairs of the L.S.E. This letter is typical of many which show how carefully Webb scrutinised expenditure, discouraging extravagance, encouraging every source of revenue and ensuring that money was always spent to the best effect. For much of its early life the L.S.E. only just succeeded in balancing its accounts.

Fyrish, Evanton, Rosshire

18/9/4

Dear Mr McKillop

Thanks for sending Mrs Shaw's letter. The £100 must, of course, be treated as she requests. I think her letter might be shown to the Director confidentially.

I hope this will enable you to avoid any actual overdraft at the bank; as you will be receiving fees early in October.

I shall be glad to have, at your convenience soon after 1 October a rough statement of all the then outstanding liabilities, and the assets – so as to show how we should stand if we wound up on 30 September.

We must try to make a little, in the coming session, out of the Railway and Insurance sections, in the way of debiting these sections with something for administration, and making them contribute freely to the Library.

Consider, too, with the Director in due course, the position towards the University courses on Sociology. If the University is to get the fees, the School ought to get something for expenses. You might also get some Sociological books for the Library out of it. It would be simpler if we could drive the University to let us keep the fees for expenses.

Sidney Webb

### 453 PP BEATRICE WEBB TO MARY PLAYNE

Shaw had just completed *John Bull's Other Island*. The play opened at the Royal Court theatre in October; on 10 November Beatrice took Balfour. He liked the play so much that he went five times, once taking Campbell-Bannerman – possibly the only occasion on which the prime minister of the day has taken the leader of the opposition to the theatre as a private guest. Writing to the theatrical manager, J. E. Vedrenne (1867–1930) on 25 August (SCL) Shaw had cannily insisted that 'it would be throwing money away to produce it before Parliament meets again. The political people will count for a great deal in the stalls'. Ruth Julia Cripps (b. 1883) was the eldest daughter of Alfred and Theresa Cripps. 'The Laird' was R. C. Munro-Ferguson. Sir Arthur Steel-Maitland (1876–1935), Conservative politician and economist, became an influential governor and later chairman of L.S.E. Stephen Hobhouse, eldest child of Henry and Margaret Hobhouse, became a notorious conscientious objector in the First World War. In December 1904 family influences helped him to a post in the Board of Trade.

Fyrish, Evanton
[September 1904]

Dearest Mary

I want to bespeak you and Miss Ross's notice of Miss Micklejohn who is going to Gloucester this week to be one of your lecturers. She is a bright clever girl – studied both at Edinburgh and London Universities; has, I think, taken both a B.A. and D.Sc. and the Sanitary Institute and Public Health certificate. She is one of the 5 pretty and energetic daughters of the

Factor of Hovar – all of whom are in professions and apparently doing very well in their respective lines.

We have had a delightful time here – fascinated with the country – the Firth and the North Sea as the background to heather and luxuriant foliage. We cycled off to the West Coast last week – 3 days constantly changing beauty and sunny weather, the 4th day 40 miles over intolerable roads through drenching rain with a head wind – but in spite of all I enjoyed it. Even that. The Bernard Shaws stayed a month in the neighbourhood but found no place that could cook macaroni and after wandering from one small inn to another fled to Edinburgh. He read us his new play, a virulent satire on English Liberalism and Irish Nationalism – laid in Ireland – very clever but destructive and derisive and lacking in any kind of hope or appreciation. Unconsciously he has in his analysis of Irish character described his own defects.

We enjoyed Alfred and Ruth's visit – an attractive young woman – one of the most attractive girls in the family? He is in excellent spirits, has given up political ambition and finds his satisfaction in [illegible] Law – at least that is my impression. I doubt whether anyone not attached to the Balfour clique will have much chance in the Conservative Party in the next years. Chamberlain will have enough to do to keep himself and his immediate entourage on the surface without pushing any stray and casual allies like Alfred. And Alfred is curiously antagonistic in interests and mannerisms to the Balfour set – he and they bore each other and in their mutual depreciation often offend each other's pride. It was amusing to see how he and the Fergusons disliked each other – Hector Ferguson, the artistic and intellectual brother of the Laird (a sort of [illegible]) almost came to words at lunch here the last day of Alfred's visit. One could see that Alfred thought him an affected and pretentious wastrel, and he thought Alfred a mere commonplace middle-class man who somehow managed to extract money out of equally commonplace men!

We leave here on the 30th, stay two nights with the Steel-Maitlands near Stirling and get back to London on Monday 3rd. Stephen comes to me that week but has not made up his mind whether or not he means to stay the autumn in London or where.

Do write me your news.

Ever yours affectionately

B. Webb

454 UI  BEATRICE WEBB TO H. G. WELLS

The Wells novel described a race of giants, raised on 'Boomfood', who were wiser and stronger than normal men and became a benevolent ruling elite. A reviewer in the *Manchester Guardian* (3 October 04) was less impressed than Beatrice by the proposed evolution of these supermen: 'One cannot go very far towards the reform of humanity with an equipment of contempt and a new drug'. Wells was currently attempting to complete *Kipps* and about to digress into *A Modern Utopia*, which appealed greatly to the Fabians: they saw themselves pictured as members of the disinterested caste of social engineers whom Wells called the 'Samurai'.

41 Grosvenor Road, Westminster Embankment
Sunday [September 1904]

My dear Mr Wells

Sidney and I have been revelling in *The Food of the Gods* – it is full of wit and wisdom – my only objection is to the particular device – *Food*! Why not imagine a complementary state of real progress – from the mystical effect of restricted diet; a gradual rarification of life leading to free and undisturbed access to all the Universe through the device of becoming mere ether? It would be quite as disturbing to the mass of unregenerate 'materialists' as the Giant Life to the Little Folk? and would have a better moral; tho' I admit the particular device is of small consequence to the truth of the allegory.

By the way, S. says that 'as an administrator' he would have suppressed Boomfood. You see the essential rottenness of the collectivist conception of the world!

When you come to London do remember us – our room is engaged for the last week in October and first of November but after that we should be delighted to see you and Mrs Wells.

Ever yours sincerely

B. Webb

455 MMLMU   BEATRICE WEBB TO BERTRAND RUSSELL

*Democracy and Reaction*, a pamphlet in which Leonard Hobhouse protested against imperialism and the negative social policy of the Liberals, was published in 1904.

41 Grosvenor Road,
Westminster Embankment
Oct. 16 1904

My dear Bertrand

It was kind of you to write to me your opinion of L.H. [Leonard Hobhouse] pamphlet and I am glad that it coincides so exactly with my own. I quite agree with you in thinking that the fact that a 'mood' (such, for instance, as the instinctive faith in a 'Law of Righteousness'; and my instinctive faith in Prayer) is felt to be 'compelling and recurrent' has no relevance, as proof of its correspondence 'with our order of things'.

I make an absolute distinction between the realm of proof (*Knowledge of Processes*) and the realm of aspiration or Faith – (*the choice of Purposes*). All I ask for this latter World, is tolerance – a 'Let live' policy. In my interpretation of this 'Let live' policy, I should probably differ with you and L.H. – since I would permit each local community to teach its particular form of 'Aspiration' and or 'Faith' out of common funds. I should even myself desire this for my own children – since I have found that my own existence would have been more degraded without it – and as I 'desire' what we call nobility of Purpose, I wish for the means to bring it about. I know no other way of discovering these means but actual experience or experiment, and so far my own experience and experiment leads me to the working Hypothesis of persistent Prayer. I do not in the least wish to force this practice on other people and should be equally glad to pay for a school in which the experiment of complete secularisation (*viz.* nothing but the knowledge of Processes) was tried or for an Anglican or Catholic or Christian Science Establishment. All I desire is that each section or locality should, as far as possible, be free to teach its own kind of aspirations or absence of Aspiration.

Can you and Alys come to lunch on *Thursday 10th* and meet Mr Balfour? I am taking him to Bernard Shaw's play. Could you not take tickets for that afternoon? It will be well for you to know Mr Balfour – in case of Regius Professorships and the like!

Ever yours

Beatrice Webb

### 456 PP  SIDNEY TO BEATRICE

Beatrice had gone to visit Charles and Mary Booth at their country house, Gracedieu, near Leicester. The earlier estrangement had been gradually overcome by some casual visits and Beatrice felt the time had come to make a friendly approach. She found she slipped into 'the old intellectual intimacy' though she found the house too magnificent, full of 'over-fed and under-occupied persons' who were 'intent on enjoying their personal existence and not much concerned as to the fate of the community they live on'. (BWD 12 November 04) Dr Frederick Rose, a research chemist, was appointed Assistant Educational Adviser to the L.C.C. on 15 November 1904 – a post he held until 1923. He had made a special study of German education, having been educated at Karlsruhe Technical University and Berlin University.

William Stephen Sanders (1876–1942), who had entered politics as an aide to John Burns in Battersea, was one of the Fabian lecturers supported on Hutchinson money. He became an L.C.C. alderman in 1904, secretary of the Fabian Society from 1914 to 1920 and Labour M.P. for North Battersea in 1929. Sir Henry Newbolt (1862–1938), the patriotic and sentimental poet, had become a member of the Co-efficients. He had lately given up his practice at the Bar to become a professional man of letters. Edward Jenks (1861–1939), after teaching law in Australia and in Oxford, became principal and director of studies for the Law Society in 1903: in 1924 he became professor of law at the University of London. Webb's scholarship scheme, which allowed those who passed to proceed to both private and maintained secondary schools, was passed by the L.C.C. in February 1905.

209

41 Grosvenor Road, Westminster

15.11.4

My own dearest

In the midst of a debate on the Building Act, I manage to send you a few lines of greeting. I woke up this morning in dense fog, thicker than ever, which at the B.M. prevented me from getting any, but 'gallery' books until late. So I found, by chance, a new print of the Salford Court Leet records from 1580 to 1669 – they have only lately been discovered. They are interesting as (a) showing the Court Leet levying rates of its own as at Manchester, (b) showing it as the only local body, giving poor relief, dealing with tramps, collecting the County Rate, etc.

This afternoon I got Dr Rose appointed as Garnett's assistant after a little struggle. I have had to see several people; and so on.

Sanders refuses as he has to lecture.

I hope and trust you will have a fine day at Gracedieu, and will have a good time and gain health and spirits. But I miss you rather badly, and it was only by a struggle that I got off to the Museum this morning in the cold fog.

Last night at the Co-efficients there were present Haldane, Mackinder, Wells, Dawkins, Hewins, Newbolt, Amery and myself. We discussed the place of the monarchial institution – general opinion in favor of it and its development, as necessary to the Empire. Wells alone dissenting and that very half heartedly. I invited Mr and Mrs Wells for Monday to Wednesday December 12–14, and he accepted. Haldane announced to Mackinder and me that the Law School had definitely broken down by the opposition of Middle Temple and Grays Inn; and advised the School conferring with the (Solicitors) Law Institution for a separate scheme – Mackinder is to see Jenks.

Goodbye dearest,

Sidney

### 457 BUL   SIDNEY WEBB TO SIR OLIVER LODGE

Oliver Lodge F.R.S. (1851–1940), professor of physics at Liverpool and first Principal (1900–19) of the University of Birmingham, was much interested in psychical research. He had stayed with the Webbs a few days earlier. Beatrice found him 'a delightful personality – large and fresh in his thought and feeling'. Beatrice had given a dinner for Lodge to meet the Russells, Mackinder, Wernher, Beit, Balfour and Harley Granville-Barker (1877–1946), the actor–producer who was making his name with Shaw at the Royal Court theatre.

Beatrice was much concerned with her own spiritual aspirations. On 20 February she noted that she was 'slipping back into conformity with the Church of England, accepting its prayers and rites as a child . . . We religious-minded agnostics feel the need for days and hours set apart for prayer, long for the strength which is given with the past and the present communion of saints, for the stimulation and relaxation of music and beautiful words'. Early in March, as a reaction to intense social activity, she was 'beginning to hanker after a period of fallowness'. (BWD 5 March 05) She was looking forward to a time when they could take a journey to the Far East: the success of the Japanese in their war against Russia had greatly impressed the Webbs and many of their contemporaries with Japanese national élan and efficiency.

41 Grosvenor Road, Westminster Embankment

12.2.5

My dear Lodge

My wife and I both thank you for the two addresses – she is specially pleased to find a good description of the Hypothesis as an instrument of discovery, and I am delighted with your sermon to the Foresters, which makes us feel in cordial agreement with your state of mind.

We are venturing to send you separately our *Industrial Democracy* – it is far too long to claim a reading through, but perhaps you could find time to look at the very last chapter, which bears on our notion of the direction in which social organisation is evolving.

Now I want to ask a favor. Would you let the Fabian Society publish your sermon to the Foresters as a penny pamphlet – with your name, and a preliminary note saying that you had permitted it, at the Society's request – so as to avoid any possible implication that you were a member? We frequently thus publish in our series things by non-members. I have consulted no one about it yet, so you are *quite* free to refuse if you are contemplating any other separate publication. We so much enjoyed your visit.

Yours very truly

Sidney Webb

458 FP   SIDNEY WEBB TO EDWARD PEASE

41 Grosvenor Road,
Westminster Embankment
2 May 1905

Dear Pease

Yours of 1st received.

Enclosed card (which I have answered and which is one of many such enquiries) induces me to make the suggestion that we might print a four-page list of the most useful pamphlets, our own and others, on Social Questions, and supply it, with a letter, to all the leading publishers agents and large booksellers – *perhaps printed on a card to hang up* – as a standing advertisement.

Yours

Sidney Webb

This letter was to the County Clerk of Shropshire. Not many letters seem to survive which relate to the extensive enquiries which the Webbs made for their local government research. One reason for this may have been their extensive use of research assistants to undertake both postal enquiries and visits to archives.

41 Grosvenor Road
23 June 1905

My dear Sir

I venture to trouble you, as a historical student, with an enquiry. My wife and I have been for years engaged on a comprehensive History of Local Government, for which we have ransacked the archives of half the counties and many of the boroughs and parishes.

We have, as yet, nothing about Shropshire, beyond the county histories of half a century ago, which are of no use for institutional history.

I believe that you have published some extracts from the records, which I have heard spoken of as useful, but I have been unable to find this volume. May I trouble you to be so kind as to send me the title and date, so that I may dig it out at the British Museum?

I fear that I cannot hope to be able to visit Shrewsbury now, to consult the original county records; so that we may be dependent on such extracts as are printed; and I should be very grateful if you could tell me of anything that there may be in print.

I feel that I am asking much, but I am emboldened to do so by having heard of your interest in such studies. I may say that I am a Member of the Senate of London University and of its Board of Studies in History, as well as of the London County Council.

Yours truly

Sidney Webb

### 460 PP    BEATRICE WEBB TO MARY PLAYNE

At the beginning of July the Webbs again went to Fyrish on the Cromarty Firth for their summer recess.

Beatrice greatly enjoyed meeting and entertaining Arthur Balfour. He 'comes into dinner whenever we ask him . . . perhaps our vanity is flattered by his evident interest in our historical and philosophical paradoxes . . . all the common thoughts and feelings of common folk seem to him ineffably banal'. (BWD 30 July 05)

Blanche Julia Cripps (1879–1921) married Thomas Faulder, a surgeon in 1904. She was the daughter of Blanche Cripps, Beatrice's sister, who had committed suicide at the beginning of June. Blanche's husband, Willie Cripps, had become attached to an Italian singer, Julia Ravogli, whom he later married. Glendaruel was the Scottish shooting lodge which Willie Cripps had taken: his Scottish home was Sir Walter Scott's house at Abbotsford.

Beatrice was much concerned with the way in which several of her sisters' children were spoiled by the philosophy 'that material comfort and ease . . . is the main end of life'. (BWD 9 July 05) This reflection was entered in her diary after visiting Alfred Cripps at Parmoor and seeing how he indulged his three sons. The youngest of these, Richard Stafford Cripps (1889–1952) became an outstanding advocate, ambassador and Labour politician.

Beatrice's nephew Stephen Hobhouse had become a Quaker.

41 Grosvenor Road<br>
Address after Tuesday: Fyrish, Evanton, Rosshire<br>
July 3rd 1905

Dearest Mary

The continuous heat makes us long to get out of London: tho' I have seldom worked such long hours as I have done the last 5 weeks – it is extraordinary what a difference not going out makes to one's comfort and efficiency. The first luxury I should indulge in, if I was forced to keep up a good establishment, would be *never to dine out* but to have little dinners, 2 or 3 times a week – the choice of the party, the dishes and the atmosphere seems to me to constitute the whole pleasure of entertaining.

Our little dinner on Wednesday went off delightfully – the P.M. was in his best form, talked about all the episodes of the last week, discussed the characters of Winston Churchill, Chamberlain and other personages, the 'game of politics' and the ethics of playing it, with little excursions into metaphysics with Mr Haldane and into 18th Century literature and political history with us. He was very glad to meet Lord Chelmsford (who has just been appointed Governor of Queensland); he thought he had never seen him before as he had evidently not noticed him when he dined here last year – and after dinner, the two, with Sidney and Mr Haldane [had an] interesting discussion [on] Colonial policy. He is certainly a most agreeable guest, partly because he manages to give you the impression that you have done him a great favour in asking him to dine with you – which is flattering to one's vanity as hostess!

I had the Faulders to dine the other night: he is certainly a remarkably good fellow – the most attractive of our 'in-laws' of the second generation I think? I am trying to persuade Julia to come for a fortnight or three weeks to Rosshire before meeting him at Glendaruel. She has evidently a horror of going there without him and he can only get away for a week or ten days. I should think she really dislikes her father and does not care much for the other members of the family – now, she seems to be devoted to Blanche's memory. I should like to get to know her, as there is a certain attractiveness in her expression and manner and this seems to want some kind of bracing influence.

We shall leave Rosshire the last week of September, stay 2 nights with Mr Haldane and then go for 4 nights to Glendaruel, returning to London Oct 1st. I wonder whether there is any chance of the Ravoglis being there: I should rather object to meeting them. Would you, *if you were me*, find out? (I could [?face Family]) and get off going, if they are there? Or is it better to go in any case? One wants to do the kind thing by the children and also by William: what do you advise?

Maggie is up in London desperately perturbed about Stephen's announcement that he intends to renounce his inheritance. She is coming to supper tomorrow and I shall try to hint to her that her extreme obsession on the material side of life is responsible for these re-actions on the part of her children and for a good deal of unpopularity with her family and friends. I am really fond of her, but she is becoming almost intolerable with her one ideadness – and such a lofty idea! Do write to me and tell me all your news.

With love to Arthur.

Ever yours

B Webb

### 461 PP BEATRICE WEBB TO CATHERINE COURTNEY

Reginald Arthur Bray served on the London School Board and then on the L.C.C. (1904–19). He was a close ally and friend of Webb on the Council.

When the Webbs stayed with Willie Cripps at Glendaruel, Beatrice was disgusted at the way he 'flaunted' Julia Ravogli before his children, 'all of us conscious that it was passionate jealousy of the woman that was the occasion, if not the cause, of his wife's suicide'. (BWD 5 October 05) She disliked Willie's 'sensual egotism': 'unless driven to it by some urgent consideration of the children's welfare, never again do Sidney and I enter that man's house or welcome him to our home'. Many years later she felt that she had done Julia Ravogli an injustice and confessed she liked her. Both Mary Playne and Kate Courtney wrote to Beatrice urging her to avoid open hostility.

Back in London the Webbs were caught up again in what Beatrice had once called the 'social whirlpool'. She noted that Shaw was much lionised 'by the smartest and most cynical set of English Society'. She added that 'some might say that we too had travelled in that direction'. Sidney, who cared less for social life, sought to curb her propensity to exhaust herself in party-giving and party-going. (BWD n.d. October 05)

Fyrish, Evanton, Rosshire
Aug. 22nd [1905]

My dear Kate

We are very anxious to hear how the cure progresses. You must have plenty of time to write us a description both of the life and its effect on you. It seems a pity that you and Mary Playne could not go to the same place and enjoy each other's society in the intervals of feeding or starving. Is it [?stifling] and what are your reflections?

We are back in this delightful country and in these delightfully quiet quarters. From our writing table we look straight on to the Firth and the German Ocean – perched up some 500 ft and quite secluded from any passers by the Great North Rd to 'John o' Groats'. Every morning we work from 8.15 to 1 o'c – and Sidney spends the greater part of the rest of the day either writing or reading in a quiet way. I am out on the moors or trotting off on my bicycle to see the Fergusons, or Clara Ryland or to the Factor's daughters or any other of my local acquaintances picking up the gossip of the place which always amuses me. Beatrice Chamberlain is with her aunt [Clara Ryland] at the manse and I had her and Hector Ferguson to lunch and we all went a mountain walk and finished up at tea at Assynt – the mother Ferguson's dower house. Bob Ferguson has brought back a beautiful bride from America and there seems to be a constant succession of smart persons calling on the Fergusons in motors on tour through Scotland. I gather from B.C. that her father is very depressed about politics and feels that he has been done by the course of events – he has gone off to take the Baths at Aix-le-Bains with his wife, her mother and his younger son. The present notion seems to be that Mr Balfour intends not only to go on the next session but to pass a Redistribution Bill, allow himself to be defeated immediately after this has passed and force the Liberals to hold office for 6 months before the formal election – thus giving time for some re-action from the reaction against his own party.

We have some echoes from W. Edinburgh: a young lawyer – Munro by name – who was lunching here said he had attended all Leonard's meetings and had a great admiration for him 'if only he would not always bring in the Boer War'! On that matter the well-to-do Scot seems unrepentant? There seems to be a general opinion that the Government has done well over the Scotch Church Question – at any rate the U.F. [United Free] and the Established Church seem satisfied – I have not seen any of the Little Frees. In this neighbourhood it is thought that of the two Churches taken from the U.F. by the Little Frees, one will have to be returned – and everyone thinks this will be a fair compromise.

Reginald Bray is coming to stay with us for 3 or 4 days early in September and we shall stay with Mr Haldane on our way to Glendaruel where we shall be for 4 days – returning to London October 2. When will you be back?

Ever yours affectionately<br>Beatrice Webb

462 UI SIDNEY WEBB TO H. G. WELLS

to 25 Sept.  Fyrish, Evanton, N.B.<br>30.8.5  Eclipse day – only there<br>ain't no sun

My dear Wells

I think you could do us a little service, and therefore venture to ask it, out of this arctic hole.

We want, for our book, to get at the archives of the Lords of Romney

Marsh. We will manage the 'getting at' them, when we know *who* is the Clerk or Secretary or other officer of that archaic body, (which is not, of course, the Municipal Corporation of Romney Marsh, or New Romney, or anything else but *The Lords* (Commissioners) of Romney Marsh) who still, I believe, profess to meet in their old hall that crouches at Dymchurch behind their long sea wall, and who affect, I was once told, the dignity of capital letters even for relative pronouns. Their Lordships, *They* do – as it indeed also the case with the Lords Commissioners of H.M. Treasury, but that is another story.

Don't *trouble* about it, as we shall go on enquiring in other directions – at present blankly hopeless, I own, but things turn up.

But if in any book of local reference at your command, or in any of your chance conversations with local officials (the Clerk to your confounded Urban District Council might know), or on any of your pedestrian or circumgyratory peregrinations – when gravelled for conversation matter for instance – to choose to enquire who the devil *Their Lordships* are, and who is *Their* Clerk or Secretary or Solicitor, and where *Their* august archives are deposited, it would be a great favor to

Yours very truly

Sidney Webb

I am to add that you must come and stay with us for the very first meeting of the Co-efficients.

### 463 HRCUT   BEATRICE WEBB TO GEORGE BERNARD SHAW

On 28 November Beatrice took A. J. Balfour to see *Major Barbara*: she thought the play was 'hell tossed on the stage – with no hope of heaven'. (BWD 29 November 05) On 2 December she called on Shaw and found him upset by the bad acting: when Beatrice complained that the play supported 'the triumph of the unmoral purpose', Shaw argued that poverty was 'the one unforgiveable crime', and defended Undershaft's attitude 'on the ground that until we divested ourselves of feeling (he said malice), we were not fit to go to the lengths needed for social salvation'. (BWD 2 December 05)

41 Grosvenor Road, Westminster Embankment<br>4 Dec. 1905

My dear G.B.S.

You made me doubt my own criticism of the ending of *Barbara* by your persuasive exposition of it. But you don't get your meaning into the mind of the audience: the impression left is that Cusins and Barbara are neither of them convinced by Undershaft's argument, but that they are uttering words, like the silly son, to bridge over a betrayal of their own convictions.

It may be the acting or it may be some lack of proportion to Undershaft's argument – I am not clever enough to tell.

I shall wait the actual printed document with immense interest.

216

Meanwhile our warmest welcome to the Shelter scene – which is really an extraordinary 'Souls' Tragedy', and useful as well.

Remember Friday 8 o'c – I fear evening dress as I have asked various types for Wells' delectation. Be so pleasant.

Ever yours

BW

## 464 GLC  SIDNEY WEBB TO W. C. JOHNSON

Webb later reversed his opinion and supported the renaming of the street, writing to Johnson, the Clerk of the L.C.C., on 14 December to say that 'Millbank' would be a unique name, easily recognised by cabmen and suitably brief to serve as a telegraphic address.

41 Grosvenor Road, Westminster Embankment
[4 December 1905]

My dear Johnson

Please don't decide on No. 16 in your agenda tomorrow – naming of the new street in Westminster Improvement. I strongly suggest that it would be a great mistake to name that bit of street Millbank, or indeed anything yet. *It will form part of a continuous line of thoroughfare facing the river*; and it ought not to be called anything but *Westminster Embankment* right up to the Tate Gallery. Pray let this be at any rate considered. This name is already in common use for this bit of it. There is a great and permanent gap in the houses at the Tate Gallery, and great confusion is caused by any other name. It is bad policy to give a separate name to a little bit out of what will be a continuous line of embankment. Pray delay it for consideration.

Yours

Sidney Webb

217

# 6. The Poor Law battle
## December 1905 – February 1909

The Balfour government had been in difficulty for some time and in the last months of 1905 it was clear that Balfour would soon go out of office. He resigned on 4 December; the Liberal leader Sir Henry Campbell-Bannerman became prime minister and immediately dissolved Parliament. In the elections which began on 12 January 1906 the Liberals were returned in an unprecedented landslide. They came back with 377 seats, supported by 83 Irish, 24 'Lib-Labs' and 29 Labour members. The Tories, now reduced to 132, with 25 Liberal Unionist allies, were weaker than ever before.

The success of the candidates run by the Labour Representation Committee, under MacDonald's leadership, meant that a Labour Party could be formed for the first time in Parliament. These gains had been secured by a covert agreement between MacDonald and the Liberal Chief Whip, Herbert Gladstone, which had given a number of Labour candidates a clear run against Tory opponents. This agreement, which allowed Labour to enter Parliament as the tacit allies of the Liberals, was not wholly satisfactory, since it was not an open and formal alliance: it led to some difficulty when local Labour enthusiasts wished to run candidates against Liberals, especially at bye-elections. It was, nevertheless, decisive in giving Labour a base in national politics which was never lost thereafter. Though the Webbs attached surprisingly little importance to this development it could be seen as the application by MacDonald of tactics learned from Webb during his active period in the Fabian Society.

The failure of the Webbs to appreciate the importance of Labour's emergence was compounded by a similar misunderstanding and dislike of the Liberal resurgence. They were more disturbed by the defeat of friends, such as Arthur Balfour himself, than pleased by the victory of many of their former Radical associates. There had been a dramatic turn in the political tide, sweeping Radical Nonconformity into power – the kind of coalition which on a smaller scale the Webbs had come to dislike and oppose in London politics. Realising that the government would now be controlled by the neo-Gladstonian impulses with which they had themselves broken over ten years previously, they were aware that they could not hope to play much of a part in the making of policy, even though a number of their old associates now held office. Insofar as the tactics of permeation could still be of use to them they pinned their hopes on influencing the younger administrators in devising administrative schemes which they might be able to sell to sympathetic members of the Cabinet. Even here their prospects were limited. Their closest contacts were with the 'Limps', Grey, Haldane and Asquith; after a futile last-minute intrigue to push Campbell-Bannerman out of the way into the House of Lords, these three had made their peace with him and accepted office. But Grey had become Foreign Secretary and Haldane Secretary of State for War – posts in which they had little influence on the issues of domestic policy in which the Webbs were most interested – and Asquith as Chancellor of the Exchequer now had his eye fixed on the party leadership and Downing Street.

In this situation it was fortunate for the Webbs that almost the last decision of Balfour's government was to set up a Royal Commission on the Poor Law and to appoint Beatrice as one of the Commissioners. She knew of the decision on 29 November, a week before the government fell.

There had been growing discontent with the Poor Law for many years. Social reformers were distressed at its harshness and by the dread in which people held the prospect of the workhouse. Officials were worried about the growing expense of relief and at the haphazard administration of the Poor Law, which was under the general direction of the Local Government Board but administered by local boards of guardians. Seventy years after the Poor Law had been reorganised in 1834 it was generally recognised that it was due for reform. Poverty – grinding, demoralising, socially infectious pauperism – still blighted Edwardian society as shamefully as in the heyday of Victorianism, and neither the Poor Law nor Victorian philanthropy, with its emphasis on thrift, self-help and moral improvement, had done more than prevent outright starvation for the masses of paupers. One person in eight still died in the workhouse; the formal stigma of pauper status remained; families were divided and the aged poor confined in near-penal conditions.

Though the Poor Law system was disintegrating, however, there was no agreement on how it might be changed or, as many Radicals and socialists had been insisting for years, broken up and replaced by a less harsh and more efficient system. On the one hand there was a powerful lobby, which included several of the senior officials at the L.G.B., which argued for a return to the full rigours of the 1834 regulations. On the other hand there were reformers who wanted to go beyond more humane means of alleviating poverty to tackle the fundamental causes of destitution.

The tension between the sharply contrasting positions was to dominate the work of the Royal Commission for the next three years. The attempt to impose a radical alternative was to become the primary concern of the Webb partnership. As Beatrice and Sidney threw themselves energetically into research and policy-drafting the balance between them changed significantly. Hitherto Sidney had been the public partner, Beatrice the researcher and strategist. Now she had to assume the public role while Sidney became her amanuensis: the situation was rather similar to that with which they had begun their partnership on the trade union book before their marriage. Membership of the Commission, moreover, was to affect Beatrice's personality, bringing out her latent aptitude for salon politics and releasing her sense of mission, with long-term consequences for both the personal and political relationships of the partnership. As they worked on the causes and possible cures for destitution they found themselves formulating a comprehensive social programme and beginning to think of the political organisation which might be required to push it through. The idea of a new political party had been generally in their minds ever since their break with the Liberals in 1894. It had led them to flirt with Rosebery and the 'Limps', to look for allies among collectivist Conservatives, to launch the Co-efficients and to become involved in the complex intrigues around the Education Acts. It had also led them to underestimate both the I.L.P. and the emerging Labour Party. They were now to seize the opportunity to demonstrate their idea of disinterested experts or social architects, devising a blue-print for society and then seeking to rally a heterogeneous cross-party body of support to impose it.

The Chairman of the Commission was Lord George Hamilton (1845–1927), Tory politician and Chairman of the London School Board in 1894. The other members were: F. H. Bentham, chairman of the Bradford Board of Guardians; Beatrice's old associate Charles Booth; Helen Bosanquet, the wife of Professor Bernard Bosanquet (1848–1923), who was an active member of the Charity Organisation Society; Charles Owen O'Conor (1838–1906), an Irish liberal politician who died and was replaced by Dr Dennis Kelly (1852–1924); the Bishop of Ross; Dr Arthur Downes (1851–1937) the senior medical officer for the Poor Law administration; the Reverend Thory Gage Gardiner; the veteran housing reformer Octavia Hill; George Lansbury (1859–1940), socialist leader in Poplar, strongly opposed to the rigours of the Poor Law, later a notable pacifist and suffragist who became Leader of the Labour Party in 1931; Charles Stewart Loch, the secretary of the Charity Organisation Society; Sir James Patten-MacDougall (1849–1919) the vice-president of the Scottish L.G.B.; Thomas Hancock Nunn (1859–1937) of the Hampstead Board of Guardians, who was a leading member of the C.O.S.; the Reverend Lancelot Ridley Phelps (1853–1936) economist and fellow of Oriel College, Oxford, who was also active in the C.O.S.; Sir Samuel Butler Provis (1857–1927), permanent secretary of the Local Government Board from 1898; Sir Henry Robinson (1857–1937), vice-president of the Irish L.G.B.; Professor William Smart (1853–1915), the economist; the Reverend Henry Russell Wakefield (1854–1933) member of the L.S.B. 1897–1900, who became Bishop of Birmingham in 1911; and Beatrice Webb. Francis W. Chandler, of the Carpenters Union was added later to represent the trade union interest. The range of the Commission reflected a variety of attitudes to the Poor Law. It included the three senior civil servants directly responsible for its administration in England, Scotland and Ireland. The Charity Organisation Society influence was extremely strong, apart from its effect on the civil servants and the Commission generally; six of the Commission members were directly associated with the C.O.S. The economists, Charles Booth and Beatrice Webb were clearly appointed as interested experts. The secretary of the Commission was Robert Duff (1871–1946), a civil servant in the L.G.B. who became a general inspector of the Poor Law in 1909; his assistant was John Jeffrey of the Scottish L.G.B.

### 465 BL   SIDNEY WEBB TO JOHN BURNS

Burns had been appointed to be President of the L.G.B., thus becoming the Minister directly responsible for the administration of the Poor Law. After he had called at Grosvenor Road on 8 February and indicated that he would be happy to receive advice from the Webbs Beatrice noted favourably: 'If good intentions, and a strong, vigorous and audacious character can make up for lack of administrative experience and technical knowledge, John Burns may yet be a success'. (BWD 9 February 06)

41 Grosvenor Road
11.12.5

My dear Burns

A thousand congratulations!

It is splendidly courageous of you to accept the L.G.B. – and I don't think it ought to have been asked of you. You will be cruelly denounced for not doing impossibilities; but you have survived this sort of thing before now.

I am sure I need hardly say that I am always entirely at your service, if there is ever any way that I can help.

Yours

Sidney Webb

466 PP  SIDNEY TO BEATRICE

Sir James Stewart Davey (1848–1915) was chief inspector of the Poor Law and assistant secretary of the L.G.B.: he was anxious to revert to the strict implementation of the 1834 principles. William H. Dickinson was chairman of the L.C.C. Herbert Samuel had been appointed Under-Secretary at the Home Office.

The Trade Union Bill was to be brought in by the Liberals in order to reverse the effects of the Taff Vale judgement of 1904 which had made trade unions legally liable for losses caused by industrial disputes. The Liberal pledge to restore the traditional protection of trade union funds helped to attract working-class votes in the elections. At the same time, the judgement had been a decisive factor in persuading the trade union movement to support the Labour Representation Committee. The number of unionists affiliated to the L.R.C. increased sharply after Taff Vale and both their organisations and their funds were indispensable in securing the Labour gains in 1906. By the time of the election the cotton operatives and the miners were the only two large groups which held back from the Labour Party and continued their close association with the Liberals. It should be remembered that the 24 'Lib-Lab' M.P.s (mainly textile and mining men) were also trade unionists, though not socialists, so that the combined 'Labour' vote in the House of Commons was 53, in addition to those Radical members who sympathised with trade unionism.

Beatrice had gone to Gracedieu to discuss the way in which the Commission might work with Charles Booth. She had decided that the officials intended to spoon-feed the commissioners with evidence supporting a preconceived policy. At the first meeting of the Commission Beatrice made procedural objections to a cut and dried scheme. (BWD 2 December 05) Striking a note that was to echo throughout her membership of the Commission, she wrote: 'It will need all my self-command to keep myself from developing a foolish hostility and becoming self-conscious in my desire to get special sound investigation . . . the work of the Commission will be an education in manners as well as Poor Law'. On 15 December (BWD) Beatrice complained 'of the absence of agenda, of concrete resolutions . . . I claimed to have a formal procedure in future . . . I shall only get my share of control by quietly and persistently standing on my rights as an individual commissioner and refusing to be overawed by great personages who would pooh-pooh a woman who attempts to share in the control of affairs'.

41 Grosvenor Road, Westminster,
London s.w.

13.12.5

My own dearest

I send a few lines to greet you. In a few words with Davy he said the Poor Law Commission had got into a dreadful muddle. He then left, so I had no more talk. But note, that a brief part of report in *The Times* about the first meeting (giving no information) says that no date was fixed for the next meeting!

Dickinson (who was grateful for the letters to Miss Addams, Lowell and Talcott Williams whom he found most interesting), says the writs will be issued about 8 January, and the borough polls will be over by the 16th. I hope therefore you will have no meetings on the 8/9th and 15/16th.

We are in the midst of an interminably long Education Committee Meeting at which everybody seems to want to talk. Herbert Samuel, whom we congratulated on his appointment to the H.O., [Home Office] asked me as to T.U. Commission Report, and said that he thought the Trade Union Bill and Workmen's Accident Compensation Bill would come first. He said he should always be glad to have hints from us. It was to be a Government of Social Reform.

Goodbye dear one. Don't work too hard.

Sidney

### 467 FP  SIDNEY WEBB TO EDWARD PEASE

'The Liberal Cabinet. An Intercepted Letter', approved by a Fabian meeting, was published in the *National Review* in January 1906. Attempting to repeat the ironic effect of 'To Your Tents, O Israel!', it was cast in the form of a letter from Campbell-Bannerman to his Ministers telling each what to do. It was, in effect, the Fabian programme – or rather, the Webb programme – for the new government, dealing with taxation, fair wages, compulsory military training, the retention of the Education Acts and other measures which were fairly commonplace among moderate Radicals.

41 Grosvenor Road
Westminster Embankment
16.12.5

Dear Pease

Here is the M.S. I doubt whether I can be at Executive this afternoon at all. At best, I can only come in very late (which I will try to do).

I have told Bland and others the M.S. is with you. Show it to as many Exec. members as you can. There is nothing in it to commit any of us to any particular proposal as all the points are put as C-B.'s personal suggestions. Practically all the things we reproached them for not doing in 1893 are put in. I have tried to make the letter reasonably correct from a dramatic point of view. It is the sort of letter that any of us might be imagined to write *if we had C-B.'s personality, and had to address such a Cabinet, in such a state of electoral opinion*. These are the limiting circumstances.

As I said, after failing with the *19th Century*, I fixed up with the *National Review* for January – we want to be free to republish in February. Copy I have promised *on Monday 19th* (as Xmas plays havoc).

Perhaps you could read some of it to the Exec. in my absence – if they desire.

It must not be made any longer. I could only get 10 pp and it exceeds that already.

Yours

Sidney Webb

468 BUL   BEATRICE WEBB TO SIR OLIVER LODGE

4 Devonshire Terrace,<br>Sandgate<br>Dec. 29 [1905]

Dear Sir Oliver

We were so glad to gather, from your little gift, that you are well again – it would be a real disaster if you were to cease to function – so please take care – we look to you as a messenger of the new Light which is breaking our poor stupid humanity.

I am interested in the story you sent us. It is well done: whether it is a true representation of workhouse training is another matter. Superficial statistics are against the author: a larger proportion of workhouse-trained children *seem* to succeed in life than of the children of the class from which they are drawn – a loose standard I admit. (Will Crooks is not a bad product in strength and unconventionality and initiative?) However I suppose the workhouse child is one of the subjects we are supposed to investigate by this new Royal Commission. How far the L.G.B. officials, who at present dominate the Chairman, will permit us to investigate *anything* that will not lead us to their foregone conclusions, I have my doubts. It will be a duel over the Soul of Lord George Hamilton – a somewhat acid subject for a fight! Meanwhile it is a somewhat serious drain on one's energies which were destined to complete the long-delayed book. I am beginning to understand Mr Balfour's remark, when I thanked him for placing me on the Commission, that 'it never occurred to me as a subject of gratitude'.

You will be excited over the election in Birmingham. Your great man (J.C.) is not strong enough, intellectually, for the job – he has too great a contempt and an incapacity for reasoning. What a splendid personage he might have been, *if* he had been endowed with Religion and Science – a Religious Purpose and Scientific methods.

We are trying to get on with the work in quiet seaside lodgings, but I have somewhat broken down and am 'lazing' it.

Ever yours

Beatrice Webb

The attached document was drafted by Beatrice as a memorandum for Lord George Hamilton to embody her procedural criticisms and to suggest a method of work.

*Private and Confidential*                                    41 Grosvenor Road,
                                                                        Westminster
                                                                 January 6 [1906]

Dear Mr Lansbury

I send herewith the suggestions which I laid before the Chairman after the first meeting of the Commission.

I thought the *procedure* most unsatisfactory as it practically left the whole control in the hands of the Chairman and the L.G.B. officials. I think we ought to have a strong committee to prepare a scheme of investigation.

                                        Yours
                                                        Beatrice Webb

Suggestions attached.


                        *Private*   please keep them private


                SUGGESTIONS made to the Chairman before Xmas

                            1. *Procedure of the Commission.*

necessary in order to come prepared with amendments.

(a) Could we not have the usual Agenda circulated before each meeting – notifying what business will be taken (what witnesses, what resolutions, drafts of circulars or other documents proposed to be issued, etc.)?

This was a way of saying that we ought to have regular minutes of the proceedings.

(b) Would it not save time at the opening of each meeting if the Minutes of the last Meeting had been circulated, and thus would not need to be read through?

This has been carried out in a somewhat perfunctory manner in regard to Mr Adrian's evidence.

(c) Most important of all, to Commissioners like myself, who start without official experience of the Poor Law, is the *early* circulation of each Witness's Proof, or Precis of Evidence, without which we who are ignorant cannot ask the right questions, and therefore would waste much of the Commission's time. Many of us need time to consider the Proof of each witness, and read up his particular subject.

*We ought to decide who are to be our witnesses.*

Would it not be possible – as regards all witnesses whom the Commission at its next meeting may decide to call – to ask them at once for their Proofs, and circulate these in a batch immediately they come in; instead of circulating them one by one with the Agenda of each Meeting?

(d) Whilst we are learning from these witnesses the legal framework within which the Guardians work, should not the Commission at once appoint a small Committee to deliberate and draw up a scheme of how to investigate the working of the Poor Law, which can only be the local practice (whether of each Union or of typical Unions) – i.e. the facts as distinguished from the law? Or is there any other way in which the *Commission as a whole* can be put in a position to make up its mind as to the kind of investigation into the facts that it will make, the methods of inquiry that it will adopt, and how it will divide this work between (1) itself, (2) its committees, if any (3) travelling investigators or (4) local agents? There is, too, the question of (a) what documents to call for; (b) how best to supplement the documents by oral evidence to the Commission, and by personal observation, either by ourselves or some of us, or by the paid officers whom the Commission might appoint.

If *we* do not appoint a Committee the Commission will be run by the Chairman and the L.G.B. officials whom he consults.

## 2. *The Investigation*

Our enquiry, I understand, is primarily into the *working* of the existing Poor Law – that is to say, we have, in the first place, to ascertain the facts of the Poor Law not merely people's *opinion* about it.
(a) The Law.
(b) The Practice.

(a) The Law.

By this I understand is meant the sum total of the legal obligation of the Guardians and their officers. I gather that comparatively little of this legal obligation is to be found in the Statutes, though I feel that I must myself begin by understanding these. I should be grateful for an expert's evidence on the Statutes.

There is a disinclination to subject the action of the L.G.B. to criticism: we want

I gather that the L.G.B. has, by statute, power to make Rules and Orders, which have the force of law. So far as such Rules and Orders have been made, they seem to me therefore part of

225

a complete knowledge of what that action has been since 1834.

the Poor Law; and I hope we shall have L.G.B. evidence as to these Rules and Orders; and as to anything else that the Guardians or their officers have to obey.

## (b) *The Practice.*

But the law is, I believe, very different from the practice in different parts of the country. How can the Commission best get a preliminary conspectus of the actual working of the Poor Law, in the practice of the different Unions. Is there for instance any one officer who can *from his own personal observation,* give the Commission the exact facts as to the variations in constitutional organization and practice of the Unions in all the different parts of England and Wales?

I imagine that the 14 General Inspectors of the L.G.B. could give the Commission these facts each for the Unions in his own district. For instance, in the few times that I have attended the Relief Committee of Boards of Guardians I have noted very interesting divergencies as to their form of composition (e.g. Committee of the whole, local Committees, open Committees, Committees excluding the Guardians of the particular districts concerned, committees composed chiefly of the Guardians of the particular districts concerned; and, in Manchester a few years ago, committees consisting of one Guardian only, with a salaried expert). I have fancied in watching the working of these various forms of Relief Committees that the form influenced the purity and wisdom of the administration.

One of the Inspectors, I understand, 'will give the L.G.B. away' and is therefore not to be called. It is most desirable that we should have all.

There must be many other forms and varieties of structure among the Unions, not noted in any text-book. I feel that I want to know what these forms are, and in which Unions they exist. Then there is the variety of practice as to the collection, verification and record of the facts of each applicant for relief. Besides the Statutory form, there is I know, the 'case paper system', and there may be others. I gather that each Inspector knows these local systems from personal inspection, as regards the Unions in his own district. Allied to varieties of local machinery is the practice with regard to Relieving Officers (e.g. whether only the Statutory officer is employed, whether he combines other offices, whether a man or a woman, how extensive is his district; whether there is a system of 'cross-investigation' by a second officer; whether the cases are again dealt with by a Superintendent Relieving Officer; which of these officers sit with the Relief Committees etc.

I cannot at present see how, until after we have heard each Inspector on the working constitution and practice of the Unions in his own district, the Commission as a whole can determine (a) the preliminary classification of Unions which is indispensable to their investigation; (b) which Unions to select for more minute investigation on the spot, possibly by statistical experts; (c) from which Unions to ask one or two years documents as to relief cases, for statistical analysis in London.

Of course, we could all of us suggest a few Unions at random; but each person would select a different set – and then they might not be typical.

It seems to me that only after the Commission as a whole has gained a vision of the varieties known to the 14 Inspectors can we refer the matter to a Committee to prepare the classification of Unions and of subjects, to say nothing of the particular points to be discovered by our travelling investigators, if the commission should decide to have such officers.

## Local Witnesses

I hope myself to learn much from the Local Witnesses – the members of Boards of Guardians, Clerks to Boards, and above all, the abler Relieving Officers, who I have sometimes found to know more about the actual working of the Poor Law, than the Guardians or even the Clerks. But I feel that I shall not be able to get the fullest advantage from their appearing before us, unless the Commission knows before hand (e.g. from the Inspector's evidence, from the classification of Unions that will have been prepared by our Committee, and perhaps also from the statistical analysis of their relief cases that the committee will by that time have got ready) what the peculiarities of the Union are – as regards the working constitution of the Board, the kind of machinery it uses, the character of the relief it gives, and the circumstances of the locality affecting the working of the Poor Law (such as trades, the prevalent conditions of the wage contract and the co-existence of other agencies for relieving destitution.) Without these facts, we shall scarcely know on what specific points it will be useful to extract from

I look to this kind of investigation to bring out the connection between Sweating and irregular Employment with the production of pauperism. I have not of course, drawn attention to this because some might object to any Enquiry into the *causes* of pauperism.

227

the witness, a description of facts within his knowledge – as distinguished from his opinions.

To sum up – would it not be well, (whilst the Commission as a whole is learning the law from one or more eminent officials and gaining from the 14 Inspectors a general view of the practice of those Unions that each of them knows personally), for a duly appointed Committee to be preparing a suitable scheme of investigation – such scheme to be reported to the Commission for its discussion and, if thought fit, its adoption as regards such Unions as the Commission may hereafter accept as typical or likely to be fertile in suggestion?

470 PP  BEATRICE WEBB TO MARY PLAYNE

Alfred Cripps, running as a Conservative, had been defeated at Stretford, where he had been elected in 1901 after his defeat at Stroud in 1901. His son, Alfred Henry Seddon Cripps, was elected for Wycombe in 1906; Beatrice's speculation that he would make room for his defeated father was justified when Alfred Cripps took over the Wycombe seat in 1910.

41 Grosvenor Road, Westminster Embankment
[21 January 1906]

Dearest Mary

What an amazing business! Poor Alfred with the 2,600 majority against him: will Seddon get in, and is he meant to retire in his favour? What fun watching C-B. with his enormous brood of ugly ducklings – all the wildest and most fantastic of one's acquaintance, old and young, are in – about 35 of the Progressive L.C.C. and a good part of the Trade Union Congress. What larks we shall have!

Probably they will 'cancel out' if C-B. is wise enough to let them stew a bit.

The Poor Law Commission is turning out rather a heavy and unpleasant business! no one except Charles Booth wants to 'Enquire'; they are all trying to lead up to some specific proposals and the L.G.B. officials are dead set on thwarting all investigation that does not directly point to these conclusions. Whether I shall get them to do anything that is worth doing in the way of ascertaining the facts, I rather doubt – if I don't, I shall be able to take it easy and go on with my own work – which perhaps will be more remunerative. Charles Booth is not strong enough to fight the position, but he is as delightful and easy to work with.

Maggie is not at all well and seems likely to be in bed for sometime. She is not wise with her health – when she became a 'Hayite' she eat most foolishly, of everything except meat. If you are going to eat and live according to impulse you had better stick to the conventional diet.

When do you come to London? Do come here?

How is Arthur?

Ever yours

B. Webb

Beatrice was anxious to push the Commission into making investigations on its own, so that it would not depend merely on material provided by civil servants. She was coming to recognise that if this kind of work was to be undertaken she and Sidney could not hope to make much progress with their own writing. She therefore began to devise lines of enquiry which could be undertaken either by staff specially employed by the Commission (which appointed such assistant commissioners or researchers) or, if the Commission would not accept her proposals, by staff whom she would employ herself. She had sensed at once that for her the central issue of the Commission would be 'the whence and whither of pauperism'. (BWD 5 February 06)

Provis was attempting to limit the Commission's access to L.G.B. papers; the Commissioners, he tried to insist, could 'not have the run of the whole' but only such papers as they specifically requested. (BWD 12 February 06) He lost his temper under pressure and Beatrice also began to reveal a truculent streak in her nature: 'if one begins by being disagreeable, one may come in the end to a better bargain'. She had already come to the conclusion 'that I shall not have the support of the Commission in my desire for scientific research into the past seventy years'. Neither Beatrice nor Sidney yet had an idea where the enquiries might lead. Their method of investigation relied heavily upon the collection of as many facts as possible and their subsequent analysis by sifting, collating and comparing. Other members of the Commission objected on two grounds – that an elaborate historical approach would be of little value and that there was no need for any large scale systematic enquiry into the current situation.

By 15 May Beatrice felt that the Commission was 'lumbering along; chaotic and extravagant in its use of time and money each committee doing as it sees fit in its own sight . . . how hard it is for a quick-witted and somewhat vain woman to be discreet and accurate'. Beatrice was already bent on exploring the causes of destitution rather than seeking means to alleviate it.


41 Grosvenor Road, Westminster Embankment

Sunday [?4 or 11 March 1906]

Dear Mr Burns

Will you come in for the dinner hour on Thursday 20th March 8 o'c – and could you not persuade Mrs Burns to meet you here? Do say yes as I want to talk to you and do not like to come to the L.G.B. lest Sir S. Provis should think I am disputing his weight on the Royal Commission. I like him much – he is a real good sort and the soul of loyalty to his office and his Chief. But he has a poor opinion of womankind. I don't altogether disagree with him – in so far as public affairs are concerned.

Do come in if you can and don't throw me over for a dramatic performance – even at the House!

Ever yours

Beatrice Webb

### 472 FP  SIDNEY WEBB TO EDWARD PEASE

The proofs were probably of 'The Abolition of Poor Law Guardians' written by Pease and published as Fabian Tract 126. 'Parish Councils and Village Life' Tract 137, was a revision of Webb's Tract 105: it eventually appeared early in 1908.

The Fabian executive was always somewhat puritanical about the Society's social occasions, ensuring that they were genteel gatherings with soft drinks: on one occasion there was a dispute as to whether the serving of ice-cream might be considered too sybaritic. The performance of folk dances and madrigals fitted the arts-and-crafts tastes of many Fabians.

41 Grosvenor Road,

Westminster Embankment

10/6/6

Dear Pease

I have been too busy to comment on your proofs. I must leave them to you and the others.

It occurs to me to remind you that *next spring*, all the Parish Councils are re-elected, having completed twelve years. What about our Tract on their work? I think the Executive should consider whether we might not usefully arrange to circulate something about January 1907, (a) To all the provincial newspapers; (b) to Clerks of Parish Councils – these are usually local amateurs; (c) To the Chairmen of Rural District Councils; (d) To Rural County Councillors. These would amount to 10,000 altogether; and perhaps we could not do so many. But it would be propaganda in a new direction; and after all, the country is still part of England.

I should think that someone could bring our Tract up to date without more than mere industry; and rechristen it Ten Years Work etc.

Something else might (also?) be enclosed; and a covering circular sent. It would be a useful advertisement anyhow, among a new set of people. Consider it.

Yours

Sidney Webb

I *shall* be at Soirée (1 ticket)

Runciman became Parliamentary Secretary to the L.G.B. in 1906. In March Beatrice had attended a meeting of the Poplar Guardians where she found their procedure for allotting contracts to suppliers 'utterly reckless', little care being taken to get the lowest price and favour verging on corruption being shown to local firms which tendered. She concluded that if the Guardians were not actually corrupt 'English human nature must be more naively stupid than any other race would credit'.

41 Grosvenor Road,
Westminster Embankment.
July 1 [1906]

Dear Mr Runciman

What I want to know is whether there are any [?valuer's] reports or other enquiries into maladministration of Guardians similar to those going on now at Poplar and West Ham? Owing to the procedure of a Royal Commission, we are getting no evidence about Boards of Guardians and of the way they have of conducting their business. If we are to Report in favour of a Reform either in area, constitution or procedure, we must have some basis for it. Otherwise we shall not convince public opinion.

Reports of Enquiries of L.G.B. *during the last 10 years* might put us on the scent and we might get corroborative evidence. (Please don't tell Sir S. Provis I am asking for this.)

My husband is always using your Local Taxation Returns and finds them of *very great value*. If you were *seriously* thinking of improving them he would sit down and consider suggestions, but it would be a task of some difficulty.

Yours sincerely

Beatrice Webb

P.S. There is one other matter about which I should like information but I hesitate to trouble you. Also I am particularly anxious that Sir S. Provis – with whom I am now on excellent terms – should not imagine that I am going behind his back. The question is this. Is there a complete edition – which could be used by a Commission – of the general orders and circulars issued by the L.G.B. since its start in 1871 to Poor Law authorities?

I have been given the task [of] drawing up from an analysis of these orders and circulars, a memorandum as to *Policy of* the Central Authority since 1834. For 1834–47 the information is complete: from 1847 to 1871 it is less complete but there was comparatively little change. From 1871 Poor Law becomes submerged in other L.G.B. work and the policy is extremely difficult to trace.

If for your own information you happened to be enquiring into this document I should much like to be informed as to the extent of the sources.

BW

The Webbs, who saw themselves as reformers of machinery as much as of policy, were strongly animated by a desire to simplify and improve administration: the haphazard evolution of English local government, on which they had become experts by their historical studies, had left a network of confused, competing and inadequate agencies which were both costly and ineffective.

41 Grosvenor Road
Westminster Embankment
July 5 [1906]

Dear Mr Runciman

Very many thanks for your letter. I know Macmillan and the other text books – unfortunately all their works give, as you say, only orders and circulars that are still *in force*. However, I daresay I may get what I require (if it exists!) from Sir S. Provis as he is now very friendly with me.

But the L.G.B. is rather a labyrinth – I doubt whether the officials themselves have a clue to its mysteries.

London Government is in a terrible tangle – Poor Law Guardians, Borough Councils, Water Board, Metropolitan Asylum Board, Thames Conservancy and presently a Dock Board – with the L.C.C. sitting uneasily on the top. Why don't you get J.B. [John Burns] to ask the P.M. for a Royal Commission on the whole subject early next year?

Yours ever

Beatrice Webb

## 475 PP BEATRICE WEBB TO MARY PLAYNE

At Easter the Webbs had visited the Playnes at Longfords; they spent Whitsun at Bramdean, Hampshire, to be near Beatrice's sister Georgina Meinertzhagen, though they found the family's rich country house life-style disagreeable. They were still able to spend some time on their local government books, though they now realised that the venture was so vast that they were committed to a series of volumes stretching away into the future.

The Commission had come to a point where each of the key figures had begun to pursue a separate special interest. Charles Booth, for instance, was occupying himself with current statistics, Mrs Bosanquet was specialising on outdoor relief and women's wages while Beatrice was reviewing Sweating as a cause of pauperism and undertaking the historical survey for which her colleagues seemed to have little taste. Charlotte Shaw had put up money for Beatrice to pay for research assistants, especially Mrs Spencer and Mildred Bulkley. Mrs Spencer was formerly Amy Harrison, who had married F. H. Spencer when he left the Webbs to work for the L.C.C.; his place was taken by Mildred Bulkley, who worked for the Webbs until 1912. A little later, a special fund was set up by the Fabians with gifts from some wealthy members and sympathisers to underwrite additional help for Beatrice.

On 17 July Beatrice was struck by what she considered an important new idea, though it bore some resemblance to a notion used by Samuel Butler in his satirical novel *Erewhon*: she thought that illness should be suppressed as a public nuisance requiring compulsory treatment.

She was still busy entertaining. In June she gave a dinner to rally support for Haldane's plan to create a Territorial Army; in July a group of young Liberals were invited to meet Arthur Balfour. In a typical week, apart from dining out themselves, the Webbs had 30 people to lunch or dinner.

Evelyn Baring (1841–1917) became Viscount Cromer in 1889 and Earl of Cromer in 1901. He was a colonial administrator who was the effective ruler of Egypt from 1883 to 1907. Edward Talbot, formerly Bishop of Rochester, became Bishop of Southwark in 1905. Lawrence Lowell (1856–1943) was a political scientist who became president of Harvard University 1909–33; Bernard Holland (1856–1926) was a barrister who served as secretary to several commissions and to his lifelong friend Alfred Lyttelton when he was Colonial Secretary; Sydney Buxton had been appointed Postmaster-General in the new Liberal government; Owen Seaman was editor of *Punch* 1906–32; Cyril Jackson (1863–1924) was chief inspector of the Board of Education 1903–06, assistant commissioner to the Poor Law Commission and a member of the L.C.C. 1907–13.

41 Grosvenor Road
July 29th [1906]

Dearest Mary

I have been meaning to scribble a greeting and scraps of news, but the pressure of the last fortnight of July in London is always severe both with S. and myself.

The P.L.C. rumbled along to the end in an amazingly incompetent way. What strikes most, looking back on these monthly sittings, is the waste of time and energy and the amazing extravagance in money, brought about by having no fixed procedure and no trained person in any position of responsibility. We are spending about £12,000 a year: I would undertake to get more information and better verified information for £1,200. We slip and slide along, massing up bulky blue books, always evading difficult points, sprawling all over the place beginning multitudinous and often irrelevant enquiries and completing and perfecting none. In despair I am undertaking 3 Investigations, into points which seem to me vital, by my own subordinates, and Charles Booth has scampered off with *all* the statistics and is elaborating tables with aid of 16 persons paid by himself. I daresay other Commissioners are doing likewise – no one knows what the others are doing – the result being that we shall all be proceeding on different evidence. No one is looking after the assistant commissioners, two of whom are hopelessly incompetent. However, I suppose something will come out of it. But it is high time we had a Royal Commission on Royal Commissions; and insisted on some sort of procedure and financial estimates, and collected a nucleus of trained persons who would consider ways and means and keep the amateurs in order!

We had an interesting visit on Thursday from Lord Cromer. He wrote out of the blue asking to come and see Sidney so we invited him to lunch.

233

He wanted S. to come over for six weeks to Egypt and report to him on the whole of the educational system of Egypt and the Sudan for a handsome fee and all expenses – anytime that suited him. I was rather tempted at the notion – it would have been such an interesting way of seeing Egypt. But S. felt he was not the man for Lord Cromer – that he knew too little about the technical side of education – buildings, plant, curriculum etc. Moreover we have not any spare time this winter. So S. suggested Dr Garnett, in default of the one or two others. But Lord Cromer was most interesting – absolutely direct and frank and without any kind of pretension to knowledge he did not possess. He struck me as a quite unusually fine administrative mind, bent on using the expert, but not allowing himself to be directed by any course of perfection in any one direction from his main object. In the evening of the same day we had an amusing little party, John Burns, the B. of Southwark, Lawrence Lowell (the American writer), Bernard Holland and one or two others – discussing the relation of the Church to Democracy – J.B. picturesque but arrogantly egotistical, the Bishop gentle and persuasive, Lawrence Lowell shrewdly well-informed and inquisitive, Bernard Holland, philosophical and non-party and Sidney acting as a sort of Chairman. On Saturday W.J. [William Jennings] Bryan came to lunch and met Sydney Buxton and Sir Horace Plunkett. He (Bryan) is a windbag – infantile in his suggestions. Thought that all offices Federal, State and Municipal should be distributed after each election between the 2 or 3 Political Parties *according to their Voting Strength*!, that the railways should be owned by the individual States (each State to have its little bit of the Union Pacific for instance) and that Trusts could be curbed by passing a law that no one firm should do more than 50% of the total trade in any article! He is a good fellow, kind and upright, but a big fool. But he firmly believes that he is going to be President and it seems likely.

Last Sunday we spent with the Sydney Buxtons – a large house party – young Liberals and Owen Seaman, the Editor of *Punch*. This evening we have come back from Cyril Jackson's comfortable bachelor establishment – meeting a bevy of Toynbee men – a first-rate lot of hardworking and hard-headed young persons – a better lot than I remember at any previous time at Toynbee Hall. On Wednesday we go to Bagley Wood near Oxford until September 5th. If you are motoring in the neighbourhood do look in on us. We are spending the afternoon of Sunday August 19th at Parmoor – Alfred is sending his motor for us and the Granville Barkers who will be staying with us. Could not you and Arthur meet us then? Write and tell me how you are – this is a gossipy scrawl – but I know you like it.

Ever yours affectionately

Beatrice Webb

What Wells later called his 'storm in a Fabian tea-cup' was already blowing up in the first months of 1906. He had joined the Fabian Society in February 1903 and taken little part in its activities, almost resigning in 1904. In 1905, reflecting the swing to the left in the country as a whole, the Fabian Society began to revive and to find new members coming in at a rate unknown since the early Nineties. Shaw, among others, felt this revival required the Society's leaders to reconsider its structure and activities. He had written to Pease on 5 June 1905 (SCL) suggesting a thoroughgoing enquiry. When Wells (at the crossroads of his own career and involved in increasing emotional problems) decided to make a bid for influence in the Society this revisionist mood made many Fabians – especially the newer members – amenable to his demands for change. On 9 February 1906 he delivered an excoriating lecture to the Society which he called *The Faults of the Fabian*. He wanted to rejuvenate and expand the Society and in the process he attacked the old guard for their stodginess and the Webbs for their unimaginative obsession with gas-and-water reforms. He had, Beatrice noted in her diary on 1 March 1906, 'broken out in a quite unexpectedly unpleasant manner . . . an odd mixture of underhand manoeuvres and insolent bluster'.

The Fabians, nevertheless, were not unwilling to give Wells a chance to make his case and a Special Committee was set up with Sydney Olivier as nominal chairman: Jane Wells was the secretary, Wells was himself a member, and four others were also his known supporters. Even Charlotte Shaw, despite her close association with the Webbs, was not unsympathetic to Wells and he had some covert encouragement from Shaw himself, who thought a shake-up in the Society could do nothing but good. The senior Fabians were as yet unaware that Wells was intending to disrupt the settled tenor of Fabian life. Before he set off on a lecture tour of the United States he wrote to the essayist E. V. Lucas (1868–1938) saying that he was engaged in 'intrigues to upset the Fabian Society by making buttered slides for an old lady'. (UI 22 February 06) Wells returned from America on 27 May. On 15 July, being worried by reports of the Committee which reached them, the Webbs went down to Sandgate to see Wells. They sensed much strain. Beatrice noted that he showed 'contempt for us poor drudgers' and that he was in a hurry to 'settle all social and economic questions in general and to run the Fabian Society in particular'. Wells coolly explained that Webb and Shaw would have to retire if they would not accept his schemes. Neither Shaw nor Webb were in principle unwilling to surrender the leadership which they had held for so many years if, as Shaw flatly told Wells, they could be sure that Wells himself would take the Society seriously and genuinely commit himself to it. They would, Beatrice noted, 'gladly give up the leadership . . . they are so full of work that they would be relieved'. But they felt that Wells had no clear idea what he wanted personally or of the future role of the Society: 'he has neither the patience nor the good manners needed for cooperative effort'. Beatrice was genuinely puzzled why Wells had stirred up the Society: she was unaware that Wells, now seeking to become a prophet rather than a novelist, was seething with frustration and inflated with self-importance.

The Webbs were spending five weeks in the Russell house near Oxford.

Lower Copse, Bagley Wood
Aug. 2nd [1906]

Dear Mr Wells

Do you remember that you half promised to find your way here for 2 or 3 days sometime in August? You shall have your morning sacred to work – a cool little room to work in. Granville Barker comes on the 15th so that you can either have us alone with our secretary who leaves on the 15th or form a quartette with G.B. We prefer not *Sundays* as Mrs G.B. will be here and we should be very rushed with a 5th. Do come.

We enjoyed our two days at Sandgate. We are excellent company now for each others' souls – as we have got safely over the mutual admiration stage and say really significant things to each other – without fear of breach of friendship.

Give my love to Mrs Wells – if you don't come, she must.

Yours sincerely

Beatrice Webb

### 477 UI  SIDNEY WEBB TO H. G. WELLS

Wells was depressed at the reception given to his novel *In the Days of the Comet*. All through the summer his apparent support for polygamy and free love had brought him under attack, notably in the *Times Literary Supplement* and other reviews. On 12 October, in a Fabian lecture on 'Socialism and the Middle Classes' he again attacked conventional marriage and sneered once more at the 'unimaginative Webbs'. He gibed at the Webbs and Shaw in his talk, *This Misery of Boots*, delivered to the Fabians on 12 January 1906, which had made Pease refuse to publish it unless Wells removed the personal innuendoes.

Charlotte Shaw protested on 4 September that Wells was turning the Special Committee into 'a Committee of Public Safety to try the Executive'; several other members joined her in objecting to the draft report prepared by Wells. (UI) Shaw wrote to Wells on 11 September: worried that the wrangle might get out of hand, though he was still friendly in tone, he warned Wells that to be 'anything more than a novelist bombinating in vacuo' he would have to take the Fabians seriously and not 'turn from your political object to criticism of the conduct and personality of the men around you'. (UI)

The Webbs paid another visit to Sandgate in late September, 'deliberately to ease the strain caused by the Wells revolt . . . properly managed he will count for righteousness in his own way and it is no good wasting his and our strength on friction'. (BWD 1 October 06) The Webbs continued their attempt to mollify Wells, inviting him to Grosvenor Road at the end of November. Wells, however, pressed his campaign. It was now necessary for the Fabian executive to produce a separate set of reform proposals (drafted by Webb and Shaw) as an alternative to the Wells document. The issue was arousing great excitement in the Society and two special meetings to discuss the rival reports, attended by a large part of the membership, were held on 7 and 14 December. Shaw had elected to be the spokesman for the executive, partly because he believed that either Webb or Hubert Bland would be too intemperate and thus play into the hands of Wells; partly because he was the most accomplished debater of them all. By a clever use

236

of procedure and with a devastating speech Shaw forced Wells to make a humiliating withdrawal. If, Beatrice commented on 15 December, Wells 'had pushed his own fervid policy . . . for vague and big ideas, without making a personal attack on the Old Gang he would have succeeded'. It was, she felt, 'an altogether horrid business'.

This victory, however, was not the end of Wells, though his defeat embittered him against the Old Gang whom he suspected of a conspiracy against him. Beatrice wondered whether he might become a nuisance, like a second Ramsay MacDonald.

Lower Copse, Bagley Wood,
Oxford
3/9/6

Dear Wells

Your draft received this morning: many thanks for the confidence, which shall be respected.

We leave here on Wednesday morning (5th) for 41 Grosvenor Road. We only stay there one night, and go off by 10.30 *p.m.* train on Thursday night. We should be delighted to see you – to lunch at 1 on Wednesday or on Tuesday, or to dinner on Thursday until our cab comes. (We are out for Wednesday dinner.) By all means come if you can during that thirty hours or so, as we are not seriously engaged. We could give you a bed.

Your report contains much that is very interesting, and well put. I think you could greatly improve its chances by some slight changes, but that is for you to decide.

Your proposals as to (i) new offices, (ii) starting a weekly newspaper, and (iii) engaging a salaried staff of persons, must, I assume, be contingent on (a) the necessary capital being forthcoming, (b) sufficient income being somehow available.

Have you reckoned it up? Frankly, I don't believe that either the necessary capital or the necessary income can be obtained. But by all means try.

Your reference to the supposed exhaustion of a policy of 'permeation' comes a little oddly after your emphatic insistence, higher up, on the need for personal propaganda of a persuasive kind – which *is* permeation. I suppose you are using the term in some esoteric sense.

I don't understand *which* policy you want – is the F.S. to aim at *being* itself the political party, or is it to aim at *influencing* politics? I gather you think the I.L.P. is to remain as the political force. Does this leave anything but 'permeation' (of the I.L.P., as of all other parties) by the F.S.? Or do you mean that the F.S., under a new name, is itself to run candidates for Parliament – clearly you do not. But you cannot have it both ways – either we are or we are not to remain an organization distinct from the political parties, and if we are a distinct body, we cannot do other than attempt to influence the others by argument and persuasion, i.e. permeation.

Or do you mean to take up the attitude that no member of the F.S. ought to be a member of *any* other organization – or of any other but the I.L.P.? [*Side-note*: I have never been against the F.S. cordially helping the I.L.P. With my assent we have done so from the first. We, in fact, helped to start it.]

By the way, you should get your titles right – there is the I.L.P., the Labour Party, the L.R.C. etc. etc. The F.S. *is* already a constituent body of the L.R.C., exactly *as the I.L.P. is*; and the F.S. corporately nominates one member out of the seven(?) supreme Executive Committee of that body.

I don't quite see how there could be also a joint committee with the I.L.P. – that body would never consent.

About the constitution I don't think you make sufficiently clear the two functions of 'official' and 'representative' – you don't like the elected person, evidently! Do you really mean that your Triumvirates are to manage the business, giving up their time and thought to running a weekly newspaper, a publishing business etc.? Can we get such work for nothing from men the Society would trust? I wonder whether you have visualised your Threes!

I think your Committee ought to make up its mind whether it wants to change the name of the Society or not – whether in fact it wants a new society. It would hardly be fair to let this be taken separately on a referendum of its own.

Of course, I see the plausibility of a new Society, with a new name – and it may be that a majority of the members of the F.S. desire this. I don't myself at all object to their doing it. I should rather prefer a new name myself. Those who did not like it would simply not join.

I can't in the least understand what you mean by suggesting that the proposed new constitution ought to commend itself to me. Of course, it is quite contrary to what I advocate. It is quite against all the lessons of *Industrial Democracy*. But if you make a new Society, you had better try your own constitutional experiments.

Frankly, I cannot believe that the Society will accept your proposals. I am sorry, as I hoped it could gain from your new impulse. I shall be quite willing to discuss them with you if you like, and do my best to help you to put them into a practicable form. It would be far better to propose them in a form in which we could get them through, than in one in which we should inevitably find ourselves on opposite sides. But come and talk about them anyhow.

Sidney Webb

478 PP SIDNEY WEBB TO GRAHAM WALLAS

The Webbs were going down to Whittinghame, the Balfour family home in Scotland. Beatrice struck up a lasting friendship with Gerald Balfour's wife,

Betty, the sister of Lord Lytton. Gerald Balfour (1853–1945) had been President of the Board of Trade when his brother Arthur was Prime Minister. The Earl of Lytton (1876–1947) was a strong supporter of women's suffrage; his sister Constance was a notable suffragette who suffered greatly from forcible feeding in Holloway prison. Beatrice's diary entry on this visit – as on all other occasions when she spent time in Arthur Balfour's company – reveal her fascination by his charm and intellect.

Lexington, now known as Laxton, was the last open-field village in England. Both it and Eakring are close to Newark-on-Trent.

41 Grosvenor Road,
Westminster Embankment
4/9/6

Dear Wallas

We leave Bagley Wood tomorrow; and shall be at home for 30 hours; going down to Berwick etc. on Thursday night next, to look at records in those parts and bicycle about a little for a fortnight.

As to materials for your lectures, I don't exactly visualize any, but you are welcome to look. The trouble is that nearly all our stuff prior to 1835 is now classified by subjects, not by localities. (It takes a month's sorting to reshuffle the pack.)

We have some continuous Nottingham *borough* records, which we are sending to you in a box. We shall want it back in a fortnight. Our West Riding stuff is 'distributed' into subjects, and also what we may have of Notts County.

But it so happens that I can put you on to a picturesque find, if you will hunt it up. At *Lexington*, near Nottingham, and also at a neighbouring village called 'Egrim', or some such name, there is still continued a very primitive sharing-up of the Common Hayfield, by the householders, who meet annually, with quaint customs, and draw lots for plots – they used to *race* to the meadows and take up their lots, and mow them instantly, etc. etc. This has never been described. If you care to go there, and interview the innkeeper etc., you could do an interesting article on it. We want to know about it, and have no one free to send. I have no more facts about it, but the above is definite and certain.

Sidney Webb

Our *Parish and County* (700 pp) is to be published on 29 September. Could you not arrange to review it for the *Chronicle* or some other organ?


### 479 PP   BEATRICE WEBB TO MARY PLAYNE

The Webbs had been to Alnwick Castle to lunch with the Duke of Northumberland, one of the largest landowners in England, whom she described as 'a commonplace stupid Englishman'. (BWD 16 September 06) The atmosphere was so frigid that they did not get to see the records which were the purpose of their visit. Lord Percy (1871–1909) was the Duke's son, Conservative M.P. for South Kensington and a notable traveller. The Duchess was the sister of Lady Frances Balfour (1858–1931), the sister-in-law of Arthur Balfour and a strong supporter of women's suffrage.

On 10 October Beatrice commented in her diary on the visit to Lord George Hamilton that he had 'public spirit, good feeling and unself-conscious dignity . . . large view or capacity for transacting business on a great scale he has not'. The Playnes were soon to leave for an extended tour in Palestine.

41 Grosvenor Road
Thursday [27 September 1906]

Dearest Mary

How horrid for you – and what a disagreeable hour you must have passed – it makes me squirm to think of it. And now these long days of confinement. However seeing Bill will be a compensation and you will have time enough abroad.

We had a fruitful time both at Berwick and Alnwick tho' somewhat uncomfortable staying in filthy lodgings and a stuffy room – glad to get back to our own dear little home. We were much amused by our lunch with the Great Personages of Alnwick Castle. We wanted to get at the Duke's manor rolls so I prepared my very best blandishments. Ignominious failure awaited me! His grace was evidently terror-struck at our reputation as socialists. The Castle was gorgeous and solemn in its state – the Duke got up as a Stage Englishman, with whiskers, countryfied clothes of admirable cut, sanctimonious expression and pompous silence – his lady a perfect Stage Duchess, in soft laces and satins, much powdered and with the most melancholy and dignified countenance – the girls commonplace and stiff and stupid. If it had not been for our persistent and cheerful friendly talk, I think we should have eaten the elaborate lunch (waited on by six magnificent gentlemen) in absolute silence. Towards the end there was a 'relaxation of manners' and if I had had another chance I do believe the manor rolls would have been forthcoming. But what an entombment of a quite worthy family – no wonder Lord Percy never goes there and one (they say the most attractive) of the daughters has gone melancholy mad. Lady Frances says her sister is an unhappy woman: and one can well believe it.

We have just come from a very different castle – from a delightful two days with the G. Hamiltons at Deal. They are certainly the most simple and homely of aristocrats – with only their real moral refinement and kindly charm to distinguish them from non-ducal mortals. I had some useful R.C. [Royal Commission] talk – also a lot of intimate glimpses into the life of conservative governments – reminiscences of Dizzy, admiration for Salisbury and somewhat acid criticism of the fascinating Arthur. In Salisbury's Cabinet, every minister was addressed (in Cabinet meetings) by his official name – 'the Secretary for the Colonies' etc. When Balfour succeeded to the Chair it became a 'cliquey' talk between 'Alfred' and 'Arthur' and 'Dick' and 'George' at the end of the table – which offended the more stately and distant members. Lord George has retained a real affection for Chamberlain – in spite of the disagreement over the tariff – thinks he has always been genuinely patriotic and a loyal colleague. Poor Joe, I am afraid it is all up with him.

We are looking forward to seeing Arthur – perhaps I might run down for a chat with you sometime before you go?

Ever yours

Beatrice Webb

### 480 BWD   BEATRICE WEBB TO MILLICENT FAWCETT

Mrs Henry Fawcett (1847–1929) had been a leader of the movement for women's rights since 1867; she was president of the National Union of Women's Suffrage Societies and opposed the militant wing of the movement.

Beatrice had discussed the suffrage question with the Balfours and they had helped to complete a change of mind. As the suffragists 'were being battered about rather badly, and coarse-grained men were saying coarse-grained things, I thought I might as well give a friendly pull to get the thing out of the mud'. (BWD 5 November 06) She sent the following letter to Millicent Fawcett with permission to send it to *The Times*: Mrs Fawcett's covering note expressed her 'extreme satisfaction' that Beatrice and her friend Louisa Creighton had both thus changed their opinions.

41 Grosvenor Road
Nov. 2 [1906]

Dear Mrs Fawcett

You once asked me to let you know if I ceased to object to the grant of the electorial franchise to women. The time has come when I feel obliged to do so.

My objection was based principally on my disbelief in the validity of any 'abstract rights', whether to votes or to property, or even to 'life, liberty and the pursuit of happiness'. I prefer to regard life as a series of obligations – obligations of the individual to the community and of the community to the individual. I could not see that women, as women, were under any particular obligation to take part in the conduct of government.

I have been told that the more spiritually-minded Eastern readily acquiesces in the material management of his native country by what he regards as the Anglo-Saxon 'man of affairs'. In the same way I thought that women might well be content to leave the 'rough and tumble' of party politics to their mankind, with the object of concentrating all their own energies on what seemed to me their peculiar social obligations the bearing of children, the advancement of learning, and the handing on from generation to generation of an appreciation of the spiritual life.

Such a division of labour between men and women is, however, only practicable if there is among both sections alike a continuous feeling of consent to what is being done by government as their common agent. This consciousness of consent can hardly avoid being upset if the work of government comes actively to overlap the particular obligations of an excluded class. If our Indian administrators were to interfere with the religious obligations of Hindus or Mahomedans, British rule in India would, I suppose, come to an end. It seems to me that something analogous to this is happening in the Europe of to-day with regard to the particular obligations of women. The rearing of children, the advancement of learning, and the promotion of the spiritual life – which I regard as the particular obligations of women – are, it is clear, more and more becoming the main preoccupations of the community as a whole. The legislatures of this century are, in one country after another, increasingly devoting themselves to these subjects. Whilst I rejoice in much of this new development of politics, I think it adequately accounts for the increasing restiveness of women. They are, in my opinion, rapidly losing their consciousness of consent in the work of government and are even feeling a positive obligation to take part in directing this new activity. This is, in my view, not a claim to rights or an abandonment of women's particular obligations, but a desire more effectually to fulfil their functions by sharing the control of State action in those directions.

The episodes of the last few weeks complete the demonstration that it is undesirable that this sense of obligation should manifest itself in unconstitutional forms. We may grant that persistent interruption of public business is lowering to the dignity of public life. But it is cruel to put a fellow-citizen of strong convictions in the dilemma of political ineffectiveness or unmannerly breaches of the peace. If the consciousness of non-consent is sufficiently strong, we can hardly blame the public-spirited women who by their exclusion from constitutional methods of asserting their views are driven to the latter alternative, at the cost of personal suffering and masculine ridicule. To call such behaviour vulgar is an undistinguished, and I may say an illiterate, use of language. The way out of this unpleasant dilemma, it seems to me, is to permit this growing consciousness among women – that their particular social obligations compel them to claim a share in the conduct of political affairs – to find a constitutional channel.

This reasoning involves, of course, the admission to the franchise of women as women, whether married or single, propertied or wage-earning.

It is, I feel, due to you that I should tell you of my change of attitude, and I thought you would perhaps be interested in my reasons.

Yours very truly

Beatrice Webb

242

Royal Commission on the Poor Laws and Relief of Distress,<br>
68 Victoria Street, Westminster, s.w.<br>
[?mid-November 1906]

My dear Mr Wells

I have finished your *America*. I can't vie with the reviewers in their extent of praise – but I *do* think it a most excellent Impressionist picture – full of illumination as to facts and suggestion as to remedies – an excellent piece of work.

We shall look forward to seeing you both on the 27th – the Courtneys want to meet you and I propose to ask the Snowdons and George Barnes.

Mrs Wells will rejoice that I have at last thrown in my lot with Womens Suffrage (see *Times* November 5th) – such a Pronouncement! See what you have accomplished by your Propaganda! far more important than converting the whole of the Fabian Society!

Ever yours sincerely

B. Webb

482 LSE   SIDNEY WEBB TO J. D. MCKILLOP

The money was for a research studentship at L.S.E. for Louisa Woodcock.

41 Grosvenor Road,<br>
Westminster Embankment<br>
17.12.6

Dear Mr McKillop

1) Referring to my note today, I find that the cheque to Miss Wood-cock should be for £50 – as per sum paid to you – not £25.

2) I assume the Director is taking all necessary steps for forming a Club, as to supply of alcohol. It is *quite impossible* for the School to have a *licence* – it would lead to the forfeiture of the building to the L.C.C. and loss of grant – there must be no question of it.

Sidney Webb

483 PP   BEATRICE WEBB TO EDWARD PEASE

The fund was that raised by friends to finance research assistance for Beatrice in her Commission work.

Court Mansions, Bexhill

*Private*
January 1 1907

Dear Mr Pease

Thanks for cheque.

I will send you a statement and balance sheet directly I get back to London to be issued to the *contributors* of the fund. If it is limited to the contributors – marked *Private* – I can go into detail. I should not like it published in the *Fabian News* lest it should become a subject of comment in the Commission itself. The C.O.S. contingent are getting very angry with me as I have forced their hand and C. S. Loch is always attacking me and they do already resent my separate enquiries and consequent memorandum. But the Enquiry from my point of view is going very well. The assistant commissioners in the relation of Industrial and Housing conditions to Pauperism have made a strong Report – casual labour the *chief* cause of Pauperism; bad housing is second; low wages and long hours creating disease, an indirect cause of pauperism. 'Bad administration' sinks to insignificance as a *Cause*: that is why C. S. Loch is so angry!

B. Webb

---

484 BL  BEATRICE WEBB TO JOHN BURNS

Sir Arthur Newsholme (1857–1943) was medical officer of health for Brighton 1888–1908: he was about to become the Medical Officer of the L.G.B., playing an important role in establishing national health services for tuberculosis, venereal disease, maternity and child welfare. Sir George Newman (1870–1948) was appointed Chief Medical Officer of the Board of Education in 1907 and did much to develop the school medical service.

Jan. 20th 1907

Dear Mr Burns

I forgot to tell you the other day the exact position of affairs in the Commission with regard to the evidence of your Medical Department in the matter of the medical assistance of the Poor.

Sometime ago the Commission fixed with Dr Newsholme to give evidence on *February 3rd* on the statement he sent in some months ago. Unless you object, this arrangement holds good and no alteration will be made. I understand that Dr Newsholme will not have entered on any duties, on the 3rd February, so he will not, in any way, be compromising his Department. Meanwhile a series of questions have been addressed to the P.H. Medical Department of the L.G.B. by the Commission. Those questions raise the whole question of the desirability of an amalgamation of the medical services. It has been suggested that they will be answered by Dr Parsons and that he will denounce any attempt to amalgamate the

Educational, Public Health and Poor Law services under the local M.O.H. on the one hand and L.G.B. medical department on the other. Perhaps it would be as well to delay the answer of their Questions either altogether or until *you* had decided whether that was the policy you desired to be expressed to the Commission as the policy of the L.G.B.? It would be rather awkward to get a memorandum from the L.G.B. Department contradicting Dr Newman's memorandum which represents I understand the Cabinet view. Dr Newman is giving evidence on the 11 February.

I merely report these matters to you, as such details are apt not to reach the Supreme authority. Perhaps you would confirm whether the R.C. has sent any questions to the Department and what it is proposed to do, pending Miss Holmes' arrival.

Ever yours

Beatrice Webb

### 485 PP SIDNEY TO BEATRICE

Beatrice, already close to collapse, went to Yorkshire for five days with the Commission and returned quite ill with insomnia and indigestion. She went down to their favourite hotel at Beachy Head while Sidney busied himself with his election campaign. She was still uneasy about her taste for social engagements 'of an aristocratic and fastidious character . . . I like brilliant little parties . . . But there are grave disadvantages to "dallying with fashion" . . . the spiteful things that are said, partly by envious folk, partly by fanatics . . . the drain on energy both financial and personal . . . Better clothes, fares to country houses, and most of all the exhaustion of living up to a reputation'. (BWD 18 February 07)

Ernald R. Warre was employed by the Charity Commissioners before becoming Clerk to the Trustees of the City Parochial Charities in 1907. The Women's Group of the Fabian Society, in which Maud Reeves was a leading figure, took part in a number of suffrage processions under its own banner.

41 Grosvenor Road, Westminster

4/2/7

My own dearest

R. B. Haldane came in on Sunday – to make sure about the dinner on Saturday, which he will attend all right. He was looking extraordinarily well, and in the best of spirits. He was full of his Army Estimates, which he has now got finally approved. He is able, somehow, to secure his full proposals, Expeditionary Army and well-equipped Territorial Army, and yet show a very large reduction – but this is to be a dead secret at present.

He was quite eager for your Medical Scheme, and generally hoped great things from the P.L. Commission.

My meeting last night was a small, but quite friendly one. I was told of a perfectly deadly device which had been used at the Borough Council Election. Every owner of weekly property was furnished with typewritten

245

letters for him to sign and send to each of his tenants, warning them that if the Progressives got in, and the rates went up, he would have to raise the rent by 6d, or 1/- a week!

But I am doing a most insinuating pamphlet for the women electors, which will, I think, do something – I think, things are looking up. This would be a rather interesting dinner! I had not heard of it before. It seems a good idea to bring all these women together.

We chose today at the City Parochial Trustees for Clerk, Warre, son of late Head of Eton – by 12 to 2 – a very rich fellow of 34, in the Charity Commission Office and *not* the nephew of Sir O. Roberts' late wife. The man we have chosen seems a very nice man.

Here are some letters. Will you march with Mrs Reeves' procession? McCleary has sent his paper on 'The State as Over-Parent' to read and return.

C. A. Whitmore, whom I met, says he thinks the Moderates have overdone it with their abuse, and that there is a reaction in favor of the Progressives. I fancy this is probably the case.

Now I must break off. Goodnight dear one.

Sidney

### 486 PP  SIDNEY TO BEATRICE

Members of the Commission made an extended tour of Ireland in the summer, with a steamer trip up the west coast as an interlude of relaxation. Sidney was becoming worried about the L.C.C. election, as a strong campaign against the Progressives was being run by the popular press. In Deptford he faced specific difficulties with the Nonconformists and with some Liberals as a reaction to Charles Bowerman's election as Labour M.P. in 1906. Bowerman, a compositor by trade, served as M.P. for Deptford until 1931. Beatrice could not bring herself to help in electioneering: 'I loathe the whole business'. (BWD 24 February 07) Sidney had, in any case, decided to retire at the next election, by which time he would have served on the L.C.C. for eighteen years; the Webbs would then take their long-planned trip around the world.

41 Grosvenor Road, Westminster<br>6/2/7

My own dearest

It was very good of you to have sent me so sweet a letter.

I could not sleep last night, and felt very lonely! There is so much to do, and so little 'sweet reasonableness'. But nevertheless the world goes on.

There are no letters to send you; and no sort of news. Everything goes on – but blankly!

I worked this morning at the revision of the proof of Manorial Boroughs – a lengthy but straightforward task. It seems all very lucid and solid, and I don't find any important alterations to make.

I am sure you are quite right to insist, quietly and steadily, on investigating whatever *you* think important – in view of the fact that the Commission will not otherwise investigate your particular points.

I must say that I rather grudge the fortnight's cruise in the summer: it will induce you to stay away a whole month! I really think I must take service as a cabin-boy. But it certainly will greatly lighten the physical toil for you; and probably the best thing will be to give a week to the land – they won't all stay the whole fortnight as you see – and then go on board your yacht. However, if I am defeated at Deptford I could come to Scotland and spend the week-ends with you. Perhaps that may be possible anyhow.

I am beginning to get replies from Fabians, offering to come for polling day – from new people, as well as from old acquaintances. There are to be 19 polling stations, instead of 14 as heretofore – which is good for us, but makes the organization a little more complicated. We may have to have more offices; but I can't yet find even 10, and it depends on whether we have really enough workers.

I have just fixed up two 'Pleasant Sunday Afternoons' on 10th and 24th at Deptford at 3 and 3.15 p.m. I think this is all to the good, whatever it may be.

But I must break off. Goodnight, dear one – don't do too much.

Sidney Webb

### 487 UI BEATRICE WEBB TO H. G. WELLS

By an odd coincidence one of the Moderates opposing Sidney in Deptford was named H. G. Wells and a number of people were confused when this was reported.

41 Grosvenor Road, Westminster Embankment
Monday [25 February 1907]

My dear Mr Wells

I am back in harness again after 4 absolutely quiet days – ever so many thanks for your kindness in writing to ask me: I am not sure that I should not have found you both too interesting for rest!

My Commission is responsible for the collapse: 'Eleven more obstinate men I never did know'. Moreover the fact that they *are* men and resent a woman with private secretaries (not to mention a husband) to back her, makes the tussles between us assume a less pleasant tone than need be. However I get my fair share of control.

Sidney is very shaky at Deptford – there is going to be a big sweep and he may go down as big game easily aimed at. You will be amused to hear that a furious Fabian wrote this morning to denounce H.G. for standing against him as a Moderate! Really the spirit of factious prejudice could hardly go further – even in the little world of the Fabians. When are you coming to stay with us – keep some time in April?

Ever yours sincerely
Beatrice Webb

As Wells recovered his spirits after his defeat in the Fabian meetings in December he sought to drum up support both within and without the Society. At the elections to the Fabian executive in April he ran fourth, behind Webb, Shaw and Pease.

41 Grosvenor Road, Westminster Embankment
[? February 1907]

Dear Mr Wells

In return for your friendly letter I venture to bore you with my paper on Poor Law Industrial Relief and Public Health on the sort of question I am asking the medical witnesses who are being examined. We have had hot times on the Commission and I came out of the tussle with the majority of my colleagues victorious but a wreck!

As for the Fabian my prophecy is Pease, G.B.S., Wells and then, I think, Webb – unless he is defeated at the L.C.C. which might put him either at the top or the bottom of the Fabian Poll. But what really concerns us just now is the L.C.C. I am not sure that we shall weather the storm – the hurricane of misrepresentation is furious and will sweep a good many of us away – possibly Sidney will most easily succumb to the onslaught against Socialism-cum-Progressivism. Personally I shall view that result with equanimity – our (S and BW) best work now is constructive thinking and the expert assistance of all and sundry who are willing to go our way.

However do not let us drift apart from you – you and we have the same faith tho' we hold it somewhat differently – we are all of us too old to change and must take each other as we are – for good or for evil.

Ever yours sincerely
Beatrice Webb

Webb scraped home in Deptford – his majority was down to little more than two hundred – in an election which saw the defeat of the Progressives. In an effort to save Sidney's seat more than three hundred Fabians had been mobilised to go into Deptford on polling day: Beatrice took charge of a committee room in a slum area, and other wards were supervised by Shaw, Pease, Reeves and Galton. George Standring was a printer who was a member of the Fabian Society and did much of its job printing.

41 Grosvenor Road, Westminster Embankment
4/3/7

Dear Pease

A thousand thanks. The Fabians saved the situation. Hundreds must have turned up. I am asking Standring to print a letter from me *to the entire membership*, old and new, London and provincial, thanking them;

I have asked him to get it addressed and posted in the office, *at my expense.* Kindly do this promptly.

Yours

Sidney Webb

Your little corner (West 5) polled 14 per cent heavier than at last election; and thus must have contributed well to our (narrow!) majority.

## 490 PP BEATRICE WEBB TO MARY PLAYNE

On 18 February Beatrice wondered how much was gained by the friendship with Arthur Balfour except 'gratified vanity and a little pleasure'. (BWD)

Fridtjof Nansen (1861–1930) had nearly reached the North Pole in 1893. In later years he had a special concern for refugees and devised the 'Nansen' passport for stateless persons.

[41 Grosvenor Road]

March 19th 1907

Dearest Mary

I have just read a most attractive account of the Holy land – your first letter from Jerusalem. As a set off, I will gossip with you. The largeness of the Moderate majority is somewhat disconcerting after 18 years uninterrupted rule. Like the last general election I don't believe it means more than a general desire to put 'the government' out and 'give the others a chance'. At present S. is fighting his own party – the remaining Nonconformist group trying to ostracise all 'bad party men' and exclude them from the important Committees – especially his friend and disciple R. C. Bray. They dare not exclude Sidney himself but they are trying to sacrifice all the other 'Webbites'. However as the Fabians have come back, as they went out, 8 strong, they will find it difficult to ignore them and S. will not scruple to call in the Moderate majority if the Progressive rank is obdurate but even they may not succeed.

The Nonconformist Liberal sector are of course horribly sore with Sidney and the Fabian L.C.C. who seem to them to have smudged the Progressives over with unpopular Socialism whilst surviving themselves in the general rout through their friendship with the Catholics and the Church. (The Catholic Priests worked splendidly for us and the Church was more than beneficent.) However I daresay matters will settle down presently.

We had a most delightful Saturday and Sunday at Stanway. A.J.B. [Balfour] bringing his motor. There was a large party of young men and maidens with just Lady Elcho and A.J.B. and ourselves as 'The Elders' – (Lord Elcho being ill in London) On Sunday we whirled to Bibury, Fairford, Cirencester, getting our lunch at a little inn at Fairford. I thought Prince Arthur was at his best with Lady Elcho for whom he clearly has a courtly devotion and whose presence seem to bring out all

249

that is most sincere and simple in his nature – all the conversation being of the frankest kind whether about religion or politics or criticism of the men and women they have both known. But directly one gets him on to the whole range of social problems we are interested in he became elusively sceptical and indifferent and seems almost to resent making intercourse anything but amusing – mere recreation like golf. That, of course, is not *our* view of social intercourse and whether the present friendly relations will survive this difference of purpose – I don't know – perhaps 'more or less'.

My last new friend – one I fear that is probably for entertainment and not for use – is Dr Nansen, who is now Norwegian minister. He is the most fascinating of Vikings, with simple crude ideas as to the futility of religion and the needlessness of anything but Science and Bureaucratic government – so fresh and artless in this complicated world! The exact opposite to A.J.B.'s subtleties of thought and feeling. Except for these 'Stars' I have been seeing endless medical officers – Public Health and Poor Law. The Royal Commission lumbers along and I dance round it sticking pins into my more obstructive colleagues! They have found it necessary to take over two of my investigations at $3\frac{1}{2}$ guineas a week each, and expenses (one was getting £2 a week and the other nothing!) which is very nice for the young ladies. The evidence as to the expediency of a municipal medical service is becoming very strong and altogether I am pleased with the direction the Enquiry is taking – all in the Public Health direction. I have cosy little dinners of medical [?witnesses] to which I ask some political star – A.J.B. came to one, Haldane to another and Burns will be asked to a third – I am acquiring, for a brief moment, a sort of leadership in the Public Health world. It is strange how one's work forces one into one set of fellow mortals – then another – a shifting scene in which perhaps the only permanent element is one's own family or a few faithful co-religionists such as the old gang of the Fabian Society. By the way the Fabian Society is booming – it has increased 50 per cent in a few months – and the Old Gang has beaten back the H. G. Wells onslaught. I am down lecturing to the Cambridge University Fabians – 100 strong – and Sidney doing the same to the Oxford Fabians last week on 'The Faith We Hold'.

Apparently the reaction against official Liberalism on the one hand and the Labour Party, on the other, is going to redound to Fabian propaganda. But I imagine it is mostly the increasing reputation of G.B.S. and H. G. Wells – perhaps even of 'Sidney and Beatrice Webb' which is leading the young intellectuals to join us in such numbers compared to the slow growth of former years.

When will you be back?

Ever your affectionate

Beatrice Webb

Three years later, reflecting on the moral lapses of Wells, Beatrice felt that his decline had begun after she had introduced him to the 'fast' country-house set around the Elchos, whose home was at Stanway, and the Desboroughs.

41 Grosvenor Road, Westminster Embankment

[? April 1907]

My dear Mrs Wells

We shall be delighted to see you for the 18th. I shall be away until the evening as I am going down to Brighton on Commission business – but I shall be back by an afternoon train probably about 7 o'c and Sidney will be here to give you dinner before the Art group begins its meetings. We could have a talk after breakfast on Thursday and perhaps you will stay over the 19th.

I am so glad you and H.G. went to Stanway – the House and its inhabitants shows the British aristocracy at its best. I am convinced that it is the business of Fabians to know everyone and be 'all things to all men'. This is especially so now that we have a tide of reaction – of popular reaction against socialism – almost demagogic reaction. About all these things we will talk on Thursday 19th.

Ever yours sincerely

BW

## 492 FP  BEATRICE WEBB TO EDWARD PEASE

The Fabians gave a farewell dinner to Sydney Olivier at the Holborn Restaurant on his departure to serve as Governor of Honduras. Though Olivier spent much time in the Caribbean he continued to take an active interest in Fabian affairs and to participate in meetings when he was in England.

Dr Ethel Williams, who undertook the children's enquiry, became president of the British Federation of Medical Women and treasurer of the Socialist Medical League: she was supervising Mary Longman, a Fabian social worker, and Marion Phillips (1881–1932), a former research student at L.S.E. who was active in the women's movement and became the chief woman officer of the Labour Party in 1918.

While staying at Bramdean and visiting her sister Georgina in mid-April Beatrice had the idea around which the Webbs were to build the Minority Report of the Royal Commission. Instead of abolishing the Boards of Guardians at a stroke she thought it might be preferable steadily to erode their functions – to place pauper children under the education authority, for instance, the sick under public health, the aged, the vagrants and others under similarly relevant authorities. Thus the old Poor Law would be broken up and pauperism would cease to be a single category: the destitute would be treated according to the cause of destitution. Tactically such a proposal had the attraction that it would tend to focus attention on specific causes of distress and possibly lead to an attack on each cause and, hopefully, to its progressive elimination. Administratively, as the Webbs were to discover, such a scheme had the drawback that a pauper family might find its members falling under different jurisdictions and needing to apply severally to them for help. There was a further disadvantage in such an effort to disperse the destitute among several agencies: it provided no obvious means of dealing with the able-bodied unemployed. For the next year the Webbs wrestled with what became their main conceptual problem – where to fit in the able-bodied and how to deal with them.

41 Grosvenor Road, Westminster Embankment
April 18th [1907]

Dear Mr Pease

Miss Woodcock M.D., 14 South Square, Grays Inn would like to join the Fabians. Will you please send her a form. (She is my medical assistant.)

I propose to come to the Sydney Olivier dinner and have asked the Graham Wallas's too as my guests. S. cannot, he has an engagement that night.

I send you my memo. on the Unemployment Question for your private information. We are to have a great discussion on it next Tuesday. Now that the R.C. has taken over my Enquiry into out-relief children I am going to start one on the boy question, 14 to 21. (Will you please look at pp 5 and 6.) I have secured the service (unpaid) of a clever Cambridge girl – Miss Dunlop – and she will make it the subject of her thesis for a doctorate. Could you give me any suggestions as *to sources*, also *persons* who might help? Could we start a ball rolling for information in the *Fabian News*?

There is a first-rate lady director appointed to superintend my two young ladies (I see they have good [*illegible*]) and the Enquiry has been extended to all children maintained wholly or partially out of the rates. The lady turns out to be an old acquaintance of mine – Dr Williams of Newcastle. She's coming to stay with me next week. My two young ladies get $3\frac{1}{2}$ guineas a week each and all expenses – a nine-months engagement. They are to carry out the investigation I have already planned. So I think that is satisfactory.

The medical question is developing splendidly. Dr Newsholme has sent in a ripping memo. in favour of free medical assistance organised by the Town and County Council. Newman, McCleary and $\frac{1}{2}$ dozen others are following suit.

Ever yours

B. Webb

493  CCO    BEATRICE WEBB TO R. C. K. ENSOR

The Reverend John Pringle (1872–1938), who later became secretary of the C.O.S., was at this time a curate in the East End: he and Cyril Jackson were working on behalf of the Commission on a study of destitution caused by unemployment.

41 Grosvenor Road, Westminster Embankment

4.5.07

Dear Mr Ensor

I want your help in respect to the Poor Law enquiry into the working of the Unemployed Acts. We begin this enquiry next Autumn. But from past experience of the work of the Commission I see that we shall get little else but 'opinions' and these mostly in the negative direction. Messrs. Pringle and Jackson's investigation did little else but discredit relief work and suggested no alternative ways of dealing with the unemployed. Moreover their investigation was limited by their reference *to the working of the Unemployed Acts* and they were not asked to enquire or report into the working of the Poor Law alternatives of the Workhouse test, and the Labour Yard. These alternatives have also been ruled out of our enquiry next autumn, as it is assumed we have dealt with them in our general enquiry into Poor Law Administration which is now practically concluded. That is not the case, and these alternatives therefore hold the field if we arrive at an unfavorable verdict on relief work. What I wanted (but was over-ruled) was an enquiry into *all ways of dealing with the Ablebodied or persons assumed to be Ablebodied*, including even the Casual Ward, and therefore Vagrancy. Only in that way shall we get a statesmanlike grip of the question. The Charity Organization Society policy, on the other hand, is to break the subject up into little bits and get a negative conclusion on each division so as to fall back on the 'Non Possumus' attitude.

Now what I should like would be some help both in suggestions as to possible reforms and actual investigation into facts. Would it be possible to form a little Committee to take each way of dealing with the Ablebodied into consideration, getting all the evidence together on each point, and looking at each by the light of the other? If then we could get a secretary (for a small salary to do the clerk's work and possibly some additional investigation) we might draw up a report of our own which the progressive members of the Commission might circulate as a memorandum.

Could you help by becoming a member of the Committee? We might have one meeting in July and then begin our work in October. I send for your consideration a Memorandum that I have circulated to the Commission. You will see that it is mainly negative, but that is the present state of the Evidence, and therein lies the danger.

Yours very sincerely

Beatrice Webb

494 BL  BEATRICE WEBB TO JOHN BURNS

Sir Leslie Mackenzie (1862–1935), a distinguished medical officer in Scotland, was the medical member of the Scottish L.G.B. from 1904 to 1919. The Webbs had decided that they wished to insinuate Robert Morant into a key position in the L.G.B. and had begun an ultimately unsuccessful backstairs campaign for him.

May 11 1907

Dear Mr Burns

I send you two more statements that I think you ought to look at. Mackenzie is the most influential man in the Scotch L.G.B. It would be a pity if the Scotchmen got hold of the notion of an organised medical service first and carried it out, because it is an English idea and we ought to have the credit of it. But whilst [Patten-] MacDougal, the Head of the Scotch L.G.B. is converted to it (tho' between ourselves this is more a testimony of Mackenzie's influence than his own insight) he is a dull conservative-minded man. I am afraid your excellent Chief of the Department remains unmoved and Dr Downes is hostile as far as such a weak kindly nature can be hostile in anything. If you ever think of carrying out any new departure you will require a really strong subordinate – a man of the type of Morant (who by the way is a great admirer of yours). I do so want your administration to stand out as constructive in the best sense. You have achieved the reputation of the strong man to *resist* foolish proposals, now you want to show yourself strong in carrying out wise ones.

Always yours sincerely

Beatrice Webb

### 495 UI BEATRICE WEBB TO H. G. WELLS

Seeking to rally support for his position Wells had circulated a rambling memorandum; it did nothing to clarify his confused position. Only 27 Fabians wrote to support him. Harley Granville-Barker, expressing a common sense of mystification about his intentions, wrote to Wells on 27 May to say that 'I have lost the thread of you over this political business', being unsure whether Wells was sympathetic to the I.L.P. or opposed to it, for political neutrality or for a socialist party. (UI) The book to which Beatrice refers was *New Worlds for Old.*

The Chestnuts,
Minchinhampton
May 25th [1907]

My dear Mr Wells

I agree with so much of the spirit of your memo but I am sorry not to be able to sign the letter of it. But I do not see my way to object to resolutions or published tracts or manifestos 'of a definitely political nature'. All social reforms are of such a nature and I understand such a [?determinated] [*?word missing*] would take out the tract on the Poor Law or Old Age Pensions or the Minimum Wage, as well as that on Fiscal policy or the War. If we were to cease to speak our mind on these economic and political questions we should cease to have even an intellectual influence?

What I do most heartily agree with, in your paper, is the expediency of non-intervention in party organisations of an electoral character. This, I understand, to be Sidney's view too. Only I gather that he thinks it undesirable to raise the question in an aggressive form among the members now that a new E.C. has been elected and a Committee is about to be appointed to consider the matter. It appears to him that there is no need to hurry to a decision and the E.C. shows no sign of doing so. He thinks that when the Committee meets the inevitable difficulty and danger of allying the Fabian with the I.L.P. or of starting a new Political Socialist party will stop the way to any foolish action.

We are hard at work on Memo. for the P.L.C. and directly we return to London I am off to Scotland to study Scotch P. Law. Only in July do we get back to our book.

I am looking forward immensely to your book on Socialism. I am longing myself to write down the 'Faith I hold' – I wonder how far it would differ from yours – not much I think – merely in perspective and perhaps a little in the way of reaching our ideals. With love to you both.

Ever yours affectionately

[Beatrice Webb: *autograph cut off*]

496 FP  SIDNEY WEBB TO EDWARD PEASE

Aylmer Maude, a Tolstoyan, was now a member of the Fabian executive.

The Chestnuts, Minchinhampton

28/5/1907

Dear Pease

I shall be here till Monday morning 3 June.

Ask Maude to conduct my report.

I have seen the Wells manifesto (which he invited Mrs Webb and me to sign!). He apparently does not in the least realise what a complete jump round *he* is making, or the lack of courtesy or loyalty to his late colleagues on the Special Committee; or to his present colleagues on the Executive Committee.

But I hope it will be treated – Shaw is aware of it – gently. If he is seeking an excuse to resign, we cannot help it; but otherwise he had better be induced to subside, or to drop out quietly.

I imagine it all arises from his not having been able to come up for the last F. and G.P. Sub-Committee and getting 'worried' at the thought of the item on the agenda as to Political Committee being dealt with in his absence; and magnifying that item into a serious plot! He may now be surprised at seeing nothing hasty or frantically impetuous on the Exec. agenda!

Yours

Sidney Webb

The Fabian leadership had made a number of concessions to Wells and his supporters. It had been agreed that Special Groups (such as the Fabian Arts Group, the Women's Group, etc.) could be set up; that more should be done to develop local Fabian societies; and that the executive should be enlarged to give more room for minority opinion. It was also proposed to establish a Political Committee, much as Wells wished, but he was suspicious of the proposed membership.

Leslie Haden Guest (1877–1969), doctor, journalist and Labour politician, later Lord Haden-Guest, did much to provoke Wells into his attack on the Fabian Old Gang but deserted him under pressure. He had an erratic political career.

Leo Chiozza-Money (1870–1944) was a journalist and Liberal politician. His most influential book was *Riches and Poverty*, published in 1905. He sat as a Liberal from 1906 to 1918 but failed to hold his seat when he joined the Labour Party in 1918.

Joseph Fels (1854–1914), an American soap millionaire, was an enthusiastic single-taxer but, urged on by his energetic wife, he also gave financial help to advanced organisations which ranged from the Bolshevik Party to the suffragette movement. Stanton Coit (1857–1944) was a leading figure in the ethical culture movement and a personal friend of many Radical and socialist personalities. Cecil Chesterton (1879–1918) was a journalist and brother of G. K. Chesterton: a member of the Fabian executive 1904–07, he was strongly opposed to Wells.

41 Grosvenor Road,
Westminster Embankment
12.6.7

My dear Wells

I am sorry you don't like the composition of the suggested Political Committee. I wish we could have had the advantage of discussing it with you at the various meetings of Sub-Committee at which the subject has been approached in a preliminary way. It is in these preliminary 'give and take' discussions that considerations (on one side or another) get weighed and sifted. If you had been able to be present, some of the points you raise now would, I venture to think, not have been put forward.

I wonder how far your knowledge of the members, and what they stand for, is quite accurate, or exhaustive. About [H.T.] Muggeridge, for instance, (who is opposed to my views) – do you really think he represents nobody?

As a matter of fact, the list now suggested – far from being packed in the interests of Shaw and myself – is representative of the *three* currents of opinion that exist; and by far the largest representation of the three is given to the political *views recommended by the Special Committee* – no fewer than five of whose members (your own choice) are included.

We will discuss the names you mention, but as regards all but one or two of them, there are conclusive reasons against them, (which would, I am quite sure, convince you, as they convinced me when they were talked over). I don't mean anything against them or their views, but reasons why they are not 'available' for this purpose. It is quite certain, for instance, that some, if not most of those you name simply would not *consent* to serve.

I don't think you are at all correctly informed as to there being any desire (except on the part of Guest, who, so far as I can learn, stands alone), to hurry on this matter. But there must be a committee appointed and it is not wise to have too much delay in so merely preliminary a step. I suppose that any committee on such a subject, starting after the summer recess (as this will), can hardly report within 6 months. This brings us to March 1908. Then the Executive has got to consider the report for itself. I doubt whether anything will be ready for the next Annual Meeting. [*page cut across*] There will only be one report, and one proposal the more.

It takes a long time, as you must have discovered, to turn talking into doing.

[Sidney Webb: autograph cut off]

P.S. To go back to your names, you surely don't suppose that Clifford and Campbell, Chiozza-Money and Fels, would have got more votes, if they had stood for the Executive, than Coit and [Cecil] Chesterton and Snell and Muggeridge did?

P.P.S. Do you *really* believe that *I* have packed this Committee 'with a strong bias in favor of this new middle-class Socialist party project'? What an extraordinary and total misconception of my bias!

### 498 PP BEATRICE TO SIDNEY

Beatrice was spending a week in Edinburgh with the Commission. Dr John McVail (1849–1926), medical officer for Dunbartonshire, was appointed as medical investigator to the Commission. Beatrice thought him sympathetic to her idea of extending the role of the public health authorities. Ewen Francis Mac-Pherson (1870–1941) was legal secretary to the Scottish Board of Health 1904–22.

[Glasgow]<br>[mid-June 1907]

My own dearest Boy

The Documents Committee – Smart, [Patten-] McDougal and myself, met in the corridor and ordered a new proof of the whole to be circulated to the Commission – McDougall added 'tell the printers to let us have it for our autumn reading' – so that is alright.

The W.H. Infirmary here is really a scandal – one girl 'medical' looking after all inmates of W.H. [Work House] 1,300 and with 300 or 400 sick on her hands – phthisical, venereal, surgical, lying-in – a 'consultant' to help with operations. The poor little thing looked as near to a breakdown as could be – she is coming to supper on Friday. Dr Downes said it was deplorable! If McVail starts with Scotch P.L. as his standard he will not criticise the English. I am just now about to have a quiet lunch (12 o'c) before going off with Lansbury to the Glasgow Distress Committee. Tomorrow I stand alone at Glasgow doing 'Mrs Webb's system' as the Commission calls it.

Men only are going to the Hebrides – the Aberdeen trip seems likely to be the most useful and I shall go there if I think it necessary to go at all and come back in the evening of the 27th so as to be rested for Kate's party. But if I feel I have seen enough to explain my scheme I shall come away from here next Saturday week so as to get back to the [?chapters]. I want to be by my boy's side when he writes those [?chapters].

I am asking two dinners Tuesday 9th and Friday 12th [July] – so keep those days free of other engagements.

It is very pleasant having these lodgings with open window and fire and comfortable meals of my own sort. Tonight I dine with the MacPhersons to talk over my plans. All the Commission is here except Provis, Robinson, Wakefield and Nunn. Lord George left today.

Ever your devoted wifey

Beatrice

You must not get headaches – darling one – or I shall come back.


499 PP   BEATRICE TO SIDNEY

Henry Lockwood was Poor Law inspector for the L.G.B. and an important witness before the Commission.

[Edinburgh]

[mid-June 1907]

My own darling

Just back from Glasgow where I have been on my own account – seeing the working of the Scotch system. Also an interesting interview with the Secretary of the Distress Committee. Exactly the same state of things in respect to the futility of Relief Works as [?education].

The crux of the Ablebodied question seems to be the 'marginal man' – the man not young enough or not skilled enough, or not well conducted enough for employment in normal times. He is not vicious, he is not ill, he wants to work: you cannot reform him, you cannot detain him as a nuisance, he has not sufficient pluck or initiative to wish to emigrate. And yet if you leave him to wander the streets he becomes vicious or ill or hopelessly indolent; if you let him into any place where he can get food and sleep and not be required to overexert himself, he remains on your hands permanently.

Here is the letter about Dispensaries, will you keep it by you for proof correction of Medical memo.

I dined with Macpherson, legal member, yesterday. He is a nice fellow, but timid and Tory; liked my scheme but did not 'dare' to accept it. MacDougall has the reputation of being a hopelessly timid man, has tried to sit on any kind of reform of Scotch poor law. Lansbury says that C. Booth is quite obdurate both about his larger areas and for retraining everyone in the P.L. except the Aged. He thinks there is a consensus of opinion in favour of taking the children out of the P.L. but not the sick. He agrees with me that the C.O.S. members are softening towards outdoor relief as 'less eligible' and less costly than institutional treatment. But at present this is no common plan except a general understanding that C.S. Loch, C.B. and the two ladies will hold together. He has hopes of Bentham as well as Thory Gardiner and Nunn – but not great hopes of any of them.

He says that Lockwood's successor is Davy's nominee – a county gentleman neighbour of Davy. He thinks that J.B. [John Burns] is completely under *Davy's* control – more than Provis.

Now darling boy, goodnight. I am taking it easy but learning a good deal which is useful.

Always your devoted comrade

Beatrice

500 PP   BEATRICE TO SIDNEY

[Edinburgh]

Saturday [?14 June 1907]

My own dear Boy

I am going to try hard to get this letter to you on Sunday morning because I do not like to think of my boy being without his morning greeting – just to hearten him up for the day. And if I do I shall expect him to take a turn in the afternoon in the Direction of the Dorking P.O. and get the letter to me before I come on Monday.

Yesterday I went for a talk with remarkable Headmaster (the 1,400 children school); he was scathing in his criticism of Edinburgh Poor Law administration as niggardly and shortsighted and is going to take me today to see some of his children on outdoor relief. He is keen on taking the children out of the Poor Law and is ready to develop an [?indirect] Day school Department in connection with his school for widows and widower's children. In the evening I had the lady medical officer of the Craigleith W.H. – it is clear from what she told me that both medical attendance and nursing is woefully scamped in the Scotch P.L. Infirmaries and W.H. – they are mere places in which to die or to rest – not for cure. The Scotch have not yet got the notion of *Curative Treatment* – they are still at the point of 'Less Eligibility' – at least the officials are, and such devices for it – that are taking place are in the direction of sentimental indulgence as of Progress. I am gaining more and more confidence in the rightness and feasibility of our scheme, and the principles upon which it is based, as the next step in the evolution of the Poor Law. There may be other heights beyond but these are at present inaccessible to us and to others. Lord George has just discovered Newsholme's Statement and is much impressed with it. 'Have you inspired him or he you?' he said laughingly – I answered 'Oh! he has inspired me – and will inspire you – I have merely got at the expert *first*'! Now I am sending him the other statements and calling his attention to our responsibility in not calling the writers of them for close examination.

Dear Boy, how happy we are in each other's love – the rest and strength this absolute confidence in each other gives us – so much more rest and strength than any degree of self-confidence. We must try to inspire others to feel it in each other, and in the community. Sooner or later the world has to be reorganised on Love shining through Knowledge. That is what you and I are striving or playing(?) for.

Ever your devoted comrade<br>Beatrice

501 PP SIDNEY TO BEATRICE

The Shaws had moved to the Rectory, Ayot St Lawrence, which they first rented and then purchased, renaming the house 'Shaw's Corner' and making it their permanent home.

Sir Francis Hyett (1844–1941) was vice-chairman of Gloucestershire County Council 1904–18 and a prominent magistrate in the county.

41 Grosvenor Road<br>Westminster Embankment<br>13.6.7

Dear One

Charlotte has just been in to say she is very likely going to take a house in Wales for three months, if she can arrange for the Hertfordshire house being taken care of: but that Shaw wants to make the date run from 1 July – she thinks she will make it 15th July. She offers to *lend* us the Hertfordshire house, and will not hear of rent. *But* Shaw is anxious to get away for three months, (and as soon as possible); not any shorter term. *She* is anxious to take all her servants, including the man who is gardener, boots and necessary to pump water. Thus, we should have to find a man, as well as take over the place from 1st (or probably 15th) July for three months.

Now, *I* should like to get away for three months. After 12 July we have only a few engagements of the Commission and County Council order. Could we manage by your coming up for Monday night, and my coming up for Monday and Tuesday nights for a couple of weeks?

It is of course not quite convenient, and not an ideal country. But it might mean a longer time in the country for you, without extra expense.

She says they will certainly take a place somewhere for August and September, and their house is at our service free (*without* the gardener, I understand); he is the husband of her cook. Perhaps you will write to her direct.

Here is a useful letter from Hyett, which needs an acknowledgement from you. We can utilise his hints and suggestions.

Today I was interrupted by a message to take Cyril Jackson's place in selecting some teachers. But I managed to begin Morpeth, and shall I hope, be able to do that one at any rate, for you to criticise.

Miss Bulkley has finished the Great Tew records – they are confirmatory but add little new. The invitation cards for 3 July have come, and I am sending all but 100 to Pease. I think he has your instructions, but I will ask him tomorrow.

The vote for the University and the School went through Education Committee without remark yesterday; so that it is pretty safe in the Council.

Now goodbye, dear one – take it easy – it is more important to have people to dinner than to see institutions, and more important to keep well than either. Adieu.

Sidney

502 PP   SIDNEY TO BEATRICE

In April Beatrice had begun to reckon up the possible alignment of her fellow commissioners. At the most she hoped to find ten allies – the chairman, Nunn, Smart, Gardiner, Booth, Phelps, Robinson, Wakefield, Lansbury and Chandler. At the least, as proved to be the case, she felt she could count on the last three to endorse the Webb plan.

Sir Henry Roscoe (1835–1915) was a former professor of chemistry and a Liberal M.P. Amber Reeves, the daughter of William Pember and Maud Reeves, was an active Fabian at Cambridge and the protégée of H. G. Wells. Arthur Hobhouse was the fourth child of Henry and Margaret Hobhouse. Leonard Courtney was raised to the peerage by the Liberal Government of 1906.

41 Grosvenor Road<br>Westminster Embankment<br>14.6.7

Dear One

It is very pleasant to think you are getting on well, and not uncomfortably. I think it will be impossible to get over the timidity and conventionality of either the 'official centre' of the Commission (which casts 5 or 6 votes), or the 'left centre' with its 4 votes or so. The utmost you can really hope for is to prevent either or both of these from coalescing with the 'extreme left' or C.O.S. 'bloc' of 4 or 5. It is not at all unlikely that they

261

will eventually all unite on some colourless common report, with individual additions. Your own strong report must stand out by contrast.

Last night I dined with the Courtneys – only the Olivers and Miss Courtney. They were all kind and friendly but I could not stand much of that kind of thing. For two hours we talked about little else but eating – what things were nice, whether peas were indigestible, whether green asparagus was nicer than giant asparagus, and so on. Then upstairs we gossiped about people, and looked at copies of Leonard's Coat of Arms and new photographs of him. He and Oliver went off to Sir H. Roscoe's party, and I came away. There is no harm in all that; but I am not yet in the mood to fill up time in that way.

Here are a few letters – one from Lady Betty Balfour to be at once answered by you. I think you have asked people for *12 July*, but is it fixed?

What am I to do with the invitation cards for 3 July (Oxford and Cambridge F.S. party)? I have sent Pease 500, and kept back 100. Do you wish to invite your own friends, or shall I send Pease also these 100?

By the way, Amber Reeves has got a *First* Class in Moral Science Tripos, beating all the men – there being no men in the First Class.

Arthur Hobhouse, on the other hand, gets only a Third Class in Natural Science Tripos; which is very poor.

Goodbye, dear one, I like my daily talk.

Sidney

### 503 UI SIDNEY WEBB TO H. G. WELLS

The Political Committee's purpose was now defined as the promotion of local Fabian groups 'with the object of increasing the socialist representation in Parliament as a party co-operating as far as possible with the Labour Party, while remaining independent of that and all other parties'. Webb was to be its chairman; half its members were known to support Wells. It was a device much more clearly related to the internal politics of the Society than to political reality, for the compromise formula meant nothing. At the same time Wells had begun a campaign to revise the 'Basis' of the Society, to which all members had to subscribe. This equally ambiguous document had remained unchanged for many years, partly because any attempt to alter it raised more problems than it would solve. The rise of the suffrage movement, however, had led to an agreement to insert a phrase on 'equal citizenship', moved by Maud Reeves and Beatrice Webb at a meeting on 22 February.

More than four hundred people turned up to a Fabian soirée at the Suffolk Street Galleries on 26 June: the company was entertained by Morris dancers. Commenting on this large turn-out Sidney wrote to Beatrice on 27 June that 'We must try to suggest activities for them and also make them pay subscriptions'. The boom in Fabian activity was embarrassing to the Webbs in their attempt to cope with Wells, partly because the excitement created by Wells was bringing in many new members and partly because the Webbs had no idea how usefully to assimilate them in the Society. Sidney was never comfortable when the

Society became larger than a number that could be cosily managed by monthly meetings.

41 Grosvenor Road, Westminster Embankment

15.6.7

My dear Wells

We have appointed that Committee, only substituting [Lawson] Dodd for [Keir] Hardie, which may please you.

I don't know whether to be pleased or not at your explaining that it is not my integrity that you suspect, but my competence! Don't you think that as this kind of thing is more in my way of business than in yours, I am on the whole likely to make a more accurate diagnosis?

But really, your suspicions are quite baseless. I have satisfied myself that there is no such danger as you fear. The Committee will be able to agree on a useful report, which will educate all of us in the preparing, and the rest of the Society in the reading of it. That, after all, is the main thing. We have got to *educate* (ourselves incidentally, and) the members. The Society never was very homogeneous because it was deliberately kept heterogeneous. But the danger now is of its becoming altogether too vague and nebulous – a mere philosophical debating society. Now it has been, since 1888 at any rate, a very definitely *political* society, with essentially *political* aims, pressing *political* proposals, and exercising a good deal of *political* influence. Personally I am not in it for anything else. I don't in the least object to other people developing an artistic side, a philosophical side, a side of individual philanthropy, or a religious side, if these things satisfy them – so long as they develop these as additions to, and not as substitutes for what has been the Society's principal business for 20 years.

I don't know whether you really differ from me in this; sometimes I think we don't use words with the same meanings. Perhaps it may not be useless to explain that by 'political' I mean simply 'state institutional'; and not all *necessarily* forming a separate party, or any party, or indeed having anything at all to do with elections or electioneering! In the ordinary use of the English language, for the F.S. to cease to be political, or to become less political, would be taken to mean that we should cease to have any-thing to do with such matters as Labor Legislation and Taxation, Local Government and Educational administration, the organisation of the State and collective action. That must necessarily imply that we should give up altogether the attempt to work out the application of Socialist theory to the facts of the community in which we live; and abandon our efforts to get these applications adopted. All this is 'political'; and nothing but 'political'. I don't think you mean this. But why use language which implies it.

Personally I do not work and strive and find money *merely* to satisfy my intellectual curiosity. Perhaps I ought to do so. As a matter of fact what moves me is a desire to *get things done*. I want to diminish the sum of human suffering. I am not concerned about this party or that, but about getting things done, no matter who does them. Elections and parties are quite subordinate – *even trivial* – parts of political action. More is done in England in politics whilst ignoring elections and parties than by or with them. Nevertheless, they, too, form a part of life which the Socialist cannot ignore.

I resisted you when you wanted to submerge the F.S. in the I.L.P. or the Labor Party; whichever it was that you meant in the report of the Special Committee. Equally do I resist the proposal that the F.S. should create a party of its own. And equally do I object to your last proposal that the F.S. should give up political action!

Let us take the new Political Committee leisurely, and make it a means of mutual education – that is its main function. It has no powers. It has only to report.

Sidney Webb

504 PP   SIDNEY TO BEATRICE

Robert Lorraine (1876–1935) was an actor and a close friend of Shaw. At the Fabian summer school in Wales that summer he and Shaw were nearly drowned while bathing: Shaw described the incident in a letter to Wells. (SCL 14 August 07) Karl Gustav Cassell (1866–1945) spent much of his career in Germany; his economics put great stress on monetary theory.

41 Grosvenor Road, Westminster Embankment<br>17.6.7

Dear One

I was glad to get your long cheery letter this morning; and to think of you as well. Your visit will have been good as preventing any doubt or uncertainty as to there being any sort of validity in the idea of 'no relief for the able bodied' – which is, in fact, only the negation of the very idea of a Poor Law.

The Shaws are very happy and prosperous – nearly persuaded to get a motorcar, and learn themselves to drive it! Charlotte has been a five-days tour with Lion Phillimore. One Lorraine, an actor, who plays Jack Tanner, was there; with his little motorcar. There is a possibility of Granville Barker being offered a big theatre and a big salary in New York, to repeat there what he has done at the Court. There is as yet no new play begun. As to availability of the house, Charlotte *thinks* she will get her Welsh Mansion, (at some large price!). It will not be until after 7 July, it is clear, because there is a public dinner to Granville Barker on that day at which Shaw plays a leading part.

Down does not know whether her sister would be able to go to Hertfordshire, but will write to ask; also as to a gardener youth; but her relatives are engaged.

Today I have got Professor Cassel, a Swedish Economist coming to lunch – he is a Marshallian, but he asked to come. He is the only Political Economist in Stockholm; and now the merchants insist on starting a Faculty of Commerce – all shorthand and bookkeeping, French and German. He turns out to be a Land Reformer, and quite reasonably 'Fabian'; much interested in getting more concrete economics.

Cyril Jackson is just about to start his enquiry into boy labor, and asks what your lady can do! I told him that I feared she had gone off into history, and was probably not going to be of any use to him.

*Per Contra* – I hear that the Liverpool Fabian Society is going to devote the coming year to studying Casual Labor there. I have encouraged them, and discreetly directed them, as to what to get and what to do, and what conclusion to come to. If the Society brings out a good report a year hence, it will not be otherwise than helpful.

Goodbye – dear one, do not get too tired – don't commit yourself to Aberdeen.

Sidney

505 PP  SIDNEY TO BEATRICE

Molly Bell, the daughter of Sir Hugh Bell, had married Charles Trevelyan. Lady Horsley was the wife of Sir Victor Horsley F.R.S. (1857–1916), a leading surgeon and professor of pathology at University College, London. George Unwin, formerly professor of economic history at the University of Manchester, had been a part-time lecturer at L.S.E. for two years.

41 Grosvenor Road, Westminster Embankment
18.6.7

Dearest One

No doubt you are right to stay for Aberdeen, or rather for influencing the other Commissioners; but it is not altogether profitable, because I am not getting on much! Sometimes I can't work, sometimes there is a rush of other things to do; but whatever it is, in the absence of my Domestic Genius I don't get on! I have not yet completed even Morpeth, and I am going to be interrupted again tomorrow.

Last night I went to the Co-Efficients – 9 present, including Lord Milner. I propounded the Poor Law Reform Scheme, not saying that was your scheme, though implying it, and not much alluding to the Commission. They were all favorably impressed and made little criticism, except deprecating the expense (Milner), and fearing medical opposition (Mackinder and Newbolt) fear of stereotyping medical practice (Bellairs). No useful suggestions were made.

I fancy Lord Milner grudges all Expenditure that is not in some way

265

'Imperial'. But it may have been only an expression of anticipated hostility.

I don't at all think a National Board for the able-bodied and Unemployed a bad idea – especially one for Scotland. But I think the practical shape would be a National Board to provide the curative institutions receiving the patients from the Local Authorities. (It must take them free or at a nominal charge, in order to encourage the Local Authorities to send them.) I doubt whether the curative institutions can get started without some such centralization. But probably Provincial Boards would be more engaging than a National Department – Scotland, London, Lancashire, Yorkshire might each have their own.

Here are refusals from Mrs Trevelyan and Lady Horsley.

Here, too, are a couple of reviews – one very appreciatory from the *American Historical Review*.

Mackinder wants to spend £1,500 this Summer on structural alterations at the School, in order to get further accommodation. I have agreed to his bringing this forward, to be conditional on our getting the Treasury Grant and appealing for donations. Our business is growing, and we must make more room to meet the demand. It seems that Unwin has declined to go on lecturing, on the ground that he wants to devote himself to writing.

Goodbye, dearest

Sidney

506 PP   SIDNEY TO BEATRICE

The photograph was possibly the earliest known of Sidney, taken at Dymchurch when staying with the Blands – about 1888–90. The Shaw volume was probably the reissue by Constable of *Three Plays for Puritans*.

41 Grosvenor Road,
Westminster Embankment
20.6.7

Dear One

Your charming letters are a great joy to me. I am fully convinced that it is well worthwhile your going to Aberdeen, if you don't visit too many institutions. Pray don't feel obliged to go through the programme any day that you are tired. The quorum of three is all nonsense: there is no requirement that there should be three; or that all three should be always together – though no doubt it looks better to pretend that the Commission has so divided up.

Here are some fragments of more or less interest, not involving any action on your part. The photograph of me I have no knowledge of. I was at Brighton with Wallas after my scarlet fever in 1890–1, but I do not remember being 'took', then or otherwise.

Last night I read through Shaw's new volume of (old) plays, staying up until I finished it (which was only till 12). It is full of amazingly clever observations and correct criticisms of persons and tendencies. But to me all this 'scrappy' and disconnected criticism lacks force and effectiveness – at least, I do not *feel* myself to be affected, and therefore doubt whether others are affected, to any great extent. It seems to me, as with his presence on the St Pancras Borough Council, that he fails to 'catch hold' of the ordinary man – just as a locomotive engine, when its wheels revolve fast without 'biting' the rails, and therefore without making the train progress. This leaves out of account his effect in stimulating people to think, if they *can* think; and in imperceptibly educating them to see that shams *are* shams. How many are capable of such education? There is thus a lack of constructiveness in the effort, which seems regrettable. But he is as he is; and I suppose all I mean is that he is not *me*!

I send you the book herewith, in case you care to read it, or *in* it, for it is all in pieces. (*Bring it back.*)

You will see from the Creighton letter that the two sons of Frederic Harrison are coming to dinner tomorrow, which is quite interesting.

Now goodbye dear one, or I shall get no work done. This is a very dreary time, but you must not go away again.

Sidney

### 507 PP   BEATRICE WEBB TO MARY PLAYNE

Edward Carpenter (1844–1929), the socialist poet, had retired to lead the Simple Life in Derbyshire. His hand-made sandals set a fashion among advanced people, though Shaw quickly abandoned them because they made his feet sore. Carpenter was also interested in esoteric thought. His *Towards Democracy* (1883) and *Civilisation, Its Cause and Cure* (1889) were widely read in the socialist movement. Beatrice noted that Carpenter 'consoled me with his ideas, made me feel not merely morally better but physically stronger'. (BWD 21 June 07) In an undated letter to Sidney in June she commented that *The Art of Creation* (1904) was 'comforting in its combination of moral fervour with mystical quietness' which offset the stresses caused by 'the contemplation of human wreckage' involved in the Poor Law enquiry.

Sir John Edward Dorrington (1832–1911) was a Conservative M.P. 1886–1906 and a Commissioner in Lunacy from 1892.

Edinburgh<br>Friday, 21 June 1907

Dearest Mary

I am writing from the night train back to my Boy – rushing through the night just for the happiness of spending 2 days and one night with him before resuming work at Aberdeen on Monday morning 12 o'c. The Treasury pays my fare so I don't scruple to take this recreation – Saturday and Sunday alone in Edinburgh was not inviting – the rest of the Commission have scattered themselves either northward or southward.

I am sending you E. Carpenter's *Art of Creation* – I have found it extraordinarily encouraging and suggestive. Also you will see in it the metaphysics of the Socialist creed as to social relations – the Faith we Hold. (I believe, I left some debt – the tin box which we never succeeded in paying the carrier: take the book in payment of it!)

Mr Hyett was very much pleased with my scheme and asked me to send it to Sir J. Dorrington who wished to see it – it will be odd if we and such conservative administrators as Hyett and Dorrington can agree on a big reform – but there is really much in common between the Tory and the Constructive Socialist.

We had a very delightful Sunday with the Gerald Balfours – A.J.B. [Arthur Balfour] joining us on the Sunday morning. They certainly are the most bewitching family taken together – combining public spirit intellect and moral refinement to a quite remarkable degree. They have also a wonderful gift of intimacy – we five talked from 8 o'c to 12 on Sunday evening (as if we had known each other from infancy). I have never seen Sidney quite so much at home with anyone as he is with these Balfour brothers. On the whole I like and admire Gerald more than I do the greater brother – there is something, I don't quite know what – that I do *not* admire in Arthur – it is a muddier nature in motive and feeling than Gerald's – perhaps A.J.B. has been spoilt by the self-consciousness of personal power and by the perpetual philandering to which he has been always addicted – apparently [*half page torn off*]

For the next three weeks I shall be leading a distracted life rushing after the Commission to the Provinces. The Bernard Shaws have lent us their Hertfordshire house for three months and we settle there July 17th until early in October. Do motor over to us – and stay a day or two – Bedfordshire is quite a good center and pretty country – Welwyn is place, about 20 or 30 miles north of London.

Ever your affectionate sister

Beatrice Webb

508 PP  SIDNEY TO BEATRICE

The Liberal government was beginning to encounter serious resistance from the Conservative majority in the House of Lords, especially in its efforts to push through an Education Bill to satisfy Nonconformist and other objections to the Education Acts of 1902 and 1903. This attempt was abandoned, the Liberal setback being a harbinger of the conflict which led to the dramatic confrontations of 1910 and 1911.

My own dearest

I can't feel sure that you will get all your letters right. Your postcard directing me to post to *Peterhead* was delivered here only after I had gone up to bed. This morning I posted a big envelope full (which I had kept back) to that address before 8 a.m. marking it to be forwarded to you c/o Dr Leslie Mackenzie Edinburgh, if you had left before it arrived (as I fear you may do). Two hours later I got your welcome letter, from which I gather that this present letter will reach you at lunch at Aberdeen.

There was nothing in the packet sent to Peterhead needing urgent reply.

I am glad you feel the tour profitable because it will make it less tiring for you! But I shudder to think of your spending day after day in this cold wet weather, and motoring too. Pray be careful.

I fear the innate Conservatism and stupidity of the Commissioners will make them reject nearly everything new. But I doubt their reestablishing the principles of 1834. What is more likely is a banal and inconclusive 'see-saw' or balancing, of considerations – not too much and not too little – resulting in nothing very definite. In this sense, C.S. Loch's prediction may prove to be right (the Status Quo, with improved administration) – as the result of a mere 'cancelling off' of each other.

Here are various letters to interest you in the train – one from Lord George (nothing important).

I think the more the Commissioners study your big memoranda, the more the ideas will sink into their minds, and prove serious obstacles to anything reactionary. I think we ought to prepare a paragraph dealing with the *cost* – showing that no particular extra cost need be involved, and that only so much need be done at any moment as may commend itself.

The Liberal attack on the Lords is, I feel, a very damp squib. It is not going to do them any particular good. It may however indirectly work for some future change in the House of Lords, carried by a Conservative Government, by consent!

Now goodbye dear one. I cannot get on whilst you are away, so this trip is a costly one. But it had to be done, and you will have learnt no end of a lot, and become ever so much more wise than your husband.

Sidney

509 PP  SIDNEY TO BEATRICE

Beatrice was on a short visit to Shrewsbury with some of her colleagues. Sir Sydney Holland (1855–1931), later Viscount Knutsford, was the dock company director and hospital reformer who did much for nursing education. Sir Francis Mowatt (1837–1919) was permanent secretary of the Treasury. Alexander Siemens (1847–1928) was an electrical engineer and industrialist. Sir Felix

Schuster (1854–1936) was a banker whose successive amalgamations produced the National Provincial Bank.

The fire screen was made at Ashbee's workshop at Chipping Campden. Abraham Levine (1871–1949) was an eminent actuary in the early years of the century, becoming President of the Institute of Actuaries in 1928.

41 Grosvenor Road,
Westminster Embankment
16.7.7

My own dear one

I have got to want a letter every morning. When I did not find one today, everything became dull and tiring. But I feel that it is unreasonable to expect a letter, as you probably got back too late. I only hope you did not do too much in the heat.

Wernher's dinner last night was of 30 men, at three tables – largely, I think, connected with the 'Charlottenburg', but with financiers added. Haldane, Sydney Holland, Morant, Mowatt, Alexander Siemens, Sir Felix Schuster etc. were at my table.

After dinner I had some talk with Sydney Holland, who was full of appreciation of you at the P.L. Commission – and I expounded to him and Wernher, the scheme for Half-Time Training for boys. Wernher thought it would put a new burden on employers.

I walked away with Holland, who asked how he could limit the patients at the London Hospital – he wanted to reserve it for the class above paupers, or else get the Boards of Guardians to pay. I suggested segregation by kinds of disease – to which he was not very sympathetic. He strikes me as a man of 'insolence', conceit and a certain falsity, yet useful for his energy and force.

The new fire screen has come, and looks well. The maker writes that it has been photographed for the *Art Journal*.

Your report on Aberdeen has come, for correction of proof. I have corrected it for printer's or grammatical errors; and now enclose it for you to consider if you want to make alterations – leaving it to you to return it.

A mass of Unemployed Statements have come – including a particularly good and full one from Beveridge.

Levine, the Actuary, works out the cost of a workman's insurance against all contingencies except Unemployment at 6/6 a week – to which I suppose 1/- a week might be added for Trade Union Unemployed Benefit. Thus 7/6 a week is what he must save, to be independent of Charitable help – this, of course, does not pay for operations or hospital treatment. I am asking Levine to send me back my questions to him.

Goodbye dear one until tomorrow.

Sidney

New Rectory, Ayot St Lawrence,
Welwyn, Herts.
1.8.7

Dear Pease

I am not happy about the Book Box Circular. I feel that we ought to make £100 a year out of the enterprise; and that we do no good by failing to exact that much.

I did not understand what you meant by saying that we should of course not charge the 10/- to old subscribers. My idea was to charge 10/- a year to everyone, from the next renewal after 1st October. Perhaps, however, this is what you meant. You can hardly make two prices.

I still think it would be most unwise to delay the issue of the circular until after 1 October. My idea would have been to issue it as soon as convenient – certainly not later than the first week in September – and to have *made much* of it, for the sake of advertisement, saying that all renewals from then onward would be charged 10/-.

I cannot see that it matters at all having several hundreds of applications. You have only to say that owing to the unprecedented demand etc. the supply is exhausted. It would give you the opportunity to get one more paragraph into the newspapers!

But, *one way or another*, you won't find it quite easy to get £100 a year out of 200 boxes; and you had better make it a favor to have a box.

Can I be of any use as to lists of books etc? £100 is a lot to spend all at once, and you will need to consider well the lists of books to be bought.

No doubt you have your plans well in mind, and I don't want to interfere. But we certainly ought to 'make a splash' with the enterprise, having now £500 capital in it, and 5,000 volumes.

Yours

Sidney Webb

## 511 PP BEATRICE WEBB TO MARY PLAYNE

The group of clever young Fabians from Cambridge meant much to the Webbs: from this time on they relied heavily on the enthusiasm of their young acolytes. Apart from Amber Reeves the group included the poet Rupert Brooke (1887–1915); Frederick 'Ben' Keeling (1886–1916), who became the first assistant editor of the *New Statesman* and was killed on the Somme; and Edward Hugh John Neale Dalton (1887–1962), who went from Cambridge to a research studentship at L.S.E. and then was appointed to the teaching staff. He became a Labour M.P. and among a number of Cabinet posts he was Chancellor of the Exchequer 1945–47. Clifford Allen (1889–1930), later Lord Allen of Hurtwood, was another member of the group; he became a leading figure in the I.L.P., a pacifist and manager of the *Daily Herald* 1925–30.

Mary Playne had developed cancer; she died of it in 1923.

My dearest Sister

I had a presentiment that all was not well with you and your letter came as a curious fulfilment of my fears. But now that I have recovered from the first shock I feel quite hopeful that all will be well with you, when the little morsel of poisonous substance is removed. There seems so much more evidence, that appears in the statistics of complete recoveries, so that if it is removed *at once* there need be no more probability of cancer than with anyone else. Most cases are *not* removed at once, and it is of the total number of cases, early and later removal, of which we have statistics. We are all of us – we sisters – living on the borderland between this life and the hereafter and anyone of us may be called before the other. I shall certainly run up to see you when you are in London – any day next week I can come up? (I suppose you would not like to take possession of my house?) We are only $\frac{3}{4}$ hour from London so it is quite easy to run up for the middle of the day.

We are having a very happy time here, working away on our volume on the Manor and the Borough and entertaining young Fabians – chiefly Cambridge men up for the Long. They are a remarkable good set of hardworking clean living youths – mostly clever and enthusiastic and who look upon us as the Patriarchs of the Movement. I am becoming more and more convinced that the Community has to take hold of the problem of clearing-up the base of society – using all its powers to improve the circumstances – physical and mental – of the lowest class. Mainly from the standpoint of material welfare we have to do that – in order to hold our own with such highly regulated races as the Germans and the Japanese. What I care for more, is that we shall not get a chance of spiritual and intellectual life for the whole community until we do make the material circumstances tolerable for the bulk of the nation.

I believe the Conservative party might take part in this work of reconstruction – so I go in with my propaganda among Conservative as well as encouragement of positive Socialists.

Do let me know what day next week I can come up and see you. I have lots to talk about and it will do you good to see me. What a strange dreamlike thing, life is, as one grows older one feels more and more of a 'wayfarer' – with a day's journey to get through and a goal to get to.

Ever your devoted

Beatrice Webb

It was probably this visit that led to the much-repeated story of later years that Wells first met the Webbs when they descended on him at Sandgate during a cycling tour. The first meeting six years earlier had in fact been formal and pre-arranged. The Barker play was *Waste*, refused a licence by the Lord Chamberlain but given a private performance by the Stage Society on 24 November and a 'copyright' reading at the Savoy in January when the Shaws, Wells, Gilbert Murray and Laurence Housman all read parts.

Ayot St Lawrence, Welwyn, Herts.
[September 1907]

My dear Mrs Wells

Is there any chance of your being at Sandgate on Thursday October 3rd, and if so may we come and demand a night's lodging? We are taking five days holiday before we return to London cycling round the south coast through the Cinque Ports or if it is wet staying at Beachy Head. We are due at Deal on Friday 4th and return to London that Sunday evening. I know you are now in Switzerland but I imagine you may be back by the beginning of next month: we should love a talk with you and H.G.

We have had an excellent summer's work, have finished our volume on the Manor and the Borough and written two weighty reports for the P.L.C. – one on the Medical Service of the Poor and the other on the evolution of Poor Law policy since 1834. If H.G. ever becomes interested in such insignificant subjects I will give him these Reports upon which to browse. At present they are going the round of the Cabinet and some Opposition leaders – all as *private friends*, of course.

We heard a glowing account of both of you from the G. Barkers. His play is first class!

Ever yours affectionately
Beatrice Webb

## 513 BEV   BEATRICE WEBB TO WILLIAM BEVERIDGE

William Henry Beveridge (1879–1963) was sub-warden of Toynbee Hall, after leaving Balliol College, Oxford. As a civil servant in the Board of Trade he worked with Winston Churchill on the development of labour exchanges. He later became the fourth Director of L.S.E. from 1919 to 1937 and Master of University College, Oxford, until 1945. During the Second World War he was the author of the notable Beveridge Report on social insurance. He first met the Webbs in 1905. At the time of this letter he had just given evidence to the Royal Commission.

41 Grosvenor Road,
Westminster Embankment
[October 1907]

Dear Mr Beveridge

Can you come to dine to meet Mr Gerald Balfour next Monday, 14th, 7.30 morning dress to discuss the question of Labor Exchanges and the organisation of the Unemployed? We can talk afterwards about your new statement which I have not yet seen.

Forgive the scrawl.

Ever yours

Beatrice Webb

### 514 PP BEATRICE TO SIDNEY

At the end of October Beatrice had an attack of conscience which exacerbated the anxiety and exhaustion caused by her work on the Commission. Mrs Bosanquet had challenged her to produce the letters from local medical officers of health on which she had based a claim that they favoured transferring sick paupers from the Poor Law to the public health authorities. Beatrice 'sent exactly what I thought fit' (BWD 29 October 07), including a few adverse letters to give an impression of balance. When Mrs Bosanquet asked for all the letters, rather than a selection, Beatrice fell back on the defence that she could not release letters written in confidence without the consent of the authors. Thinking Mrs Bosanquet guilty of 'a mean little tricky attempt to trip me up', and replying in kind, she had in fact put herself in a vulnerable and scarcely honest position. The episode preyed on her mind. It recalled a similar fear of exposure years before over her exaggeration of her East End experiences before the House of Lords committee on Sweating. As on the earlier occasion she broke down with strain and remorse. She went first for a few days to Mary Playne at Longfords and then to Beachy Head.

[Longfords]
Friday [early November 1907]

My own darling

Here I am being nursed – fire in my room all day and a most pleasant friendly atmosphere surrounding me. I have not mentioned the P.L.C. since I came as Mary taboos the question as she says wisely that I better not think about it. I have hopes that after my letter – there will be Peace for sometime. I really don't want to be more objectionable than need be and we must consider how I can avoid it best. Anyway I will try and not get obsessed by the personal aspect of the matter. In the end solid work will prevail and one must try and keep friendly towards one's hostile colleagues and credit them with good intentions. You will help me to do so.

I saw your letter in *The Times*, it reads well. Do you see that the *Daily Mail* is going distinctly socialist, much to Arthur's disgust?

Ever your devoted wifey

Beatrice Webb

Beachy Head, Eastbourne
Nov. 12, 1907

My own Boy

All is right except that He is not here. The hill was safely rounded, under the lee of the wind – lunch, rest, another saunter, in the Hollow, a cup of tea, and just two words of love to my boy.

I wish I were giving that lecture tonight – but clearly I must reserve all my strength for this big affair of the P.L. Commission. How our ideas have grown – first the transfer of Poor Law Medical Relief to the P.H. authorities, then the break up of the Poor Law, now nothing short of clearing up the base of society – no wonder the poor Commission is a bit breathless and inclined to kick out at its female jockey. However with my boy's help we will pull the whole programme off in so far as presenting it to the public is concerned.

I am steadily getting better – I shall not be quite well until I am back at work again – then will be shown the real advantage of the slow cure of rest in good air, instead of drugs, stomach aches and forced food. But I don't think I shall do Seaford.

Darling, God bless you, while you sit at work this morning send me a *good long letter*.

BW

Beatrice had written to Professor William Smart asking to be released on grounds of poor health from her undertaking to produce a series of reports on local authorities between 1834 and 1907: in fact she offered the excuse because she felt the Commission would not tolerate the reports if written. She made it clear that she intended to continue her own line of enquiry on the able-bodied unemployed. (BWD 15 November 07) The letters mentioned are missing.

When Beatrice next turned up at the Commission it was clear that she had a draft scheme which might command support from four or five members. She therefore agreed to prepare a substantive memorandum on 'The Break-Up of the Poor Law'. This, she noted on 26 November, was 'a bold move . . . but I think, on the whole, a wise one. The majority of the Commission are tired of wandering about the subject without a leader . . . the planting down of an attractive and logical scheme of reform will make the other members nervous of being contented with muddle-headed generalisations'. At the subsequent meeting the manifest polarisation of feeling led Beatrice to reveal that she, Lansbury and Chandler were thinking of a comprehensive minority report. She noted 'the most distinct consolidation against me . . . a discourteous coldness . . . I think they are somewhat justified in their dislike of me – I have played with the Commission'. (BWD 9 December 07) She was frank about her aggressive independence: 'investigating, inventing, making an atmosphere favourable to my inventions and, where possible, getting the person with right opinions into high places, and persons in high places in the right state of mind'. From this point she no longer had scruples about her role. 'All I have to do is to get on with my own work and leave them alone to settle their own report; merely use the Commission to get the information I need and they can give me . . . without bothering myself about the Commission as a whole . . . they have absolved me from obligations of good fellowship.' (BWD 12 December 07) The best she could expect was that her pressure might, on some points, have shifted the Commission towards a more radical set of conclusions.

[Beachy Head]
Thursday [? 14 November 1907]

My own darling boy,

So many thanks for your *most satisfactory* letters – your talk with Lord George gets me out of the difficulty. I have sent him the enclosed letter and a copy of the report to Professor Smart. This I trust clears up the whole situation.

I know it is probable I shall have to face some discussion and questioning on the Commission but that I shall quite easily do. The plain truth is we are quite detestable colleagues on a R.C., for those who are against us – and I must expect some buffetting. With your advice and consolation I think I can stand quite firm and endure any little pin-pricking they may have recourse.

My [*illegible*] came in the post satisfactorily. I shall have lots to talk about on Saturday afternoon – but my hand is tired with comparing and copying letters to Lord George.

Ever your devoted

B

517 BL   SIDNEY WEBB TO R. B. HALDANE

This covering letter and the memorandum were passed on to Asquith and are in his papers at the Bodleian Library.

41 Grosvenor Road, Westminster Embankment
12.12.7

Dear Haldane

I hope you will not think it altogether too presumptuous of me to have written the enclosed Memo. on Old Age Pensions; when you read it you can judge whether any of the ideas are likely to be of any use or not. By this time, you have probably got more exact figures than I have time to work out.

What may be of more interest to you is the Poor Law position. Beatrice was called upon to produce her scheme; and I enclose the Memo. which now gives it in perfected form. In this form, it has secured widespread private approval from county administration and other experts.

Its effect on the majority was like the bark of the shepherd's dog. It drove them helter-skelter into the Chairman's fold! Sinking their differences, they have *provisionally* adopted – rather than accept anything from her – a blurred outline which may not unlikely work out to the same thing! viz. abolition of all Boards of Guardians, adoption of the County and County Borough area, County and County Borough Council to be the supreme authority for Poor Law, some sort of stipendiary officer to sit with nominated local committees to hear applications etc.

This, as you see, comes very near to Beatrice's plan; but fortunately it just leaves her an excuse for a Minority Report in favor of the Break-up of the Poor Law, in which we are going to do in the grandest style.

Now, it is quite impossible for the P.L. Committee Report to be out *before* next Autumn, probably not before Christmas 1908.

Yet, it seems to me that the C. of E. [Chancellor of the Exchequer] will almost necessarily want to adumbrate something for Poor Law Reform, in unfolding his Pension Scheme.

That being so, we leave it to your discretion how far you make use not only of the typewritten memo., but also of the printed P.L. Committee Memo. and of this information – only, we can't get further copies!

Yours

Sidney Webb

518 PP  BEATRICE WEBB TO MARY PLAYNE

The Commission had gone to visit an experiment in the use of a residential colony as a means of coping with the unemployed.

Hollesley Bay Colony,<br>Suffolk<br>January 1st 1908

Dearest Mary

I am so glad to see your writing this morning and to read your letter – now you will have your face turned towards home and I imagine this will meet you in Europe – I wonder whether you see the Olivers!

We are settled down in this wild weird place – a large red brick building on the open moor with stretches of sea and river on each side of it and 8 miles from a R. Station – merely a little coastguard station a mile away from the nearest neighbour. There are the 300 unemployed living in the establishment – a crowd of general labourers – unintelligent and unhappy looking, angry with the cold wind and unaccustomed work and longing for wife and child or the Public House in the London slums. They are all married men and are supposed to be training for emigration or land settlers but the greater bulk of them are simply destitute men who accept the 14 weeks residence as one job like another, but rather an unpleasant one as they only have 6d a week to spend on beer and tobacco and nowhere to spend their leisure. The experiment has its good side and might be improved by better organisation of the men's leisure. It is quite worth while watching it carefully, but this contemplation of these 300 low-typed sore-minded men is not pleasant – it gets on your nerves. The Superintendent, [?Hilton] Smart, is an excellent fellow – a sort of Quaker and wonderfully devoted – perhaps he needs rather more iron in his nature, but certainly he keeps the men well in hand by moral influence. I doubt whether he quite checks the slackness of the labour.

We return to London on the 10th, spend that Sunday with the Sydney Buxtons in Sussex and settle down to P.L. Commission work on the 15th. We shall be desperately busy for the next 6 months.

Ever yours

B. Webb

519 BL   BEATRICE WEBB TO JOHN BURNS

The deferential tone of this letter contrasts with the critical note Beatrice made in her diary on 30 October 1907, when she declared that John Burns 'has become a monstrosity . . . enormous personal vanity feeding on the deference and flattery yielded to patronage and power. He talks incessantly and never listens to anyone except the officials . . . he is completely in their hands and is becoming the most hidebound of departmental chiefs . . . When issues of the gravest character are at stake ought one to damage the chance of his taking the right course by frankness that offends him? Ought one to increase the chances . . . by ministering to his vanity? Or ought one to forego all influence by merely avoiding any connection with him?'

41 Grosvenor Road, Westminster Embankment
January 15th 1908

Dear Mr Burns

Here is our scheme for dealing with Unemployment. Could you let me have it back again? My Commission is very jealous of our showing even our old productions, so we are limited to one or two copies. *You* can always procure the evidence and as I think Sidney will be called you will get the revised copy and the evidence thereto in due course.

I have been thinking seriously of your coming to give evidence. Don't. If you are ever going to introduce a big scheme, or help to introduce it (perhaps the P.M. would do it!) it would be precious awkward to have stray answers to silly or ridiculous questions brought up against you. At least that is our suggestion.

I will look in upon you someday – but I always hesitate to intrude on the guarded privacy of a Cabinet Minister.

Ever yours

B. Webb

At the end of January Charles Booth resigned from the Commission: his health was poor, he sensed that he was making little impact on it, and – in Beatrice's opinion – felt that she had usurped his standing as a social investigator. The Webbs had already worked out the main themes of the report they were to spend most of 1908 writing and were busy sending selected drafts to Cabinet ministers, senior members of the Opposition, Labour leaders and public servants.

Beatrice had gone to see the Salvation Army colony in Essex which she found much more acceptable than the miserable establishment at Hollesley Bay. Greatly impressed by the 'spirit of love and personal service' on the part of the Army's staff, she was amazed 'that these wondrous beings should be ordinary English citizens brought up in ordinary English traditions'. She was, nonetheless, troubled about subjecting derelicts to moral exhortation supported by regular meals: 'Is it right to submit men weakened by suffering to this religious pressure exercised by the very persons who command their labour?' (BWD 2 February 08)

> Park House, Hadleigh
> [? 31 January 1908]

My own dearest

Perhaps this will reach you Saturday evening – just to greet you.

Colonel Laurie met me at the outlying farm and we drove and tramped about for some hours – talking all the while. He is the same direct ascetic type as other Army officers – a man with whom you can talk as an intellectual equal – and a religious superior. The colonists are a grade lower than at Hollesley Bay. The grading arrangements seem the answer and they at any rate break up the men and prevent the tone sinking to the lowest level. There are far more 'drink' cases, more wreckage and not so much mere casual labour.

This is the house of the officers – the one that superintends all the eating arrangements. It is very comfortable and I have a bed and sittingroom to myself with a view of the sea over the marsh – an old castle standing out in front. Altogether quite a pleasant week-end place where you might have worked quite comfortably. But it is just as well you did not come and you would hardly have avoided the services.

Now I am about to have a comfortable supper at 7.30 – everything that I could wish.

> Always your loving old lady
> Beatrice

The dinner was for the Advisory Committee on Army Education: thirty officers attending a course at L.S.E. came in afterwards.

Beatrice's spirits always rose when she seemed to have the ear of the eminent. 'The net impression left on our mind', she noted during this round of parties, 'is the scramble for new constructive ideas. We happen just now to have a good many to give away, hence the eagerness for our company.' (BWD 10 February 08)

Sir Edward Stafford Howard (1851–1916) was Commissioner of Woods and Forests.

Hadleigh Farm Colony<br>February 2 1908

Dearest Mary

Here I am among the Salvationists watching their methods for dealing with the Unemployed and Unemployable, and incidentally observing the characteristics of this new religious order. I had seen something of them in London and am glad to add to my knowledge. The officers of the army are quite the most remarkable body of men and women that I have yet come across – remarkable because they are of one type, at least they appear so to the layman. There is absolute equality between the sexes – there is a real practice of poverty, abstinence and obedience, there is family life but an aloofness in family relationships from all who do not belong to the body, no Salvationist being permitted to marry anyone but a Salvationist, and no officer being permitted to marry any Salvationist who does not undergo the training of an officer. That training seems to result in an extraordinary sweetness and reasonableness of disposition, combined with fervour and power of command over others. They represent in part a true 'Samurai' class. To the outsider they are uniformly courteous and tolerant and intelligently open-minded tho' I imagine they would refuse any degree of personal intimacy to anyone who was not one of themselves or who did not appear to be likely to become so.

As for their social work they have been acting without economic training and without any thorough study of the larger learnings of the problems they attempt to handle. But the leaders are already aware of this and are beginning to look around for the proper framework of State action in which to set their efforts at personal redemption. And I can see that they will be a quite invaluable agency to which to entrust the actual treatment of different sections of the residues of unemployed and unemployable labor; when once we have definitely ascertained the surplus, and separated it off from the body politic. If the State undertakes the drainage system the Salvationists are quite the best agency to deal wisely with some of the products of this drainage system. Their spirit of persistent work, their extraordinary vitality – even their curious combination of revivalist religion, with the technique of a very superior and reformed 'Variety Artist' exactly suits the helpless, hopeless, will-less man, a prey to sexual impulses, to recover his virility and faculty for regular life and regular work. Also they have developed an extraordinary shrewdness in inventing devices for stimulating personal self-respect and ambition to become self-dependent. So I am seeking allies in the movement.

We have been pushing our ideas among the politicians of late – especially our scheme for breaking up the Poor Law and dealing with Unemployment. Mr Haldane and Mr Balfour came to dine to meet the military contingent but I had a good deal of talk with him about my scheme. This by the way turned out a brilliant affair. The generals came in their stars and ribbons and the thirty young officers when once they had overcome the awe of the 'dinner company' talked at a terrific rate – both Mr Haldane and Mr Balfour having little groups around them, with the generals and the lecturers chatting to the others in between. On Wednesday, we dined with Mr Haldane and I went into dinner with Mr Asquith and had a long and satisfactory talk – more intimate than I have ever had, about P.L. reform and unemployment. I also renewed my acquaintance with Winston Churchill who was very anxious to be friends and asked to be allowed to come and discuss the long-term question. We are seeing something of the Labour Party who seemed inclined also to take up our views, despairing of the practicality of their own. Altogether we are feeling rather happy about our chances of 'Permeation' – everyone seems convinced they have 'to move on' and are really grateful to anyone, whose knowledge they trust, telling them exactly which way to go.

Meanwhile my Commission is floundering about – in the most amazing manner. Dr Newsholme, who is now Head of the L.G.B. medical Department, is coming tomorrow for cross-examination; McVail on medical investigation has reported strongly in favor of transferring from P.L. to P.H. Sidney is coming also tomorrow to be cross-examined on our great scheme for dealing with unemployment – which strange to say the Commission is very taken with! (The Labour men insisted on Sidney being called.) Mr Hyett and Sir Stafford Howard have been asked to send in statements! Charles Booth has resigned, partly on grounds of health, partly I think because he feels that he cannot influence the Commission without fighting it, which he is not strong enough to do. Meanwhile S. and I and four secretaries and some other assistants are hard at work preparing reports on each of the classes. I cannot make out what the majority are doing – no one seems to feel any responsibility for the result except Lord George who really is lightheaded in his lack of appreciation of the gravity of the task of coming to conclusions and setting them before the public in an efficient and dignified way. My only hope is that he and his majority will get so sick of the whole business that they may, after much troubling, hand the whole thing over to me.

Ever yours affectionately<br>Beatrice Webb

## 522 BEV SIDNEY WEBB TO WILLIAM BEVERIDGE

Though the Webbs much liked the idea of labour exchanges, especially if they could be linked to a relief scheme for the unemployed, Beveridge was already beginning to think along lines that led him away from the Webbs and towards an unemployment insurance scheme, of which he had seen some models on a municipal scale in a number of European cities.

41 Grosvenor Road
Westminster Embankment
13.2.8

Dear Beveridge

As I have to talk about Labor Exchanges, I always ascribe the idea to you, and yet I have to say you have no responsibility for 'Utopian' plan that Mrs Webb and I are now pushing.

But the latter you have not actually seen. Here are two printed statements, on which I have recently been examined by the Commission.

*Please return both within a week.*

If you would add criticisms etc., we should be grateful.

This scheme will be pressed forward, *and in due course* 'boomed'.

Sidney Webb

### 523  BEV  SIDNEY WEBB TO WILLIAM BEVERIDGE

The Webbs were overtly opposed to the idea of 'deterrence to the idler' which continued to dominate the thinking of most of the Commission members. They emphasised the social rather than the individual causes of unemployment but they were far from sure how to deal with the unemployed who seemed to lack capacity or will to work. The best solution they could find when they wrote the Minority Report was to suggest that training might deal with the first category and that the second, consisting largely of 'malingerers', required fairly stiff sanctions which, at the ultimate, came very close to penal labour colonies.

41 Grosvenor Road,
Westminster Embankment
17.2.8

Dear Beveridge

Enclosed card was among your papers.

Many thanks for all your criticisms and suggestions. Some of them quite embody our own views, which we have failed to make clear.

Speaking generally I may say I would allow no man freedom to *choose* his grade or training: he must be 'appointed' to a particular course of training. The first class reserve, in particular, would be a highly selected strictly limited set of men; who (as you say) would always be passing off into permanent employment. Others would then be promoted from the lower grade to fill the vacancies thus caused.

It is essential that the men should be always moving up *or* down, by promotion or degradation.

But there is much to work out, in which all your hints will be useful.

Yours very truly

Sidney Webb

By now Beatrice had reconciled herself to the fact that no one but Wakefield, Lansbury and Chandler would sign the report she and Sidney were drafting. Miss Key was a Webb secretary for some years. The original text of this letter is unusually obscure.

Bradford
20/2/8
about 7 a.m.

My own dearest

You will be just waking up and very soon sipping your cup of tea without your 'little Bee' to cheer you – I have had my cup of tea some hour ago and have been waiting for the light wherewith to write to my boy.

Quite a comfortable journey – Bentham remaining with me until his dinner at 7 o'clock.

He does not believe in an early report – not before Xmas – and feels no responsibility for it. He says that the chairman is very optimistic and pleased at their progress. He assumes that the government will accept their plan and thinks that there will be some difficulty in passing the [?minor nominated committees] through Parliament. Gardiner and Downes still object and insist on elected local committees. He regards Loch's notion of Public Assisted and no classification or regulation and 'any case on its merits' as sheer lunacy and altogether despairs of getting any help out of Loch. He is very disappointed in Provis: thinks he ought to help them more than he does. But Bentham is thoroughly enjoying himself and has no special desire to see things ended.

He told me that the last thing Charles Booth said to him at the Commons was after the morning discussion when they accepted the Chairman's scheme, 'You have made a momentous decision. By taking the County area and County authority you have laid the foundations for Mrs Webb's scheme – that would not have been the case if you had accepted my proposals'. Which shows how fundamentally hostile Charles Booth was to my view! The general impression left on my mind is that there is no stronger mind in the Majority than the Chairman and that he virtually controls them when he has himself made up his mind. He has no consistent views as to Policy – so they will drift into anything that is at all consistent with their Scheme of the Authority – which they will adhere to. They will be prevented from taking the sick or the Able-bodied out of the Poor Law for fear of leading inevitably to my Proposals. They are determined to go no further in that direction and all the rest must be fitted in somehow or other. It is really now a question of drafting: Status Quo policy with the new authority.

We spend the morning going over the institutions, the afternoon at the

Relief Committee. I shall try and get away to Sheffield by an earlier train so as to have a rest before supper.

Ever your

BW

P.S. I am afraid the sorting will bore and bother you; don't do more of it than you feel inclined. Tie the bundles up with tape, which Miss Key will give you. Other slips will have to be added. I have not the remotest notion of what value that painstaking analysis will prove to be; but one has always to risk analysis not bringing out much that is new.

BW

### 525 PP  SIDNEY TO BEATRICE

Auberon Herbert's son, Auberon Thomas Herbert (1876–1916) succeeded to his uncle's barony as Lord Lucas in 1905; he was an active Liberal politician until he was killed in 1916.

John Seely (1868–1947), later Lord Mottistone, had been elected as a Conservative in 1900 and in 1904 he became a Liberal. He became Secretary for War in 1912 and was involved in the Curragh mutiny in 1914. Hamar Greenwood (1870–1948), later Viscount Greenwood, was a Canadian-born barrister who was elected as a Liberal M.P. in 1906. He became Chief Secretary for Ireland in 1920 and established the 'Black-and-Tan' military auxiliaries to fight the nationalist guerillas. John Alfred Spender (1862–1942) was editor of the *Westminster Gazette* from 1896 to 1922: he was a leading press spokesman for the 1906 Liberal government and a biographer of Campbell-Bannerman and Asquith.

C. F. G. Masterman (1874–1925) was under-secretary at the L.G.B., later Financial Secretary to the Treasury and Chancellor of the Duchy of Lancaster, R. C. Lehmann (1856–1929) a member of the staff of *Punch*, was Liberal M.P. for Harborough 1906–10.

41 Grosvenor Road<br>Westminster Embankment<br>21.2.8

Dearest One

I found your scribbled pencil letter when I got home late from Winston's dinner; and I rejoiced to sit up reading it, though its arrival deprives me of anything this morning.

It is strange that Bentham should think that the Government will adopt the Commission's plan. (I think *we* can prevent that, by argument.) But it is probably a delusion of all majority members of the Royal Commissions that their reports will be acted upon!

I went on with the sorting all day, and did a great deal – perhaps in a rough sort of way, but at any rate it will enable you to revise it without much difficulty. I will get on again this morning and tomorrow.

Last night Winston's dinner was 12. Most distinguished! There were Sir E. Grey and Runciman, Lords Lytton and Lucas; Colonel Seely,

Masterman, Lehmann and Greenwood M.P.'s; two other M.P.s whom I didn't know; and J.A. Spender. Winston made me sit next him and was most obsequious – eager to assure me that he was willing to absorb all the plans we could give him; that he would read anything we sent him and so on. He had nothing particular to say. Now I must finish, or I shall not get on with the sorting! Goodbye dear one; don't work too hard.

Sidney Webb

### 526 PP BEATRICE TO SIDNEY

Beatrice was now paying her own expenses since the Royal Commission refused to reimburse her for research activities it had not approved in advance. She found workhouse visits 'a horrid business: ah me! when will all this wicked misery cease?...Oh! ye politicians, What a work before you if you could only be forced. every one of you, to realise the needlessness of this abomination'. (BWD 22 February 08)

Leeds<br>[late February 1908]

My own darling

I am going to try to get a letter to you tonight.

I had quite an interesting day – spent the whole morning with the workhouse masters and the afternoon with the Labour Yard Superintendent. The Labour Yard dealing with unmarried men, the Workhouse with married men in the workhouse [*illegible*] Yard if the families are respectable. The workhouse is almost like a colony – a large strip of land under cultivation – the buildings being scattered about. These buildings – include 1,500 or more persons – all except the sick and the children. The inmates are classified into A B C D and Test cases. A B and C are old or infirm (including prematurely incapacitated) and all graded according to character, the A having complete liberty and being dressed in tweed suits and living as couples, the B ditto but living in one establishment, the C (unknown character) being promoted or degraded, and the D being ablebodied or semi-ablebodied or persons of bad character, living in their own block, corduroy suit without tea or other luxuries and being constantly subjected, on medical certificate, to 'The Test'. The Test House is really a little penal enclosure for 30 persons, seldom more than 8 in it, as they always take their discharge in a few days. These men have the roughest accommodation – are not allowed to smoke, are kept at severe task work from 8 to 5.30 – no maximum task – increased if they have finished before the time, time lengthened if they have not – altogether they prefer Wakefield Prison and either discharge themselves or get committed to prison. Every ablebodied man is subjected to this if he remains in the D block, or comes again, and as many of the semi-ablebodied as the masters can get certified. The medical man and medical assistants who had charge of the

Infirmary, refused to certify men as A-B – out of spite, the master said. So he got another medical man appointed who took a stricter view. I saw there D. Nutt, a thoroughly good fellow – not particularly hard. Both he and the master favoured labour colonies – they realised that tho' they saved the rates, they did not solve the problem. An interesting point in the discipline is that the master changes the Labour Superintendent of the Test House every month as he finds that one man gets tired of 'driving the men' – (there are 3 and they take the Test House in turn). It is a brutal business and only fit for bad characters for short periods.

The Labour Yard is managed on much the same principles. No money is given only food and a ticket for lodging house. But of course the discipline cannot be so severe and men are constantly leaving – sometimes they are sent to the Test House. Here they only had 8 men. Certainly Sheffield applies the 1834 principle to the A-B more successfully than any other Union. But it is significant that neither the Superintendent of the Labour Yard nor the Workhouse master felt that they had solved the problem. Another interesting point was the number of officials concerned in the treatment of these 140 A-B or Semi A-B. The Labour Yard had two, the D block and Test House 4 – thus 6 officials were necessary to keep the driving up to the requisite standard so that only 16 A-B men were on the rates.

I had a talk with the Clerk, who is rather a swell and would have been offended if I had not gone to see him. He is rather the Vallance sort of official and a little bit suspicious of me. But I disarmed him by giving him your scheme of unemployment. All these officials were, by the way, not at all averse to the break-up of the Poor Law.

Now darling goodbye – I shall take it easy today and be with you tomorrow. This is a very quiet pleasant hotel, but I expect expensive. I had a really good night – a good long sleep and feel refreshed. The hotel at Sheffield was horrid and a Ball until 3 a.m.

Ever your devoted wife<br>Beatrice Webb

527 PP    BEATRICE WEBB TO MARY PLAYNE

Leeds<br>Feb. 22 1908

My dearest Mary

I am stranded at a Hotel on a Saturday afternoon waiting for a Police Magistrate to come and talk to me about P.L. prosecutions – so it seems a good opportunity for a talk with you.

I am paying a flying visit round some Yorkshire and Lancashire towns, at which they have special Test Houses and Labour yards for Able-bodied men. I have been to Bradford, Sheffield, go to Manchester tomorrow, and on to Liverpool on Monday, back to London on Wednesday. This sort of knocking about in Hotels, trudging through streets and over institutions I loath, more than I used to in old days; but it has to be done if one wants to pick new ideas and points of view. It is a great comfort, as one gets elderly, to feel how completely one has oneself and its faculties under control – never hesitating to do, at once, exactly what one thinks to be best to get the work done. I often think this complete self-control is the one great additional happiness of elderly existence. That state of indecision one used to suffer from was most uncomfortable – it meant so much loss of working capacity.

The Commission has begun to consider its Report – or rather resolutions upon which the Report will be drafted. They cannot bring themselves to accept my scheme tho' most of them are prepared to admit that the break-up of the Poor Law must come in the end – [*side note: Private*] they think they will propose a half-way house in the abolition of the Guardians and the transfer of all their functions en bloc to the County Councils and County Borough Councils with a wonderful system of nominative committees to give outdoor relief and manage institutions. Their scheme is quite impracticable but I think they will stick to it. I am rather glad because it just gives me room for a minority report in which I can make a strong statement leading up to definite and well-thought out conclusions.

Did I tell you that we have made friends again with Winston Churchill – Sidney dined with him the other night and he is dining with me on the 11th to discuss our scheme for dealing with unemployment? He is much improved in appearance – more healthy and less bumptious, and most anxious to give us to understand that he will weigh and consider all our suggestions. I don't much believe in his concern for economics and social problems, but of course he may have become aware that no government can now ignore them.

About Easter – I grieve to say that we cannot come then. I go to Ireland with the Commission on the 21st April and am starting 3 days before, in order to spend the weekend with Horace Plunkett. Sidney is going to stay with the Phillimores during my absence. May we come at Whitsuntide? If that is really as convenient to you it would be delightful to have 3 weeks down at the Chestnuts the end of May. If not we must come for a weekend whenever it suits you.

How are you? I often ponder over your case and wonder whether you are living the ideally healthy life so as to ward off recurrence of the mischief. All one hears of cases such as yours makes us very hopeful that you will have no more trouble; and may even be all the healthier for the enforced care. I wonder when we shall get any insight into the cause – I should like to hurry up that investigation. I don't believe they are putting enough energy and thought into it or exhausting the material that lies to hand to be investigated. Goodbye, dear sister, it is a blessing to think of you, resting and happy after that Hurricane of last August. Which of us sisters will be the next to be overtaken by a storm? – may we all sail out of it as bravely and as well. You will be able to help the one to whom the storm comes.

Ever yours affectionately<br>Beatrice Webb

## 528 PP  SIDNEY TO BEATRICE

Sir John Cockburn (1850–1929) had a political career in South Australia, supporting women's suffrage and educational reform; he became vice-chairman of the L.S.E. governors after settling in London. Sir George Dashwood Taubman Goldie (1846–1925) was the organiser of the United Africa Company and the founder of Nigeria in 1897: he was much involved in the struggle with the French and Germans for the partition of Africa. Arthur Henderson (1863–1935) became a Labour M.P. in 1903 and secretary of the Labour Party from 1911 to 1934. He held Cabinet posts in the Lloyd George wartime coalition and the two Labour governments of Ramsay MacDonald, serving as Foreign Secretary in 1929–31. He was awarded the Nobel peace prize in 1934. Peter Curran (1860–1910) was one of the new trade union leaders to emerge after the 1889 dock strike. He was for a period a member of the Fabian Society and a Labour M.P. from 1906 to 1910. Sir Dyce Duckworth (1840–1928) was a prominent physician and treasurer of the Royal College of Physicians for fifty years.

41 Grosvenor Road,<br>Westminster Embankment<br>22.2.8

Dearest

Your very long interesting letter came last night, and was very welcome – your postcard this morning. I enclose some letters.

I hope today will be partly a rest – at any rate in the evening. Let us be not too eager! 'He that believeth shall not make haste'.

Yesterday we had only a small meeting of the Finance Committee at the School – Cockburn, Pease and Charlotte only. There is still no definite prospect of getting the £2,000 we want. I have impressed on Mackinder that everything must now be subordinated to this in his mind. Unfortunately, things press on us in the way of enlargement (Ethnology etc.) which it is unwise to refuse; and though they bring their own resources, every enlargement involves not only responsibilities but even some margin of expense. He and I discussed plans; and the best course seemed to be to go for an even further enlargement by increasing Geography, *if* we can get Sir George Taubman-Goldie (his friend; President of the Geographical Society; and a new Moderate Alderman of L.C.C.) to take it up, and get us the money. We may thus be able to make Geography *and* Ethnology together, with the several subsidies that they bring, pay well for both, and also our deficit. It is a hazardous game; and I am alive to the risks. But the commitment will not be great or irrevocable; and we shall not move without help. We cannot afford to let University College cut in. And we cannot make an appeal without some new feature.

The debate on the Wages Boards Bill last night was very significant – practically no opposition. The Labor Party, speaking by Henderson and Pete Curran, were wholly favorable. But it is referred to the Home Work Select Committee, on which J.R. MacDonald is sitting. I hear that Aves *is* back in England, but nothing is known of his report.

The sorting that you left me to do will, I think, be all finished by tomorrow – at any rate in a state for you to revise.

Here is an interesting report of Medical lecture by Sir Dyce Duckworth which reinforces your view of future preventive work.

Now goodbye dear one, until tomorrow when I shall be at the Grosvenor by 5 p.m. (I am to be called for at 6.30 p.m.)

Sidney

By the way, *I* have had no reply from the Grosvenor. Perhaps I told them to reply to Queen's Hotel, Leeds.

If, perchance, the Grosvenor is shut up, you had better meet me at *Victoria Station* – North-Western train due 4.30 p.m. There are the Midland, the Victoria, the Grand, and the Queen's.

529 PP   BEATRICE TO SIDNEY

Derwent Lodge,
Wavertree, Liverpool
[?25 February 1908]

Dearest

Here I am in luxury – a charming suburban villa looking out to country.

Nothing at Liverpool but three distinct and contradictory accounts of why the A-B Workhouse was transposed into a huge mixed establishment of 1,100 persons – sick, aged, children and A-B.

(1) *Clerk of West Derby* The A-B Workhouse, established 1890 for two to four hundred persons was a great success and cleared both parishes of A-B men with which class they had been infested. It was given up because it had accomplished its object and A-B ceased to apply.

(2) *Master of Workhouse* When he came in 1902, found the place a real happy hunting ground of the A-B male pauper, 400 of them living content, principally street-corner boys 18–30. He 'tested' them out of the place, principally because the extensions of the premises to other classes and the cellular vagrant system enabled him to isolate the hard cases. Now he has hardly enough A-B men to do the work – wants all he can get (100 in House now).

(3) *Clerk of Liverpool* Was never a success because all the men were semi-ablebodied and could not be tested.

I looked at the minutes of the Committee which managed the W.H. but there was nothing in them, so I have had Miss Bulkley to do the Manchester minutes and come back. I shall have cleared up these A-B W.H., I think.

I went over the *ci-devant* A-B W.H. – the men and women associating freely in the kitchen and laundry. I gather that the A-B really keep themselves by doing the whole work of the establishment. In that sense the arrangement is an excellent one – the cost of the sick and the aged would go up considerably if the A-B were abstracted. But it is terribly demoralising.

Darling we shall be together again.

Send Miss Bulkley an introduction to the Salford Clerk.

Ever your

Beatrice Webb

530 BOD   BEATRICE WEBB TO HERBERT H. ASQUITH

Beatrice believed that the majority of the Commission might be publicly committed at least to the abolition of the old Poor Law. If Asquith and other politicians could be induced to take that line, without tying themselves to a specific alternative, she felt that her own schemes might then fill the gap that could be left by the failure of the Commission as a whole to provide an acceptable solution.

*Private*                41 Grosvenor Road, Westminster Embankment

March 2 1908

Dear Mr Asquith

The Chairman of our Commission – Lord George Hamilton – has asked, and attained, the consent of the Commission to communicate to you the present proposals of the majority of the Commission. I am therefore free to do likewise!

These proposals (of which I enclose a copy) are so impracticable in their detail that I doubt whether anything will survive discussion, except the broad principles of transfer, to County and County Borough Councils, of all the services now performed by the Guardians. I enclose you some notes pointing this out, in order that you may be able to estimate the possibility of these proposals being embodied in a final Report; or being such as could be drafted into law, should the Commission persist in them.

I am more than ever convinced that my scheme for the Break-up of the Poor Law (of which I think you have a copy?) is the only alternative to the Status Quo. The chaos at present developing in the medical services, on the one hand, and in the provision for children, on the other, will force on the consolidations of these two services under the Health authority, and the Education authority respectively. To illustrate this necessity I send you the statement of Dr Newsholme (just recently appointed to the Headship of the Medical Department of the L.G.B.): it is one among many other statements by responsible medical officials – all in the same direction. As for the children, even the Moderates of the L.C.C. have decided to ask the Commission to hand over all the Poor Law Schools, as well as the superintendence of the children on Out-Relief, to the Education Committee of the L.C.C. In fact, by adopting the County Councils, and County Borough Councils as the future Poor Law authority, the Commission has made 'the Break up of the Poor Law' quite inevitable.

Some influential members of the Commission have suggested to me, that if you could adumbrate the inevitability of the Break-up of the Poor Law into the combined services, and the distribution of these among the various committees of the County Councils, in your introduction of the Pension scheme, the Commission *might* be induced to accept the only practical and logical outcome of the proposed transfer to County and Borough Councils.

This is a tiresomely long letter in my dreadful writing, but I meant to have written a clear note and send all else in my husband's round clear hand. I have run on incontinently – pray forgive.

Yours sincerely

Beatrice Webb

## 531 UI SIDNEY WEBB TO H. G. WELLS

Beatrice could not shake off her exhaustion and depended upon Sidney's 'blessed strength and capacity' which enabled them to sift their mass of evidence and draft memoranda based upon it. This left Sidney little time for other business. (BWD 24 March 08)

Writing to Wells on 22 March Shaw complained that after ignoring a new draft of the Fabian Basis written by Shaw and Webb for a whole year Wells had suddenly come up with a new version of his own and was impatiently demanding a response. 'You are forgetting your committee manners', Shaw wrote, 'if a man can be said to forget what he never knew.' (SCL)

41 Grosvenor Road<br>Westminster Embankment<br>9.3.8

My dear Wells

I have been trying to write, but have failed. I simply *can't* give any time or thought to amending the Fabian Basis just at present. We are crushed with urgent work; and besides, have had to spare three days for Beachy Head to avoid a breakdown.

What you have written seems to me void of offence. Perhaps it is for this reason, partly, that it seems to me not at all suited to the Basis. But I can't write all my suggestions. Nor does your plan of campaign seem to me a right one. I can't imagine anything more regrettable than to turn the

291

local Societies and Groups away from work in order to spend some months of time discussing a Basis. This may be my incurable habit of regarding the F.S. as an actively militant body, getting things done; not as a 'mutual improvement' or debating society.

But, as I said above, my chance for helping in this has, for the moment, passed. I don't think I *can* be available yet awhile. Does it press?

Sidney Webb

## 532 UI  SIDNEY WEBB TO H. G. WELLS

41 Grosvenor Road,
Westminster Embankment
10.3.8

Dear Wells

I am sorry my conduct strikes you as uncivil. I really am very much occupied just now for a little while, with business that I ought not to neglect.

I did not object when you were equally occupied, and I not.

If we are to get anything through, there must be some joint action.

It seems to me that new members are joining pretty fast, month by month. Nevertheless I am honestly willing to confer about the Basis. Only – just as you could not take it up some months ago, so I can't very well take it up now. I hope that is not unreasonable. We can't all be disengaged at a particular moment when you are.

Sidney Webb

## 533 UI  SIDNEY WEBB TO H. G. WELLS

41 Grosvenor Road,
Westminster Embankment
13.3.8

Dear Wells

Let us – for the sake of what we have at heart – try patiently to understand each other, and see how we can best co-operate. It is not to be accomplished offhand. We shall be meeting shortly and can talk it over.

I may be wrong, and I will try my best to be open to conviction, but I do not believe that the *method* you propose for the instruction of members is either practicable, or likely to result as you intend. This is a judgment as to a matter of fact – possibly an erroneous judgment, but not an issue as to Socialist definition or policy.

I am, I believe, at one with you in your desire. Will you not, when we meet, try to be open to conviction as to the most efficient and practicable method?

Until then,

Sidney Webb

While Beatrice went off with the other Commissioners to Ireland, the Grosvenor Road house was to be cleaned and decorated. Sidney went out to stay with the Phillimores in Hertfordshire.

41 Grosvenor Road,
Westminster Embankment
18.4.8

My own dearest

Here are the letters – all satisfactory and two newspaper cuttings. There is nothing else to send you but my love; and that you have had for more than 18 years.

Today all seems blank because you are not there, and the morning has not been very profitable. But I like to think that the sun has been shining and you will be having a fine crossing.

It occurs to me that we ought really to have some little reference to foreign experience in the able-bodied book – even if only a short chapter just mentioning some sources of information. To issue a big book on 'Able-bodied Destitution: its Prevention and Treatment' – and then to make it as purely insular as if no other country existed, seems to me lacking in culture.

I think we ought just to save ourselves from that reproach, whilst at the same time admitting our ignorance of how things *really* are in other countries, and suggesting the limitations of possible copying from them. And in dealing with Labor Exchanges and Farm Colonies we must have the Continental experience in view.

The men have come for the carpets and rolled them up. I have packed up, and somewhat tidied up the place – and it looks desolate indeed without its mistress, and mine. I will try to get out the Unemployed Scheme in the best possible way, and do my various jobs also – though I am rather inclined to read miscellaneous books all day for a rest. However, I am taking 10 volumes of L.G.B. Reports also.

I wonder what you will discover in Ireland. I wonder whether scheme of ensuring constant employment or maintenance is possible in a country of peasant cultivators. We could not omit Ireland from our Unemployed Schemes but it might well be restricted to the towns. But what about the Ablebodied Destitution of independent peasant cultivators? They clearly can't be allowed chronic outrelief so long as they are paying any rent or interest on their holdings.

Goodbye dear one.

Sidney

Sir John Francis Horner (1842–1927) was married to Frances Graham, a beauty of her day and one of 'The Souls': their daughter married Asquith's son. Robert Chalmers (1858–1938), Chairman of the Board of Inland Revenue, was later governor of Ceylon and Master of Peterhouse, Cambridge. Dr Hugo Münsterberg (1863–1916) was professor of psychology at Harvard University and wrote extensively on educational matters.

Beatrice's itinerary, after a visit to Horace Plunkett, took her to Connemara, County Clare and the coastal islands.

c/o R. C. Phillimore,
Battlers Green,
Watford
20.4.8

My own dearest

It was an unexpected pleasure to get your letter this morning – I had scarcely thought it possible that the post was so good. I fear it is slower from here.

Here are two letters. One from Sir J. Horner, to be destroyed: and the other from Chalmers, unable to come. We have not yet heard from Dr Münsterberg, but I assume he is settled.

I shall be all right here for health and comfort, but not quite so well for work, as I haven't yet made the hours quite fit. And I have brought down much more than I shall manage to accomplish. After all, things do take time to do, and we can't cram a quart into a pint pot.

We shall have definitely to live for the P.L. Scheme, and put aside everything else for nine months. It is, as you say a great responsibility and at the same time a magnificent opportunity.

Lion is giving a party to young Fabians on Sunday week, which I shall just come in for. The Wells are coming for the weekend, and perhaps the Shaws, whilst a young lot are coming to tea. We did go out for a little walk yesterday, in between the snows. Today the fields are white, and it is still very cold, but it looks like being fine, so I shall actually go out two days running. Dearest, goodbye.

Sidney

536 PP   SIDNEY TO BEATRICE

C/o R. C. Phillimore,
Battlers Green,
Watford
21/4/8

My own dearest

No letter from you this morning was a disappointment, but I realised that you had probably been away on your expedition, and unable to write in time for post. This can hardly reach you by the morning post, as it has first to go to London, so I shall address it to the Hotel.

Here is a letter from Dr Münsterberg showing that he will arrive on the *Wednesday* before he gives evidence; in the afternoon – the day that you thought of returning. But I can deal with him for that evening, so that please feel quite free to stay until the Thursday, if it saves you any fatigue. I have noted the Courtneys for Friday, the 8th, but I think you had decided not to go. It is probably Olivier at the Fabian Society.

Yesterday it snowed at intervals, all day, but I really did go out for a brisk walk in the afternoon for a little while. It is very comfortable here and I am quite well, and only lacking one thing – which is everything; namely my dear companion and helpmate, on whom I am so dependent. I am struggling to get through my tasks. I have done the greater part of my Secondary Education article, somehow; and have put it aside now pending the arrival of bluebooks and statistics for which I have sent. And I am now beginning my address for the Social and Political Education League on the National Minimum. In a day or two I will put this also aside, and grapple with the Unemployed Scheme.

This is quite a nice house, in much better country than Kendalls, though of course merely common routine rural scenery; it is three hundred feet high, and will gradually get a pretty garden etc. round it. Mrs Phillimore offered to lend it us for the Summer, but I said we had already fixed up for Leominster. It is still horribly cold and sunless; but this weather probably does not extend to Ireland, where I like to think of you among the Wicklow Hills in Spring warmth and sunshine.

I shall think of you tomorrow at the Viceregal Lodge – send me an account of your doings when you can. I hope you will remember to take 'a day off' on Thursday or Friday, staying quietly at the Hotel, and going for a walk about Dublin, or in Phoenix Park. You will need the rest from talking, and being always in company with people.

It was nearly 16 years since we were together in Dublin – you so unwell, and I still bewildered with my good fortune, and wondering how I could make up for my manifold shortcomings, and learn how to be at any rate a serviceable companion and friend to her who had trusted herself to me. I do hope she has not found it so bad a bargain. Dearest, goodbye.

Sidney

537 PP BEATRICE TO SIDNEY

The Rt Hon. W. J. M. Starkie (1860–1920) was a classical scholar who was Commissioner of National Education in Ireland from 1899. George William Russell the poet and economist, edited *Irish Homestead* from 1906 to 1923. 'Taylor' was Alice Green's friend whom the Webbs had known during their engagement. Maurice Joy was an author who later emigrated to the United States. In 1916 he edited a book of essays on the Easter rebellion.

My own darling

I got your budget of letters yesterday – letters posted at 5 p.m. one day arrive here the morning of the next day, Sunday included.

I am really having a quite pleasant and useful time here. The Secretary of the Royal Commission on the Congested Districts is staying here with his draft Report – clearly the question of able-bodied destitution (and poverty) is mainly a question of land cultivation and already enormous sums have been spent on 'relief work' to relieve this destitution. He says Labour Exchanges in the big towns would fit in very well with the organisation on the land and give them another string to their bow. Of course H.P. [Horace Plunkett] disapproves of the Recommendations of the R.C., because they advocate the compulsory and mechanical cutting up of estates and settlement of the persons of the congested districts *without training*. Our idea of training of the residue before dealing with it would appeal to him immensely – he wants farm colonies for the purpose. It does seem to me that if *you are actually going to settle certain persons on the land at the public expense* – if that is determined on, these farm colonies are justified and a method of testing and training their capacity. The difficulty in England is that you are *not* going to settle there. A *National Authority* for Able-bodied Destitution seems to me just as much required in Ireland and Scotland as in England. From the standpoint of our scheme the difficulty is the children. I saw Starkie, the Head of the Education Board – a man whom everybody speaks well of – a sturdy but unimaginative man. He is the paid member of a Board of 20 who manage Primary Education through the intervention (as local managers) of the priests and other clergy. The Christian Brothers are outside the organisation, with about 7,000 out of 700,000 children. They look after the secular education but the Priests would not let them meddle with the home life of the children; they have no boarding schools – the industrial schools being under another department. He does not think they would be allowed to touch the P.L. children. These seem to be in the workhouses, mainly taught there with shocking bad instructors – very few going to the parish school. It seems a clear case for reform but no one knows where the children ought to go, if there were no P.L. authority.

H.P. is arranging to upset the R.C. report on Congested Districts and apparently with the Secretary's consent – he was communicating his opposition to the conclusions to the Editor of the *Irish Times* who came out to lunch – a shrewd and able journalist. I can hardly imagine Duff bringing the draft report to the House with a view of having its conclusions discounted! My imagination falls before it!

But the great object of destructive energy on the part of H.P. and his friends is the Irish University Bill with which they are very angry because of the constitution of the governing body. It seems a pity that what is proposed is always opposed by everyone else, in this unhappy country.

Tell Lion that two men she probably knows and likes have been here – one the *Homestead* Editor – Russell – who *looks* and is thought by H.P. a most undisputably moral and intellectual genius. I did not think what he said was remarkable – he seemed like Taylor, of old, up in the clouds – talking strange abstractions about 'Human Nature' in rather a grandiose way. He is a Co-operative Idealist and devoted friend of H.P. Also a young and attractive creature – Maurice Joy – the son of a peasant, with a beautiful face and a clever turn for writing.

Now I think I have told you all the news of yesterday. Today we go up into the Wicklow mountains to lunch with a friend – tonight some men friends coming out to dine.

Goodbye my own Precious Boy. Take care of yourself for your own Bee's sake.

BW

538 PP   SIDNEY TO BEATRICE

c/o R.C. Phillimore,
Battlers Green,
Watford
22.4.8

My dear dear one

Your letter of Monday arrived here today Wednesday, which shows that it is a two day's post to this hamlet; and I fear it must be reckoned *three* days when you leave Dublin.

The difficulty as to the disposal of the Irish P.L. children seems to me a serious one in our way. You cannot destroy the Board of Guardians in Ireland until you have arranged for all its duties; and it may even be an obstacle to doing it in England if you cannot do it also in Ireland. Can you not get any suggestions from the Irish officials as to what could be done with the children? There are probably ten or twenty thousand of them under the P.L. altogether. If there are enough private institutions – in the nature of our certified schools – to which they could be sent on payment, this might be, under the circumstances, the best way out of the difficulty. This plan suits the Catholics in England, and should suit them also in Ireland.

This would leave two unsolved problems
(i) the children on Outrelief
(ii) the children of 'Ins and Outs'. How would it do if no better plan can be devised, to make the Stipendiary responsible for the children on Outrelief? But he is probably a Protestant!

The only other way I can at present think of is to create a 'Children's Care Committee' in each county, by agreement with the R.C. Church –

297

perhaps appointed by the County Council, with provision for there being always due representation of the religious Minority.

Yesterday I actually went out for a brisk walk of four miles at least, quite an expedition. Bobby and Fitzpatrick came back at dinner time: they had got as far as *Thame*, on the outward journey, when it became too dark to proceed as they had no lamp on the car! (They had also no licence for the car; and neither of them was a licensed driver!) They left the car, and took train to Oxford, and found their way in the dark to the Russell's, arriving at *midnight*. (Bertrand is away at a Mathematical Congress at Rome; and Alys had various friends with her.) They spent Monday with her and Logan etc., and travelled back Tuesday after various breakdowns, purchase of new tyre, etc.

I get on with my various tasks with difficulty, missing my inspiration, my companionship and my joy! It is really terrible to think how dependent I am on your constant presence.

I shall want to know *by return of post* exactly where you stop on Monday, and Tuesday nights etc., if you are to get a letter from me in the mornings. You may start too soon to receive the post at some places. I must not post to Dublin *after* Friday *from here* (which is not London); so that unless you have sent me an address *before* you receive this, I shall be in a difficulty. But you will get letters at Mallaranny anyhow.

Dearest, goodbye.

Sidney


539 PP    BEATRICE TO SIDNEY

[Dublin]
7 a.m. [23 or 24 April 1908]

My own Darling one

I have just had my cup of milk-tea in preparation for a cold motor ride.

Yesterday as the snow storm continued I remained in Dublin and went with Bentham and Duff and Macdougall to the South Dublin Workhouse. It is a monstrosity – 4,000! inmates, a very bad edition of Liverpool – squalor, dirt, disorder and idleness and promiscuous [?indecencies]. We spent 2½ hours going over it and I came back to lunch and rested quietly and had little chats with my colleagues. In the evening we entertained 5 inspectors – two clever go-ahead women – [*illegible name*] and Dr Stafford and another man.

Bentham is determined to acquiesce with the Chairman's report. He hopes I shall only get Lansbury to sign my report. He wants to get the majority out as he says I am rapidly permeating the country with my ideas – he meets them everywhere! He is not helping with the Report and assumes the chairman will do the whole thing. Macdougall objects to *any* change in Scotland and is ready to sign any English report if he is allowed to write the Scotch report. I made him realise that once the case had been given away for England he could not resist the change for Scotland. He would join a status quo party but not initiate it until we had finished England. Downes seems obdurate against the Chairman's proposal and will I think not sign. Nunn says he disagrees with *all* resolutions. Phelps is a chairman's man and pretends to think that we are all arriving at agreement. Meanwhile the Chairman, with whom I had a friendly talk, is evolving an entirely new scheme – Commissioners appointed by the L.G.B. acting in conjunction with local committees. I don't know whether he means to spring this upon us in his Draft Report! He has made up his mind that the *Whole Report* must be submitted at one time, otherwise we shall get inconsistent changes introduced. He thinks he can get the Report drafted by July or the middle of July and then he proposes to sit until the middle of August in order to get it agreed to, leaving the secretaries to smooth it out and I suppose the minorities to add their dissent and publish in the autumn – coming back to sign it only.

He thinks if we don't agree before we part, we shall all have changed our views when we come together again. He is very optimistic of getting agreement, barring me, as he well may be judging by the past – but of course he does not realise that he has not been getting agreement all round! the dissentients are merely silent. He is fully impressed that the Report must be out by Xmas – or it will be useless. I am inclined to think that their fear of my wicked permeation will drive them to publication – so we must be ready.

Meanwhile the Commission at the very end of last sitting has decided to send a Committee abroad – Loch, Nunn, Bentham and perhaps Lansbury. This without giving notice to any Commissioner who was not present, in spite of the fact that they had settled not to last winter when I raised it. Duff is very angry, as he told the Treasury that we were not going abroad. Also he says it will delay the Report.

Now darling one – Councillor, Friend and Lover – goodbye – take exercise and be careful. With fond love to the Phillimores.

Beatrice Webb


540 PP    BEATRICE TO SIDNEY

Dublin
6.30 am Saturday April 25 1908

My own dear Boy

It is still snowing and is very cold – but I am quite well and enjoying the *change* of scene – tho' perhaps there is not much change of idea. Yesterday the Chairman, Duff and I motored out to Celbridge, where we saw the best workhouse I have ever seen – a workhouse of 150 aged, sick, and a few mothers with children, kept by 8 nuns. These Vincent de Paul sisters were delightful creatures, the Sister Superior, handsome and brimming over with love and interest, and the others not quite so handsome but equally attractive in their universal kindness and courtesy. Every corner of the place was cared for – they had got the house well painted with all sorts of little comforts manufactured by tramps in return for the unaccustomed kindness of the sisters. The only bad spot was the tramp outhouse, which was filthy – apparently this is the settled policy of the Irish Union – a filthy outhouse for tramps. The sick wards were used as a general hospital and the M.O. [Medical Officer] who was a first-rate man had persuaded the Guardians to fit him up a little operating room, with all the newest appliances, in which he did all the operations of the countryside – he being the Dispensary Doctor. The children and the inmates were taught by a nun and their schoolroom was a perfect museum, but it would have been better for them to go out to school. There seems to be a great prejudice in the villages against having the 'pauper' children with their own children, and the nuns, when they manage the workhouse, prefer to keep the children in. We came back to lunch and had some witnesses for an hour. But perhaps the most useful part of the day was my talks with colleagues. Dr Downes is wholly disgusted with the majority proposals and definitely said he 'had got out of the coach and did not intend to get in again'. He said that there was a great feeling against anything that I suggested on the ground that I was 'so clever and that however harmless my proposal *looked* it meant socialism'. Clearly Bosanquet and Loch have persuaded the bulk of my colleagues that I spell the break-up of the family and destruction of property, etc. But he talked in a quite friendly way and asked intelligent questions. What I did with him was to suggest a really sound status quo report – the difficulty is he cannot write. Then I had a long walk with the Bishop. He said that he could not sign my report because we differed fundamentally on the constitution of the family, that he would prefer that children should die than that the family should be broken up. I tried to show him that my proposal was less subversive of the family than the others, but it was clear that he feared association with me (as with the Devil: tho' he likes me personally), and would not consider anything I wrote, *on its merits*. Then after dinner, the Chairman, Phelps, Bentham, Downes and Nunn and I had a little informal palaver, and when we had finished the Irish plan, we asked the chairman exactly what he proposed to do about the Report. He said he *hoped* to get the whole report drafted by early in July – he might circulate the parts as they were done, but he thought we must discuss it as a whole. He was sanguine that he could get it finished by the middle of July. He proposed then to sit until we had passed it – and Phelps and he suggested the Commissioners should go to *Deal* where he would entertain them. He thought that for *this* stage they must have a young draughtsman to embody the changes made – Duff was not skilled enough. I suggested Steel-Maitland – but

300

they agreed 'he could not write'! They all agreed that they must not separate until they had finished as if they did they would find *their opinions changed when they returned in October*!

We then drifted into a general discussion and I tried to make them understand my scheme – Phelps supporting me. But it is curious to see how they *dislike* discussing it. I answer all their questions but they, with the exception of Phelps, almost run away from my answers. The chairman did literally run away and the Bishop was absolutely silent. Downes made little half-humorous remarks. He was the most friendly, except Phelps, because having made up his mind to the status quo, he is as friendly to my scheme as to theirs. Of course his game is the same as mine – the more reports the better.

What is clear is that there is no kind of preparation to get expert assistance in drafting the report in its first stage and they have no notion of the magnitude of the task. I am inclined to think that the chairman will hold a majority to anything that he and they muddle out between them, and that there will be 2 or 3 dissentient reports – but the fear of me will make them less critical than they would otherwise be. We must be ready with our report by the middle of August at the latest.

Ever your devoted old wifsey

Beatrice

I do not go until 7 a.m. Monday. It is too cold to motor on Sunday.

541 PP  SIDNEY TO BEATRICE

Tract 133, *Socialism and Christianity*, was written by the Rev. Percy Dearmer (1867–1936), an active Fabian who was later secretary of the London Christian Social Union and Canon of Westminster. Mrs Henrietta Barnett was an old friend of Beatrice's.

c/o R.C. Phillimore Esq.,
Battlers Green, Watford
25/4/8

My own dearest

Your dear letter came at breakfast this morning. I have got them to breakfast at 8 – but this one cannot reach you by first post tomorrow, and therefore must go to the Recess Hotel.

I think you must put yourself in a position to have a few hot words about these *monster* workhouses – of which I suppose that at Dublin is the chief and worst. It would be well to get their printed report for exact statistics.

It seems pretty clear that the Commission will manage somehow to report by Christmas. The Chairman will probably get something through; or if not, he will fall into the arms of Robinson. As you say, we must be ready, by the end of July at any rate, with the main body of a draft for possible use as an alternative. The Treasury may make difficltiues about the Foreign trip. Meanwhile, how can we *increase* the permeation? We might well spend some money on it. Not much occurs to me straightaway, but it would be well to think out something for the next six months.

E.g. (i) We might present the F.S. with Dearmer's tract, so that each member had it. I don't think this has been done.

We might send 100 copies each to a dozen of the local Fabian Societies telling them to send them with letters to the most influential local citizens.

(iii) Could we get a corresponding pamphlet written for Scotland? This would stir up Macdougall from behind!

I am inclined to think that a little thought and money put, *now*, into stirring up local agitation of this sort, would be very remunerative.

Here is an enthusiastic letter from Mrs Russell, to whom I sent the Oxfordshire and Berkshire M.P.s. Also one characteristically unre[ce]ptive, from Henry Hobhouse.

I enclose result of Fabian Executive election – with which I am not altogether pleased – as it is a pity that Standring is rejected, and Ball; whilst the Wells's and women nominees have done too well!

Here, too, is a letter from Georgie which you had better answer.

And one from Mrs Barnett, which also requires an answer. I enclose her article, cut from the *Cornhill Magazine*.

At Grosvenor Road, yesterday I found a box containing a *score* of press cutting *books*, from Miss Mason! So you will be well supplied on the Boarding-out side – when we get time to read them. Her address seems to be 5 Vincent Square, Westminster.

It is still snowing hard, and bitterly cold. We have asked Shaw down for this weekend, and Keeling to lunch Sunday, but don't know whether either will come. Charlotte was to go to Brittany last night; she looked worn and plain and old. They have both been badly ill.

Now goodbye dear one. I do hope Ireland is warmer, but I fear it will be cold enough. You can skip some of the days' outings, and stay at home resting.

Sidney

542 PP  BEATRICE TO SIDNEY

Dublin<br>Sunday morning<br>April 26 1908

My own Darling one

Your letters are short, but very *very* sweet. I like to hear that you do not get on *quite* so quick, or so well, without me: sometimes I fancy that you are doing all the work, that I am a mere bit of furniture to which you have grown accustomed – a good habit and nothing more! But it is something to be a good habit.

We had a day of evidence yesterday – the Head Inspector and the Medical Commissioner and His Excellency, who insisted on coming to tell us about the Tuberculosis Exhibition. Dr Stafford was even more decided than Leslie Mackenzie, Newsholme, and Newman in favour of a complete division of medical from Poor Law. So all the Heads of Medical Departments are in our favour. Both the officials like the Stipendiary. But I don't see light about the chairman. I am going to lunch with Mackenzie. I gave him my scheme to consider and shall hear what he has to say. No more news of my Commissioners except that Phelps was doubtful whether he ought to read any report (I offered to show it him) – he is very loyal to his majority, means to try and bring them round but won't part from them. He relies on Duff to write the Report – dismisses the idea of the chairman doing it. Downes says that if they stick to their present proposals, he will not go down to Deal in the autumn; he thinks that the chairman is under a delusion as to amount of support he has got – Thory Gardiner, he is sure, is not 'content', nor is Nunn. He cannot make out what Provis is about – thinks he does not care, as 'he is going in a couple of years'. Altogether the whole business is, as you say, still uncertain. What is still amazing to me is the optimism of chairman and Phelps as to getting a Report drafted by July and to getting this Report accepted in a month's hurried sittings, with a large section of the Commission neglecting to consider it before the evidence was finished. It will be the Report of a clique or sort of drafting committee and will not be discussed by the Commission as a whole until October.

Yesterday I went for a walk to Phoenix Park – it was very beautiful with the snow-covered hills, and parkland seeming to stretch to their base. I thought of the time we were in Dublin together and of a walk we took in the Park, I feeling very ill, and I thought how glad I should have been then, if I had known of our successful work together, of the way in which we two are able to think out plans for making life happier and nobler for the rest of our poor kind. It is a pitiful business now compared to what it might have been – every day I live I become more of a revolutionary – more confident that changes are coming because of the good will of our fellows and ourselves. But what sustained work it will mean, to contrive and to carry out, in spite of indifferences, or selfish opposition.

I go tomorrow by the 7 o'c with Robinson and Downes but instead of stopping with them at Galway to go over institutions I go straight on to Recess, get there for lunch and spend a quiet afternoon. I propose to come back to England on Tuesday week night – it will be less tiring, I believe, to go straight through from Castlebar, having only a few hours at the Hotel on Tuesday afternoon and catching the night mail. It will be more convenient to have Wednesday quietly before Münsterberg comes.

Now my darling boy goodbye – I shall write a letter to send you by tomorrow's mail – though I fear you will not get me again for a day – but I shall try to arrange to send one as soon as possible.

Ever your devoted wifsey

Beatrice Webb

### 543 PP   BEATRICE TO SIDNEY

Recess is a village west of Galway. Belmullet, Mayo, is on the extreme north-west corner of Ireland. Sidney contributed the chapter on 'Social Movements' to Vol. XII of the *Cambridge Modern History* (1910).

Recess

Monday [27 April 1908]

My dearest one

Saturday's letters came here by the same train as I arrived – so I found it awaiting me when I came from lunch. Do not post anything to Belmullet after *Thursday* – send to Castlebar after that as Belmullet takes a good couple of days from *London* and we leave before the post on Monday morning.

I left my colleagues at Galway to go over institutions and came on here, a most comfortable hotel, in a wild moorland country very much like the W.C. [west coast] of Scotland. The weather has turned warm and rainy – but I had a delightful walk on the moors and am now sitting in a large light bedroom with a fire and the windows opened. Robinson and Downes are very pleasant companions. Smart is a poor creature, of no account. He is trying to wheedle a trip to Arran out of Robinson in a comfortable District Board steamer after we have left (there being no Poor Law in Arran as they cannot collect the rates). We discussed the Report on the train and Robinson and Downes said emphatically that they regarded the resolutions that were passed as of no authority and were waiting to see what sort of Report the Chairman drafted before they expressed their dissent. They both want to see one report – and Downes is making over-tures for a joint Report which would give as alternatives my scheme and an amended status quo; I am 'flirting' with his proposal but, of course, it would not suit us to do that. Lord George by the way in our last talk together (we are *most* friendly) said that if his Majority threw him over, he should have his 'own Report', which he could then make much better than if he had to consult 'them'. I think I have managed to foment dissent! A litter of reports would not be altogether bad for me, as mine would be the best, and perhaps even the Majority among many.

I should like to get something done in Scotland in the way of propaganda. What about Miss Leonard and the Edinburgh C.O.S. – the Edinburgh Fabians would not be a good platform. I wonder whether there is a Presbyterian C.S.U. [Christian Social Union] I must ask Prof. Smart. But I think we must not spend much time or money on anything until we have got our present jobs done: the General Report and the Able-bodied Book and the Cambridge History chapter. Those will take all our strength. We will finish the A-B P.L. chapters and then go straight at the General Report. Probably it will not be wanted until the autumn but we had better have it ready to show. I want to finish the A-B P.L. chapters so as to get the first part off to the printers to have it in proof; also the extended scheme if possible. Morant wrote to ask whether he might take a copy of the P.L. scheme: I answered by all means, in slip proof if he liked, so long as my name and the P.L.C. imprint did not appear on it. The more study given to that scheme – the better.

Will you write and ask Sydney Olivier to dine on Thursday *12th* [May] (Robinson can't come) to meet Balfour and Münsterberg? That will make up the 10, which I think is enough.

Now I am going down to see my colleagues who have just arrived and to post this letter. With my dearest love

Beatrice Webb

### 544 PP   SIDNEY TO BEATRICE

Reginald Brett, Viscount Esher (1852–1930) had been a Liberal M.P. before becoming a senior official at the Court: his main interest was in army reform, where he was supported by Edward VII and acted as a liaison between the King and Haldane as Secretary of State for War.

c/o R.C. Phillimore,
Battler's Green,
Watford, Herts.
27/4/8

My own dear one

I am sorry you have not had my letter every day: it is evidently impossible to secure this, with provincial posting here. I have written each morning with absolute regularity. But just as I have had from you, sometimes two letters within three or four hours, and sometimes none for forty-eight hours, so mine must, I fear, reach you irregularly. I am writing this on Tuesday morning, but I cannot hope to get it to London in time to catch the evening mail. It will therefore not reach you until the morning of Thursday, when I hope it may still find you at the Recess hotel.

Here is a letter at last from Lord Esher, which I have answered. This leaves a vacancy for 11 May.

Here, too, is one from Fels. I think you might ask him and Mrs Fels to supper *after* the 12th May – not the 14th, 19th or 22nd – and on the 28th we may go to Longfords. I don't know that Fels is quite hopeless; he must be getting somewhat uncertain as to his own course, and he may possibly be turning to other ideas or possibilities. Anyhow we may as well give him what we have, as he approaches us at last, and *may* be willing to listen.

Yesterday it rained all day, but at 6 p.m. I started off in the mist for a good hour's tramp, which made me very tired, as walking alone always does. But I thought that if I did not go, my dear B. would not approve, and this comforted me in the wet and muddy walk. Bobby spent the afternoon in the rain, helping a man to load straw or manure or something. He farms himself some 80 acres, and evidently does a lot of things with his own hands, pottering about, which he enjoys immensely. All Sunday afternoon he spent trying to repair a small petrol engine in his carpenter's shop, which had broken down, and which left him smeared all over with black, which remained on his face after two successive washings. But he is really a charming boy, filled with both modesty and a silent conceit about himself, and determined to go on living his own life, and doing lots of good to the neighbourhood.

The house was bitterly cold all last week, as the hot water apparatus was out of order. At last, yesterday, it was mended, but the weather had become 'muggy' and warm, so we were pretty well baked in the evening. Today I have got the apparatus mitigated or stopped. Lion is, of course, very kind; but she is evidently very unstable in health. She has only been out once since I have been here, and complains of her heart whenever she does anything, mental or physical, and stays upstairs mornings.

I think it is quite impossible to forecast how your Commission will finally divide up. If Robinson can carry Provis, as I should think he could easily if he tried seriously, those two could control a majority – because they could arrange to give you enough to secure the adhesion of your group; and at the same time convince the Chairman and Phelps that only in that way could they be in a *good* majority – thus also carrying Wakefield, Smart, and Bishop and doubtless Bentham = Eleven, besides MacDougall, Gardiner and Nunn, who *might* eventually fall in.

On the other hand, Loch and Mrs Bosanquet will certainly make it impossible for the Centre Party as a whole, if it attempts to form at first on that nucleus; and the outcome might conceivably be 5 reports, viz. Chairman, (counting about 7 or 8), your 3 or 4, Loch's 3 or 4, Downes 2 or 3, and Nunn by himself. It may come to this; or develop into this before a final struggle for rival coalitions. After all, I cannot believe that Loch would, in the end, not be prepared to compromise with the Centre Party; and thus the Chairman may probably win, and come through with something like his present majority – *I* expect with something like the Fabian plan!

Anyhow, your course is clear, viz. to have your Report ready as though you had a majority. We must begin this at once when you have had time to look about you, and got rid of Münsterberg and his dinners.

Now, dear one, goodbye, so that I may struggle on with the Unemployed,

which I *can't* get on with properly. I write, and write and write; and look
through the boxes again and again, but it won't get over the footlights as
I want it to do. You will be profoundly disatisfied with my progress when
you get back, but I shall at any rate have earned 15 guineas by my Secondary
Education article, and more or less written my lecture for 14 May.

I have not yet heard that Miss Key is back at work. I have sent her some
letters to write to most of the remaining English M.P.s – Adieu.

Sidney

545 PP   BEATRICE TO SIDNEY

Recess<br>[29 April 1908]

My own darling

We are leaving at 11 a.m. in a leisurely fashion, to attend a Board of
Guardians and then go and inspect the Marconi Station, returning here in
the afternoon – not more really than a pleasant motor drive – the sort of
thing that quite suits me.

I have been thinking that on the whole it would be wisest to begin on
our general Report directly I come back. We have broken the thread of the
Able-bodied and it will be no more difficult to piece it together after we
have finished the general Report than to do it now. So I suggest that we
put all the A-B stuff on one side and go straight ahead at the Report – that
will only leave us $2\frac{1}{2}$ months before the end of July. It will also enable us
to know what exactly we want to take down to 'Chestnuts' for our 3 weeks
and what we want in the way of statistics from the office. It will be a big
job that Report, because every word must tell – it is style in its best sense
that is needed.

5.30

Just back from our excursion. The Board of Guardians was most entertaining – G.B.S. would have found it most exhilarating – a lot of corrupt
and rowdy shopkeepers and little farmers – the workhouse a sordid handful of aged sick and some $\frac{1}{2}$ dozen desolate children who were going to no
school and having no schooling. Then to the Marconi Station which was
an impressive display of Electric force – booming and flashing like a great
spirit of fire on a desolate rocky coast and then back in the rain to find
your dear long letter. We have settled not to go to Castlebar but to return
from Belmullet to Mallaranny by the Congested Districts steamer round
the islands. Tomorrow Sir H. and I take it easy and skip the Board of
Guardians, going quietly in his motor to Mallaranny – a 60 miles drive.

Dear One – I don't like to think of you as pounding away alone – but
it is a sweet thought to feel that you do really depend on me for some of the
quality of your work. Latterly I have felt somewhat of a fraud.

I am really enjoying myself – the motoring through the wild scenery is

307

a complete change and Sir H. is certainly the most agreeable of companions. Dr Downes too is pleasant – Smart is a dull dog and the Irish clerk who accompanies us and the Irish Inspector who is in attendance are both unattractive mortals.

It will be an early start from Mallaranny – 7 o'c – arr. Dublin 2.15 but I shall find it less tiring to come straight on to London than to stay the night and come over in the daytime. Also I shall want a good talk with you before Münsterberg comes in the evening. Mind you ask Olivier for the 12th to meet Balfour.

Now dear one goodbye

Always your devoted wifsey<br>Beatrice Webb

### 546 PP SIDNEY TO BEATRICE

Webb had earlier argued against the schemes of Wells for Fabian expansion on the grounds that they were too expensive: he feared that this argument would be undermined if Wells knew about the Hutchinson Trust – and he feared, too, another MacDonald-type row about the way in which he had managed the Hutchinson money. Wells dropped the matter, however, when Pease simply told him that the Trust had been wound up 'years ago'.

Wells had lately created bad feeling by supporting Winston Churchill, running as a Liberal in a bye-election at N.W. Manchester, where the socialist Dan Irving was also a candidate. (Wells had written an article, 'Why Socialists Should Vote for Mr Churchill' in the *Daily News* for 21 April o8.) Wells was keen to defeat the Conservative nominee, William Joynson-Hicks (1865–1932), who became a notably puritanical Home Secretary. Hicks had been one of the leaders of the 'moral purity' campaign against Wells for publicly advocating free love. Webb defended Wells at the Fabian annual general meeting but when he mildly reproved Wells for not informing the executive in advance of his support for Churchill Wells simply walked off the platform. The next day he wrote to *Fabian News* saying that he was ready to resign from the Society. This was his last formal appearance at a Fabian meeting.

c/o R.C. Phillimore,<br>Battler's Green, Watford<br>30/4/8

My own dearest

Your letters come now regularly every morning, which is very pleasant. I am glad to think of your having such a complete change of physical life, which must be healthful, if you don't get too tired.

It is again raining steadily and the wind is blowing wildly, and I can't help feeling sad without my dear companion and helpmate. Yesterday it was fine, and Lion drove Bobby and me out for two hours through a smiling Spring landscape, and afterwards I tramped about a little with Bobby over the farm and his new buildings. Among other things he is breeding Shetland ponies, and flocks of chickens, and so on. Lion declares that he has really greatly increased his income by all his enterprises. The manager of his brickworks gets £350 a year, and a quarter of the profits, which seem to exist genuinely, besides a royalty on the clay to Bobby as landlord. He is building a bank in Kensington on his father's land, with granite which he has quarried in Donegal – the work being managed by Lion's brother, Fitzpatrick. So he has a good deal to do, and he has lately become a J.P. for Herts.

They have offered the loan of this house to the Granville Barkers, but they cannot take it until the middle of August. Lion is very anxious to lend it to us for that fortnight or three weeks, as she goes away at end of July. Would this perhaps suit you; as you will almost certainly have to attend the Commission frequently in the first fortnight of August?

H.G. Wells *is* breaking out again. Without any sort of intimation to us, he has sent in to Pease a series of 4 resolutions, which he intends to move at the first meeting of the new Executive on 8 May: *viz.*

1. The Committees each to consist of 2 members only!
2. *Fabian News* to be changed in form and content.
3. Any such post as Organiser to be held for a year only; on no account for more than 3 years; to be advertised in *Fabian News*; *and reserved for members under 28 years of age* (which is the limit of age for the 'Nursery' Group).
4. Full accounts of the Hutchinson Trust and Will to be circulated!

We shall fight and defeat Nos. 1 and 3; refer No. 2 to Publishing Committee to dispel and I shall volunteer full information as to No. 4 to any enquiry, but deny *right* of Executive as such.

Bland hears that he announces that 'if defeated, he will chuck it'. I will *try* to be peaceful and conciliatory.

Dearest, goodbye: this will doubtless still reach you at Mallaranny.

Sidney

547 FP  SIDNEY WEBB TO EDWARD PEASE

C/o R.C. Phillimore,<br>Battler's Green, Watford<br>30/4/08

Dear Pease

I had, vaguely, prior intimation of part of Wells' intentions; and that is why I suggested your asking members which sub-committees they wished to serve on: I assume this has gone out. Please have ready on 8 May tabulation of the replies; including lists of the sub-committees as they were last year.

You must I think, circulate Wells' notices of motion *exactly as he* sends them in. (His reference to the Hutchinson Trust is not actually so improper and out of order as to warrant any suppression of it.)

I propose to volunteer myself, as an act of courtesy, all possible information as to the Hutchinson Trust, but to point out that it closed up in 1904; and to deny any *right* of the Executive to control it. As you rashly mentioned the No. 2 A/C in your draft annual report (I struck it out, and I hope you have now), I think we shall have to instruct you on 8 May to circulate the original minutes as to this, and the accounts.

I propose to defeat A. and C. and to refer B. to Publishing Committee.

Yours

Sidney Webb

### 548 PP BEATRICE TO SIDNEY

Sir Joseph Ridgeway (1844–1930), soldier and colonial administrator, negotiated the Afghanistan border with the Russians: he was under-secretary for Ireland 1887–92, Sir Antony MacDonnell (1844–1925), Indian administrator, was permanent under-secretary for Ireland 1902–08. Attempting to reform Irish administration on Indian patterns, Beatrice wrote, 'he found the law, the custom, the habits of the people wholly different. Moreover, he was face to face with a new factor – one he had never before encountered – the democratic institutions of Great Britain, which baffled and perplexed him'. He was 'broken in health, broken in spirit and much worsened in fortune'. (BWD 3 May 08) Doherty was MacDonnell's subordinate on the verge of retirement. Augustine Birrell became Chief Secretary for Ireland 1907–16.

Mallaranny
Friday 7 a.m. [1 May 1908]

My own Darling

I am writing now in case we do not get back in time to post this to catch the evening mail. I want you to get it on Sunday morning. Then it will be only 3 more nights and you will wake to see your Bee standing by your bed rather worn by 24 hours travelling, but really quite rested by the pleasant little trip. I am sure I needed the holiday, I was losing my nerve and suffering from a sort of chronic brain-fag. And this has been just the sort of holiday I needed, luxurious travelling, with everything arranged for me, and the stimulus of just a pretence of investigation, to give a little flavour to our motoring. And I have learnt a good deal from Robinson. Yesterday he told me the whole story of relief works in Ireland by successive Chief Secretaries – each anxious to distinguish himself by concern for the condition of the people. It really makes me believe in Home Rule. Morley seems to have been the worst and to have done the work most recklessly and with least attempt to prevent demoralisation – which is just what one would expect from that pedant individualist. Also R. says they have suffered much from 'Indian' administrators, who imagine they know exactly what to do – Ridgeway and Macdonnell he says were both ignorant of Irish character and Irish ways and both equally have utterly failed to understand Irish problems. I tried hard to find out what was Robinson's standpoint – but he has no philosophy of life or of government – directly one touches assumptions, his expression becomes dead – he is simply bored. I asked him straight out, yesterday, whether he had any idea of what state of things he wanted to bring about and after looking puzzled he said he had never thought about it: he had always been living at 'concert pitch to keep his Chiefs out of trouble'. We also discussed the scheme. I showed him Morant's reprint and he read it very carefully. For Ireland, there are only 2 points he dislikes – he prefers not to use the word '*Court*' – would like to make the Superintendent an administrative officer, and he fears the introduction of a '*Receiving Home*'. About this he is very persistent even for England; he thinks it would be the mixed general workhouse, over again, there ought to be O.R. [Outrelief] until the stipendiary comes along and 'observation wards' at the specialised institutions. He thinks there is no difficulty about the children, he would give them to the Committtee of the District Council which would still continue to be the Municipal Sanitary Authority [?for roads etc.] and to the Borough Councils in large towns. We settled that he should write the Irish Report, directly he has seen my report for England. About Morant, what he was fearing was that he would be sent to Ireland! and he was quite relieved when I told him, in strict confidence, that I hoped he might be translated to the L.G.B. He is of course rather sore about not being made Under-Secretary and still has hopes if Doherty is appointed and can hold out until Birrell is about to go, or has gone – and he might still be U-S. He is great friends with Birrell personally and thinks he would get the appoint-ment if Birrell had no trouble to fear for himself. I think he will do his best to promote my scheme inside the Commission. He realises that it will be difficult to get it for Ireland, unless we have it for England, and he thinks we are influential people with both sides. He is convinced that Provis will not put his name to a complicated absurdity and thinks he is playing for a *Status Quo* as a last resort from disagreement. But on the whole R. thinks we shall still be wrangling this time next year.

I really did begin to think out the order of the Report yesterday morn-ing. Downes gave me a good idea as an Introduction. I propose to begin with the [?Reference] and an analysis of its breadth extending it to new P.L. methods of relieving A.B. distress and the cause of unemployment. Then, as Downes suggested, stating what *led* to the Enquiry – we will describe in this paragraph the Break-Up of the Poor Law – the introduc-tion of new authorities – this will strike the *note* at once but in an indirect manner – then end the Introduction by describing the Commission's own methods of investigation *very shortly* and the breadth of our Enquiry, more in detail. In this Report we must let every paragraph tell for one point – even if it gives mere formalities. The first chapter after the Introduction I thought of making a description of P.L. administration and the General

Mixed Workhouse and indiscriminate outdoor relief – I have [?not got farther than that.]

Now dear one goodbye. Are the Wells with you? If so ask them if they will not dine with us on the *19th* and meet Runciman and the most delightful and [?typical] of Bishops – Talbot – [tell him] an ideal type for a novel.

Now my own dear Boy goodbye. Send me a welcoming letter to the Hibernian Hotel, Dublin, on Monday with any letters to me. Of course if I am very tired I shall stay in Dublin overnight.

Ever yours

Beatrice Webb

The sun is coming out and the clouds are lifting, we shall have a lovely day. Adieu.

BW

### 549 PP BEATRICE TO SIDNEY

Beatrice was oppressed by the contrast between the beauty of the scenery and the misery of the people 'who crouch in their filthy hovels and toil hour by hour on these boglands in a listless fashion . . . There is Heaven and there is America – and according to whether they are the children of this world or of the next, they desire to escape to one or the other . . . one realises for the first time the grim fact of the existence of a whole community on the margin of cultivation'. (BWD 3 May o8) She returned to England convinced, after her conversations with her colleagues, that she and Sidney needed to press on rapidly with the draft of the minority report they planned.

Mallaranny

6.30 a.m. Saturday [2 May 1908]

This will greet my own dear Boy as he looks through the great heap of letters on the table of our working-room on Monday morning – think of his good fortune that I am coming back to him after only one more morning's work, refreshed and ready again for our joint work. What a fussing round there will be on Wednesday morning trying to get things into order but feeling sleepy and demoralised with the long journey and the echoes of holiday feelings.

Yesterday was gorgeous sunshine, so hot that we could not bear our coats motoring – but a fresh invigorating heat. The sea and cliffs and islands and stretches of brown bogland looked extremely beautiful as we pottered about in our two motors over Achill Island. And the day was quite interesting. We attended a Petty Session at which an unfortunate woman was being convicted for infanticide – a married woman who had gone to Scotland for potato picking. The R.M. [Resident Magistrate] was most kindly and tho' the guilt was obvious they say she will be let off by Assizes with some months' imprisonment. The case, they say, is very rare and the feeling against the woman very hot, not for murder, but for interfering with 'the Will of God'. Then we saw the notables of the Island and visited a squalid village of stone huts by the shore getting back here about 5.30. Today we motor to Belmullet to attend a Board of Guardians and see relief work: sleep the night there, and steam back through the Islands and round Achill Head, sleep here on Sunday and Monday night, and spend the day steaming to Clare Island all of which will be very pleasant if the weather is fine and it is not too rough. But my heart is now full of getting back to my boy. It has been a first-rate holiday for me, exactly what I needed but 3 more days will be quite enough for me as I am longing to get to work on my Report.

I tried yesterday to 'draw' Smart, but he evidently feels quite bewildered and lost and will therefore tend to drift with the majority. The only chance would be for him to know that this is a first-rate Report, which will throw the other completely into the shade. With seeming impartiality and moderation every word of that Report has to tell in the direction of Breaking-up the Poor Law, the argument has to be repeated in any conceivable form so that the reader cannot escape from it. It must be a real work of Art; we can dismiss Science! It will be High Jinks doing it and we will get to work at once. The more saturated it is with argument the less will they be able to adopt any part of it without the conclusions – but the argument must be cunningly wrought – so as to seem a mere recital of facts. The Wood shall absorb the Trees.

Robinson is very anxious to get MacDonnell's place: and certainly he seems the best man. He implied that Birrell had a great opinion of our judgment and will evidently appreciate a good word for him tho' he fears it will be impossible for Birrell to appoint him. But we might perhaps have Birrell to dine quite alone on the excuse of talking Irish P.L. and I must intimate H.R. [Henry Robinson's] devotion to him. I think I should appoint Robinson – he at any rate knows all the conditions in Ireland and would do his best to keep his chief 'out of trouble' and if I had any policy of my own I should pick his brains to carry it out. But I don't see that much is possible in Ireland so long as the government is English and bound to be spasmodic and ill-considered. Moreover I believe the Bishop is right and that there is not more than a living for 200,000 and that the process of deportation will be a hateful one anyway and especially hateful under English Rule. Home Rule would quicken the process and Ireland would cease to be more than a Tourist Resort run by Scotchmen and Americans with a patch of vigorous Industrialists in the North – which must end by dominating the whole.

Now Dear One, goodbye, one more morning and I shall be back.

Beatrice

It looks a beautiful day – not so hot as yesterday, but the clouds are few and far off.

One hundred copies of the Webb memorandum were privately printed and sent to Asquith, Lloyd George, Winston Churchill, Sydney Buxton, Herbert Samuel, Arthur and Gerald Balfour, civil servants and journalists: they were run off by Morant on his official press, with a dummy front as a safeguard against a leak. Such big schemes, Beatrice noted on 15 May, 'have to sink in to the minds of those likely to carry them out if they are to become practical politics within a generation. And to my schemes of reform there are, at present, no rivals; they have the field to themselves. The sort of conglomeration of disjointed changes, which the majority are likely to agree on, will seem mere scraps and scrapings by the time they appear'. (BWD)

A few days after this letter Beatrice saw John Burns. She attempted to make him accept her idea that the able-bodied unemployed must either be given a work test under penal sanction or there must be created 'a great national authority for the unemployed'. (BWD 19 May 08) The persistent belief that the causes of destitution must be tackled, coupled to the assumption that relief without tests either of conduct or willingness to work was demoralising, led Beatrice to underrate the political attractions for the government of schemes of social insurance which at least alleviated destitution.

H. J. Mackinder resigned as Director of L.S.E. in order to devote himself to Conservative politics. Though he had not been personally close to the Webbs they had respected him as an administrator. They considered, among other possible successors, H. A. L. Fisher, W. J. Ashley and G. M. Trevelyan. At the end of May their close friend William Pember Reeves accepted the post, giving up his position as the New Zealand High Commissioner in London and becoming Director of L.S.E. until 1919.

41 Grosvenor Road, Westminster Embankment<br>
May 8th 1908

Dear Mr Burns

I am very sorry that Dr Münsterberg was not able to get to the German Embassy in time to procure a ticket and came on to the H. of C.

I send you, of course in strict confidence, the scheme which I showed in typewritten form last spring, and which I circulated some little time ago to the Commission.

Are you too busy for a talk? there are many matters arising out of the P.L.C. I should like to tell you about? If you can spare the time shall I come to the L.G.B.? – if so when? or would you prefer to look in here on your way to and fro? – letting me know when to expect you – so I may be in.

Always yours sincerely<br>
Beatrice Webb

Sure of the support of Wakefield, Lansbury and Chandler for the proposed minority report, but convinced no other allies could now be won, Beatrice decided that it was a waste of time to take part in any further formal meetings of the Commission and that it would in any case be embarrassing for her to sit through drafting sessions of the main report. She therefore left Lansbury and Chandler to conduct a delaying campaign; the longer the majority took to complete its report the more time there would be for the Webbs to be ready with a finished alternative – for their document was to be a fundamentally different scheme, not a series of dissents on specific points.

The Webbs spent several weeks working on their draft in a guest house on the luxurious estate of Sir Julius Wernher at Luton Hoo: Beatrice reflected on the 'unpleasant' paradox between the 'machine for the futile expenditure of wealth' and the 'drunken, sensual, disorderly' streets of nearby Luton. (BWD 27 July 08) They went on to stay near Leominster, briefly visited the Fabian summer school at Harlech and returned to London early in September. On 12 August Sidney wrote to Pease (FP) to say that their report was 'going to be a terrific document . . . covering the entire field; and mapping out a complete revolution of the whole system'. He told Pease to prepare for 'a big concerted "boom", organising every member of the F.S. so as to go full tilt at the walls of the confounded old Elizabethan Jericho, which we must destroy. "The Break-Up of the Poor Law and the Abolition of the Workhouse" will be one good cry; and "The Final Solution of the Unemployed Problem" another'.

The Webb practice of circulating drafts led to comments appearing in the press and to complaints of a breach of confidence from Lord George Hamilton. 'The net result of our indirect, or, as some would say, unscrupulous activity', Beatrice noted, 'has been to damage the Webbs but to promote their ideas. We seem destined to use ourselves up in this breaking-up of the Poor Law – the fate of capacity and good intentions combined with bad manners!' (BWD 15 September 08)

On 9 October the Webbs went to breakfast at 11 Downing Street for a meeting with Lloyd George, Churchill and Haldane. They argued against Lloyd George's scheme of social insurance on the grounds that it would leave the real problems of the Poor Law untouched. Beatrice recorded that she had 'tried to impress on them that any grant from the community to the individual beyond what it does for all ought to be conditional on better conduct and that any insurance scheme had the fatal defect that the state got nothing for its money – that the persons felt they had a right to the allowance whatever their conduct'. This failure to make any effort to meet Lloyd George's proposals or to seek any compromise position had serious consequences for the Webbs, cutting them off from influence on government policy at a crucial moment in the development of new social legislation: it left them with no alternative but to come forward as the public champions of their own scheme, opposing the government as well as the majority of the Commission. Their inflexible tactics, which reflected Beatrice's determination to impose her solution at all costs, contrasted with the success of Sidney's efforts in shaping and lobbying through the Education Acts in 1902 and 1903.

In her diary entry on the Fabian summer school Beatrice noted that 'a somewhat dangerous friendship' was developing between Amber Reeves and H. G. Wells. This affair, as it intensified over the next two years and led to the birth of a child fathered by Wells, brought Wells close to social ruin, disrupted his relations with many friends and embittered him towards the inner group of Fabians. He convinced himself that the Webbs had gossiped and conspired against him.

Sir Edward Priaulx Tennant (1859–1920), later Lord Glenconner, was Liberal M.P. for Salisbury 1906–10. J. E. Raphael was defeated as Liberal candidate in a bye-election at Croydon in 1909.

41 Grosvenor Road, Westminster Embankment<br>[September 1908]

Dearest Mary

Here we are back in our little home after our pleasant recess of country life and strenuous work. After you left us we had 7 Cambridge men spending 3 days on their way to the Fabian School – all nice fellows and two remarkably brilliant persons. Also Amber Reeves, the 'double first' in Moral Science, an extraordinarily vital little person – but egotistical and vain and a dreadful little pagan. One of the Cambridge Fabians, Dalton (the son of the Dean of Windsor) is one of the most astute and thoughtful of our younger members – by nature an ecclesiastic – a sort of lay Jesuit – preparing for political life. We spent 4 days at the school in N. Wales – some hundred members of both sexes and all ages living in 3 Houses and camping out roundabout there, listening to lectures in the morning, and bathing and rock-climbing in the afternoon, discussing in the evening – food almost vegetarian and clothes of the most unconventional – ladies in 'Gyms' and men in any description of flannels. Among them was a rather pleasant cricketer – Raphael, an Oxford Blue, who plays now for Surrey, (and is standing for Parliament as a collectivist radical for Croydon) attractive and quite intelligent. Mixed up with these university men and girls, were some score of elementary teachers and minor civil servants – some of the new pension officers – the whole making a most varied little world, living in intimate companionship one with the other.

We find all our affairs rumbling on satisfactorily. Reeves has taken hold of the School and promises to be a more staid and conscientious administrator than Mackinder tho' often not so brilliant. We are trying hard to raise the £3,000 needed to pay off debt and make some small alterations and we are also making a large demand for £30,000 to extend our premises. Yesterday Sir Edward Tennant called to see Sidney in response to one of Sidney's insinuating letters suggesting that he should give us the £30,000 and establish a great Colonial library in connection with the School. He seems half inclined to do it.

We are still at work at The Report – my three colleagues in dissent are delighted with what they have seen – but we want a good three months to finish it off in style. The majority report came rolling in and some of the majority believe they will get it through by Xmas. It is diffuse and impracticable and seems to us most unconvincing and unconvinced.

The infantile mortality returns are turning out most interesting. The death rate among the 8,300 infants in workhouses of which we have particulars is more than *twice as much* as in the general population – in some, it is terrific, in others, it is comparatively light. The death rate in the Maternity Hospital, is about the same as in the general population. The death rate in the Plaistow Domiciliary [*illegible*] is $\frac{1}{2}$ as much as the general population. It looks as if domiciliary attendance was far better than institutional treatment – as the Plaistow nurses go into the poorest homes. I wonder if I could get the statistics of other nurses and midwives? Would it be possible to get some of your nurses to fill in the forms for their own cases? The nurse at Birchen Knoll is doing it for me – among the 60 cases she has had in 3 years there have been no deaths.

I am ashamed to send this scrawl but I wanted to write to you and my hand is tired with scribbling.

When exactly do you come in October? Could you let me have the dates? I want to have a little party to meet the new Principal of London University and might as well have it while you are here.

Ever yours affectionately<br>Beatrice Webb

## 552 UI BEATRICE WEBB TO H. G. WELLS

Wells had sent the Webbs a copy of *New Worlds for Old*, which he called 'a plan for the reconstruction of human life'.

[41 Grosvenor Road]<br>[October 1908]

My dear Mr Wells

I have read your book from the first word to the last. It is, indeed, a contribution 'to your degree' – which, as you know, I have always thought, and felt, to be a very high one. I liked your insistence on The Child as the starting point – this is new and fresh and applicable to all Humans far more than the communist basis of Socialism. Also I like your tone throughout – and tone is a most significant matter. Perhaps what I least sympathised with – tho' possibly it is only the phraseology that annoys me – is the recurrent emphasis on the evil of what you are pleased to call Bureaucracy. Of course officialism has its faults – but we in England commonly overestimate these faults – our objections to them have become rather ignorant shibboleths of the market place. I know so many officials, of high and low degree, and I am perpetually amazed at their unpretentious self-subordinating devotion, and with the amount of initiative and experiment they are capable of. But this is an old quarrel of ours! What I felt most in reading your work was the amount of genuine intellectual and moral sympathy between Wells and Webb. Also your references to me are most kind and flattering. But what a lot of constructive thought in constructive action there is for all of us to do, if we are really to produce a genuinely state-conscious collective mind and the machinery to carry this Will into effect.

317

You will get our two volumes on The Manor and the Borough in their [*illegible*] – an impossible work for anyone but the student of the subject. But it is quite extraordinary how this minute and, some would say, meticulous study of the past, has helped us to devise bold schemes for Breaking up the Poor Law, and for grappling with Unemployment. When you come you must just look over these schemes – they are really catching on in an extraordinary manner with Ministers and ex-Ministers. These gentlemen show a quite remarkable avidity for being fed with ideas. We have made friends again with Winston Churchill and are cramming him with stuff. Love to Jane.

Ever yours affectionately

Beatrice Webb

### 553 NUL  BEATRICE WEBB TO CHARLES TREVELYAN

Beatrice felt that the Webbs must hurry on with their work 'before this mad dog of a Commission rushes at the public with its report'. (BWD 24 October 08) She was overworked to the point of hysteria and despised her colleagues to the point where her judgement was plainly distorted. She knew she was close to collapse and kept going by the thought that they could take a long holiday once the reports were published. By 15 December the first part of the Minority Report was finished, running to three hundred pages: Beatrice gloated that by comparison the Majority Report would seem trivial and imbecile. 'If I ever again sit on a Royal Commission', she wrote, 'I hope my colleagues will be of a superior calibre – for really it is shockingly bad for one's character to be with such folk – it makes me feel intolerably superior.' (BWD 15 December 08)

41 Grosvenor Road,

Westminster Embankment

Dec. 2 [1908]

Dear Mr Trevelyan

A fortnight hence will be quite time enough to talk over the children's chapter. Pray do not mention that I have lent it you – especially to J.B. [John Burns] of the L.G.B. who is in close alliance with the reactionary elements of the Commission, and could repeat to them anything he heard about me!

The minority will be 4 – the 2 Labour men, Russell Wakefield and my-self.

Ever yours

B. Webb

### 554 BEV  BEATRICE WEBB TO WILLIAM BEVERIDGE

The Beveridge book was *Unemployment, The Problem of Industry*, published in 1909.

Dear Mr Beveridge

Congratulations on your book which seems to me excellent. Will it be sufficiently near publication by the beginning of January for me to quote you? It would be a small advertisement of the book – there seem to be some passages from the 'penal Factor' chapter that we must carefully quote? If so, let me have the proofs early in January and we will give the book a big mention.

We are terrifically pressed getting our two last chapters written. Part I dealing with the Non-able-bodied devoured our time – but it was worth it. We will break up, once for all, that nasty old Poor Law.

If Liberals don't like it the Tariff Reformers shall!

Ever

Beatrice Webb

Is there any chance of your coming to dinner one night for a talk 7.30 – any night *except* Monday or Tuesday? Very many thanks for notes which will be most useful.

---

555 FP  SIDNEY WEBB TO EDWARD PEASE

The Commission met at the beginning of January for a formal photograph, signing blank pieces of paper because the Majority Report was still being pieced together and no copies were available. Beatrice was 'in a state of complete exhaustion' and so hostile to the Majority that she could see no virtue at all in the report, believing that it would 'get a bad reception from all sides' in contrast to the favourable reaction she expected for their own elaborate proposals. (BWD 1 January 09) The anti-climax after so much effort left her feeling blank: 'there is nothing to pray for, nothing particular to do'. (BWD 17 January 09) She hoped for another 'Call' and that 'I must be strong enough to answer "Yes, we will come and do it"'. She felt remorseful about her conduct on the Commission but believed her intrigues and hostility had been justified by the manner in which the Commission had been run. The next problem, she noted, was how to mobilise public opinion behind the Minority Report.

The Webbs believed that the Minority Report was their copyright and that they were entitled to publish it separately from the complete official version. If they were to run a successful campaign they needed a cheap edition which could achieve a far wider circulation than the formal documents of the Commission.

41 Grosvenor Road,
Westminster Embankment
1.1.09

Dear Pease

I think the Executive should decide on 8 January whether it will publish *its own* Edition of the Minority Report of Poor Law Commission – see enclosed, which please hand to Sanders. We shall try to publish a Library Edition with Longmans, 'edited' by my wife and myself, with added preface, appendix notes etc. in two volumes, at 6/- each or thereabouts. I am offering to the I.L.P. to let them publish an edition of the Report alone, without our editing, and with their name on title page, supplying the copies to them from our Stereoplates, paper covers, on thin paper, to be published at 3/- in one volume; or, as we strongly advise, two volumes (one on Poor Law, 2/-; and one on Unemployment, 1/-). It will make *1,000* pages 8vo in all! We supply it at 2/- a copy absolutely net (or 1/4 and 8d).

I want the F.S. also to have its own Edition, with its name on titlepage, on the same terms; and to get rid of two or three thousand copies.

Of course, this will spoil the sale of our own edition as a bound book; but we don't mind that. Only the I.L.P. and the F.S. must *order* their copies in January; as we must strike them all off together. So big a book at so low a price needs careful organizing of the printing.

Yours

Sidney Webb

### 556 PP  SIDNEY TO BEATRICE

Beatrice had gone to stay with Mary Playne to rest. The Webbs suspected that the official proposal to publish in two volumes was not a convenience of printing but a device to prevent the automatic circulation of the Minority Report along with the Majority Report.

Sir Samuel Sprigge (1860–1937) was the editor of *The Lancet* from 1909 to his death. Alfred George Gardiner (1865–1946), a prominent Liberal journalist, was editor of the *Daily News* from 1902 to 1919.

41 Grosvenor Road

Westminster

29.1.9

My own dearest

Here am I after a whole day in the fog, on the Report business. As no copies came yesterday, I went round at 12 today, and found Duff had kept them for me. He was very civil, and eventually agreed to *send* the (a) proof and M.S., (b) office copy of all the investigation reports (as he says they had altered them in some cases). I did not press for duplicate proofs, but contrived to make him send *four*. They are to be called for at *2 p.m.* on Saturday next, when I have promised they shall be ready. He also sends me office copy of the Majority Report; and promises the other dissents on Saturday (Downes has rewritten his: he signs the Majority Report also, as do they all). The dissent on Settlement is, I gathered, withdrawn.

But I subsequently got a note from Duff (with all the above parcels *enclosed* – saying the Stationery Office wanted to print in *two* volumes and asking to see me about it. I am going to see him tomorrow morning.

320

I don't see how we can formally *resist* printing in two volumes; if it is pressed, as it is plainly reasonable. But I propose to temporize, and to play for retaining one volume, if it is decent to do so. Of course, if two volumes be decided on, I shall stipulate that both volumes should always be issued together.

If you have any other instructions, please telegraph. Tonight I will begin the revision of the Report. (I *don't* propose to send the copies to the other signatories.)

Duff raised the question apologetically as to your being offended, and aggrieved at the action of the majority and the Chairman. He explained that he was sure the Chairman did not do so knowingly. I took the opportunity of saying all over again what you said, and saying that we wanted to let things sleep, but that if any reflection were made on the Minority, we should make a smashing reply, impugning the procedure and conduct of the Commission. He, of course, deprecated any idea of recriminations, and was most polite.

Haldane came in this morning, to talk at large. He wanted another copy of Part II, which I gave him. He signified that the Government were going to do something on the Report, but must proceed cautiously, so as not to scare the well-to-do people. I pointed out that he could do nothing without moving Burns (and explained about the Post Office). He said Asquith was fully aware of the situation: he *seemed* to indicate that nothing could be done in that matter, but did not state so, clearly. I explained how popular the scheme would be, and urged its adoption.

He is going to be Chairman of the Royal Commission on London University – when that comes – which is excellent.

I then saw Dr Sprigge of the *Lancet*. He is *quite eager*, and will do everything possible.

Also Gardiner of the *D. News*, who will be very glad to do the same.

Goodnight, dearest. I have had a busy day.

Sidney

557 HRCUT  SIDNEY WEBB TO J. L. GARVIN

The essential difference between the Webbs and the Majority lay in their insistence that there was no undifferentiated mass of paupers which should be dealt with by a single agency, such as the Poor Law. The old system, in their view, inevitably led to the classification of paupers by the type of person rather than the type of need. They also pointed out that the Poor Law expenditure of about 30 million pounds a year was only part of the total amount spent by various branches of national and local government on the aged, the sick, the unemployed, vagrants and defectives. They proposed, instead, the concept of a National Minimum and argued that a number of specialised agencies should cope with the specific deficiencies of those who for any reason fell below the minimum. They thought, for instance, that Public Health should deal with sickness – a great cause of poverty – whether the claimant was young or old, in or out of work.

Similar services should cover Employment, Mental Illness and Pensions. The Education services should be concerned with the social problems as well as the schooling of children. This notion of a network of welfare services seemed far too complex for contemporary politicians and administrators. One strong objection was that needy families would need to relate to several rather than to a single relieving agency; another, more emotive, was that public money might be spent on persons who were not formally categorised as paupers. The Webbs themselves felt that there was a risk of discouraging thrift and personal responsibility. This awareness had plagued them all along as they attempted to find a solution to the problem of the able-bodied unemployed. They therefore sought to bolster their case by proposing fairly severe action against malingerers. Believing that destitution was a public danger they wanted drastic measures to 'drain the morass'. Such action in their view was essential to a programme of national efficiency.

The Webbs, however, had misjudged the immediate appeal of their own proposals – though over the next forty years their ideas were increasingly woven into the pattern of the emerging welfare state. The day after publication of the report Beatrice confessed 'we turned out to be quite wrong . . . the Majority have got a magnificent reception. We have had a fair "look in", but only in those papers who had got to know of the existence of a Minority Report before the issue late on Wednesday night. If we had not taken steps we should have been submerged completely'. The Webbs felt 'a trifle foolish' for having crabbed the Majority Report in advance and exalting their own scheme. (BWD 18 February 09)

J. L. Garvin (1868–1947) was editor of the *Observer* 1908–42.


41 Grosvenor Road
Westminster Embankment

*Confidential*                                                                      31.1.9

My dear Garvin

I had hoped to have met you at one place or another. I hope you are now recovered from your influenza.

What I wanted to discuss with you was the forthcoming Report of the Poor Law Commission, which is to be expected on or about the 18th February.

This will be an important document, but hugely cumbrous – some 1,300 bluebook pages. *In strict confidence* (for it is really important that no 'adumbration' or forecast or gossip should be published), I may say that the Majority and Minority Reports agree in their revolutionary destructiveness, on which there is absolute unanimity. They will make a great sensation; and compel early political action.

The Majority Report, headed by Lord George Hamilton, and signed by the L.G.B. officials and the C.O.S., is, however, so far as constructive proposals are concerned, an 'Individualist' document, on the old Whig and Free Trade lines, thoroughly 'anti-popular' in tone and proposals.

The Minority Report signed by Mrs Webb, and the Labor Members, has been very carefully prepared, with expert advice on each chapter, on the contrary line; containing a comprehensive scheme for Poor Law and another for Unemployment – but definitely negativing Relief Works; and not violating either the Four Rules of Arithmetic or the Ten Commandments, which I say we must always take care to have on our side!

Of course both Reports have been in the hands of the Cabinet for some time; and the indications are that Ministers and the Liberal Press will try to debit the Conservatives with the Majority Report (for Mr Balfour appointed the Commission); whilst accepting what they choose from the Minority Report, as being the popular and 'Democratic' one.

Now, I don't see why this should happen. *There is not a single Tariff Reformer among the Majority*, which, in fact, is largely Liberal. And there is no 'Liberalism' in the Minority Report.

What can be done to make it a non-party affair? As it really is and ought to be. Mrs Webb has no belief that the Liberals can or will carry out the necessary reforms, and rather counts on the Tariff Reformers being more constructively minded. Could you come to lunch one day at 1 p.m. and talk it over?

Yours very truly

Sidney Webb

## 558 UI BEATRICE WEBB TO H. G. WELLS

Wells made a habit of sending copies of his books to a wide circle of acquaintances. Beatrice, tired and reading *Tono Bungay* casually, upset Wells by this unfavourable comparison to his 'invasion' novel.

41 Grosvenor Road, Westminster Embankment<br>Feb. 10th 1909

My dear Mr Wells

*Tono Bungay* came just in the nick of time – when the Report was finished and I was longing for a friend to talk to about something fresh – different. Unfortunately I had been tempted to read two instalments in the *English Review* (a rotten system from the artist's and not the moneymaker's point of view) which just took the keenest edge off my delight. Still I thoroughly enjoyed a good lazy day over it.

The first part is quite the best thing H.G. has done – but all is – what *is* the adjective? – it is not exactly stimulating, because its human nature is such poor stuff – entertaining is too small a word – interesting is 'banal' – so I give it up.

Do you know I almost wrote you my admiration for *War in the Air* – which combines a really magnificent political pamphlet with a most invigorating flight of one's imagination. I am not sure whether it will not outlast *Tono Bungay*.

I know that is heresy to the author of both.

Ever yours

Beatrice Webb

When the Treasury Solicitor claimed that the cheap Fabian version of the Minority Report would be an infringement of Crown copyright, the Webbs were greatly put out. They subsequently discovered an earlier Treasury minute permitted republication in the absence of any formal and advance embargo. Haldane intervened on their behalf and the Treasury letter was withdrawn. The Fabian paperback was published at 3s. as against the official price of 5s. 6d.

41 Grosvenor Road,
Westminster Embankment
Feby 17 1909

My dear Mr Lansbury

I do not know which gave me the most pleasure – your letter or the charming gift that reached me late last night – taken together they are a real joy to me. Your choice was excellent as I do not possess a tea-caddie and have often thought of getting one. The silver box would serve equally well as a cigarette box – so that it represents my two Vices!

The R.C. certainly has not been an altogether pleasant business for the minority – but I believe we have done a good day's work and that it will be a turning point in the history of English Collectivism.

Did you hear that our chairman (I think I am not doing him an injustice) had got hold of the Treasury Solicitor and the Fabian Society had received a peremptory order not to publish the Minority Report? However an application from us to 10 Downing Street secured an immediate withdrawal of the letter and the Fabian Society and Longmans will publish tomorrow! The reduction of the price of the blue book is the last little kick. But of course it is all to the good, and will not hurt the Fabian Society 3/- edition in the very least, and will transfer the Longman's Edition into an '*edition de luxe*'. Moreover, the sillies have not sent the communication to the Press which they ought to have done, at once. Meanwhile the Chairman and I have exchanged quite affectionate letters. I really like the man and am sorry I have been such a troublesome colleague. If you had not been there I am not sure that I should not have 'succumbed'.

Always yours sincerely
Beatrice Webb

### 560 UI BEATRICE WEBB TO H. G. WELLS

Wells replied with what Beatrice called 'a real gem' of ill temper. (BWD 24 February 09) 'It is, of course, H.G. at his worst; just now he is at his worst in anything that concerns the Shaws or us or the Fabian Society – conceit, bitterness, and an element of treachery to past intimacies'. In her diary she justified her preference for *The War in the Air*. She found that *Tono Bungay* bored her with its 'absurd impression of meaningless chaos'. She felt that Wells was 'going through an ugly trouble, and I would like to help him through it, instead of serving as a source of bitterness and antagonism'. The novel on which Wells was working was *The New Machiavelli*, which included a savage satire on the Webbs as 'Oscar and Altiora Bailey'.

41 Grosvenor Road, Westminster Embankment
Feb. 24th [1909]

My dear Mr Wells

What an interesting letter – quite the most interesting you have ever written me – I enshrine it with due honour in my diary! Lots of people will agree with you in all you say – and you say it so well.

Now we are off for a nice holiday – taking the boat to Naples on March 6th and then spending 4 weeks in Rome and the Hill Cities. When we return we must manage to meet and go on with the discussion of how best to get some more sense into human affairs? I am delighted to know from Amber that you are at work on a novel which is to combine all the great qualities of *Tono Bungay* with a study of the more ideal elements of human character. I watch for it with eagerness.

Always yours sincerely
Beatrice Webb

561 UI  BEATRICE TO H. G. WELLS

Wells was not appeased, writing back to accuse Beatrice of being 'wilfully unsympathetic' and insisting that 'you and Sidney have the knack of estranging people'. Beatrice thought it 'strange that he seems obsessed with the notion that we have some scheme to undo his influence. Bless the man! We never think of him now he has resigned from the Fabian Society. While he was there we *had* to think of him, because he spent his whole energy attacking us. But I can honestly say that our one thought was to stop him doing mischief, but to avoid doing him or his influence any harm. We wanted to keep him as an asset to the cause; but we could not let him simply smash the thing up without having the least intentions of working out a new plan of campaign'. (BWD March 09) Wells had resigned from the Fabian Society on 16 September 1908.

41 Grosvenor Road, Westminster Embankment
Feb. 28th [1909]

Dear Mr Wells

Don't shake us off altogether: it won't be good for either the Webbs or the Wells and will be very bad for the common cause. I am conscious of having written a stupid letter about *Tono Bungay* – all the stupider because I had just written to a friend that it was your greatest work! What I meant to express was my quite spontaneous admiration for *War in the Air*, which you had told me was a pot-boiler, and which seemed to me a magnificent Allegory-cum-Parody, as to human affairs, combining Truth with Irony. The only criticism I have to make about *Tono Bungay* is that I think you 'crab' the business world – it is not so bad as that – and in doing so, you 'crab' human nature.

As to the Report, we have put our best work into it, and I am too tired to care a little 'Damn', what you, or any one else, thinks about it. I *know* it is good – and that the ideas embodied in it will, in the end, prevail.

Ever yours sincerely<br>Beatrice Webb

# 7. Leading a crusade
## June 1909 – May 1911

The Webbs had always seen themselves partly as explorers of social problems and partly as missionaries preaching a solution to them. In 1909, however, their lives entered a new phase. They were now to lead their own revivalist movement in an effort to destroy the old Poor Law and impose their utopian solution in its place.

The decision to launch a national campaign, in which they would for the first time come forward as agitators rather than wirepullers, was prompted by both personal and political motives. They had become obsessed with the virtues of the Minority Report and frustrated by the failure of lobbying and salon politics to latch it upon either the Liberal government or the Tory opposition. They had antagonised many of the powerful vested interests, especially the Charity Organisation Society, and fallen out with some of the key ministers, notably Burns and Lloyd George. Beatrice, moreover, seems to have been determined to score off her former colleagues and to vindicate what she felt were her unsuccessful tactics in the Commission by arousing public opinion against its proposals and behind the Minority Report.

In one sense the moment was propitious for such a campaign. The publicity created by the work of the Commission had stimulated interest in the problems of the Poor Law and fed the growing desire to do something about the haunting problems of poverty and ill-health. When the Webbs launched their campaign they were able to appeal to a substantial body of middle-class opinion which saw it more as a general crusade against poverty than as an agitation to secure official acceptance of the particular remedies proposed by the Webbs – later there was the significant change in the title of their National Committee from 'for the Break-up of the Poor Law' to 'for the Prevention of Destitution'. The Minority Report, in effect, was more a symbol than a programme. A national campaign also provided an outlet for Fabians who felt the Society should be more active: the impetus aroused by Wells, and the new recruits attracted in the last three years, needed an outlet. If frustrated enthusiasm were not to be released into socialist political action an alternative was needed. It was ironic that the organisation and methods of the Webb campaign, as it developed, came to resemble very closely the plans which Wells earlier had proposed for the Fabian Society itself in the face of determined opposition from the Webbs.

In another sense, however, the situation was much less favourable than the Webbs assumed. They were sadly out of touch with the growing Labour Party and with the I.L.P.; they had gone off on a very different tack from Lloyd George and the Liberals; and they had little influence over a Tory Party which had been caught up in the excitement of Tariff Reform. They also failed to realise how much support the Liberal government would be able to drum up in the country for its social legislation and its radical tax proposals as the House of Lords steadily moved to block further progress. The stage was already being set for the great battle between the Liberals and the Lords which was to absorb the energy of both parties and distract the public for the next three years. In such a context a campaign for the Minority Report, however strongly it might appeal to the progressive professional and middle classes, was bound to remain a side-show.

Looking back later in life Beatrice wrote in *Our Partnership* that what she called 'this plunge into propaganda' had two consequences which, if the Webbs had anticipated them, might have been a deterrent to their attempt to run their own political movement. One was the diversion from their research into local government: it meant that they were still labouring with their planned series of volumes for another twenty years and that the original grand design was never completed. The second was that with the loss of contact with both Liberal and Conservative leaders they abandoned permeation for propaganda. This shift prefigured their ultimate commitment to the Labour Party. Once they had decided upon a great scheme of social reorganisation they moved increasingly, though at first with great reluctance, into the orbit of the Labour Party they had hitherto ignored or neglected. In the course of 1909 and 1910, as they threw themselves into what proved in the short run a propagandist success and a political failure, they began to lead a new kind of life as campaign strategists and itinerant agitators. The evangelical impulse – the sense of a 'civilising mission', so strong among the early Fabians – had become a crusade to convert England to a policy of 'complete communal responsibility'.

Beatrice sketched out the Webb plans at a testimonial dinner for them attended by 200 Fabians on 19 May 1909, after they returned refreshed from a holiday in Italy. She told the gathering that the Webbs intended to make a new start 'at the head of a contingent of young men and women'. (BWD 15 May 09) Believing there would be a reaction against the Liberal Party she deliberately appealed to the young, recruiting a corps of voluntary workers who would undertake research and propaganda. The National Committee's offices in Norfolk Street, between the Fabian Society and the L.S.E., were 'a sort of middle-term between avowed socialism and non-partisan research and administrative techniques'. (BWD 27 September 09) Within a few months the Committee had enrolled 16,000 members, set up its own publication arrangements, and was busy organising public meetings, conferences and summer schools. It also established its own organ, *The Crusade*.

### 562 BUL   BEATRICE WEBB TO SIR OLIVER LODGE

Beatrice was energetically enlisting prominent sympathisers and enlisting suitable speakers. Philip Snowden (1864–1937) was a leading member of the I.L.P. and Chancellor of the Exchequer in the Labour governments of 1924 and 1929.

41 Grosvenor Road, Westminster Embankment
[? June 1909]

My dear Sir Oliver

Mr Balfour dare not take the chair for any of our meetings, partly on the grounds of health and partly because he fears to offend G. Hamilton. Now will you help us, so far as to preside at one of these meetings? We have secured Sir Frederic Pollock, Bernard Shaw, Winston Churchill, and Philip Snowden. I am asking Gilbert Murray. *Now is the time that help is valuable* – don't fail us. If we are really to carry this new conception of personal and social obligation, we must all pull together.

You see the Majority has come out at last (read *Times*) and cannot make up their minds whether they will or will not stand by the Status Quo. If they adhere to their *One Authority* it means the retaining of the Board of Guardians and the Old Regime. There is no conceivable reason for sweeping away a directly-elected Poor Law body, if the principle of the relief of destitution is to be maintained. Why Professor Muirhead failed to see this, I cannot understand. I suppose it comes from not knowing the facts of local government, on the one hand, and being unable to shake himself free of the old categories of the Poor Law, on the other.

Will you write to us – as the time is short – let us know which date would suit you – the first lecture would suit us very well as Sir F. Pollock will be out of England and perhaps also Bernard Shaw.

Ever yours sincerely

Beatrice Webb

563 PP  SIDNEY TO BEATRICE

By the middle of June the Webbs had realised how much time the campaign would demand in the next year. Beatrice had even begun to envisage the emergence of a permanent organisation 'to maintain the standard of life in all its aspects' – a new version of the idea of a party of national efficiency which had never been far from their minds in the past decade. She was the more inclined to speculate on the possibilities as it became clear that their former Liberal associates were beginning to drop them socially and politically. (BWD 18 June 09) This falling away was in part offset by the rallying of other progressives, some of them, such as Wallas, old associates with whom they had recently differed. Some of them were new acquaintances from the universities, the professions and not least the theatre. Beatrice, for instance, wrote to John Galsworthy, Granville-Barker and John Masefield and other authors asking them to write plays in support of the campaign. None of them did so. The only apparent outcome of this notion was a playlet called *Our Little Fancies* briefly produced at Manchester in 1911: it was reported to have dealt with the problem of the General Mixed Workhouse. Lionel Holland (1865–1936) had been a Conservative M.P. until 1900, when he switched to the Liberals on the temperance issue.

At the beginning of July Beatrice went to Manchester to receive the honorary degree of D.Litt.

41 Grosvenor Road

Westminster

2/7/9

Dearest

Here are two letters, one from Lionel Holland (sending a cheque for £1.1.0); and Masefield – which are both very satisfactory.

329

I just manage to scribble you this greeting for tomorrow, in the hope that you will have had a good journey, a pleasant evening and a good night. I shall think of you tomorrow midday going up the hall in your scarlet gown. I am proud to think that this recognition has come, and come so spontaneously.

I propose to go round by the office before I go home, just to see if anything is wanted. I think we shall have a lot of members in the next few weeks. I am inclined to think that in October we shall have to consider a *petition* to the Government, as numerously signed as possible, begging them *not* to create any new Poor Law Authority – giving the reasons against it. I fancy that such a petition to the *Cabinet* – not to the House of Commons – would not be without influence; and it would educate our own members.

Now, goodbye dearest.

Sidney Webb

### 564 PP SIDNEY TO BEATRICE

Clifford Dyce Sharp (1883–1935) was an active young Fabian who, in 1909, married Hubert Bland's daughter Rosamund. He was one of the main organisers of the Poor Law campaign and editor of *The Crusade*. After this experience he was the natural choice of the Webbs as first editor of the *New Statesman* in 1913. Mary MacArthur (1880–1921) was secretary of the Women's Trade Union League in 1903; in 1911 she married William Crawford Anderson (1877–1919) a trade union leader and prominent member of the I.L.P. John Robert Clynes (1869–1949) became president of the General and Municipal Workers' Union from 1912 to 1937. He was a member of the Labour Party Executive in 1909–39, Home Secretary in 1929–31 and deputy-leader of the Labour Party in 1934.

41 Grosvenor Road
Westminster Embankment
3.7.9

My own dearest

I was very glad to get your pencilled greeting, and to know that you were comfortable.

Here are some letters for you to read in the train. Also there have come two letters, each enclosing cheque for £1.1.0, from two sisters of Buxton (Miss Mabel Buxton and Mrs Constance Hawker), which I do not send. And all but two or three sections of the Scottish Report, which is admirably written. The recommendations are as we already knew. (Phthisis is to remain a Public Health function!)

I saw Miss Bulkley for a moment through the window; she said she had taken the whole day to deal with the correspondence, i.e. applications for membership from the *Christian Commonwealth* and *Clarion* people, mostly enclosing 2/6 or 5/-. She could not say what the number was – possibly a hundred.

There may be some use in Clifford Sharp's suggestions, especially as to getting signatures to a petition, later on. But I fully believe we can get 100,000 members, merely by working on the membership as it grows, by pressing each person individually to enrol others, *if only we can organise the office* effectively *enough* to be able to write to each one. This would be of extraordinary propagandist value in itself; and of ever growing range. If we *can* in this way get anything like 100,000 members in six months, that 100,000 might grow to any number, of its own weight. I am much inclined to believe in the value of the office work *on each member* – writing to them all again and again.

I shall try to go on to the office this morning, as I want to see (from Pease and Sanders) whether I cannot write usefully to the Labor people in the two bye-elections now current. We ought not to let it be said that the question was not even raised.

By the way, Lansbury has been elected as one of the four new members of the N.A.C. [National Administrative Council] (central executive) of the I.L.P. – with Miss MacArthur, J. Clynes M.P. and another man.

Now goodbye dear one. I can't do anything without you; nor settle down to any useful work. It is nice to think you will come back tomorrow, and not Monday – but if there is any reason or pleasure in your staying till Monday, of course do so, and send me a telegram (arranging for Sunday delivery if necessary).

Sidney Webb

565 PP   BEATRICE WEBB TO MARY PLAYNE

41 Grosvenor Road,Westminster Embankment<br>[?July 1909]

Dearest Mary

The flowers, fruit and vegetables were both decorative and delicious – I had a pleasant party to enjoy them, among others a great admirer of yours – Mr Christopher Turner, a Lincolnshire landlord, who said you made a quite admirable speech at the conference! (He is a 'Minority man' and has written a clever report to the Chamber of Agriculture in support of our Report.)

We shall be very glad to get away next Saturday – from London tho' we are going to lecture a good deal the first week. I have had 2 lessons on Voice Production in view of the amount of talking I shall have to do in the next 6 months. We shall be practically 'campaigning' all the autumn – organising and speaking – from Edinburgh to Plymouth – from Bristol to Bolton. It is a new life for us both, especially for me; on the whole, I think, less straining than the life of thought and writing, that we have been living for about 3 years, combined with the friction on the Commission. But I sometimes look back with regret on the days of quiet undisturbed study we had before I became a Royal Commissioner. I am afraid it will be long before we get back to that more pleasurable existence. This organisation with its almost mushroom growth is going to absorb us almost entirely. All sorts of persons are joining – from Peers to Relieving Officers – even L.G.B. officials! and quite a number of County administrators. We have now over 1000 members and nearly £1,000 – all in 7 weeks.

Ever yours affectionately<br>Beatrice Webb

<br>

### 566 PP  BEATRICE WEBB TO GEORGINA MEINERTZHAGEN

Beatrice's niece Beatrice was known in the family as 'Bobo'. She married Robert Mayor in 1912. J. W. Hills was elected as a Protectionist for Durham in 1906. Sir Gilbert Parker sat as a Conservative for Grimsby 1900–18.

The campaign had begun well. 'We are living in a veritable turmoil' Beatrice noted on 22 July. 'The little office we took is crowded with literature and active workers: members are streaming in and a good deal of money. Sidney and I spend our lives writing, talking and organising.' She liked the sense of leadership so much, comparing 'the atmosphere of administration and willing obedience to my will' to the 'perpetual hostility and disparagement' of the Royal Commission, that she felt it necessary to remind herself of the dangers of self-satisfaction and demagogy. She thought the campaign might be the last active phase of the Webb partnership: 'the best way to spend the remainder of our two little lives'.

The Webbs spent five weeks at the Fabian summer school.

Bryntirion, Llanfair,<br>Harlech<br>Aug. 8 [1909]

Dearest Geo

I am glad to hear my charming namesake is recruiting for her elderly aunt – one of the hopeful signs is the number of young folk who are throwing their energies into the movement. We are also gathering quite a number of Conservatives – that nice Mr Hills M.P. for Durham and Sir Gilbert Parker are our latest recruits. Will you tell Bobo that we are having a quiet meeting in St James Hall October 12th with the Bishop of Southwark in the chair – can she bring a big party to reserved seats – persons who might be converted? It is the sound-off meeting to our autumn campaign. S. and I are speaking all over the country from Edinburgh to Portsmouth – Cardiff and Newcastle – a regular going 'on the stump'. As a preparation I practice voice presentation between 6.30 and 8 a.m. every morning on the beach – orating to the Waves! I want to be able to speak without effort, which is really certainly a question of proper tone of the voice. It is rather funny to start on a new profession after 50! But I have come to the conclusion that one only becomes thoroughly 'adaptable' after 50 – before that age, one is so terribly handicapped by one's body. (I suppose one's strength argues a well-spent youth!) Certain it is, that one's body becomes less and less of an incubus as the years roll on.

This place is very lovely – we are in lodgings perched up on a hill overlooking Barmouth Bay. The Fabian School is about 2 mins off – with 100 students who change week by week – we gave 7 lectures during the first week – now we look in once or twice a week and give a talk to the newcomers. They are rather a nice set – almost exclusively professional men and women – medical men and women, teachers, nursing Inspectors, with a sprinkling of Oxford and Cambridge young men. We shall be here until the 28th August when we pass through London to get to the office on our way for a fortnight at Longfords, settling in to London September 15th.

Our office at Clements Inn (which Bobo must come and see) is crowded with work: we shall have a paid staff of 5 as well (as my own two paid secretaries) and some 10 volunteers. We have between 2 and 3,000 members now and have collected over £1,000. We hope that our membership will rise to tens of thousands in the autumn. I really do believe that if we get a sufficiently strong public opinion, we may, in the course of a decade, clean up the whole bad business of a class of chronically destitute persons. Incidentally we shall increase both Rent and Interest – as, sooner or later, the wealthy have to pay for a demoralised and degraded slave population.

However, I won't run on!

Ever yours affectionately

Beatrice Webb

567 NLS   BEATRICE WEBB TO ELIZABETH HALDANE

*Earlier in the summer Beatrice had noted after dining with Haldane and his sister that they were 'estranged or constrained' by the Minority Report: she suspected that they might also have been made jealous by the admiration of the Webbs for Winston Churchill.*

[Harlech]
Sept. 5th [1909]

My dear Miss Haldane

Ever so many thanks for your kind and frank letter.

Your criticisms of our crusade would, I think, be quite valid if our aim were to alter the law, as soon as possible, to ever so slight an extent, in our direction. Then, no doubt, the cautious 'management' of this person, or that, together with a general atmosphere of minimising differences, and readyness to [amend] 'the law' would be most likely to be successful. But rightly or wrongly, we are after something bigger than that. After 20 years hard study and practical administrative experience, we really *do* see our way *to abolish Destitution if it be desired to do so*. But we realise that to carry out this Scheme, something more than changes in the law are needed. We need to change *the assumptions* upon which the ordinary man now proceeds in his dealings with Poverty – we need to make him feel wholly intolerant of what he now complacently accepts as inevitable. Without the change of thought and feeling, any little reform we might screw out of this Parliament, or the next, even if it pointed in our direction, would not attain our End. That is why we prefer to state our case boldly and fervently and with logical completeness. When the time comes for considering any legislation that is actually proposed we shall, of course, be ready to accept, gratefully, any small instalments in our direction whilst resisting, with all our strength, proposals which make the carrying out of our reform more difficult.

I sometimes wonder whether Liberals have, in the past, been altogether wise in walking so *stealthily* along the path of progress – trying to look, as if they were prepared to stand still, if all sections of their followers did not unite to push them on! The success of this Budget with its somewhat brilliant, if not blatant, signboard painting, rather points to the bolder attitude?

However, you are the government – we are merely a little bit of leaven in the doughy mass of Public opinion, which we hope will make something possible, that would otherwise be impossible, and other things impossible, that would otherwise be possible.

Anyway it will be an interesting adventure.

Ever yours sincerely<br>Beatrice Webb

We return to London on the *15th* for good.

BW

### 568 PP  BEATRICE WEBB TO AMBER BLANCO WHITE

While the Webbs were in Wales they learned of the sexual relationship between Wells and Amber Reeves and of her pregnancy. It meant 'the end of our friendship with H. G. Wells' Beatrice wrote. (BWD early September 09) In a number of diary entries over the next few weeks Beatrice summarised the progress of the scandal, which greatly upset the inner group of Fabians, expressing her disapproval of Wells 'as a Goethe-like libertine'.

The matter was complicated by spiteful letters from Wells accusing the Webbs of malicious interference in his personal affairs. Though the Webbs wished to support Amber, the daughter of close friends, they found themselves in a difficult position, for Amber in a state of bravado refused to break off relations with Wells despite the fact that in the summer she had married an old suitor and fellow-Fabian. Amber was living in Surrey in a cottage provided by Wells and was visited by him while her husband remained in London. The Webbs and Shaw were involved in efforts to save something from the wreck; both for Amber personally and for the Fabian Society, whose reputation could well be affected by a public scandal. Wells, indeed, was using the threat of publicity as an attempt to ward off intervention by Amber's parents and friends. In the event the pressure was too much for Wells and he agreed resentfully to break off relations with Amber before the child was born in January 1910.

*Private*                                            Sept. 11 [1909]

My dear Amber,

We will certainly see Blanco White and talk to him about general matters – we have the warmest appreciation of both his character and his intelligence and hope great things from him, if he keeps up his courage and his faith in himself and others.

Now as you have written to me quite frankly let me write to you quite frankly. You will have to choose – and that shortly – between a happy marriage and continuing your friendship with H.G. Wells. *That is the one essential fact in the present situation.* Therefore you see, I had better not and shall not, talk to Blanco about his marriage – because you and you alone can decide whether that marriage is to continue or not. I do not propose to utter another word about your affairs to anyone – willingly – and when I am challenged about them I shall shut people up as quickly and conclusively as I can. But that will not prevent me from realising that there can be only one end to continuance of your friendship with H.G. Wells – that is a breach between you and Blanco.

I may of course be wrong, but I do not think so.

Shall I come and have a talk with you – or do you prefer to work out your problems alone? I have the warmest affection for your parents, and *real* liking for you and a respect for Blanco. I have even a quite genuine desire to see H.G.W. saved from a big smash. But I don't want to interfere, if you prefer that I should not.

Yours affectionately

Beatrice Webb

### 569 HSP   SIDNEY WEBB TO MRS JOSEPH FELS

A number of wealthy sympathisers ensured that the Webb campaign had adequate funds. At its peak it employed more than a dozen full-time staff in London alone. On 3 October the Webbs had Winston Churchill to dinner to meet some of their younger supporters. On this occasion Churchill said: 'You should leave the work of converting the country to us, Mrs Webb, you ought to convert the Cabinet'. Beatrice replied revealingly that the Webbs did not wish merely to change the law: they proposed to change 'the mind of the people with regard to the facts of destitution – to make them feel the infamy of it and the possibility of avoiding it'.

Frances Greville, the Countess of Warwick (1861–1938), the companion of Edward VII when Prince of Wales, was converted to socialism and thereafter put her money, her mansion at Easton Lodge in Essex and her somewhat eccentric enthusiasm at the service of advanced causes. She was known as 'Daisy' Warwick or 'the Red Countess'.

41 Grosvenor Road
Westminster Embankment
Oct. 20 1909

My dear Mrs Fels

The £1,000 has taken a weight off my mind because now I can look ahead for a good year and refinance the movement with efficiency. We must take the country by storm and there is every sign that we may do so if we are sufficiently energetic in the next two years, before the reactionaries realise what a big job it is to become responsible for preventing Destitution! Once we get the country to accept the responsibility for all neglected infancy, childhood, preventible sickness and Unemployment and they will be forced to go on to the bitter end whatever that end may turn out to be. Perhaps Mr Fels may be in at the end!

So I accept the £1,000 with grateful gladness. If you do not object I am going to keep the fact rather quiet as I don't want to stop the flow of other subscriptions and diminish the role of our underpaid and volunteer staff! I shall tell the Treasurer and the Finance Committee but no one else at present. I am appealing for a special fund to start the Journal and have written to Lady Warwick to ask her for £500.

The 2 -5/- tickets shall be reserved for you.

Ever your devoted

Beatrice Webb

### 570 PP SIDNEY WEBB TO LORD COURTNEY

Courtney continued his propaganda for proportional representation for many years.

[Dundee]
4.11.9

Dear Leonard

I am afraid that I cannot consent to add my name (quite unimportant in this connection) to the draft memorial. In many respects it fails to express my convictions, and the only value of such a collection of signatures is falsified if those who sign are not really in agreement about what they sign. I am a little flattered by your evident feeling that I must be converted, because you would be the last to suggest any laxness with regard to such signatures! But I am *not* in agreement.

I am not sure whether I understand the philosopher's distinction between the 'general will' of the nation, and the sum of the individual wills; but it seems to express a truth. I am not in the least convinced that the arithmetical sum of the individual wills at any moment is equivalent to that 'general will' which lies at the root of real Democracy.

Anyhow, if I *did* think the arithmetical sum of the individual wills of such

336

vast consequence (not for truth, because *that* at any rate, does not depend on votes; but for the education of the citizen and convenience of administration), I should be concerned about what seems to me more important matters than P.R. [Proportional Representation] If we are to look to votes for the will of the nation, I don't think it nearly *so much* matters *how* we count the six or seven millions of electors, as our continued exclusion from the electorate of three or four million adult men (33 per cent of the total) – not to speak of our continued omission of all the women! How can I be enthusiastic about methods of counting the votes of what is, after all, only one-third of the adults in the nation? No amount of error this way is comparable in magnitude with the error of omitting (from the voice of the nation) two-thirds of its sane and adult citizens.

I am not at all convinced that the adoption of P.R. methods with regard to the present electorate – this being only one-third of the adults – would make the result a *truer* representation of the 'general will' of the adult community than the present methods. Indeed, I cannot help feeling that most of the influential members of the P.R. society *do not want* a truer representation of this 'general will'. They seem to me to shrink back in horror from manhood suffrage, or adult suffrage, and indeed the very last thing they desire to bring about is a strictly numerical counting of heads. They may be justified; but if they are, I confess that I do not think they ought to talk so much about the unfairness of the under-representation of existing minorities. I cannot respect their intellectual clearsightedness or their moral honesty, so long as they do not take just as much interest in getting represented the 15 millions of adults, who have at present no vote at all, as in getting an enlarged representation for *the minority* of the 7 millions, who at present *do* have votes.

I began this at Dundee; but addressing 10 meetings in 5 towns within 7 days hinders letter writing. Beatrice has stood it very well, (as I have also). We have had large and most enthusiastic meetings, and collected money and members. I think we may be quite assured that the Majority Report is politically quite impossible.

Yours

Sidney Webb

P.S. As regards other possible signatories, have you thought of

| | |
|---|---|
| Sir Oliver Lodge | Sir W. J. Collins, M.P. |
| Prof. Karl Pearson | Sir Edward Busk |
| Sir Wm Chance, Bart. | Sir Gilbert Parker |
| Alfred Marshall | Mrs Sidgwick |
| Prof. Starling (of University College) | Mrs Humphry Ward |
| Sir W. Ramsay (ditto) | Sir Francis Galton |
| | Lord Reay |

Archbishop Bourne (Westminster)   S. H. Butcher, M.P.
Sir Felix Schuster              Lord Hugh Cecil

I don't know their views: and I *don't suggest your using my name in approaching them.*

### 571 PP   BEATRICE TO SIDNEY

The 'raging, tearing propaganda', which Beatrice noted on 14 November, meant a great deal of travelling to the main provincial cities.

Sir Charles Eliot (1862–1931), soldier and colonial administrator in East Africa, became Vice-Chancellor (not Principal) of Sheffield University in 1904. A number of persons mentioned in letters as hosts or supporters of the Webbs during their campaign have not been positively identified.

In *Ann Veronica* Wells fused the story of his elopement with his second wife and his affair with Amber Reeves, glossing the facts so little that the novel was embarrassingly indiscreet. On 20 November the *Spectator* denounced this 'poisonous book' and said that the 'muddy world of Mr Wells's imaginings' was 'a community of scuffling stoats and ferrets, unenlightened by a ray of duty'. Other supporters of literary censorship joined the hue-and-cry against corrupting books.

> Endcliffe Holt,
> Endcliffe Crescent,
> Sheffield.
> [late November 1909]

My own dearest

One line to say that my meeting was a great success – about 700 persons and a great many guardians and councillors. Miss Eliot came with me and the young man who is temporary lecturer on Economics – a pleasant and good fellow, but of no authority. He wants to be a Factory Inspector – and I advised him to come up to the L.S. of Economics if he gets a Cardiff fellowship.

Mrs and Miss Eliot are good looking well-bred women – the mother devoted to her son and terribly concerned at his being here instead of in the Diplomatic as Administrator – feels him to be a misfit in every sense of the word as Principal of Sheffield University.

I read over the *Spectator* review of H.G. Wells – evidently written with knowledge of the story – it is an unfair review because it is a review of the Wells–Reeves episode and not of the book. H.G.W. has no conception how hard he will be hit by that story getting about. What a fool the man was not to go away and delay the publication of *Ann Veronica*! He had such a splendid chance of escaping scot-free if he had only taken it. But I shall not regret if he is permanently 'broken up' as a social leader. Perhaps I shall get a letter from you tomorrow?

> Ever your devoted wifey
> Beatrice Webb

338

Ernest Darwin Simon (1879–1960), later Lord Simon of Wythenshawe, was a Manchester industrialist, Liberal and later Labour politician. He became an expert on housing and local government. In 1947 he was appointed Chairman of the B.B.C. He and his wife Shena remained on friendly terms with the Webbs all their lives.

41 Grosvenor Road,
Westminster
17.12.9

Dear Mr Simon

Your letter calls for a longer answer than can easily be given. You will have seen that we believe in Piecework as a method of remuneration, *provided that* Collective Bargaining (or the legal enactment of Common Rules as to wages) is not thereby impaired. This necessarily involves a bargain (or a legal determination) that is precise in its terms.

Our point is that Timework involves just as precise a definition of terms as Piecework, if it is not to be open to silent and insidious perversion to the men's disadvantage. In the Timework trades, the men more or less consciously seek this definition (in which they are quite right) by having in view a definite *quantum* of work, or rate of speed, which is really one of the terms of their bargain. I think it a very imperfect and somewhat objectionable expedient; but it is, in my view, *indispensable to Collective Bargaining* until someone invents a better.

Your letter seems to make two distinct criticisms, one, that the introduction into the Collective Bargain of this condition of the normal quantum of effort, or normal speed is wrong in Timework trades; and two, that the Engineers ought to adopt Piecework rates at no increase of daily pay. These demand separate treatment.

So long as Timework prevails, I think the men are right to introduce the condition of quantum of effort, or normal speed. Otherwise the bargain is indeterminate, and it is open to the employer to vary it at his will, whilst professing not to vary it. A persistent course of 'speeding up' and a succession of improvements in subsidiary processes might gradually lead the workman to be giving, for an unaltered daily wage, twice as much 'work' (energy, force) as that for which he was formerly paid.

You would never dream of entering into such a contract yourself, if, for instance, you were letting out a steam engine for hire and *supplying the power* (as is done in some trades). You would never let this engine at a lump sum per day, leaving the user to get as much work out of it as he chose within the specified hours. You would know that the amount of 'work' got out of the engine and the speed of working would determine, not only the wear and tear (for which you would want to be paid), but actually also the amount of fuel etc. that you would be called upon to

339

supply. Now, the workman is – in terms of mechanics – an internal combustion engine, used as a prime mover. The more 'work' you make the human engine do, the more fuel it consumes, and the greater is the wear and tear. How can you expect the owner of that engine (having to supply its needs and keep it in repair) to enter into a contract to lend it for a fixed lump sum per day, without making some stipulation as to the amount or speed of the 'work' to be got out of it?

Now, I grant two things at once. First, that the workman's stipulation is vague, is not always a wise one, and so on. Second, that the human machine may be run in such a way that the attempt to avoid increase of effort may cause more wear and tear (in the shape of moral deterioration – 'ca canny') than the increased effort would have done. Nevertheless, the men are essentially right in refusing to enter into an indeterminate bargain – exactly as you would yourself refuse in the instance of the steam engine let for hire.

I need not remind you that it would be equally absurd to enter into such a bargain with a person whom you trusted for benevolence. You cannot rely on even the most benevolent persons *when the matter is one of contract at all* – least of all between different social grades, because they *cannot* see things with the same eyes. And it is (as Denny discovered) not the benevolent employer with whom the man is dealing. It is with the foreman anxious to cut down labor cost in his department. But as the men's stipulation is so indeterminate and inconvenient, we all prefer Piecework when it can be safely resorted to. Failing a proper Standard List of Piecework Rates, which employers and workmen alike declare to be impossible (I doubt this), the A.S.E. has sometimes been induced to stretch a point, and admit Piecework without any such security for its Collective Bargaining. But then it naturally asks that increased pay shall be given for the increased effort, and makes a rough shot at it by the demand for guaranteed Time and a Quarter. I cannot see that this is wrong.

If you ask that the men shall work at the admittedly higher speed, and therefore give the increased effort (of course, to work *unremittingly* is far greater effort than working slackly), at the old rate, you are, in effect proposing a reduction of wages per unit of effort. You may say that this is necessary in face of German competition – but I should naturally want to see how much you pay for rent, interest and profits before I could admit this. [*Side-note*: It may be that the German employer gets his managerial and directing ability at a lower rate than our *employers* choose to work for.] Even then, I should want to know why you did not propose to reduce the rations of the horses you employed, or (in the alternative) to make them draw heavier loads or draw their loads more continuously. You would then reply that to do this would mean that the horses would be worked out on an average in five years instead of seven. *That is the men's case.*

My wife bids me thank you most sincerely for the very handsome donation you sent for the National Committee. It is a big 'Crusade', and we feel
that it is worth all the effort that we can give – without bargaining, by the
way!

Will you not give us the pleasure of coming to see us when you are all in
London? We could put you up in our garret 'prophet's chamber', with
latch key *appartenant* – or we are mostly accessible at lunch or dinner.

Yours very truly

Sidney Webb

### 573 PP  SIDNEY WEBB TO EDWARD PEASE

W. V. Osborne, a branch secretary of the Amalgamated Society of Railway
Servants, successfully sought a judgement that it was unlawful for a trade union
to spend its funds on parliamentary candidatures, on maintaining Labour members elected to parliament, or on any political object whatsoever. When the House
of Lords finally upheld this claim the Labour Party was faced by a severe
financial crisis. Without trade union money it could not expect to finance its
election campaigns or, in the period before the payment of M.P.s, provide sub-
sistence for its members in the House. Though the Party managed to scrape
through the two elections of 1910 and slightly to strengthen its representation,
the only immediate relief was the Liberal measure of 1911 which provided a salary
of £400 for M.P.s. In 1913 the adverse effects of the Osborne judgement were
partially offset by an Act entitling trade unions to spend money for political
purposes if they first secured the specific approval of their members and then set
up a distinct fund to hold the money.

41 Grosvenor Road,<br>Westminster Embankment<br>18.12.09

Dear Pease

[*First paragraph crossed out*]

(2) H. of Lords on Tuesday will, I am told, unanimously and emphatically confirm decision in ASRS and Osborne, and a majority – perhaps all –
will also say that T.U. support of a candidate bound to a party is against
public policy. I assume the Labor Party Executive is prepared for this – if
not, this early intimation may be useful.

Yours

Sidney Webb

### 574 PP  BEATRICE TO SIDNEY

The Webbs had hoped for Cabinet changes which would have led to the removal
of Burns from the Local Government Board and his replacement by Winston
Churchill who seemed, at that time, amenable to their influence. Having failed
to induce Burns to take their ally Robert Morant into the L.G.B. as a senior
official they thought that Churchill, then President of the Board of Trade, might

agree to accept Morant and initiate a vigorous attack on the Poor Law. Burns, however, remained at the L.G.B. and he appointed Sir Horace Monro as permanent secretary to replace Sir Samuel Provis, while W. T. Jerred (who had been private secretary to Burns) was moved up to assistant secretary. The Webbs rightly inferred from these appointments that the government did not intend to take any early action on the Poor Law – not even on the Majority Report – and that Burns had successfully resisted an attempt to displace him. The government strategy, devised by Lloyd George, was to bypass Burns and the L.G.B. and to press forward with its plans for unemployment insurance as politically more attractive and easier to implement.

The Webbs had been too optimistic. Despite the great response to their agitation they had not moved the Liberals, the Tories or the administrative machine; and the supporters of the Majority Report, led by Lord George Hamilton, had formed the National Poor Law Association to press the case for a single Poor Law authority and vigorously to criticise the Webb proposals. It was this counter-attack that led the Webbs to shift their emphasis from 'the break-up' of the Poor Law to 'the prevention of destitution', seeking new allies in the education and public health service whose jurisdictions would be extended if the Minority Report were to be adopted.

It had, nevertheless, been a stimulating but tiring year. 'Our comradeship has never been so complete', Beatrice wrote on 30 December 1909. 'Hitherto, we have had only one side of our work together – our research and book-writing. But this last year we have organised together, spoken together, as well as written together.'

Sir Walter Tapper Jerred (1844–1918) was assistant secretary to the Local Government Board from 1910 in succession to Sir Horace Monro (1861–1949) who became permanent secretary. Sir Noel Thomas Kershaw (1863–1930) was also an assistant secretary. Sir Douglas Adrian (1845–1922) was legal adviser to the Board 1899–1910.

41 Grosvenor Road, Westminster Embankment
[January 1910]

My own dearest

Just a line on the chance of it finding you at Wakefield.

You will see *Jerred's* appointment to Assistant Secretaryship vacated by Monro. This, I think, makes it clear that J.B. [John Burns] intended this stroke from the first and kept it secret from his colleagues, to the last moment in order not to be ordered *not to do it* by the P.M. I cannot believe that the P.M. would have sanctioned the two appointments! Probably that also accounts for Morant believing in Winston's proposal to take him to the L.G.B. If Asquith has consented it means a *status quo* government in regard to Poor Law itself. Probably the legal appointment goes to Kershaw or Adrian will be pressed to return.

J.B. has done us! But then he was in a position to do so.

Come back darling one.

Ever yours

Beatrice Webb

In the general election of 1910 Lansbury fought Bow and Bromley, running second to the Conservative in a three-cornered fight. The Liberal candidate was the celebrated preacher Stopford Brooke (1832–1916), who was supported by many Progressives, including Dr John Clifford who urged Nonconformists to vote against the socialist Lansbury.

The government, supported by Labour and the Irish, came back with a clear majority, the country broadly dividing between the Tory south and the Lib-Lab industrial north. Beatrice still had hopes of persuading the Tories to match Tariff Reforms with Poor Law Reforms, but a weekend at Stanway with Balfour and other Conservative leaders convinced her that they were too fearful of 'the downward course towards a collectivist organisation'. (BWD 15 February 10)

41 Grosvenor Road, Westminster Embankment

[January 1910]

My dear Mr Lansbury

We were grieved with the result – but we did not ourselves expect more than you have done – prove yourself to be the proper Progressive candidate for Bow. If you stick to it you will get in next time – and that will probably be within a year. But next time we must all make an effort to organise the campaign scientifically – work up your electorates and appeal to each section separately, with Nonconformist backing.

However, as far as our P.L. policy is concerned, I think you can do more good outside Parliament. There are plenty of voting machines to go through lobbies – it is outside public opinion that we have to convert. Parliamentary parties will never be more than sounding brass. That is why Sidney has always declined to stand for Parliament.

The next year *will be very vital* for the crusade against Destitution – so unless we bestir ourselves everyone will be engulfed in the constitutional issue and the existence of Destitution will again be taken for granted. You must *work up* the T.U. and I.L.P. into favor. Cannot you come for a talk over propaganda when you are rested?

Ever yours

Beatrice Webb

The National Committee had drafted a Bill embodying the main proposals of the Minority Report and looked for a sympathetic M.P. to introduce it. Robert Harcourt, M.P. for Montrose Burghs, and a journalist and playwright, was the Radical son of Sir William Harcourt (1827–1904) the Liberal statesman. Sir Robert John Price (1854–1926) Liberal M.P. for East Norfolk introduced the Bill on 8 April 1910. No division was taken after a debate in which Asquith, Burns and Balfour spoke.

Sir Edward H. Verney was the husband of Lady Verney (1844–1930), the historical writer who produced *Memoirs of the Verney Family*.

Sidney had ceased to play a leading role in the L.C.C. in the past few years, all his energies having been devoted to the support of Beatrice in the drafting of the Minority Report. He was also less active in Fabian affairs (even during the Wells agitation) and in L.S.E. business. The period of the Commission and the ensuing campaign was the climacteric of the Webb partnership, changing much in both their private and public concerns. 'The progressive movement which the Fabian Society started in 1889 has spent itself. The machine that has been created goes grinding on all in the right direction – but it has become more or less automatic. A fresh impetus will, I think, come from our propaganda, from the new principle of the national minimum as a joint responsibility of the individual and the community for a given standard of individual life . . . for the present we can do more in persuading the country at large than in the administration of London's municipal business.' (BWD 1 March 10)

41 Grosvenor Road, Westminster
23/2/10

Dearest

Harcourt ran in to say that one of 'our' members had drawn the best private member's day whatever it is. He is Sir R.J. Price, of Norfolk and he was to meet Harcourt then and there to consider whether he would give notice of our Bill, for some likely day after Easter. He *hoped* that Price would agree, but said that of course many others would be at him with Bills. It would be excellent to get a second reading debate.

I see from collating various scanty newspaper reports, that you and I were much referred to at the Guildhall Conference of Poor Law Unions Association. A Mr Stone of Canterbury said that M.R. [the Minority Report] reminded him of the vision of Dante in that the spirit of Beatrice was over it all!

But we had one or two backers besides Lansbury (e.g. Sir E. Verney), amid much abuse.

It occurs to me, though no one else realises it, that this is my last afternoon at the Council or any of its Committees.

Yours
Sidney

577 PP  BEATRICE WEBB TO MARY HANKINSON

Mary Hankinson, a games mistress, was 'the secretary for physical education' at Fabian summer schools and a dominant character in their organisation for a number of years. Beatrice disagreed with her conception of the summer school as a jolly combination of exercise, education and entertainment. While conceding that games should have a modest place, Beatrice feared that such high jinks might become an end in themselves, distracting from the more serious business of intellectual debate. Since the Webbs had undertaken to run the 1910 school at Harlech for six weeks, devoting it in part to the encouragement of university Fabians and in part to the Poor Law campaign, Beatrice was insistent that the domestic arrangements should not be haphazard and onerous. A long entry in

Beatrice's diary for 4 September reviews in detail the conduct of the summer school and draws conclusions about the way she felt such events should be conducted in future. Sidney later told her (7 October 10 PP) that the school had made enough profit to pay off all the outstanding debts of the Society (£191). In the following year the Fabians took Barrow House, near Keswick. This letter is in Sidney's handwriting: it may be a fair copy retained for reference.

[41 Grosvenor Road]

10/5/1910

Dear Miss Hankinson

I really must ask you not to go back on the arrangements quite definitely made with regard to the service at Caermeddyg. When we undertook to act as Directors and to pay for our own board, I expressly stipulated that as a quid pro quo I should be permitted to have an extra servant over and above the four servants as my parlourmaid, and that I should also have my private secretary, if there was no paid housekeeper other than the cook. Now I have generously given up my private secretary, and you immediately suggest that I should give up the extra servant too. The voluntary helper would be really quite useless to me as I could not ask her to act as my personal servant. Now pray let us be quite clear about it, I must have five paid servants at Caermeddyg – one of them must be my house-parlour-maid, because I depend on her attendance for my personal comfort. Who the other 4 servants are I do not care. But I am willing to bring my own cook as one of them if you like, and she agrees to come.

Will you let me know by return of post whether you will stand by this arrangement? Otherwise we must discuss the whole question afresh on another basis. You might entertain us, and I might pay for my parlour-maid as my maid. But I am not going to pay for my board, and be 'sweated' as Director, lecturer and working housekeeper with insufficient service.

BW

578 PP    SIDNEY WEBB TO ROBERT SILYN ROBERTS

Robert (Silyn) Roberts (1871–1930), Methodist minister at Blaenau Ffestiniog 1905–12, was a notable Welsh bard and author, a member of the I.L.P. and Fabian Society, and the founder of the Workers' Educational Association in North Wales in 1925.

41 Grosvenor Road

30.5.10

Dear Mr Silyn Roberts

Mrs Webb and I are looking forward to seeing something of you during the Fabian Summer Meeting at Llanbedr.

Dr Lawson Dodd and I have been talking over the question of Sundays during those six weeks; and we have wondered whether something could not be done to induce one (or more) of the chapels in the village to have one (or more) special sermons on The Problem of Poverty, or The Crusade for the Prevention of Destitution. It would be very useful if the congregation could be made aware that what the Fabian Summer School wants is the same as what the congregation wants done(!)

We don't know how to deal with the matter; but if there is anything to be done with any of the chapels in this way, *you are the man*! Could you arrange to come over and preach? Can you put the matter in hand, and get the necessary arrangements made? Or shall I write? (If so to whom?) Shall I offer that you would be willing to preach a special sermon if invited?

We want to do whatever is possible with the Chapels.

Yours very truly

Sidney Webb

## 579 PP  BEATRICE WEBB TO MISS ROWSON

Before the summer recess, when the Webbs took a Swiss holiday and went on to the Fabian summer school, Beatrice reviewed the organisation and progress of the Poor Law campaign. She concluded that the Webbs had so far done what they set out to do – to put the Minority Report clearly on the agenda of public discussion. They had won much support among social workers, church interests, miscellaneous middle-class progressives, Labour supporters and Co-operators. The number of volunteer workers was such that the National Committee was forced to move to larger offices, to set up committees to control the work – there were now over four hundred lecturers on the list of available speakers – and to cope with the growing total of rather sloppily-organised branches. 'Can we develop this organisation into a really big national movement to do away with destitution as a chronic and wholesale state of millions of our people?', Beatrice asked. (BWD 27 May 10) She felt that the non-partisan platform of the Minority Report was 'concrete, comprehensive' and had 'a philosophic basis in the whole theory of an enforced minimum of civilised life'.

The problem the Webbs now faced was that the movement depended almost entirely upon their personal leadership: Beatrice wondered whether they could ever give it the independent life which they had created in the L.S.E. If they could not, she realised, the movement would eventually collapse – especially as they had to establish the necessary momentum before they left for their long-planned sabbatical journey round the world. Beatrice found herself enjoying the sensation of leadership (though it evoked her customary self-searching about vanity and arrogance), feeling regret only at the physical demands the campaign made upon her and Sidney and at the diversion of effort from what she always considered their preferred existence of research and writing. The effort was justified, she felt, only in so far as it served two ends – the diversion of national wealth from the rich to the poor and, at the same time, '*an increase in personal responsibility on the part of those benefited classes*'.

Apart from a fifty-member executive, which controlled finance, publications and meetings, Beatrice had set up a Volunteers Council with committees for press, social, propaganda and office work. There was also a separate Lecturers Council.

This is the earliest surviving letter from Beatrice which was typed (by a secretary) in the original.

41 Grosvenor Road, Westminster Embankment
4th Oct. 1910

Dear Miss Rowson

In case I do not see you at the Office today, will you let me have a draft of the Minutes of the Volunteers' Council before inserting them in the Minute Book? I think they might be circulated (after correction) to the members of the Volunteers' Council as it keeps those who were absent informed. Will you see that the resolutions referring Numbers 1 and 4 on the Agenda to the General Purposes Committee, and Numbers 2 and 3 to the Propagandist Committee are placed on the Agenda of those Committees with instructions that they bring up proposals on all these points to be submitted through the Honorary Secretary to the Finance Committee and Meetings and Membership Committee of the Executive Council respectively.

I thought it better to suggest that the Committees of the Volunteers' Council should proceed to elect Chairmen and Secretaries as until they have done so they cannot be properly constituted. At each Volunteers' Council the Chairman of each Committee ought to report as to the work of his Committee during the interim, and these reports ought to come first on the Agenda of the Council.

I do not know whether you will act as Secretary for any of the Committees? I am inclined to think it is better to distribute the work so as to interest more members of the Council. Also I think it is hard on you to have to do all the work, as I look forward to a great extension of the Volunteers' Council – it is conceivable it might turn into a Club. Also, I think the Secretary of the Volunteers' Council should be able to keep a general oversight on the work of the Committees and to some extent look after their relationship to the Volunteers' Council, which would be impossible if the Secretary were also the Secretary of the Sub-Committees.

We are all very grateful to you for undertaking this work. If we can make a success of the Volunteers' Council and keep it straight in its relations to the Staff, on the one hand, and the Executive Council on the other, we shall have solved a very difficult problem in the administration.

Yours very truly

Beatrice Webb

## 580 PP   BEATRICE TO SIDNEY

The autumn campaign began with meetings ranging from Bournemouth to Darlington. Sidney returned to London while Beatrice went on to Scotland, staying with Haldane and his sister at Cloan.

Haldane had carried through a series of important and much-needed army reforms, including the creation of the Territorial Army, but he had encountered persistent covert opposition from diehard interests in the Army and War Office.

Beatrice feared that Haldane was 'eating himself into the grave' and would not have 'much longer to work in the world of edibles'. (BWD 9 October 10) She felt that like many of his colleagues in the Liberal leadership his life was 'so rounded off by culture and charm, comfort and power, that the misery of the destitute is as far off as the savagery of Central Africa'. Her despair at the languor of both party leaderships made her doubt whether either had a real will to effect social change: 'We may have, in the end, to establish a real socialist party if we want rapid progress'.

Sydney John Chapman (1871–1951) was professor of political economy at the University of Manchester from 1901 until 1918. He was a supporter of the Webb campaign.

R.B.H. seemed rather depressed about the Territorials and the W.O. generally – he can't get them to carry out his policy when his back is turned.

Cloan, Auchterarder, N.B.
[?8 October 1910]

My own darling one

Your letter was a delight this morning and though I cannot post this to you before tomorrow and then only to find you at Prof. Chapman's on the 12th, I am noting down before I forget it the results of a long talk with R.B.H.

First, I gather from him and also from Elizabeth that he *is* in favour of the distribution of the services and would gladly accept some sort of compromise which would give us the substance if not the form of the Break-up. (The only objection which was raised either by Elizabeth or R.B. was that the *Public Health* Authority ought to be made supreme in all matters of Health, from birth to old age, and that they objected to the Education Authority having the medical treatment of children.) I agreed that that would be ideal so long as the E.A. was master in its own house. Secondly he told me that, both Asquith and Lloyd George want him to go to L.G.B. and that he will go if there is another Liberal administration. Thirdly, that being the case he does not want to take the chair for us as he does not want to be committed. So I must not ask him for February. Meanwhile he is quite ready that we should go ahead with our agitation and does not at all object to our sending out an appeal about the Midwives Bill. It was 'John Burns who was at fault', but he does not say that they are going to over-rule him unless we make a fuss.

About general politics. He anticipates, I think, an agreement – he thinks they will remain in for one more *year*. In that case he thinks they will be beaten and the Tories will have their chance.

That is what he *wants*. He thinks he will have done all he can at the W.O. by that time and that he will then need a complete rest. (He is ageing very rapidly and looks to me on the point of another breakdown.)

348

With regard to Osborne's judgment – he is really in favour of it. But I think they intend to come down with qualifications – earmarking the *extra* subscriptions to other funds if there is conscientious objection.

My general impression is that he wants to ride for a fall so as to bring in the Tories and have a rest and then come in again and do something like the Minority Report Scheme. He ridicules the idea that the Labour or Socialist movement could prevent them from coming in after a spell of Tory Government. He believes the old see-saw between the two front benches as at present constituted will go on indefinitely and that they can always refuse the demands of Labour by letting the Tories have a spell of office and counting on an anti-Tory [?pact] to bring them back again.

But on the whole he is in favour of the Minority Report.

I have promised to stay with the Whites on the 26th.

Now darling one goodbye – I do miss you, my friend, colleague, and lover. Write nice long letters to me.

Ever your devoted wifey<br>Beatrice Webb

### 581 PP  SIDNEY TO BEATRICE

The campaign, in its first five months, had cost £1,200 and donations had reached £1,550; it was never handicapped for lack of money or volunteer workers.

Sir Maurice Amos (1872–1940), was a barrister who served in the Egyptian administration and later became professor of comparative law at University College, London.

41 Grosvenor Road,<br>Westminster Embankment<br>10.10.10

Dearest

Your *two* letters were very reassuring – though you must not give up eating altogether! (Get some Sanatogen in Edinburgh).

As to Edinburgh I have written to Wilson, the secretary person who was at Llanbedr, telling him you would be at the Roxburgh, and *would lie down on arrival*; that he was to *call* for you *just in time to walk* to the meeting, and not let you talk too much or too long. I enclose Edinburgh addresses.

Now, don't trouble about money support for the National Committee. You could at any time raise some hundreds of pounds now by a personal appeal to all your members. The money seems coming in quite well; and I see no reason to doubt you receiving in subscriptions (renewals and new) anywhere between two and three thousand pounds. You may count confidently on leaving them at least £1,000 in hand when you go, and a good list of subscribers.

I think there is no doubt that we are getting accepted in the country.

The question now is, how to get into the mind of the governing class and the governing clique? That I feel less hopeful about at the moment.

The house goes on all right in your absence, but it is very lonely; and I do not find that I can sleep. But I have done a lot of writing work, and cleared off some things. It will be a great joy to be together again on Saturday, even though it is only for 24 hours, and I must go out to the meeting after lunch. The Amos's and Reeves's came yesterday, all very cheery, but with no particular news. Amos is very anxious we should spend a week with them in Cairo on our way home in March or April 1912.

I enclose a letter from Mrs Macrosty, which is not very important. But it does not cost much to get incorporated as a Company not for profit (like the School); and as it makes for permanance, you might well do it, *when* you give yourself out for permanent. I doubt doing it now, when people believe in carrying the reform with a rush in a year or two. There is no real difficulty about legacies: they may always be left to the Treasurer for the time being.

Also letters from Lady Constance Lytton as to midwives. I have sent *her* an answer for the other lady.

Now goodbye dearest.

Sidney

### 582 PP BEATRICE TO SIDNEY [*incomplete*]

On 17 September, in the course of a talk to the executive committee of the Amalgamated Society of Railway Servants Sidney made a critical comment on the recent Osborne judgement. On 17 October three governors of the L.S.E. with railway interests – appointed to reflect the School's special concern with railway economics and the companies' support for the training of their staffs at the School – resigned from the governing body and sent letters to Webb which they simultaneously released to the press. They complained that Webb had prejudiced the impartiality of the L.S.E. The three governors were Lord Claud Hamilton (brother of Lord George Hamilton, chairman of the Poor Law Commission), who was chairman of the Great Eastern; James Inglis, manager of the Great Western; and Oliver Bury, manager of the Great Northern.

*The Times*, in an editorial comment on 19 September, had already accused Webb of stirring up trouble between capital and labour at a critical time and attacking a court of law, saying that 'Mr Webb's political passion had latterly outrun his economics'. Since the start of the campaign against the Poor Law, it said, Mr Webb had 'preferred agitation to science'. It urged that he should either resign from the L.S.E. or refrain from taking sides in the class war. Beatrice attributed these attacks to their Poor Law campaign: 'The Hamiltons know that we care for the School and that it is our child, so to speak'. (BWD 19 October 10) Shaw wrote to Beatrice on 24 October urging her to restrain Sidney from hitting back at the railway directors: Sidney, he said, 'has only preserved his reputation for being a prudent and moderate man because he has never yet met with a really embittered opposition . . . He never suffered fools with any real gladness; and when the fools begin to injure him and hurt his feelings as well as bore him there will be wigs on the green . . . The moral of all this is that you must not let this campaign overwork him. He requires a certain amount of fat not so much on his body as on his temper; and if you let him get too much overwrought he will make the air ring with more liars and scoundrels and thieves than Hyndman in his wildest moments ever ventured on'. (SCL 24 October 10)

[?Edinburgh]
[17 October 1910]

My own dearest one

You will be upset by the Railway Governors' letters. I think it probable that Lord George has something to do with it and that it is a determined effort to oust you from the London School of Economics as unfair to institutions. You will have to be very cool and careful in what you do and say. My advice is don't write off in a hurry. It is clear that it would be intolerable if even Professors let alone Governors were debarred from expressing their views on current topics. The great thing however is to let the matter blow over. Whether or not it would be desirable for you to resign the chairmanship for a time (as you are going away) is open to question. But I am inclined to sit still and say as little as possible except that [it] is clear that individual members of the governing body must be allowed to have their own views on political and economic questions. You may lose your railway class!

Anyhow, dear one, don't worry about it. We have got to go straight forward to our goal as discreetly and wisely as we can, but without fear of consequences. There is going to be a great back-up against the advancing tide and it is not surprising that the Railway directors are angry with you. We may have to sacrifice one aspect of our work to another – or let it go into abeyance. It is wonderful how long we have been able to carry on both departments simultaneously.

I had a pleasant little gathering yesterday. The office is working at full swing.

583 PP SIDNEY TO BEATRICE

This letter was written before Sidney received Beatrice's letter written on the previous day. The Webbs met in Glasgow on 22 October and jointly composed Sidney's answer to the railway directors. The Social Democratic Federation went through several changes of name, becoming the S.D.P. (Social Democratic Party) and the B.S.P. (British Socialist Party) – one faction later reverting to the old title of Social Democratic Federation.

Ashbrook, Arbroath
18/10/10

My own dearest

I had quite a good meeting last night – some 500 people. Mostly men, of working class, but with all the local Councillors and School Board, some

351

clergy and teachers and doctors and so on – quite non-party. I gave a good stiff lecture on the Unemployment Scheme, and dealt with the S.D.P. hecklers all right – Harcourt and others of all sides spoke on vote of thanks. This morning is fine and sunny, but cold; and I go on to Dundee presently.

The announcement of resignation from the School of Lord Claud Hamilton, Inglis and Bury is a blow; but it cannot be helped. There is, of course, no ground for their resignation – Lord Claud himself makes violent speeches, and I don't see how we can get Governors who will not do so. However, we have lately secured definite pledges from all the Companies to renew their fixed contributions for three years, so that I hope it will not mean any collapse of our Railway Department. No doubt I might have been more prudent and guarded in my language, but even then I could not have prevented the short reports in the newspapers which are what has been resented.

After all, I am that sort of person, and what is wonderful is that we should have gone on so long, and got on so far. It is lucky that there is no ground for connecting my speech with the School; and that the trouble has not arisen out of anything about the School as such. It is lucky, too, that it comes just at the moment when we are financially prosperous. We will consider whether, in view of the fact that we shall be going away next year, it may not be just as well for me not to be re-elected as Chairman in December, and let Sir John Cockburn take my place as Chairman for a couple of years. He might do better as a money-raiser; and it might help us with the present majority on the L.C.C., without doing any harm elsewhere.

It is interesting that it is said that there is to be a 'Majority' meeting got up here in Arbroath, but it will be a small affair, and it may not come off.

Harcourt and I will stay for Thursday night at Esk Park, Brechin, at the house of another wealthy manufacturer – in case you get this in time to use that address.

This man here (Webster) is an acquaintance of Leonard's, and Leonard [Courtney] came to see him when staying at Bervie. They knew the Olivers, and have New Zealand connections. It was he who got John Morley to stand as M.P. here, when he was without a seat. He is a very good specimen of the enlightened Liberal successful manufacturer (of canvas and coarse linens), an ancestral business of a hundred years standing. They have three sons at Rugby, Clifton and Winchester respectively.

I have of course no letter from you, but I shall find one at Dundee in a few hours. It is terribly lonesome without you, and this whole business of lecturing is a horrid nuisance. But it is only in this way that we can get the thing 'over the footlights', and probably the most valuable element is the general prospectus which we have thereby been able to circulate all over Scotland. You will be having a busy time at the office, but I hope not overdoing it, and managing to eat and sleep. Dear One, I shall be very glad to get to you on Saturday afternoon, whenever it may turn out to be, even though we shall have to separate on Tuesday. We shall soon be through with this job, and in December we can get back a little to our home life.

Goodbye

Sidney

584 PP BEATRICE TO SIDNEY

A meeting of L.S.E. governors was held in London on 29 October.

[?Edinburgh or Glasgow]
[18 or 19 October 1910]

My own dearest

I was glad to get your two sweet letters. We must go straight forward with our work without fear or favour but with the wisest of discretion for all the interests we have at heart. You will have to have some sort of reply but I do not think there is any hurry for it and I should limit it entirely to the freedom of Governors. Indeed there ought to be freedom to express them *inside* the institution tho' of course, one set of opinions ought not to dominate. But apart from the reply which ought to be as dignified and restrained as possible I think it might be desirable to consider the position on the governing body of the School. I should advise the unqualified acceptance of the resignations by the Board of Governors on the ground that they could not enquire into the sayings of Governors or Chairmen of Governors. But I am inclined to think it might be desirable for you to retire from the Chairmanship for a year or so. What is desirable is to keep a good majority on the Board and therefore it is best to *accept resignations* but to remove the most obvious cause of complaint in your chairmanship.

The *Times* article which I send you (please keep it as I want to put it into my diary) lets the cat out of the bag. It is the Minority Report agitation which has led to this attack. It is another indirect reply from Lord G. Hamilton – an attempt to injure us as he cannot fight us.

Of course we always did know that agitation would interfere in more ways than one with our scientific research. But it is clear to me that the time has come for agitation and that we have to go through with it. Public opinion is in a ferment and we have to guide that ferment – as we are the only people with sufficient knowledge and a sufficiently consistent philosophy. We have got to use ourselves up in this and in all our other work, and the opposition which is raising against us is in itself a testimony to the success of our work.

Lloyd George's striking speech at Campbelton is significant. Also the miserable manifesto of the '[*illegible*] Tories' – they will never win on that

353

– the philosophy of it is fear and dislike of any collectivist movement in favour of the working class.

Now darling goodbye

Ever your devoted wifey<br>
Beatrice Webb

P.S. Reeves has just been here and we have discussed the situation produced by the *Times* article. He thinks that you ought to reply in very measured terms pointing out that the views objected to had nothing to do with the School and were expressed in your capacity as a private citizen and that it would be [?intolerable] if difficulties were raised with regard to the expression of opinion by Governors. That it would be better to avoid *all* controversy as to the subject matter.

Also he wants a meeting of the Governors and that you should attend it. It would be possible for you to let me or *Harcourt* take the meeting on Friday 28th at Greenock and for you to go down by the next mail on Thursday and to come to Whittinghame by the next mail on Saturday. Could you not arrange that? I have no meeting on Friday 28th and could take it or Harcourt could take it if he would do us the favour. Let Reeves know what you will do. I think it is desirable to see the Governors and go into the matter. My own feeling is resist quietly the attack and after that is done make matters easier by resigning the chairmanship before *next session's* negotiations. It would be a mistake to resign now as that would be giving way to the attack and presently they would ask for Reeves' resignation. I have advised Reeves to give up his speechmaking.

BW

### 585 PP   SIDNEY WEBB TO LORD CLAUD HAMILTON

The meeting of L.S.E. governors unanimously passed a vote of confidence in Webb and the railway interests did not press the threat to sever relations with the L.S.E. Beatrice concluded from the row that when the Webbs returned from their coming world tour they would have to play a less prominent role in the affairs of L.S.E. if they proposed to continue public campaigning for their advanced ideas. In another long letter on the same theme to Sir Alfred Lyall, a governor of L.S.E. (n.d. PP), Sidney confessed that his speech was 'somewhat indiscreet' and claimed that he was 'badly misreported'. He was at pains to clear himself of the charges that he opposed arbitration of industrial dispute. But he again insisted that L.S.E. must accord 'belligerent rights' to all opinions.

41 Grosvenor Road,<br>
Westminster<br>
October 22nd 1910

Dear Lord Claud Hamilton

It was, I need hardly say, with the greatest concern and regret that I read in the newspapers of the 18th inst. the letter which subsequently reached my house, resigning your position as a governor of the London School of Economics. Simultaneously I read, also in the newspapers, the letters of Mr Inglis, dated October 15, and of Mr Bury, dated October 17, which seem to have been forwarded at the same time. The reason given for this concerted action was not any dissatisfaction with the London School of Economics or with any doing of mine as its chairman, but the disapproval of the opinions expressed by me in an address to the Executive Council of the Amalgamated Society of Railway Servants a month previously.

That address, which had not the remotest connection with the London School of Economics, was one that I was invited to deliver as historian of the trade union movement. It would have filled four columns of *The Times*, and the newspaper reporters could naturally give only about one sentence out of every thirty. Almost inevitably, therefore, the reports gave a false idea of what I said. Some of the misrepresentations were grotesque. One that I have seen gives a sentence uttered (in connection with payment of members) explicitly about the House of Commons, expressly as applying (in connection with the Osborne Judgement) to the House of Lords. Even the fuller report subsequently published in a weekly paper inevitably omits much, suppresses parenthetical qualifications and explanations and cannot avoid some positive inaccuracies. But apart from all this, there is, of course, as we have both always known a fundamental difference between your opinions and mine as to the functions of trade unionism, its relations to employers and to the State, the legal regulation of the conditions of employment, and the expediency of the direct representation of Labour in Parliament. This fundamental difference of opinion in economics and politics has not prevented our cordially working together for the past five years in the business administration of a university institution, during which you, as chairman of its Railway Instruction Committee, have done so much to organise the higher education which both you and I think necessary for railway administrators. During those five years you have expressed – and quite rightly expressed – both to your shareholders and to your parliamentary constituents, the views that you take on the economics and politics of railway administration, in public speeches which (if you will forgive me for saying so) have seemed to me to contain many statements 'at variance with the facts and calculated to mislead the minds' (to use your own words about my less important utterances). But it never occurred to me, notwithstanding the strong, and as I believe erroneous views on the economics and politics of railway administration that you publicly expressed, to question the ability, public spirit, and impartiality of your chairmanship of our Railway Instruction Committee; or to resign my position as a member of that committee, in protest against the public utterance of views so contrary to my estimate of what is in the public interest.

355

## Free Speech

But your letter raises a larger issue – nothing less, in short, than that of freedom of thought and freedom of speech in university administration. By common consent, the London School of Economics has from the first been organised and administered without a shadow of partiality for one set of opinions or another, as its first director, Mr W.A.S. Hewins, has so aptly and generously testified in *The Times* of October 22. Owing largely to this strict impartiality and genuine freedom of teaching, it has in 15 years attained its present unique position. Whilst for the first 12 years of its existence its successive directors and many of its professors happened to hold militant Tariff Reform and Conservative opinions, it received the constant support of a Progressive and Free Trade county council, as well as that of Government departments presided over by Liberal Ministers. This impartiality of administration and freedom of teaching, indispensable in a university institution, have been rendered possible only by the presence among the governors of men of every shade of political and economic thought, who come together (knowing each other's views) on the common basis of organising the best available instruction and the most open-minded research in the science and technique of administration in its widest sense, whether governmental, municipal, railway, or commercial. And if freedom of thought and freedom of speech are vitally necessary to the salaried director and professors within the institution, it is plain that a like freedom cannot be denied to those men and women of public position or specialised attainments who, without fee or reward of any kind, give up some portion of their time to serving on the governing bodies of these educational institutions. On this point I speak as one having had many years' experience in the difficult task of recruiting a sufficient number of these indispensable volunteers for the couple of hundred governing bodies of the higher educational institutions of the metropolis. If such governors or chairmen of governing bodies or committees are to be precluded, outside the institutions with which they are connected, from making speeches on public issues that some of their colleagues think inaccurate, indiscreet, or against the public interest, the administration of educational institutions by unpaid men and women of position will become impracticable, and we shall have to depend on a bureaucracy paid to be silent, or paid to express only such views as are agreeable to the national or municipal government for the time being.

## In a Dilemma

There remains the comparatively unimportant question of my personality. It is of course desirable that the chairman of any corporate body should not (whether for good reasons or bad) be personally distasteful to any of his colleagues. The unanimity of my successive re-elections as chairman, and the unbroken cordiality of my relations with every one of my colleagues – not least with those of them whose political and economic opinions differ most fundamentally from those that I am so well known to hold – made your letter (published without a word of previous inquiry or explanation with me) come as a painful shock. If it had been intimated to me at any time that some other governor would be more acceptable to my colleagues, or even to any fraction of them, I would gladly have made place for a more popular business head. The School is now so well established that it is of little consequence who among the fifty governors acts as chairman of the Court or of any of its committees. As a matter of fact, in the course of 1911–12 I expect to be away from England on a prolonged tour of the East, which would, in any case, have necessitated some arrangement of chairmanships among the governors. But your public denunciation of my chairmanship on the express ground of the opinions that I hold – supported by a leading article in *The Times* explicitly requiring me to resign on account of the opinions of myself and my wife – places me in a dilemma. If I follow the natural prompting of good manners, and tender my resignation, I shall be responsible for submitting to the ostracism of particular views which a great financial interest thinks objectionable; and for thus bringing to an end the reign of tolerance and impartiality which has hitherto prevailed at the London School of Economics, and which, in my judgment, is indispensable to a university institution. If, on the other hand, I retain the post to which you and the rest of my colleagues unanimously elected me last December, you compel me to feel that I have, through your personal dislike of me, caused the school to lose the services, in the conduct of its business, of such able and experienced administrators as Mr Bury, Mr Inglis, and yourself. In this dilemma I can only consult with my colleagues as to what is best for the permanent interests of university education in the subjects in which you and I are concerned.

Under the circumstances I think that you will not object to my sending this letter to the Press.

I am, yours faithfully,

Sidney Webb

## 586 PP  SIDNEY TO BEATRICE

Both the Webbs were busy with speaking engagements; several omitted letters from Sidney deal with minor details of meetings and contain descriptions of families with whom he stayed. On 2 November (PP) Beatrice wrote him a mild reproof. 'By the way, will you be *very urbane* over questions: it appears that you sometimes frighten people by snubbing them – Prof. Seth is very anxious we should answer questions sympathetically however silly they may be.' Andrew Seth (1856–1931), who changed his name to Pattison, was professor of logic and metaphysics at Edinburgh 1891–1919; he was a prominent supporter of the campaign in Scotland.

On 18 November Asquith announced the dissolution of Parliament on 28 November. The general election, the second within the year, produced a similar result: the Liberals and Tories each won 272 seats, but 84 Irish and 42 Labour seats gave the government a majority against the Lords so long as it remained committed to Home Rule. Will Crooks in Woolwich and Harry Smith of Huddersfield stood as candidates sponsored by the Fabian Society; this was a gesture towards Fabians who wished the Society to take a more positive attitude towards parliamentary contests.

41 Grosvenor Road
Westminster Embankment
18.11.10

My own dear one

Your very nice letter came last night. I have ordered Book box to go to Miller, and answered Brockhouse of West Bromwich. I hope you will get your galoshes today at Walsall – but the weather here is bright and sunny, though very cold.

I send you *The Times*, in case you care to read the fullest reports of the speeches. You will notice that Balfour is emphatic about maintaining the Osborne Judgement and keeping the T.U. out of politics; and that he stops at only *mentioning* Poor Law, without a word of actual commitment. I gather that the dissolution *is* to be on 28 November (without any 'guarantees'!) The first polls may be in the first week of December – how about

| *My lectures* | | *Your lectures* |
|---|---|---|
| 5 December | West Bromwich | Brighton Libs. |
| 6 ,, | Oxford Young Libs. | Battersea |
| 7 ,, | F.S. | |
| 9 ,, | | Rugby |
| 10 ,, | Plymouth | Battersea |
| 11 ,, | ,, | |

This, however, involves the very minimum of interference with our lecturing.

I shall go to the office this afternoon on my way to Woking, to speed things up. We must 'keep cool', and let things happen – the education of the country with our ideas goes on.

Farley (whom I saw yesterday at one of my Seminars – the gentle ex-Unitarian minister) said that Offor (late of the Progressive League) declared that Burns had told him that 'eventually we should come to the Minority Report'! But this means nothing, and is probably untrue.

I saw Graham Wallas for a few minutes at the School, full of energy – his child steadily improving in health. He said the School was flourishing, and that Reeves had told him that the Midland Railway Co. had decided to send students to our Railway Dept. in January next, apparently by way of (Liberal) protest against Lord Claud! Reeves had also (very rashly!)

told Wallas that he hoped to get £2,000 surplus out of the School in the present and next year, and begin building with it.

The Fabian Executive decides today to issue appeal to its members for funds (£800) to support Crooks and Snell, as its contribution to the Labor Party. I think we must subscribe £5 or £10. The Society is committed to finding the money at once – I enclose some interesting and satisfactory letters as to Nat. Committee work.

Goodbye, now, dearest. Your lecturing job will soon be over now, and you have only to hold out for a few days more. We are getting on very well, I think, and it is bound to have its effect. Courage!

Sidney

### 587 PP   SIDNEY WEBB TO EDWARD PEASE

41 Grosvenor Road
Westminster Embankment
18.11.10

Dear Pease

I ought before to have asked to be excused from Executive, for previous meetings and today, (when I have to speak at Woking). I think I am of more use lecturing about than merely attending Executive meetings, though I hope now to return to them.

I hope the Executive will do their utmost at this contest – *for* Labor or Socialist candidates where they are really serious (notably our own two), and elsewhere whatever is most effective *against* the House of Lords. We have a very powerful tide of general reaction to resist, and unless we do stem it now, we shall have to fight every single issue at a grave disadvantage.

Sidney Webb

### 588 PF   SIDNEY WEBB TO SIR HORACE PLUNKETT

Beatrice had decided to set up a research department for the Poor Law campaign, employing some of the bright young university graduates who had come in as Fabians or as supporters of the movement.

Sir Francis Hopwood (1860–1947), who had served in the Colonial Office, was appointed vice-chairman of the Development Commission, of which Sidney had been a member since April.

41 Grosvenor Road
Westminster Embankment
25.11.10

My dear Plunkett

My wife and I are overwhelmed with gratitude for your generous kindness in sending £100 in aid of the research side of the Prevention of Destitution work. This is real helpfulness, and we thank you sincerely, as

359

much for your trust in us, as for the substantial aid – because it is that kind of appreciative confidence which gives encouragement and stimulus. We *do* need the money, because we are spending all that we have of our own, and all that we get given to us, and yet we cannot pay for all the expenses that come along.

Now (unless you signify objection) this is how we propose to deal with your donation. We propose, after Christmas, to put it to the credit of a new fund, to be called the Research and Education Fund, to be expended solely on the objects indicated by the title. But we propose to keep back the item from the official accounts *until after Christmas* (and therefore not to send you official receipt); because we hope then to try to get some more money for this and other purposes from other potential donors. One other donor has already half promised to give us £100, *on condition that nine others do likewise*. We want to use your £100 to induce him to confirm his proposal, by telling him that we can guarantee at any rate, a seconder! This will help us, also, to find the eight others. I feel sure that you will not object to our getting the utmost value out of your donation – especially as nothing useful can be done in the present month, amid the election turmoil.

I am interested in the rumour as to Sir Francis Hopwood. If there is a vacancy I will remember Mr. H. [?] but the appointment will lie with the Chancellor of the Exchequer (I assume) – certainly not with the Development Commissioners themselves.

My wife and I are both sorry to have been out when you called – we were both lecturing, in different towns!

Yours very truly

Sidney Webb

589 PP  SIDNEY TO BEATRICE

Charles Whitley and Edward Whitley were strong supporters of the Webbs: they were, Sidney told Pease (FP 5 December 10) young Fabians 'of great wealth and no occupation'. Charles was killed in the First World War; Edward became one of the main financial backers and a director for many years of the *New Statesman*. Frederick James Marquis (1883–1964), later Lord Woolton, was involved in socialist activity as a student at Manchester University. He first became Warden of the University Settlement in Liverpool and later the head of a large department store and Minister of Food in 1940. Sir James Sexton (1865–1938), leader of the dockworkers and a founding member of the I.L.P., became president of the T.U.C. in 1905.

[Blackburn]

28/11/10

Dear One

I am to lunch at 6 Croxteth Drive, but stay with *Charles* Whitley (whose address I have not got!), so unless you can find his address (it is at Neston,

I think) I shall not get your letters on Wednesday morning. (But I will try to post you the address today.)

Last night's meeting was a great one in numbers – the theatre crowded (over 2,000 people). But I doubt whether that kind of meeting is of much use. The local I.L.P. runs a regular Sunday Evening Meeting all through the year – with songs and choir, just like a Pleasant Sunday Afternoon affair, with the lecture thrown in. The audience comes as to evening service and not to learn! Most of them are I.L.P. members, and many are young people taking it as an alternative to Chapel. I gave a good enough lecture, and had to answer the usual S.D.P. questions, but I did not feel that it was of very much use. However, these people probably don't read, and this is the only way of getting to them, and moreover, the literature was on sale. I got my 3rd Class return fare.

It has occurred to me several times that it might be well to make a rule to have *in all our pamphlets*, a Membership Form perforated for detaching. It seems a pity to be circulating hundreds of thousands of tracts, which go into all sorts of corners, without a detachable Membership Form. The adoption of the coloured cover seems a good opportunity for beginning this plan.

I don't feel at all confident now that the Liberals will hold all their present majority – the attack seems too fierce to be withstood in the weaker places. I see it is said that the Conservative Central Office expects to reduce the adverse majority from 120 to 70. This gain of 25 seats is probably their utmost hopes. Anything like that would inevitably mean a compromise on the House of Lords, and probably a 'marking time' Liberal Government for a year or two, which would do nothing (except the compromise) for 1911, and nothing very 'party' in 1912; i.e. *not* Home Rule, Welsh Disestablishment or Education. It *might* therefore do Insurance and Poor Law, conceivably. This *might* therefore be as good for our particular interests as a Liberal victory. At any rate, we could not be sure that it was a calamity. On the whole I prefer to hope for a Liberal gain of a few seats.

Dear One, it is wet and cold and dreary, and I am lonely and dispirited without my companion and partner. I shall go for a little walk presently, just to see the town, and because you say I ought to have a little exercise; and then I shall go on to Liverpool. I think I have had about enough of this provincial lecturing with its perpetual separations. And tomorrow you have to start again, in the cold and wet. Pray be careful of your dear self. Goodbye.

Sidney

I am to see Marquis and perhaps Sexton at lunch.

George Lansbury, after losing Bow and Bromley in January, was given a clear run against the Conservative in December and won easily. A good deal of covert arranging, especially with Dr John Clifford and the Nonconformists, had secured the Liberal withdrawal in his favour.

41 Grosvenor Road
Westminster Embankment
1.12.10

Dear One

Your very charming letter came late last night, but this morning I got the one you sent to Croxteth Drive. I hope you surmounted the fog all right and got in safely to Bolton. Here it rained in torrents and blew in great gusts, amid which I sallied out to Deptford, to find an excited meeting of workmen, all supporters of Bowerman, being addressed by a very eloquent mob orator of a Catholic priest – a certain Father Hopkins, an ex-naval Chaplain with land and a motor car, living in Hampshire who had come up to London to help any Labor candidate. We ought to try to get hold of him for the M.R.

Charles Whitley telegraphs that he cannot come, so we shall only be seven tonight, and one to sleep.

I will do what I can with the Executive, as regards money etc. We must evidently try to raise a fund of £1,000 as you say; and with £300 promised or given we *may* be able to do it – I don't feel that we have yet got people convinced about Part II, or indeed even really aware of it. I see the General Federation of Trade Unions and the Parliamentary Committee of the T.U. Congress do not, in their Manifestos, evince any consciousness that Unemployment ought to be *prevented* – they are still only at relief of one sort or other.

I am getting more and more uncomfortable about the Election. I should not now be surprised if the Unionists win a score of seats on balance wholly in London and the South and Midlands. This would make them the strongest single party in the House, and leave the Government only a composite majority of 84 – possibly, therefore, open to defeat by the changing over in a division of the Labor Party alone. This would mean a compromise on the Constitutional question, with the revolt of all the extreme section; but it might mean also a complete stagnation of legislation, even social legislation. However, we can only strive and wait.

I am glad you wrote to Dr Clifford, and that he replied favorably. I don't see what more we can do for Lansbury (to whom I wrote yesterday, saying you had written to Dr Clifford). I don't suppose Hugh Smith has any real information, or that the sanguine hopes of Amery and his friends are based on much actual knowledge. But of course the 'moderate' men may abstain, and a proportion of the poorest electors may be lost by removals. I have just been interrupted by a visit of a young lady of Manchester, a Miss Reiss, daughter of a cotton person, along with her French governess(?), who had heard you somewhere, and wants to 'hook on'. I gave her appropriate advice, and retained her address for your use.

Now goodbye dearest – until tomorrow.

Sidney

591 LP  SIDNEY WEBB TO GEORGE LANSBURY

Aware that public interest was focused on the constitutional crisis and the general election the Webbs ended the year feeling 'weary and somewhat dispirited' about their campaign. (BWD 10 December 10) Membership was falling off and, Beatrice noted, 'our friends are beginning to melt away'. She estimated that they could continue on the same lines for another six months, collecting sufficient money to tide the movement over during their long absence abroad, but she felt that they would probably have to abandon their hope of establishing a permanent organisation. 'In case we had to wind up the National Committee, I should throw the remnant and some of our energy into revivifying the Fabian Society.'

Henry Schloesser, later Slesser (b. 1883), Fabian and lawyer, later held legal office under MacDonald and became lord justice of appeal. He drafted the Poor Law Bills prepared by the campaign as a propagandist device.

41 Grosvenor Road
Westminster Embankment
12.12.10

Dear Lansbury

1) The L.C.C. resolutions as to Mentally Defective are all right. If there is any chance of speaking on them, I should utilise it to point out that they would mean the 'taking out of the Poor Law' of about one-sixth of the present paupers, and the transfer from the existing workhouses of (in the U.K.) tens of thousands of imbeciles, and (even in London) of many hundreds, who are now there.

2) You are quite right about Separate Bills, as well as a general one. Schloesser is getting them ready. There will be one on Unemployment, one for the Sick, one for the Mentally Defective, one for the Children and one for the Aged. We must get different M.P.s to introduce these: we can hardly hope to draw the first day in the ballot this time again! Robert Harcourt M.P. will gladly help to arrange with you.

3) Subject to what he may advise, I think there ought to be a meeting of sympathetic M.P.s of all parties to form a 'Minority Report Group', with its own three Secretaries – one Liberal, one Labour, one Unionist – to take advantage of any chances that arise.

4) But I doubt the wisdom of an Albert Hall Demonstration on the M.R. just at this moment. After all, the M.P.s must do the House of Lords business first!

The newspapers and the public won't think of anything else, just when the new House meets. I think we should reserve this until later – we may be able to get a debate on the M.R. somehow – and just before the debate would be a better moment.

When the moment comes, might it not be better to make it an Unemployment demonstration, instead of M.R. generally, to demand that the Government should do something (i.e. take over Hollesley Bay and add others) which they can [do] administratively without legislation, on a mere vote in Supply. This might be easier to get the I.L P. to take up.

5) We are more pleased at your election than at *any* other. It is great.

Sidney Webb

P.S. I did your job at Plymouth Saturday and Sunday – four meetings.

### 592 PP  SIDNEY TO BEATRICE

Joseph Thorp, dramatic critic of *Punch*, later (1917) established the Romney Street Group as a luncheon-club for liberally-minded civil servants and intellectuals temporarily in government service. His Agenda Club was an attempt to create a prestigious group to sponsor socially useful projects. Sidney reported to Beatrice (9 October 1910 PP) that Thorp had appointed him as a sponsor.

Ayot St Lawrence<br>Sunday morning [? 18 December 1910]

Dearest

I write this at Ayot, in brilliant sunshine. I hope you have the same weather, and the same comfort, if not quite the same friendly surroundings.

Yesterday I wrote a lot of letters and did sundry work. But it is not easy to grapple with big jobs in this distraction – which happily will now soon be over.

The Shaws are both feeling that the Fabian Society has been a little left behind by the National Committee and that a new departure must be found for it – there is a Committee sitting to try to evolve some new items of programme. I think I must help them with suggestions.

Did I remember to tell you that Thorp of the Agenda Club replied that he would put in anything I like. I thought I had better draft a paragraph for him, and he now writes hoping to get it included. We shall see. *If* it goes in, I think I am justified in adhering.

By the way, it is a pity that the King and Queen are going to India just when we shall be there. We shall have to keep at the other end of the country in order to avoid the crowd and the expense, which rather hampers our route.

We are going to motor over to the Phillimores to tea this afternoon, which will be a convenient way of seeing them. For this reason Shaw and I are going out for a walk this morning, which will bring my letter to an untimely close.

Shaw read his new little play *The Dark Lady*, which is a very short scene to be acted at a Shakespear Memorial Theatre function this week. It is a most amusing scene between Shakespear (who had gone to meet his 'dark lady' of the Sonnets) and Queen Elizabeth (whom he at first mistakes for her), and the dark lady herself who interrupts them by suddenly boxing both their ears on discovering her Shakespear with an unknown woman. It will take the public fancy as a *jeu d'esprit*. I have also read his preface to *Doctor's Dilemma*, a most scathing attack on the general practitioner and on vivisection, ending up with glorification of the salaried Public Health Service.

Now goodbye dear one. I hope this will get to you in time.

Sidney

### 593 FP   SIDNEY WEBB TO EDWARD PEASE

A number of Japanese socialists had been accused of a plot: some were executed and others sentenced to long prison terms. The Webbs learned more of the case, which aroused widespread protests, during their visit to Japan later in the year. Sidney was clearly anxious at this time to do nothing which might embarrass that visit.

41 Grosvenor Road<br>Westminster Embankment<br>5.1.11

Dear Pease

Our 'acquaintance' with the Japanese Ambassador is not such as to warrant our writing to him about the Japanese Socialists; and it is not easy to see how anything can be gained by anyone writing to an Ambassador on such a point.

Moreover, the enclosed in today's *Times* seems to knock the bottom out of the particular allegations. We may think the procedure objectionable, but Japan copied Germany, not England, in these matters; and we cannot expect them to see that our procedure is so Divinely inspired as to make the other inherently unfair.

Personally I think we should be careful how we assume that people *called* Socialists (or even people who call themselves Socialists) in other countries are our friends. I don't want to see even murderers deprived of a fair trial etc.; but every enemy of a government is not a collectivist.

Sidney Webb

The Webbs spent Christmas at Fisher's Hill, Woking, the home of Gerald and Betty Balfour, which was loaned to them for a holiday. They took several of their young friends with them, including Amber Reeves and her husband, now reconciled. While there Beatrice realised (BWD n.d.) that the victorious Liberals were unlikely to take up the Poor Law case, preferring to press on with the 'most unscientific state aid' in the form of a national insurance scheme: 'if it were not for the advantage of proposing to transfer the millions from the rich to the poor, we should oppose it root and branch'. She saw some virtue in combining voluntary unemployment insurance with the compulsory use of labour exchanges (rather than the converse proposed by the government), but she rejected the sickness scheme as 'wholly bad' and likely to lead to malingering. She intensely disliked measures which were a 'mechanical way of increasing the money-income of a wage-earning class' without attempting to secure 'an advance in conduct in return for the increased income'. The Webbs, she felt, were handicapped by the fact that Lloyd George and Winston Churchill, the ministers most likely to attempt a reform of the Poor Law, were directly responsible for the insurance schemes which the Webbs felt obliged to attack: 'we have to dance on eggs without cracking them – we shall have to try and invent some way out for L.G.'.

Early in February the Webbs, trying to devise such 'a way out' for Lloyd George, had concocted an alternative policy to combine sickness insurance with the public health administration. They pressed it on Lloyd George and his colleagues, and also on Arthur Balfour, but with a sense that it was merely a symbolic parting shot. In March they let their house for a year, spending five weeks in Eastbourne and two months at Luton Hoo before sailing for Canada. During these spring months they worked up their campaign material into *The Prevention of Destitution*, published later in 1911, as a textbook for their supporters.

Beatrice was coming to see that the emphasis of the Webb campaign was changing from an attempt to push the proposals of the Minority Report to a wider concern with destitution and social reform. While she hoped on their return to England to resume their local government research she thought it likely that their younger supporters might be diverted to 'a big campaign for a socialist party with a self-conscious collectivist programme'. (BWD 16 January 11) Indeed, as she noted three months later, the Webbs might initiate such a campaign. The attitude of the government and the leaderless state of its radical opponents made Beatrice feel that 'our duty, when we return, *may be* to throw ourselves into the democratic movement'. Though Sidney disliked public speaking and agitation, she thought that unless some new leader emerged in the Labour Party or the Fabian Society, 'we are doomed to offer ourselves as officers of the larger crusade to conquer the land of promise'. (BWD 18 March 11)

41 Grosvenor Road
Westminster Embankment
29.1.11

Dear Professor Brentano

My wife and I send you cordial greetings!

We venture to introduce to you our young friend Rupert Brooke, a distinguished Cambridge graduate, full of charm and poetry, who is temporarily at Munich studying German literary criticism of English literature.

But he is also interested in Economic problems, especially Poor Law; and he is a keen supporter of what we call the Minority Report campaign for the complete supersession of the Poor Law by the newer Municipal authorities for dealing with Sickness, Children and the Aged etc.

Will you kindly allow him the privilege of some talk with you?

Yours very truly

Sidney Webb

595 PP   BEATRICE WEBB TO GEORGINA MEINERTZHAGEN

By some backstairs efforts Beatrice managed to secure the approval of Lord George Hamilton for the proposals of a Poor Law Committee set up by the County Councils Association. She and her three co-signatories of the Minority Report also approved the suggestions. The scheme proposed by the Association would have broken up the Poor Law, putting the unemployed and defectives under specialised agencies, the sick under the public health authorities and children under education. It was possible for all parties nominally to subscribe to this scheme, since it saved the face of the Majority by leaving a single Poor Law authority to oversee the whole system while giving the Minority its essential concession of specialised agencies. Beatrice considered this manouevre a great victory. But the new scheme was still opposed by the powerful C.O.S. and disregarded by the government: in the event it came to nothing, for the moment for such a compromise had been lost in the last months of the Commission when Beatrice had brusquely written off her colleagues and pushed for the undiluted proposals of the Minority.

Beachy Head

[? March 1911]

Dearest Geo

Ever so many thanks for contribution – it is very generous of you and I hope you will be rewarded by seeing the fulfilment of our scheme of reform. I have a great idea of making our National Council the real Charity Organisation Society – that is to say, getting all volunteers and voluntary institutions grouped under the public authorities concerned with neglected infancy, neglected childhood and adolescence, old age, feeble-mindedness and unemployment. If we could get all our effort, *Public* and *Private*, really organised and registered, I believe the money we are already spending in a chaotic and spasmodic way would be more than sufficient to do the job efficiently. But we must have behind all this good will and expenditure, the element of compulsion and *disciplinary supervision* – of the persons who are aided, and that could only be exercised by a Public authority. At least that is the philosophy of the Minority Report. It is no use letting the poor come and go, as they think fit, be helped or not – helped as the charitable choose. That is really pauperism and encourages persons to be parasites.

Destitution must be prevented and where necessary penalised as a public nuisance.

We are up here for three days. We had a crowded meeting of Eastbourne residents – 300 persons having paid 1/- for the privilege of hearing us. The politicians make a great mistake in assuming that the Budget is the only interesting subject!

Ever yours affectionately<br>
Beatrice Webb

### 596 BL  SIDNEY WEBB TO GEORGE BERNARD SHAW

'The Fabian Society is going through a crisis, not of dissent, but of indifference', Beatrice noted on 7 March. The Old Gang had beaten Wells but, with Shaw busy with his theatrical life, the Webbs taken up in their Poor Law campaign, Olivier abroad and Bland in poor health, they had done nothing with their victory. The Society had simply drifted through a period of intense political excitement in the country at large without doing anything distinctive. In March 1910 Hubert Bland had written to Webb complaining that 'our members are fed up with defeat' and pointing out tartly that 'the Fabian policy of delay is to delay the enemy but not to delay yourself'. (FP 27 March 10) On 22 March 1911 Shaw made a similar protest: 'apart from pure routine', he wrote to the Webbs, 'there has been absolutely no *raison d'être* for the Society' in recent years. Provoked by Sidney's proposal to resign at last from the Fabian executive, on the grounds that he would be away for nearly a year, Shaw suggested that all the older leaders should resign and make room for younger people. He put forward a scheme for something like a Fabian senate, formed from the senior members, who 'wearing togas if necessary' should attend executive meetings without the power to vote. Webb responded with a plea for a class of consultative executive members, co-opted for three years by the elected members. This proposal was bitterly attacked at the Fabian annual meeting as undemocratic: though Webb's motion was passed by a narrow majority he refused to press it on the grounds that it was apparently too contentious. Shaw and Bland nevertheless retired from the executive.

4 Derwent Road<br>
Eastbourne<br>
6/3/11

Dear Shaw

I still prefer the Consultative Members. It might be added to the rule that they might at any time (a) meet to confer, and (b) memorialise the Society. This meets your *only* objection to them. The Senate idea seems not only ridiculous but also incorrect. It implies *regular* separate meeting, and *habitual* collective action of the Senators as such. That we don't want.

And I still think we had better retire separately. The shock argument disappears if there *is* no shock. And there will be none if we are merely one by one printed in italics!

Yours<br>
Sidney Webb

I have sent your letter to Miss Gillmore.

F. Lawson Dodd, not Ensor, replaced Hubert Bland as Treasurer: Bland, his eyesight failing, dropped out of activity and died in April 1914.

> 4 Derwent Road, Eastbourne
> 8.3.11

Dear Pease

I enclose my proposal, which you may perhaps be able to circulate to Executive (which I cannot manage to attend in person). If Bland insists on retiring, it is quite graceful that he should become the first Consultative Member. I strongly deprecate any other retirements, beyond that of Chiozza Money already announced, as he obviously cannot attend. Two vacancies, with more in prospect, is enough for immediate ventilation.

I strongly deprecate any simultaneous retirement of the Old Gang. It would inevitably be misunderstood; be taken to imply a diminution of the Society's influence; and be a discouragement to recruiting and work.

We can drop one by one on to the shelf of the Consultative Member without all this shock, and such a procedure has the merit of being in accordance with the facts.

For this reason, as at present advised, I intend to stand for election. If no one else is *simultaneously* retiring in June, I may then do so. But if anyone else retires, I will harden my heart and not resign, leaving my seat to lapse by absence!

> Sidney Webb

I agree as to Ensor for Treasurer.

> 4 Derwent Road, Eastbourne
> 23rd March 1911

Dear Mr Pease

I understand that G.B.S. had nominated me for the Executive. Please withdraw my name. But will you please be so kind as to remember that I want to be nominated for the Executive next year and should be very glad to have G.B.S.'s nomination and your own.

> Always yours sincerely
> Beatrice Webb

Lloyd George had presented his insurance proposals. The first part, dealing with unemployment, was to come forward in the autumn session of Parliament; the second, dealing with sickness, in 1912. The Labour Party, especially its trade union majority wished to support a scheme which plainly benefited its members. Beatrice, however, scathingly dismissed the proposals as 'costly and extravagant' and as irresponsibly handing over twenty million pounds to wage-earners without any conditions, 'to be spent by them, as they think fit, in times of sickness and unemployment'. (BWD 13 May 11) She was also upset by the immediate popularity of the scheme which, she realised, would take the steam out of their own campaign; and she could not dismiss her 'rooted prejudice to relief instead of treatment' or her belief that social distress should always be tackled 'in such a way as to improve conduct'. Despite Sidney's initial opposition to Lloyd George's scheme, Beatrice noted later that he 'wishes the Bill to go through', since he believed that it was capable of useful amendment. In her heart Beatrice knew the battle was over, though she left her supporters to conduct a rearguard campaign against it in her absence: Lloyd George held the initiative and all the high ground.

The Hermitage, Luton Hoo

17.5.11

Dear Sanders

Thanks for letter.

Will you please represent to the Committee on Insurance Bill that unless they are efficient and prompt they will fail to get out even the first of their letters to trade unionists before the Bill is read a second time. They must certainly put something into type *at once*, or it cannot be circulated in paged revise to the Executive on Wednesday 26th, for meeting on Friday, 28th. It ought to be issued on Saturday 29 May.

I hope the F.S. is not going to be as disgracefully incompetent over the Bill as the Labor Party has been!

As to consulting Henderson, let Pease do as he thinks fit. But I do not think that Henderson, who has always been a politician, at all represents the opinion of the great Trade Friendly Societies such as the A.S.E. and A.S. Carpenters.

My feeling is that the working class is being in this matter abandoned by those on whom it ought to rely for advice. There seems no one in the Labor Party able to watch its interests in any complicated matter.

My view of the Bill is 'unfit for publication'!

Sidney Webb

# 8. Round the world
## June 1911–May 1912

The Webbs took almost a year to complete their journey round the world. The record of their travels is substantial but largely unpublished. It consists of 530 pages of typescript in Beatrice's diary, which she never had the time or much inclination to work up into a planned book on the Far East, and a considerable number of letters. Most of these letters were written to Beatrice's sisters, Catherine Courtney and Mary Playne, and to members of the staff of the Poor Law campaign. The letters were intended to be passed around for reading and some extracts appeared in the campaign journal, *The Crusade*. The contents consist largely of travelogues, describing the scenery and conditions seen by the Webbs as they journeyed successively across Canada, through Japan, Korea, China, Malaya, Burma and India. They are interspersed with social and political comments, though none of these are singularly original or important. The letters, moreover, are inordinately long: pressure on space has made it impossible to publish more than a representative selection. The majority may be found among the Passfield Papers and some letters to Clifford Sharp are in the University of Texas collection.

It was an exhausting odyssey. Beatrice later claimed that it had a powerful influence on the partnership's conception of the past, present and future of the human race. It certainly preceded a change of political direction as decisive as the shift in attitude which followed the Australian visit in 1898 and the expedition to the Soviet Union in 1932. Though the Webbs missed the great wave of strikes which ran across Britain while they were away, when they returned they were more sympathetic to militant trade unionism and to the ebullient politics of the I.L.P. and the intellectual syndicalists who called themselves Guild Socialists. They were also more critical of imperialism and aware of the rising tide of nationalism in Asia. Their stay in Japan confirmed their *a priori* liking for Japanese efficiency; they were openly contemptuous of China and the Chinese. Beatrice, moreover, returned home with some understanding of the Indian nationalist movement, of the shortcomings of British rule, and of the conflicts that lay ahead; and the Webbs maintained contact with both British and Indian acquaintances met on their tour. Yet the overall impression left by the thousands of written words in diary and letters is one of curious detachment for a couple of social investigators who had a unique opportunity to travel at leisure through Asia in the heyday of the British Empire. They seldom afterwards referred to their experiences or made any serious effort to evaluate them. In retrospect the journey seems like a long ante-room to the next phase of the partnership. When the Webbs arrived back in London they would have to make another fresh start.

In the spring of 1911 Bertrand Russell began his long and complicated relationship with Lady Ottoline Morrell (1873–1938), who became the patronne of the Bloomsbury group. At first his wife Alys agreed to preserve appearances but by the summer she decided to make an open break and to set up house with her brother Logan Pearsall Smith. The Russells were divorced in 1921.

This letter was sent from Kyoto. The medical superintendent of the Toji temple was Dr Kobayashi. The president of the Government University was Baron Kikuchi.

Sept 18th [1911]

Dearest Kate

I have just got your letter of August 17th – (I think I have had all your letters) and it was delightful to hear all your news. Alys Russell wrote to me before we left England to tell me of the catastrophe. Ten years ago, when I took her abroad, there was trouble between them, but we hoped that all this had passed over and that they had settled down. Bertrand Russell has a queer nature, and he is always deceiving himself about his own conduct and motives – he is a bit of an 'A' – Artist, Anarchist and Aristocrat, and inspite of his acquired puritanism, is apt to be swept away by primitive instincts. I think it quite probable, and I hope likely, that when the present impulse has passed away, they may come together again. It is very hard on Alys, as she is a really charming and good woman, and we, who have lived with her, know how easy she is to get on with and how she has always respected Bertie's freedom. Her family are rather trying, but Bertie had only to speak to be delivered from them. They are an excuse for, and not a cause, of the separation. I am sorry now that Bertie went to Cambridge – there is a pernicious set presided over by Lowes Dickinson, which makes a sort of ideal of anarchic ways in sexual questions – we have, for a long time, been aware of its bad influence on our young Fabians. The intellectual star is the metaphysical George Moore with his *Principia Ethica* – a book they all talk of as 'The Truth'! I never can see anything in it, except a metaphysical justification for doing what you like and what other people disapprove of! So far as I can understand the philosophy it is a denial both of the scientific method and of religion – as a rule, that is the net result on the minds of young men – it seems to disintegrate their intellects and their characters.

We have been staying here for the best part of a week and we have rather collapsed in energy in this comfortable and delightfully quiet Hotel (in European style) – sauntering out to see the Temples – and Palaces of Kyoto and having University Professors to talk to us. Tomorrow we start off again for the mountains – spending some six days in Buddhist temples seeing what we can of Buddhist Priests. We try everywhere to get in touch with the leaders of native religious Kyoto thought. There is a great deal of religious feeling in the villages – enormous sums are contributed to support the temples and priests by the peasants and the little shopkeepers and craftsmen, but the enriched classes are mostly of 'no opinion', and wholly materialist. The Buddhists are broken up into rival sects and until lately the priests have had a very bad reputation. Now there are some men of light and learning among them, and a certain revival of interest among the professional classes in Buddhist philosophy. Yesterday we went to see the one Buddhist Hospital of Japan in the grounds of a great and famous temple. The Medical Superintendent was a well-known Surgeon who was also a pious Buddhist, and who seemed to have three grades of treatment according to whether the illness was 'ideal' or 'real' – thought + healing, thought + medicine, thought + medicine + operative surgery. Each patient had a separate room and looking on to a beautiful garden, and when well enough, attended the services of shrine or temple – the hospital was very popular and the government were beginning to subsidize it. Afterwards we were taken over the House of the High Priest and entertained, and shown all the treasures of the Sect – some magnificent sculptures from India brought over 1,200 years ago. We also went to the Buddhist university college of another sect and watched the Priests instructing the young men who want to become Priests – they were simple-minded learned men but not men of affairs or even propagandists. On the other hand, there is no sign that the Christian missionaries are making any headway – they are used as teachers of English, and patronised when they start night school or boys clubs and the government usually subsidizes and to large extent control the Y.M.C.A. – but no one seems to take their doctrinal teaching seriously and they themselves are becoming very 'broad' in their theology. We have seen something of the President of the Government (secular) University who is exactly like the President of an American university – and the University Professors are rather more like English than like American Professors perhaps because of their 'classical' training. They are all civil servants and have to be careful not to incur the reproach of 'dangerous thoughts' – but certainly in their talks with us they were quite free and easy in their criticism of the Government and the status quo. Nearly all the professors of Political Economy in Japan are 'Socialists of the Chair'; and we were pleased to find that they had all our books, even those on English Local Government! Now goodbye dear sister.

Ever yours

Beatrice Webb

601 PP  BEATRICE WEBB TO LADY COURTNEY

The Webbs had let 41 Grosvenor Road to William O'Brien (1852–1928), the Irish nationalist M.P. whose arrest in 1887 had been the immediate cause of the Trafalgar Square riot known as 'Bloody Sunday'.

Sontag's Hotel
Seoul
Korea
Oct 18 1911

Dearest Kate

We are listening with anxiety to the rumblings of revolution in China – wondering whether we shall be allowed to go from Mukden to Pekin – there is a rumour that all passenger traffic has been suspended so as to expedite troops. Anyway our plan of taking the train from Pekin to Hankow and from thence down the Yangtsee to Shanghai is, I fear, doomed, and even if we get to Pekin, we shall have to return to Tientsin and take the steamer from thence to Shanghai – which is annoying! If we change our plans *considerably* we shall telegraph to the office as to dates for letters to be sent to Shanghai and Hong Kong.

We finished our tour in Japan by a steamer down the Inland Sea and two nights at the beautiful Temple Island of Marugame. We were both exhausted by the 11 days at Tokio, suffering from too much entertaining and colds in the head – certainly the Japanese are extraordinarily hospitable. In return Sidney gave them a first-rate lecture on 'How the administrative experience of the British Empire might be made useful to Japan', which seems to have been much appreciated by an audience of Ministers, officials and Professors. What the representatives of the B.E. [British Embassy] thought of it I do not know!

Now we are seeing something of the Japanese administration of Korea. The Koreans are a horrid looking race, and the country is badly cultivated and all the woods cut down – the towns are masses of insanitary mud huts – there are no Temples and no decent Korean habitations – not even tombs for the bodies or spirits of their Ancestors. And yet a few hundred years ago these people were great artists and architects with a fine literature of their own. The whole race seems to have gone into decay. The Japanese seem to be spending a great deal of their own money, and putting a great deal of thought and work into getting the place into some sort of order and teaching the people to work and to save. They are sufficiently like the Chinese in appearance to make intermarriage possible and if anyone can raise the Koreans out of their present state of barbarism I think the Japanese will. The officials have much less 'side' on than would be the case in any European dealing with a coloured people and so far as we can judge, they are really anxious to adapt their administration to the old customs and even to the old superstitions of the Koreans. Apparently the Japanese have secured law and order and the people are beginning to build better houses, and to put more work into their rice fields; and the trees are beginning to grow on the mountain ranges. But the Koreans have a sullen suspicious look; and the men lounge about smoking their long pipes, directly they have made a few pence as coolies. They never wash, and

374

clothe themselves in dirty white cotton shapeless garments and absurd little senseless black hats. We spend tomorrow here seeing more sights – and lunch with the governor-general, then to the more decidedly Korean town of Pyongyang, then 2 days journey to Mukden and then the Unknown, to be decided by events in China. One reason we want to get to Pekin is to find a budget of letters from Home with all the news of our dear ones and of the 'causes' we are interested in. I wonder whether you have thought of going to our office and seeing our secretary Miss Bulkley? I know she would immensely like to see you – she is a very devoted person and quite able in her way and has been with us now for six or seven years as research secretary. We left her, on loan, to the National Committee to which she has given the better part of her time for the last 2 years or more. Our little typist clerk, Miss Key, had secured a very good temporary position with American millionaires before we left. I wonder whether she is still with them? Our cook was, I think, going to the School of Economics Refectory and our faithful Emily is with her father and mother I suppose. We shall not be back till May. The O'Briens want to take our house on for the remainder of the session – we have offered them it for 200 guineas from March till August or so. I suppose we shall settle down in the country somewhere and collect our thoughts. The Playnes I think want us to go to them for three weeks in May or June. It will be delightful to see you all again.

Ever yours affectionately<br>Beatrice Webb

602 BL   SIDNEY WEBB TO GEORGE BERNARD SHAW

The Webbs had a disorganised stay in Peking, leaving on the last train before the revolutionary troops overthrew the Manchu dynasty. Beatrice complained that the British diplomats were so absorbed in the wedding of the ambassador's daughter that they took no notice of the revolutionaries or of the Webbs! (BWD 1 November 1911)

Peking, China<br>29.10.11

Dear Shaw

We have failed so far to write to you and Charlotte, because the added fact that you were yourselves travelling without known address, combined with all other reasons to prevent it. Psychologically, I find it almost impossible to concentrate, when travelling, the requisite energy for writing to anyone!

Now you will be back in England, and I feel ashamed that you will find no letter awaiting you.

We have thought and spoken of you innumerable times. First, perhaps, at Grosse Ile, the quarantine station in the St Lawrence, where our steamer

375

was 'held up', with that awful yellow flag flying, because we had two cases of smallpox in the steerage. The French Canadians always have smallpox going; and perhaps for that reason they are rigorous in excluding it. The whole 1,500 of us, from captain down to the youngest infant in the steerage, were peremptorily put to the option, of either instant revaccination, or disembarking on Grosse Ile, amid miscellaneous infective patients, for three weeks; and perhaps be refused permission to land in Quebec even then. So we were all – 1,500 of us – revaccinated, in 24 hours, except some 200 of the steerage who were refused even that option, and were compulsorily landed at Grosse Ile! I wonder what you and Charlotte would have done. We submitted without a murmur, the gentlemen baring their arms in the smoking room, the ladies in the music room. Fortunately it did not take with Beatrice (who had not been done for 20 years); and only made a painless sore for a week with me (who had not been done for 38 years). So we were protected. As smallpox is always rife in China, I am told that it was inexcusably foolhardy of us not to have been done before we started. In fact, I felt a little like an undetected Jonah. Perhaps the two cases were sent by God just to get me revaccinated. As Peer Gynt once said, on a memorable occasion, 'God is Just. But economical he is not'!

Well, at last we landed in Canada, and spent a very agreeable five weeks in that land of extraordinary material prosperity and 'boom', in spite of an unparalleled tropical heat – 107° in the shade at one point they said – we stayed with a charming History Professor on Lake Memphremagog (U.S. border); on a twenty-year-old wheat farm on the Saskatchewan prairie; and on an attractive fruit farm in British Columbia. What we think of Canada socially you will see from our article in the September *Crusade*, which kindly deign to read.

Then we cross the wide Pacific – 16 solid days at sea (and *so* cold) without anything more than a glimpse of the Aleutian Islands on the horizon – fortunately we were not ill either on the Atlantic or the Pacific – and landed at Yokohama. We had a most delightful two months in Japan hardly ever with Europeans; almost entirely spending our time with Japanese statesmen, officials, philanthropists, bankers, landlords and peasants; with a charming little man who acted as interpreter, to whom we became personally much attached, and who took all trouble off our hands. We had a most enjoyable walking tour in the mountains between Nillko and Nagano, walking 12 to 18 miles a day, over passes 7,000 feet high, clothed with luxuriant subtropical vegetation to the top: all this in the tropical heat of a Japan August, very much like the atmosphere of the great palmhouse at Kew! But we found it unexpectedly possible and pleasant; reducing our clothing to a minimum and our luggage to the one basket carried by a coolie; staying in tiny villages, at native inns where no white woman had stayed before; and drinking cup after cup of their weak tea, leading to endless perspiration, which made the daily hotbath most refreshing, even if one *could* not lock the bathroom door! We have put our impressions of Japan into an article which Sharp may print in the December *Crusade*, if it reaches him safely.

Then we crossed over from Japan to Korea – 11 hours in a fearful storm, during which we both lay sick in our cabin. We had six days in Korea, virtually as the guest of the Japanese Administration; met at each railway station by bevies of bowing officials in gorgeous uniforms; taken out in the Governor's State Carriage, the only one in Seoul; and shown palaces and schools and prisons and hospitals and tombs etc. The Koreans are 12 millions of dirty, degraded, sullen, lazy, and religionless savages, who slouch about in dirty *white* garments of the most inept kind, and who live in filthy mudhuts. This race the Japanese have at last annexed (after failing to get them along by Advisory Residents, and then by a Protectorate), to the world's advantage, as there is at any rate law and order now; and they are now spending a couple of million pounds a year of Japanese Government money in trying to equip them with the elementary institutions and habits of civilisation!

Then we crossed over into China – that is Manchuria – where the Japanese had a long thread of civilisation in their wonderful railway; but which is otherwise quite Chinese. Here, indirectly by the ex-students of the London School of Economics, the Chinese Viceroy took us up, had us to tea, and sent us round with Chinese officials in shades of blue, to see Palaces, Tombs, Schools, Prisons etc. Oddly enough, it was the prisons that were really excellent (as prisons go); quite up to European standard, and even better in the variety and extent of real work provided. (The prisoners were actually printing off tomorrow's issue of the local daily newspaper!)

Now we have just got to Peking, which is in a 'panicky' stage; the Chinese fleeing from it in crowds which not only cram the carriages of the trains, but actually travel on the buffers. The Europeans profess no fear, and the Hotel is full of nondescript trippers. But we cannot go to Hankow; it is doubtful whether we shall be allowed far beyond the walls; and we are relying on the line to the sea by Tientsin being kept open by the Powers, even if the Revolutionists (whom most people sympathise with) do overcome the very sulky Imperial troops, whom we have seen going to the front.

We got here this morning, and have had our first walk in the dirty, crowded, noisy Chinese city, accompanied by a Fabian (one Adderley), a mild Irish youth, who is teaching the Chinese how to be customs officers – which an Irishman ought to know how to do, considering how many of them get Customs appointments in U.K. We are already engaged to dinner three successive nights, and to spend tomorrow morning at the University.

We go on to Shanghai, Hongkong, Singapore and Calcutta. Miss

377

Bulkley, 87 Norfolk St, will readdress any letter sent to her to be forwarded. We should immensely like to hear from you and Charlotte.

We find it adds greatly to travel if, in addition to the scenery, one can get to see and talk with all sorts of native people – officials, teachers, philanthropists, bankers etc. – and we have found it easy to do this by taking a little trouble to get introductions. Certainly it is the only way to enjoy Japan; and the fact that it can be done in China to so small an extent, is a great drawback.

Well, goodbye now. We are quite well, and hope you are also.

Yours

Sidney Webb

## 603 PP BEATRICE WEBB TO CLIFFORD SHARP

Travelling by way of Hong Kong, Singapore and Rangoon the Webbs arrived in India at the time that the Royal Durbar was being held in New Delhi. The rajah they met at Benares was Madhava Lal; his son-in-law was named Das Vyasa. The Collector at Buddhgaya was named Whitty; at Benares the Webbs discovered that the Collector (C. S. Streatfield) was the brother-in-law of one of their volunteer workers in the Poor Law campaign.

Annie Besant, the former Fabian turned Theosophist, made a significant contribution to Indian education and to the development of the Indian National Congress.

Allahabad<br>India<br>January 15th [1912]

My dear Mr Sharp

Since we left Calcutta a week ago we have seen so many 'sights' and talked to so many people – (and I have been struggling through it all with a chronic cold) – that I hardly feel that I can write to you an intelligible letter. India is a desperately baffling place which leaves you gasping at the questions it presents, and confused with multitudinous impressions – squalor and picturesque beauty, piety and vice, starvation and magnificence – administrative efficiency, and gross administrative carelessness – one impression following so quickly on another that one almost despairs of any net result to hand on to other people. All I can do is to give you one or another of the scenes we have passed through.

At Benares we had an introduction to a Hindoo Rajah, (Nobleman) a large agricultural landlord and a great local magnate. He was old and was too ill to see us, but he sent his carriage to meet us at the station, and his son-in-law to show us everything we wished to see. So the son-in-law (who was also a country gentleman on his own account) motored us first to the family's City Palace, then to the family's country house and finally took us right into the country to see him administrating the family estate. The City House was a strangely picturesque but barbarously ornamented

378

mansion, rising out of the dark narrow streets of Benares with dark and dirty rooms, innumerable servants – the only liveable part of it being the five or six separate roofs at different levels from where you could watch the brilliantly coloured life of the narrow and tortuous alleys. On these roofs were the bedrooms of the men of the family. The ladies were in 'Purdah', living in closed courts, and he did not offer to let me see them – which perhaps would have been useless as none of them could talk English. The country house was another rambling palatial establishment with the same odd combination of European furniture and pictures of English hunts and races in the men's quarters, and the same bare and comfortless dark rooms for the ladies' accommodation. There was a Temple and a great water tank with flights of steps descending into it, from out of a large garden, where the family and its retainers perform their religious exercises. The family belonged to a strict sect of the Brahmins.

But the most interesting sight was to watch this Hindoo Landlord among his villagers. We had to walk a mile or so from where we left his carriage, across the badly cultivated fields with their bare stretches of uncultivable or uncultivated sand – the wells and irrigation works in disrepair – the ploughs quite clearly of the same sort that Adam invented, just scraping off the surface of the earth – the inhabitants listless and gaunt – picturesque but unpleasing picture. Arrived at our landlord's bungalow, we watch him settling the disputes between his tenants and his agent, and between the tenants themselves. There was an aged tenant kneeling before him for at least half an hour in the attitude of prayer – the agent has let his acres to a man who had offered 5 per cent more, the poor old man having failed to ask for a renewal at a higher rent because he thought no one would offer for the land. There was a bitter controversy between 'the Brahmins' and the 'Ascetics' in one of the villages over an extension of a mud cottage – the Brahmins contending that the Ascetics would defile their yard [?food] if they advanced into their domain. We accompanied our Landlord to look at the site – it was a squalid hamlet of low mud huts with mere holes as doors and windows; to judge by the gaunt figures, they were all Ascetics! The whole of the men and boys were gesticulating wildly and the women peering out of the huts, veiling themselves whenever you looked in their direction. The feud between the two castes packed closely in one tiny hamlet was evidently of old standing and our Landlord said unless he settled the matters there would be a fight and a Police Court case. Then as we were departing the 'Fighting Caste' from another group of huts appeared all armed with sticks just as big as the Police would allow under the Arms Act and accompanied us to a neighbouring village that was already inhabited by the same Caste, with whom they were going to have a Palaver. Altogether the whole day of incidents revealed to us the curiously discordant character of Hindoo Village life, broken up into these innumerable castes. To think that there are 60 millions belonging to the

'Untouchables' – who are bound to cry out that they are at hand, so that their shadow shall not fall on a Brahmin! These cultivators are of all castes and cannot ever combine against their landlord as they are perpetually quarrelling among themselves. Only 20 per cent of our landlord's tenants had fixity of tenure – the others were all tenants at will.

Another scene of amazing beauty and interest are the Ghats (great stairs down to the Ganges) of Benares, with the steps down to the sacred river crowded with worshippers and surmounted by Temples and Palaces. At one of these Ghats some half-dozen bodies are burning each on its own platform, and we watch one corpse being laid on the funeral pyre, wood heaped up over it, and then the poor little boy (as the nearest of kin) fetching the fire from the Temple and setting his parent alight – trembling all the while, but receiving no kind of consolation from the matter-of-fact cremators of the bodies. Very wonderful is the strange hysteria in the excitement in the killing of the sacrificial goat, the crowded temples and the bestial hideousness of the idols that are being worshipped – the mercenary importunity of the Brahmins who are officiating – and the weird vanity of the naked Ascetic 'making up' his dishevellment, with a little hand glass, an adept in the artistic use of grey ash and white paint.

From these native haunts to the House of the Collector, and to a tour in the Collector's motor! At Buddhgaya we stayed with one Collector and at Benares we saw a good deal of another – two excellent English University men living in a great comfort – even luxury – and keeping up the correct 'State' of English Rule. We were shown at Benares magnificent Police Offices, and fine water works. But the 'Free Municipal School' consisted of a mud hut with 85 boys crowded into a few square yards 'taught' by a private Venture – a Brahmin receiving a government grant of a few rupees a month, who could not tell us what time the school opened or was shut, and looked an awful scoundrel.

The Collector seemed vastly amused and scoffed at giving 'the natives' any better education – they were much better left alone. The Collector we stayed with at Buddhgaya however, was only too anxious to do anything he could, but Police and Justice and Roads were all he had time for. When we remembered the Japanese Schools in Korea – a far more depraved population – one feels a bit depressed with the results of a hundred years British administration! On the other hand, the English official as Magistrate is unimpeachable – his very aloofness keeping him impartial. All Indian gentlemen, Hindoos and Mahomedans alike will tell you 'they want more Indians in the Civil Service' – but none of these want an Indian as a Collector of their own district! And the feeling in the United Provinces against the Bengalee, or in the Punjab against a 'Man from Madras', is intense, whilst the Hindoo and the Mahomedan clamour for the Englishman as Arbiter – that is to say when they are in the Minority – when in the Majority they clamour for Home Rule!

380

We spent one afternoon with Mrs Annie Besant at the Hindoo Central College at Benares. This is the most hopeful institution we have seen. There are 1,000 students – it is supported almost entirely by voluntary subscriptions from wealthy Hindoos and very moderate fees from the students. Mrs Besant has gathered together a staff of 50 teachers – only 3 European (all women for the little boys) and many of these accomplished Hindoo scholars work for love. There seems a great corporate spirit among them and a most friendly relation between teachers and students. Of course some of the Christian Missionaries are bitter against it, as a successful attempt to reinstate Hinduism and they scoff at the sight of Mrs Besant going round the Temples offering rice or flowers to the Hindu Gods! The Government College presided over by a great Sanskrit scholar, a great believer in historical criticism and with a staff of able Englishmen, but with high fees and no enthusiasm is dwindling rapidly. There may be some shoddy in the Central Hindu College, and I cannot in talking with Mrs Besant quite believe in her intellectual sincerity. But she has managed to call out the patriotism and the self-respect of the educated Hindu public, and she has combined traditional Hinduism with liberal views, and a faith in conduct as a necessary element in life. And she has certainly a quite extraordinary personal hold over all these people – the feeling towards her almost amounts to worship. The Central Hindu College is to be nucleus of the New Hindu University. The great difficulty before this is not the money – that has been subscribed, but 'what constitutes Hinduism'? Mrs Besant's modernist interpretation is not accepted by the Pundits and orthodox Brahmins, and what with Castes and Sects and different territorial races of Hindus, some common ground – sufficient for a denominational University to serve all India – is difficult to get. It is strange that the dominant personality of an English woman is the only chance of securing common action among Hindus for the teaching of the National Religion.

I must not run on. Next week we go into Camp with a Collector for ten days and then for the best part of a week with a Forest Officer. The only drawback to our enjoyment is the cold – I had not realised that India was just as cold as England in winter – colder as there are no arrangements for heating and you have the midday sun to enervate you. However I am gradually adapting myself to it, but I have had to throw over Vegetarianism – or die of starvation. No European eats anything but fish and meat and they breakfast at 9.30 and dine at 8.30! Even in the summer heat.

Ever yours

Beatrice Webb

604 PP  BEATRICE WEBB TO MILDRED BULKLEY

John Hope Simpson, whom the Webbs thought 'pro-native' and a first-rate administrator, was later appointed by Sidney Webb to a special post in Palestine when Webb became Colonial Secretary.

Beatrice noted that the annual government expenditure in the whole district, which had a population of 3.5 millions, was £20,000; this had to meet the cost of roads, bridges, schools and health measures.

The Moslem leaders whom the Webbs met in Lucknow were Aziz Mirza, secretary of the Moslem League, the Rajah of Jehangirhad and a number of local barristers and attorneys. The Hindu group was led by Ganga Prasad Varma, editor of *The Advocate* and a local councillor.

In Camp<br>
United Provinces<br>
January 24th 1912

My dear Miss Bulkley

Here we are 'in camp' with Mr Hope Simpson – a Collector – the Administrator of a fertile plain in the United Provinces, with a population of 3½ millions. We stayed two days with him in his station near to the largest city of his district – Gorakpur – 60,000 persons crowded into narrow alleys of mud huts, lined with booths and little shops for food and hand-made articles of common use – every craftsman working in his open shop and trying his best to encroach on the narrow lane just as little crafts-men used to do in the English medieval towns. The streets are always densely crowded with men and boys and little children, and here and there a low caste woman – the more respectable the streets, the fewer the women. Directly a Native of India – Mahomedan or Hindu, rises in life, his women kind 'go into Purdah' and are seen no more. The few resident Europeans – civilians and Railway officials – live in comfortable bungalows in large attractive grounds some half mile away from the native city. And well they may as Plague, Cholera and Malaria are always present in the native city and sometimes sweep thousands away in a few months. Our Collector had all his four children down with Plague – they just pulled through because they had been inoculated, so he said! and out of 11 years married life, he has only had five years with his wife and children. Every European expects to suffer from malarial fever and habitually takes Quinine. We are now taking six grains every other day on the advice of our host. Close to the native city is the settlement of the [?Dermos] – the criminal tribe of the neighbourhood. This settlement is run by a devoted Salvation Army Officer and his wife with two native converts who actually live with this lowest type of 'outcaste' – untouchable to any Hindu. They are a dark talkative little race – all the men are hereditary thieves, all the women are prostitutes. The Salvation Army has had an extraordinary success with them – we went to the Sunday evening service – they were all shouting and singing and clapping their hands – the men looked really touched – but the women looked indifferent and obdurate. What a life for the refined English man and woman who live year in and year out in their midst.

Our Collector – Mr Hope Simpson – is an ideal one – perhaps he was chosen by the Government of India to take us around for that reason. He is a tall good-looking middle-aged man – the son of a Liverpool Bank Manager – educated in France and Germany and eventually going to Oxford – a good sportsman, and a Patriarchal Head of his district, speaking the various vernaculars with perfect fluency and associating almost exclusively with the natives. The first afternoon he had a garden party to celebrate the opening of a Club at Gorakpur for Indians and Europeans and there we met all the Rajahs (noblemen and landlords) from fifty miles round and all the Europeans and Indians Judges and Government servants of the district. Both evenings at his Bungalow we had Indian gentlemen – Government officials to dine. But he much prefers to be 'in camp' and spends at least 3 months touring through his district, and all his leave shooting Tigers in the jungle that borders this province.

The life in Camp we find extraordinarily interesting and our time is so fully occupied that it is difficult to read or write. The Camp (which consists of some half-dozen well furnished tents and a whole retinue of servants, horses and bullock waggons in a shady grove of mango trees) is always there, in full swing, when you leave and when you arrive – even though you left it two hours before some 12 miles away – for there are two complete camps one of which goes on in advance the day before. The day begins early – tea and toast are brought you by your own servant at 6.30 and you have your bath and all your dressing arrangements as comfortably as in your own house. At 7.30 you start off for the day's march. I ride with the Collector (I made myself a habit with a few yards of holland). Sidney drives with the Assistant Collector. The day is brilliantly fine with a cool, even cold wind, and the great plain of wheat and sugar cane of blue-flowered linseed seed and yellow-flowered dal, broken in its lines by mango groves, mud walled villages and Pagoda Temples, stretches right to the distant Himalayas – every now and again giving you a glimpse of the snow peaks. On the road are, at this time of year, streams of bullock waggons carrying the sugar cane to the village sugar-boiling houses. But you are not allowed to ride far. At the corner of a village or at the crossway corner of a rough track there are some thirty or forty village elders, their heads and shoulders draped in white – their arms and legs bare – waiting to waylay the Collector, bowing and 'salaaming' and sometimes even kneeling. He must visit their school – no 'sahib' has yet seen it. So we turn off the main road and trot along the narrow paths dividing the various crops or through groves of mango trees, accompanied by the Headman of the village and probably by some of the little landlords on shaggy ponies, until we find ourselves in the crooked courts and alleys of a village made up of various types of mud and brick huts and houses. In one of these courts – usually that of a little landlord – is the village school. The Villagers have started the school themselves – sometimes built a shed for the boys in wet weather sometimes the Zemindar (local landlord) lends his Verandah – they have subscribed for books and slates and engaged a teacher. They always have 50 boys on the roll (as this is the Government limit for one teacher) but actually there are 60 or 70 being taught. And these 60 or 70 youngsters of all ages from 6 to 20 are there awaiting us – shivering in their cotton garment in the cold morning air – got up at least an hour earlier than usual in order to be inspected by the Collector. No school in India starts before 10 o'clock and it goes on till 3 or 4. They are being taught to read and write in the vernacular and also to do mental arithmetic. But the accomplishment they and the teacher are most proud of, are gymnastic exercises and wrestling. I have never seen such exercises! The whole school strips, except for a loin cloth and begins a series of rapid and graceful contortions that no European except a professional gymnast could possibly get through. And the wrestling is really a joy to look at – they show so much pluck and good nature and such dogged persistency. One feels what splendid materials these village boys would make for the Boy Scouts. The teacher is usually a young man – he knows no English and is only paid 5 Rupees (6/8) a month – but he is a much better sort than the Brahmin teacher of the big city. What the villagers want from the Collector is that the school should be made into a Board School. And as our Collector knows he is going to get an increased grant from the new sum promised for Education at the Durbar he delights them by promising to consider it favourably. One wonders how the village managed to scrape the money together to start the school, as there is no sign of comfort – the mudhuts and the one good house is that of the moneylender, who has got every little landlord or occupier in his grip. Our twelve miles march lasts some three hours as we are always turning aside to inspect village schools – police stations or a new road. On the dried-up pasture land are herds of cattle and that terrible pest – the Brahmin Bull – wanders unchecked among the cows and even in the crops. (These are bulls dedicated to the Gods – they are always the halt, the maimed and the blind, and they keep the breed low as well as doing untold damage – but no one may kill them!) Another sad sight are the villages sunk in unhealthy holes – (the country is absolutely flat except for holes big and small) – with perpetual pools of stagnant water breeding mosquitos, because the villagers will make their huts of the earth actually on that particular spot. Indeed the only progressive spirit shown by these village folk is the immense desire for schools for their children.

Arrived at the new Camp we have our breakfast. This is a great function and there are always five courses and we sit and smoke and talk until about 12 o'clock. Then begins the business of the day. Seated at his desk with two native officials squatted down beside him the Collector hears appeals from the Sub-Collectors Court. So far as I have yet heard, these appeals almost always concern the partition of property in the Hindu Joint Family or the primitive village community – both of which are breaking up under the influence of English ideas of individual property. Usually in the Camp Courts, the two parties and their friends alone appears – but to-day two native lawyers come to argue the case. The villagers seem to delight in these cases and will bring suits about the ownership of the 3rd part of a tree. Having been prevented from fighting with each other physically they take refuge in litigation. Revenge unfortunately plays a great part in these suits – especially in the criminal suits heard by the local judges. Only the other day an old man was beaten to death at his own desire by his two sons in order to accuse another man of the murder, against whom the family had a grudge. False accusations and false witness seem to honeycomb the life of the village. But they don't steal each others crops like the Chinese!

After the hearing of the Appeals we have afternoon tea. Then there arrive from all the four quarters some 200 village headmen. The Collector sits under the largest mango tree and the Headmen squat on the ground in a semi-circle with an outer circle standing – for a real talk with the Collector. Very striking is this scene – the big burly Englishman with his paternal kindly authoritative manner talking about all the events of the last three months – the repeated burglaries in one village, the defective drainage in another, or the desirability of inoculation for Plague. As he begins this last subject there is an uneasy movement in the squatting and standing crowd – some of them slink away – then he roars with laughter and explains that there is no Doctor present – that he is only recommending them to have the village inoculated – the whole crowd laughs at the timid ones. All through the Collector's talk Headmen intervene to explain or to agree. To look at, they are not orientals – they resemble almost exactly an Italian crowd, some of the Brahmins are exactly like Raphaels' picture of the famous Cardinal, whilst others have the features of Beatrice Cenci. It is only the low castes that look negroid or mongolian.

After the Conference is over we go, accompanied by the whole village at a more or less respectful distance, to inspect the institutions of the little town – the Hospital, the secondary or English School, the Police Station and the drains or absence of drains and the innumerable encroachments in lane and market place. Sometimes we finish the day with having the native officials to dinner. We fare sumptuously – the local landlords sending in fruit and vegetable fish and game – (even we had a present of nuts and fruit brought to our Tent). The Collector may not accept any other present but these native fruits – and he often sends most of the fish and game back again just taking one to show politeness.

We have seen something of the native officials – from the well-to-do Hindus and Mahomedans – generally Oxford and Cambridge graduates who pass into the Indian Civil Service to the native police men at 5/- or 6/- a month. The former are not altogether successful as Collectors – though they frequently make excellent judges. As administrators they seem to lack moral and sometimes physical courage (notably in dealing with Plague and Cholera) and though they are said to be absolutely honest financially they show favouritism to their own caste or creed. The Assistant Collector who is travelling with us, is one of them. He is a nice good-looking boy, the son of a wealthy and very distinguished Mahomedan judge. But he is glibly talkative, and decidedly 'slack' and he combines English snobbishness with Mahomedan prejudice. There are some dozen others in the *administrative* service in these Provinces but only one has been a success. At the other end of the scale there is a perpetual difficulty with the exactions of the lowly-paid native officer, and the amount they 'squeeze' out of the villagers would constitute a valuable source of revenue. The real success among the native officials seem to be the middle class – men who are relatively well paid and who are working under the direct supervision of the English officials. These seem to be in many cases quite first rate – far better than Europeans paid at the same rate – loyal, devoted and intellectually subtle, with a great knowledge of their own people. Also as I said before some of the Hindu and Mahomedan Judges are said to be great lawyers and incorruptible. The passive Act of judgement seems to suit their mental make up – much better than the direction and management of men. *Executive back-bone* is what they seem to lack – and the sort of Education they get either in India or in England does not seem to give it them.

Before I end this long letter, I must tell you something about our doings at Allahabad and Lucknow – where we stayed about a week. We managed to see the principal English officials in both places. But in Lucknow we had a long talk with the little group of leading Mahomedans who run the All-India Moslem League and also with the rival Hindu Nationalist organisations. The Moslems are a slower and duller race but they are waking up in emulation of the Hindu Nationalist organisation and starting all sorts of schools, as well as political agitations. They are bitterly opposed to 'Home Rule for India' – they do not really feel they are Indians, and pride themselves on being Persians or Arabs even when they belong obviously to the Hindu race! Their real allegiance is to Islam and just now they are terribly upset about Tripoli and Persia. They feel they have been humiliated by the rehabilitation of Bengal – not because they care about it, but because it is a political victory for the Bengalees. They don't really like us and resent our social exclusiveness even more than the Hindu, who wraps himself up in his own caste exclusiveness. They hate democracy and really dislike Education and all that is modern. On the other hand, the Hindu Caucus was made of cultivated men who were eager to discuss political devices and economic theories – and whose whole thought in life was to fit themselves for self-government. They are full of hopefulness just now and recognise the change of spirit in the British administration. They admire us immensely – but they want to take our place.

By far the most wonderful sight we saw was the Magdmela at Allahabad, the great religious Hindu festival held once in six years. On the sandy banks at the confluence of the Ganges and the Jumna were assembled some hundreds of thousands of Hindu Pilgrims from all parts of India. Innumerable flags were flying each with its own device over little booths signifying the presence of the Brahmin who directed the devotions and received the offerings of the pilgrims from particular villages. Provided with a boat by the Collector we drifted down the Ganges right into the midst of the bathers. Here was a scene of extraordinary picturesque confusion – men and boys and children scrambling in and out of the water, boats of bathers of every description struggling to get to the meeting of the waters – Purdah ladies creeping out of their silken awnings to bathe unseen, aged folk borne by pious sons, and babies of mothers of low caste into the river – whilst the Brahmins on the river edge shouted their directions and sang the appropriate sutras. We managed to struggle on to the belt of sand and we wandered up between the booths. Presently there was a great commotion in the crowd and two or three young English Police Officers cantered up to direct the coming processions of 'Saddhus' or holy men. These processions were wonderful to look at, weird music from strange instruments played by gaily dressed men – wild dancers executing wonderful contortions preceded some hundred Saddhus two by two, hand in hand. These Holy mortals were stark naked – their bodies covered with ash dust, their faces painted with lines of yellow ochre and white paste, their heads elaborately dressed with coils of platted hair – or a mass of matted dishevelled dirt. Some of the men were miserably thin and looked genuinely ascetic – others were enormously fat and looked like satyrs – for the most part they seemed merely naked dirty vagrants. Following them were their Brahmin Directors, well dressed, carried in gaudy palanquins – then a rabble of adherents – devotees of this or that Saddhu. Directly the procession had passed the crowd closed in behind it, and grovelled in the sand over which the Holy ones had passed. Three separate processions we watched, each one escorted by the young English officials, to prevent a fight between them for precedence to step first into the Holy River. Mixed up in the crowd were all sorts and descriptions of idols and little improvised altars kept by most blackguardly-looking Brahmins. The crowd was most incontinent in its devotion – throwing its mites of coin and grain or rice before every idol or decked out stone. It was also naively fraudulent – cows and calves were tethered here and there – bought from a Brahmin for a few pence in order to acquire the merit of presenting the Holy animal to the same Brahmin. In the course of an hour the same cow would be bought from the Brahmin and presented to the same Brahmin some twelve times. This Hindu religion is certainly the most amazing vision of mysticism and incontinent 'other worldliness'.

Now I must really stop – the Collector is discussing an interesting case with a local judge and I am probably writing rubbish – you, at any rate, will be tired of reading my scrawl. We shall be in Camp for another week. Then go on to the Camp of a Forest Officer on the slopes of the Himalayas, then to stay with the Native Ruler of a small state in the Central Provinces.

You might get this letter copied and sent on to Mrs Drake for any of my family who care to read it.

With best wishes

Ever yours

Beatrice Webb

We are both very well.


605 PP   BEATRICE WEBB TO CLIFFORD SHARP

Mrs Kirkwood and Hamilton Fox helped organise the Poor Law campaign workers; Glynne Williams, a wealthy landowner in Argentina with progressive views, helped finance the campaign; Reginald Pott was a Fabian businessman and a member of the London County Council for some years. Beatrice noted that 'the Gaekwar of Baroda and his Consort struck us as real enthusiasts for social reform'. (BWD 3/5 April 1912) The Governor of Bombay was Sir George Clarke; the Native Ruler was the Jam of Nawanagar, better known to cricketers as Ranjitsinji. Gokhale was at Poona; Ferguson College was a centre of Hindu higher education run according to the Vedas by a brotherhood who lived in commune-like simplicity. The Servants of India, run like a monastic order, sought to train Indians for public service. Since only a typed copy of this letter survives it is uncertain whether the bracketed phrase ('all Jesuits') was intended or whether this is the typist's misreading of 'Arya Somaj' in Beatrice's scrawled original.

Government House<br>Bombay<br>April 7th 1912

My last letter! After this Postcards and telegrams.

I am lying on the most comfortable of sofas, on a balcony overlooking the Homeward Ocean – and thinking with pleasure that in another five weeks I shall be back again in Norfolk Street and that I shall find at the office many of our fellow-workers of a year ago. That is the most delightful thought! When we left last year I wondered whether the office would not be deserted when we returned – and as I have listened to exciting news from England my anxiety has increased – whether Mr Sharp and Mr Lloyd might not have escaped and taken refuge in a Government Office or in Parliament, whether Miss Bulkley might not have been enticed away to superintend the penal servitude of the Suffragettes, whether Mrs Kirkwood might not be managing the information bureau of the Syndicalist Movement – and whether all the other workers might not be either striking or smashing windows, with Mr Hamilton Fox registering and cataloguing their numbers and activities, and Mr Glynne Williams and Mr Pott paying all the fines or standing bail for them. It is a great testimony to the goodness of the staff, and the permanent usefulness of the work, that the organisation has endured in spite of all these splendid 'other attractions', to able and energetic minds, during the last six months. All these exciting events must to some extent alter the character of our work – give it perhaps a new direction – or add other departments to its existing activities, but the purpose of the National Committee – the getting of a civilised life for every individual citizen – stands out still as the one imperative necessity if our civilisation is to progress and endure.

For the last few weeks we have been visiting the native states of Rajputana, ending up at Baroda – the seat of the naughty Gaekwar who was so rude to the King Emperor at Delhi. Medieval India, with its magnificent fortresses, within them Palaces, Mosques and Temples, sometimes dead and deserted, in other cases, alive with the picturesquely armed soldiers of native rulers, the naked Saddhu, and the trader's booth, are a veritable joy to the antiquarian or artistic sightseer. But if you are staying in the Guest House of the native ruler or in the sumptuous British Residency – you see little of the leading inhabitants and find yourself lunching and dining with the little set of English folk – not very interesting and rather prejudiced editions of ordinary English officials. At Baroda we saw far more of the Indian Officials – as the British Residency is now vacant and we had personal introductions to the Gaekwar and his ministers. The Gaekwar and his Rani are just now in disgrace – he is a sympathetic, intelligent public-spirited man – vain and underbred (one of the only Rulers who belongs to a low caste) – also ambitious of becoming a popular Prince and leader of 'Young India'. From what we gathered from his Ministers, his disloyal feelings began with Lord Curzon's somewhat insolent interference with the public and private life of Ruling Chiefs, accentuated by the tactless intervention of a meddlesome resident, who insisted on touring round the Gaekwar's State hearing grievances. But I rather think his fascinating and clever wife is the centre of the disturbances – the Government of India insisting on the grandson of the first wife inheriting the throne instead of her eldest son. We lunched and spent the afternoon with them – the Gaekwar was nervous and the Rani defiant until they discovered that we were loyal subjects of the House of Hanover and believed that criticism of Government was justifiable, however silly rudeness might be. And I think the poor Gaekwar is very penitent: he is in mortal terror lest his 'Salute' shall be knocked down from its present 21 guns. To have your Salute diminished is the Horror of Horrors to the Native Ruler. The whole family struck us as in a state of chaos from the clash of Western and Eastern ideas – the Gaekwar has broken all the rules of caste, the Rani has thrown over Purdah, the son has returned from America with hideous manners and accent and the young lady has broken off her engagement and is temporarily in retirement. As for the poor little grandson he is jealously guarded by his widowed mother, and every one asking 'Will he survive?'.

Here we are enjoying two days dignified rest – talking at stated intervals with 'Their Excellencies' and more frequently with the retinue of A.D.C. and secretaries or with the Europeanized Native Ruler who is staying here.

It is a most fascinating place – a series of charming bungalows in beautiful groups with great central reception rooms. Our bungalow hangs right over the rocks and I slept last night on the verandah in the moonlight – with fishing smacks sailing close under me and the waves breaking on the very wall of our abode carved out of the rock. Tomorrow we go to stay with Mr Gokhale ('the most dangerous man in India' the political Secretary informed me) at his monastic institution – The Servants of India ('all Jesuits') – then we come back for five days to the Taj Hotel to be spent in seeing sights and people. As the Governor and his staff leave for the Hills we shall be able to consort with all and sundry, without causing scandal. On Tuesday week – we sail – there are plenty of pleasant people going on our steamer. Then a week at Cairo with Maurice Amos – a judge of the Supreme Court – two days at Venice and we shall appear on the platform of Charing Cross or Victoria probably on Monday 13th – but we will send a wire to the office when exactly we shall be back. The very next morning will see me at Norfolk Street. So goodbye until then. We are looking forward to the evening meeting sometime in the next week.

Yours

Beatrice Webb

# List of recipients

The figures refer to the Letter numbers

# Index

Users should also consult the index of Volume I for biographical references to individuals first mentioned in that volume.

Jackson, Cyril 233–4, 252–3, 261, 265
James, Lina 110–11
James, William 62–3
Jeffrey, John 220
Jenks, Edward 209–10
Jerred, Sir Walter Tapper 342
Jersey, Earl of 81–2
Jersey, Lady 81–2
Johnson, W. C. 217
Joy, Maurice 295, 297
Joynson-Hicks, William, M.P. 308
*Justice* 5, 49

Keeling, Frederick (Ben) 271, 302
Kekewich, Sir George 147
Kelly, Dr Dennis (Bishop) 220
Kershaw, Sir Noel Thomas 342
Key, Miss 283–4, 307, 375
Kikuchi, Baron 372
King, A. W. W. 97–8
Kingston, Charles 92–3
Kirkwood, Mrs 388
Kobayashi, Dr 372–3

Labour Party ix, xi, 9, 10, 35, 118–19, 218–19, 221, 250, 262, 264, 281, 327–8, 331, 341, 343, 349, 358–9, 362, 366, 369–70
*Labour Elector* 5
*Labour Leader* 5
*Labour Prophet* 4
Labour Representation Committee 118–19
*Labour Tribune* 5
Lal, Madhara 378
Lamington, Lord 84–5
*Lancet* 320–1
Lang, Cosmo Gordon 150, 201–2
Lansbury, George, M.P. 220, 224, 259, 261, 275, 283, 298–9, 314–15, 324, 331, 343–4, 361–4
Laurie, Colonel (S. A.) 279
Lehmann, R. C., M.P. 284–5
Leon, A. L. 154
Levine, Abraham 270
Levy-Lawson H. L. W., M.P. 109–10
Liberal Imperialists ix, 117, 119, 131, 134, 137, 145–6, 172, 183, 185, 188, 199, 218–19
Liberals: Webbs and ix–x, 1, 3, 9–11, 35, 50–1, 109–11, 198, 202, 204; and L.C.C. elections 28, 60, 198, 249; and social reforms 35, 222, 334, 348; and education 44–5, 48, 147, 174–5, 181–2; and 'Limps' 117–19, 137; and Labour Party 119; and tariff reform 183–5, 188; and Campbell-Bannerman 140, 199; Balfour and 199, 215; compla-

cency of 208; 1906 election 218; and T.U. Bill 221–2, 341; and Conservatives 202, 268–9; and Poor Law 323, 327, 330, 342, 349, 366; Churchill as candidate 187–8, 308; and the Lords 268–9, 327–8; and payment of M.P.s 341; and L.S.E. 356; 1910 general elections 358; future of 361–2; and National Insurance Bill 366, 369–70
Liberal Unionists 35, 119, 137, 147, 164, 362
Library Association 180–1
Lincoln, Robert 71
Lloyd George, David, M.P. x, 148, 193, 315, 327, 342, 348, 353–4, 366, 369–70
Lloyd, H. D. 49–50, 114–15; *Wealth Against Commonwealth* 49; *Newest England* 114
Local Government Board 103, 219, 223, 225–6, 231, 244–5, 253–4, 342, 348
Loch, Charles Stewart 220, 244, 259, 269, 283, 299–300, 306
Lockwood, Henry 258–9
Lodge, Sir Oliver 210–11, 223, 328–9, 337
London County Council: and Deptford ix, 28, 60, 107, 163, 196, 199, 201, 246–9; education policy and Webb ix, xi, 44, 94, 141–2, 148–9, 164–5, 172–5, 209; and L.S.E. xi, 33, 47, 83–4, 98–9, 102–3, 113, 128–9, 133, 141–2, 154, 161–2, 166, 169, 173, 175, 261; chairmanship T.E.B. 181; Webb as member of 1, 3, 27, 39, 98, 105, 126, 133, 344; and factory tailoring 8; elections for 28, 123–4, 135, 137, 192–4, 197, 201, 246–9; and Liberals 28, 60, 198, 249; and 17 Fleet Street 127; and tariff reform 186; and Imperial College 188–9; naming of Millbank 217; London administration 174–5; and Poor Law 291; resolutions on Mentally Defectives 363
London Reform Union 26, 98
London School Board 11, 26, 44, 133, 138, 165, 172–3, 191
London School of Economics: founded x–xi, 1, 49, 94, 170–1; aims of 1, 30–1, 37, 158, 176–9; finances 12, 33, 47, 105, 113, 125, 143, 159, 162, 173, 176–81, 205–6, 288; and Hutchinson legacies 20, 33, 38–9, 204; appointment of Directors 29, 31, 33, 314, 316; and L.C.C. 33, 38, 83–4, 98–9, 102, 125, 129, 133, 141–2, 261; premises for 34–5, 46, 97–9, 101–4, 106, 113, 126, 128, 183; and Bertrand Russell 38–9; and Charlotte Shaw 40-3, 45–8, 104; the railway department 43, 206, 350–7; and Ramsay MacDonald 44, 141–2, 154–7, 159,

398

Box House,
Minchinhampton,
Gloucestershire.